I0558180

PICKUP ARTIST BIBLE

CORY SMITH

CORY SMITH @PUA_DATING_TIPS

Conversation Casanova Mastery 2.0

48 CONVERSATION TACTICS, TECHNIQUES AND MINDSETS TO START CONVERSATIONS, FLIRT LIKE A MASTER AND NEVER RUN OUT OF THINGS TO SAY, THE BOOK

Cory Smith

Introduction

Did you ever see a beautiful woman, only a few feet away, but you were too scared to say or do anything?

A decade ago, that was me! I felt TRAPPED like a thirsty man in a desert surrounded by water he can't drink. There were women all around me, but I didn't know what to do to start an interaction, and sustain it long enough to seduce her. IT WAS TORTURE to see a sexy, young woman only 6 feet away, but NOT KNOW WHAT TO SAY TO HER TO START THINGS OFF.

It took years of painful, heart-breaking trial and error to crack the code, but when I did figure it out then the sex was as abundant as sand on a beach. WHEN I COULD FINALLY GET RESULTS IN THE FIELD CONSISTENTLY, IT MADE ALL OF THE YEARS OF EXCRUCIATING PAIN WORTH IT.

He who has game-related-skill-sets will find beautiful women as abundant and accessible as OXYGEN, but he who lacks game skills will ponder bullshit thoughts such as:

- "all the beautiful women are taken",
- "no woman will suck my dick",
- "what's the point of trying if I'll fail anyways", and
- "all hope is lost. I am completely fucked."

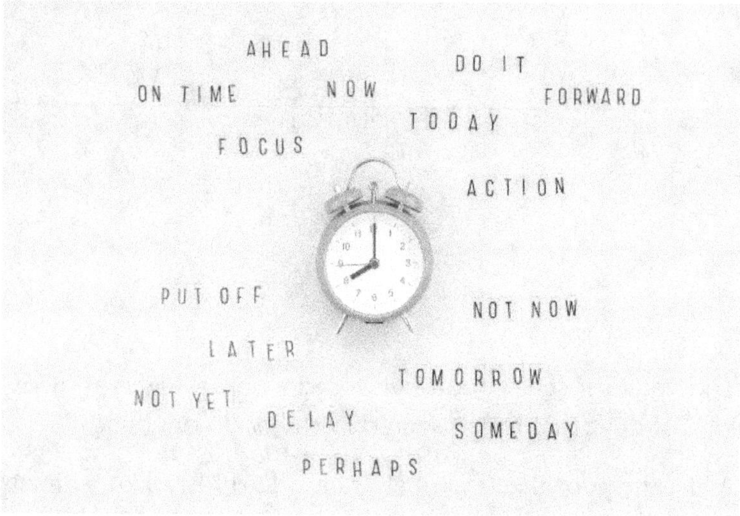

The lazy man always has a convenient "perfectly logical" excuse ready to justify his lethargic, cowardice behaviors. He uses these rationalizations to avoid feeling guilty for behaving like a pussy.

CREATE A POSITIVE FEEDBACK LOOP.

When you have success in the field, motivational and inspirational thoughts find you. You become invigorated by your results and find yourself hitting the field more often. You start looking forward to interacting with women. It becomes a positive feedback loop that gets stronger with time. Success breeds MORE SUCCESS. **The rich get richer and the sexy get sexier.**

However, when you have repeated failures in the field, your confidence and self-esteem levels take a hit. This leads to even less results and generates a vicious negative cycle that can take someone into the depths of depression. When one has repeated failure, he starts to expect failure - creating a self-fulling prophecy. If this is you, you must SNAP OUT OF IT NOW!

A woman doesn't give a fuck about your excuses, sob story, lack of a strong male role-model, abusive childhood or victimhood. She cares about the bottom line: did you emerge as a WINNER in the game of life? Can she trust you to be a powerful leader?

HE WHO DWELLS IN THE PAST, MISSES OUT ON OPPORTUNITIES IN THE PRESENT.

LISTEN TO ME, SON. I don't care what your past is. I don't care how many mistakes you have made. I don't care how much of a "loser" you think you are.

THE PAST IS DEAD.

And from the ashes, arises a NEW YOU. This moment right now is a NEW CHAPTER IN YOUR LIFE. Let go of the past, and start over RIGHT NOW.

Every mistake is an opportunity to learn something new. Everyone makes mistakes. The difference between those who are successful and those who are not: is the ability to quickly gain the lessons from the experiences and move on forward - without a loss of intensity of purpose.

THE FIVE FUNDAMENTALS OF GAME

FUNDAMENTAL I.

The number one secret is to GIVE ZERO FUCKS WHAT ANYONE THINKS - just like a dangerous psychopath would.

- FUCK what society thinks.
- FUCK what people will think of you.
- FUCK being a sheep conforming to the popular culture that the masses are enslaved to.
- FUCK what her opinion is.

THE ONLY THING THAT MATTERS IS WHAT YOU THINK. It is the ability to make a decision and act upon it - regardless of external approval or disapproval - that will take you far in life.

99% of men are sheep following other sheep. Be the wolf. A wolf does not care about the opinion of sheep; he eats sheep for breakfast. Don't live like a prey animal; embrace the seductive, primal predator within. **Be highly aggressive in going after what you want in life and FUCK anyone who disapproves.**

❄

FUNDAMENTAL II.

Accept that you might feel intense anxiety and APPROACH ANYWAYS. Don't let emotions control and dictate your destiny. HARNESS THE FORCE OF YOUR WILL POWER.

Just because you don't feel like approaching a beautiful woman, doesn't mean you should give into those emotions. Just because every ounce of your being is telling you to not approach, doesn't mean you should give into those feelings.

Develop the self-control to do that which you have logically, consciously decided is the best course of action for you - regardless of how you feel like in the moment and despite any possible intense emotional resistance.

❄

FUNDAMENTAL III.

<u>DEVELOP THE ABILITY TO CREATE A GOAL FOR YOURSELF AND STICK WITH IT NO MATTER WHAT.</u> IF YOUR GOAL IS TO DO AT LEAST ONE APPROACH FOR THE DAY THEN YOU HAVE TO IMPLEMENT THAT - NO MATTER THE EMOTIONAL OR PSYCHOLOGICAL RESISTANCE.

What's the difference between people that are successful in the game of life and soy boys that suck at it? It is the ability to set clear long term, short term and daily goals; then, execute these goals with FULL FORCE - regardless of any anxiety or fear that they may feel along the way.

<u>Goals allow the aspiring master seducer to stay focused on what matters most</u> in a chaotic, distracting world filled to the brim with noise.

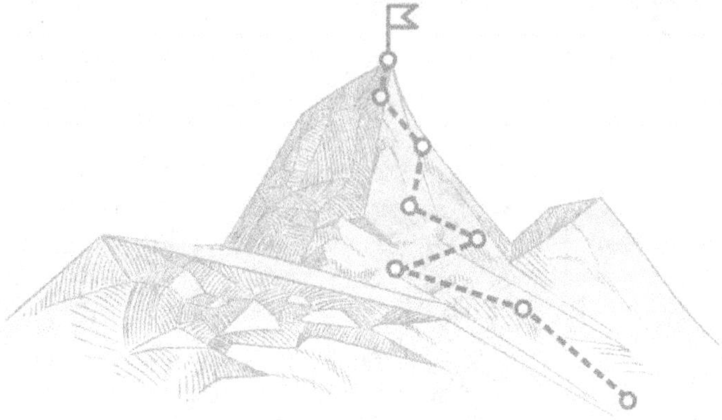

❄

FUNDAMENTAL IV

DOMINATE EVERYTHING THAT YOU DO.

Meeting women during the daytime is a medium to help you develop the character and habits of a successful, high-status MAN WHO FUCKS and then transfer those same skills to other fields such as business, networking, fitness and dominating life in general.

If you don't even have the balls to approach a beautiful woman then what does that say about the size of your balls, and you ability to approach a successful business man at a networking event to pitch your mutually beneficial/lucrative business idea?

DON'T YOU GET IT!?! HOW YOU HANDLE YOURSELF IN THE SEDUCTION FIELD, REVEALS HOW YOU HANDLE EVERYTHING.

If you are a pussy soy boy in the field, who interacts with women with

- evasive eye-contact,
- downward eye-contact,
- stuttering,
- fidgeting,
- touching of the face due to nervousness,
- a high-pitched whiney voice,
- rushing your words without any pauses,
- folded arms or arms over crotch (defensive body-language),
- filler-words,
- incoherent rambling,
- awkward hesitation and perpetual procrastination,
- general intense anxiety around women,
- incel-level lack of situational awareness and socially inept calibration,
- hateful bitterness and emotional baggage, or
- lacking the KILLER INSTINCT TO CLOSE,

then you are most likely that kind of guy in the business realm. **By developing yourself in the seduction game, you indirectly improve yourself in the business game and the game of life in general.**

The same character traits, correlated set of skills, and conversation techniques that make one successful with women for sexual purposes ALSO make one successful with men for networking/business purposes. In addition, when you have hot girls around you: wealthy men are more inclined to hit you up for business related discussions because they perceive these hot girls as "evidence" that you are a winner, and winners like to associate with other winners.

YES, this is a book about conversation skills, but how you learn these skills serve as a model for how you learn new skills, in general. **Learn how to learn. The most powerful ability a man can develop is the ability to learn new skills FAST.**

Further, how you handle yourself in socially and sexually charged situations has implications far beyond just pickup and if you can stick your long stick into a living hole.

- Fundamental game skills (such as approaching, conversation, flirting, closing),
- bold charisma,
- enticing charm,
- fierce courage,
- humble patience,
- passion for a meaningful purpose in life,
- being a visionary,
- posessing self-control,
- emotional state regulation skills (EQ),
- self-intitiave and being proactive (not reactive),
- dominant leadership,
- being a calculated risk-taker and adventurer,

will get you laid with women, but more importantly will get you far in life.

GAME SKILLS aren't just about getting laid. They are about building your life. **Women should be a supplement to**

your already amazing life - not the purpose of life itself.

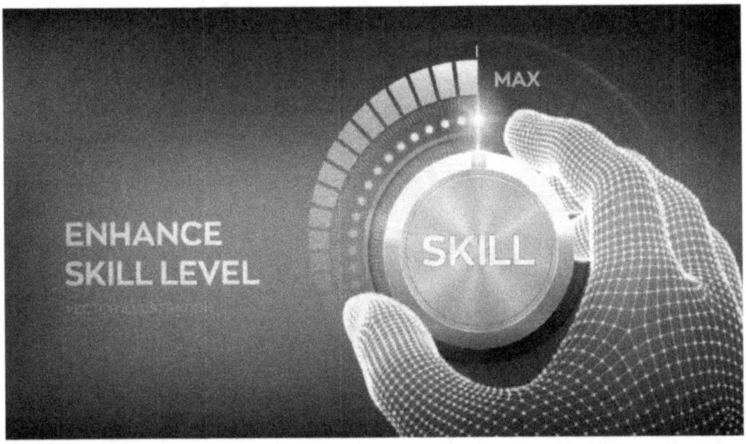

❄

FUNAMENTAL V

Pickup artists are able to walk up to anyone, at anyplace, at anytime and strike up a conversation. They are very good at quickly forming social connections. This is a valuable ability to have that has multiple benefits including sex, money, and power.

And starting now: embrace the identity of being a pickup artist. Verbalize these words:

"I am a man who takes what he wants out of life. If I see a twenty dollar bill on the sidewalk, I'll pick it up because ***I TAKE WHAT I WANT****. If I see a beautiful woman, or anyone that I want to be more intimate with, then I'll approach and strike up a conversation because* ***I TAKE WHAT I WANT****. I am a pickup artist!"*

WHY LEARN CONVERSATION SKILLS?

Attraction is not a choice. Attempting to logically negotiate desire is silly. Sexual attraction is merely a primal response to certain external stimulus such as:

- dominance,
- leadership,
- powerful body-language,
- impeccable high status style and elegant fashion,
- leading (*display of leadership*),
- strong frame (*display of leadership*),
- flashing elite status,
- flashing wealth,
- vibing,
- touching,
- emotional spiking,
- arousing (a horny woman will lose control),
- "I am the prize to be won" frame,

- social proofing,
- sparking jealousy, and
- general escalation.

In between these tactics is a glue that keeps the interaction alive. Without this glue, the mutual engagement will die and there will be no "time" to implement the aforementioned seduction-tactics.

Conversation is the glue that keeps interactions together. It is what fills the space between the tactics. Conversation is the ultimate meta-skill that makes everything else in the human mating ritual possible. It's what keeps her around, so that you can play your game.

In contrast, if the conversation dies then the interaction dies. So it's important to be emotionally engaging enough in conversation to keep women hooked in to interacting with you, and thus "buying you time" to win over mind, heart, and physically escalate on her body. Hence, conversation skills are imperative to learn.

Escalation happens through different mediums:

- Logistics,
- Physicality,
- Mental, and
- Emotional.

These same conversation skills will be useful to help one:

- network with influential millionaires,
- to create mutually beneficial friendships with men (***that have access to things that you don't, or are experts in fields that you are not***

knowledgeable in),

- keep you entertained every time you leave your home and encounter people along your commute, or they can be used to
- create ENDLESS sexual opportunities with very young women (18+) despite the fact that you are a guy in your 30-50s+.

They create a foundation for a successful life. **Pickup related skill sets are transferable skills that give will you benefits that exceed merely sticking your penis into a woman's lubricated hole for the purpose of temporal pleasure. Women are inspiration for you to be the best version of yourself, and build your empire.**

CONVERSATION SKILLS ARE A MAJOR PART OF THE PUZZLE WHEN DEALING WITH WOMEN.

You can be a master approacher, but if you suck at conversation skills, then good luck, because approaching her is just step 1. Step 2 is being able to give emotional value and carry a conversation which sustains the interaction long enough to convey high status (and eventually getting her PSYCHOLOGICALLY HOOKED to being with you).

You can approach a woman and have an amazing opening line, but if you don't follow that up with further observations and conversation then the interaction will most likely DIE RIGHT THERE on the spot. Upon approaching, BRING THE FUCKING VALUE.

THE DARK SIDE OF CONVERSATION

Keep in mind that conversation is not a means unto itself, but rather a medium that buys you time in the interaction to develop a connection on a physical end emotional level. The goal is NOT to have endless conversations that lead to nowhere; THE GOAL IS TO FUCK. THE GOAL IS TO CREATE A LONG-TERM SEXUAL RELATIONSHIP.

You don't want to be:

- the endless texting penpal,
- the perpetual "do-nothing" conversation-guy,
- the eager-to-please, dancing-monkey, juggling-try-hard clown,

but rather A GUY WHO FUCKS WOMEN IN THE PUSSY. VISUALIZE SUCCESS.

She could be down to fuck right now, but you're too busy having a nice guy conversation (trying to spark more perpetual attraction) to notice and capitalize on the sexual opportunity. Have conversations that spark attraction and foster a genuine connection, but when it comes time to close, fucking close. It's counter-productive to always be in "elevator pitch mode". Sharpen your KILLER INSTINCT. **Always be closing.**

HOW TO USE THIS BOOK

When developing your conversation skills, you want to aim for CONSCIOUS practice - not mindless practice. Focus on developing at least one of the tactics mentioned in this book every time you practice your skills on a woman. By small chunking your learning, you ensure that you are not overwhelmed.

I recommend printing out this book and reading through it with a highlighter. Highlight the sentences that really resonate with you. Then verbalize out-loud those collection of highlights every day for the next 30 days; this will assist you in internalizing the mindsets of a sexy conversationalist. When you have the mindsets down (internalized into your bloodstream), the behaviors will flow effortlessly.

- - Getting out of the house,
- - going to a place where there are women,
- - approaching some cute ones,
- - saying an opener to break the ice,
- - starting up a conversation,
- - flirting to create a man-to-woman frame,
- - throwing in field-tested teasing lines,
- - escalating the vibe,

is just the first phase of the mating dance but it's where most guys are stuck at.

This book will discuss 48 conversation techniques and mindsets to ensure that you always have something to say, and you will never again be in the situation where you see a pretty girl but you can't approach her because you are lost for words.

LETS GET STARTED RIGHT NOW MOTHERFUCKING, MOTHERFUCKER. IT'S ABOUT TIME YOU RADICALLY CHANGED YOUR LIFE FOR THE POSITIVE.

Yours truly, Cory Smith

P.S. Also see the other books in the series, "The Sexcalation System", and "Womenese 101" which discuss different aspects of seduction.

YOU CAN APPROACH ANYTIME AND ANYWHERE. YOU CAN START A CONVERSATION WITH ANYONE. THE ONLY THING HOLDING YOU BACK ARE YOUR LIMITING BELIEFS.

HOW TO NEVER RUN OUT OF THINGS TO SAY, THE DEFINITIVE ULTIMATE GUIDE

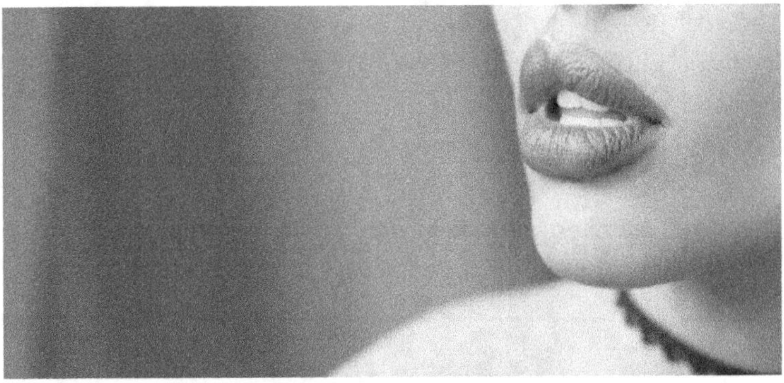

"Men are seduced by what they see; women are seduced by what they hear." - Russian Proverb

In this chapter, I will teach you how to NEVER run out of things to say in social and sexual situations; this is also known as, HAVING A GOLDEN MOUTH PIECE. Be willing to review the key points in this particular chapter multiple times (even once a week) for the concepts to really sink in. Verbal repetition is the key to internalization, and internalization is the key to lifestyle integration. Now let's MAKE IT RAIN VAGINA.

If you find that you have difficulty keeping a conversation going then it's because of:

- - social inhibitions,
- - nervousness,
- - insecurities, and
- - filtering yourself.

You don't run out of things to say with your close friends because you are **FEARLESS** and **SPEAK YOUR MIND FREELY.**

Have you noticed then when you are with your bros then you always have something to say? When you are with these close friends, you don't panic, or think "Oh my gosh, I don't know what to say next! I AM FUCKED." The right things to say just come to you. Why is that? It is because...

Always having something to say comes from a being in a resourceful emotional state.

Repeat.

Always having something to say comes from a being in a resourceful emotional state.

Again!

Always having something to say comes from a being in a resourceful emotional state.

This "talkative state" is a certain state of mind that is conductive to having something to talk about. It is "BEING IN THE ZONE". When you are in this "FLOW STATE", you are ON-POINT and the right things to say come to you naturally.

Good game comes from learning how to leave non-resourceful emotional states (such as anxiety, nervousness, fearfulness, panic, stress, tension, being overly self-conscious, being self-filtering and self-judgmental), and...

ENTER ON COMMAND into a resourceful emotional state (100% in control of yourself, calm as an unmoving mountain, fearless like a lion, empowered, energized, and inspired).

When you are with your male friends, you are in a relaxed empowered emotional state. Apply the same to women. Assume familiarity. Treat her as if you've known her your entire life. The added benefit of this is that by assuming rapport, you create rapport. This is how women come to feel "it's as if I have known him forever."

When you treat a woman as if you've known her for years, then it will naturally make you feel relaxed enough to speak your mind freely. When you are in this relaxed flow-state, you will always have something to say to keep the conversation going, and the interaction alive. Women feel what you feel; when you're relaxed and comfortable talking to her, she will mirror that contagious emotional state and behavioral patterns.

Knowing what to say is based on having the right emotional state.

In contrast, being in a nervous state of mind fucks guys up because anxiety shuts down the brain. Being nervous leads to the mind going blank, and lacking the ability to come up with interesting/emotionally-engaging things to say on the spot.

Being fearless and in a "talkative state" puts someone into THE ZONE where the right things to say naturally come up. Strong conversation game comes from being able to put yourself into this talkative, positively charged state of mind.

The following behavioral sequence can help put someone into that resourceful emotional state of FEARLESSNESS and having ENDLESS THINGS TO SAY TO WOMEN. You can implement this brief ten minute behavioral "ritual" prior to going out to meet women.

While I point out a behavioral sequence that has helped me personally (**which incorporates a combination of**

several techniques at once), I recommend that you tailor (and experiment with) your own behavioral sequence based on empirical results gained in the field.

- Setting a timer for ten minutes[1],
- listening to motivating instrumental rock music: https://www.youtube.com/results?search_query=rock+instrumental[2]
- screaming the affirmations "I AM THE DANGER!! I AM THE CHAOS!!! I DON'T GIVE A FUCK WHAT ANYONE THINKS. I AM FEARLESS."
- verbalizing the affirmation "I take action every day to become competent in a field that I value. I will have a good time and every approach is a WIN - regardless of the specific results."
- doing push-ups and/or hitting a punching bag,
- utilizing affirmations in the field,
- utilizing self-suggestions in the field,
- singing a tune, and then when leaving one's home
- doing at least three simple warmup approaches.[3]

The big secret to starting a conversation with a woman is to simply assume you already are in one, and act accordingly. When your frame (perception of reality) is strong then women will just accept it. In any interaction, the person who has more conviction in his perception of reality will create the mutually acknowledged frame. He who controls the frame, controls the game.

No wonder it's difficult to find things to talk about with women if:

- you're operating from an anxious place (instead of using mindfulness and deep breathing relaxation techniques),
- stuck in your head over-analyzing the situation,
- have unrealistically high standards of what is acceptable to say, and
- TRAPPED in hesitation, bullshit excuses, and fear.

Every time you give into fear and illusions, they develop a stronger grasp over you. Every time you feed limiting beliefs with actions, they limit you even more. Every time you don't approach out of the fear of rejection, your balls shrink.

❄

If you want to always have something to say and never run out of things to talk about:

- operate from a relaxed state of mind,
- be fully attuned to what is happening in the situation at the moment,
- talk about that which personally excites you,
- let go of self-censorship,
- destroy the self-filter,

- speak your mind freely,
- express yourself fully,
- shine your personality without fear of being judged,
- approach immediately as soon as you see the girl, and
- don't be afraid of "what I have to say isn't good enough".

Write this down: nothing kills conversations more than social inhibitions!

- **He who hesitates, masterbates.**
- **He who doesn't give a fuck, fucks.**
- **To fuck pussy, don't be a pussy.**
- **Sexual fortune favors the bold.**
- **Sexual opportunities are abundant.**

❄

The Six Fundamental Mindsets to Having the Golden Mouth Piece

I.

OVER-ANALYSIS AND OVER-THINKING KILLS CONVERSATIONS. BE MINDFUL.

Be in the present moment and pay attention to what is happening right in front of you - the reality that is mutually shared between you and her. Pay attention to what she is saying, to who she is, what she is doing, and to the situation in front of you. **It's hard to have a conversation with someone who is in their own world STUCK in their**

head paying attention to OTHER IRRELEVANT THINGS.

It can be difficult to have things to say if you are too busy:

- analyzing game dynamics ("does she like me? am I dressed properly? what if I get rejected?"), or
- thinking too much about things that are NOT relevant ("what am I eating for lunch later? what time is my doctor's appointment again? what are other people thinking about me talking to her?").

What kills conversations? Being stuck in your head, overanalyzing and overthinking the situation - instead of entering an emotional state of free, uninhibited, confident full expression. Instead of spending time "on a different planet" in your head, bring yourself to the here and now.

EMPTY YOUR MIND OF ALL THOUGHTS and **FOCUS ON WHAT IS GOING ON IN THE CURRENT SITUATION**. Focus on what is happening in front of you and thoughts will naturally come to you. When the thoughts come to you, speak them freely.

II.

KILL THE OVERLY SENSITIVE SUPER-EGO. USE FREE ASSOCIATION.

When a thought POPS into your mind, don't stop yourself by thinking "is this appropriate to say?" Don't even ask that question. JUST FUCKING SAY IT!

One of the easiest ways to start talking to everyone and not run out of things to say is to just speak out your immediate thoughts without any filter or personal censor. Say whatever POPS into your mind - even if it seems random or somewhat inappropriate.

Let go of needing to always say the perfect thing and simply think out-loud!

You can say almost anything; as long as you have the confidence and enthusiasm behind it then it will work.

III.

UTILIZE PASSION

If you're running out of things to say then you're probably trying to talk to her about things that you don't care about instead of focusing on your greatest passions in life. When you talk about what matters deeply to you, you'll never run out of content. In fact, you *almost* won't be able to stop talking!

Talking about what you're passionate about TURNS WOMEN ON because they feed on that enjoyable energy, and get a spike of adrenaline for being "high on life". Successful seducers make women feel happy through this method.

IV.

SELL CONVERSATIONAL VALUE TO THOSE WHO ARE BUYING THAT WHICH YOU ARE SELLING.

Take this to a higher level by becoming highly knowledgable and skillful in the subject that you are passionate about.

Assuming that this is a field that women find intriguing and you meet those type of women by going to a social club/organization (such as yoga, spirituality, salsa dancing) that specializes in that field, then you will have hours upon hours of content when teaching a woman the path to mastery that you took.

Example: if you are passionate about career development, then you are more likely to meet women who are interested in hearing what you have to say about that subject matter in a college social event than in the street. If you are passionate about spirituality, then hitting up drunk eighteen year old teenagers at 2am at a sorority/fraternity mix event is less than an optimal mating strategy.

V.

LISTEN.

Listen to what she says; then use that information as fodder for what you will say next. The key is to pay attention that topics that she is most passionate about. Making your remarks relevant to topics that she sincerely cares about and that will keep the conversation going for miles.

VI.

SPEAK YOUR THOUGHTS OUTLOUD.

When you listen attentively to what a woman says, you'll experience certain impulsive thoughts in response to what she has said. The key is to speak these thoughts out-loud verbalized with confidence when they occur.

SUMMARY OF HOW TO NEVER RUN OUT OF THINGS TO SAY TO WOMEN:

- **Enter a resourceful emotional state.** Achieve this through emotional regulation techniques (such as affirmations).
- **I. Be mindful.** Focus on what is relevant.
- **II. Kill the inner-critical.** Use free association.
- **III. Utilize passion.** Talk about what you enjoy.
- **IV. Listen**. Use what she says to assist you.
- **V. Think out-loud.** Ride emotional waves.
- **VI. Meet the type of women** (in a location where this type of women hangs out) that would be interested in hearing what you have to say about subjects that you are knowledgable and passionate in. You'll fuck her mind and then fuck her body.

❄

When you are in bed, FUCK HER HARD. HOLD NOTHING BACK. In a similar manner, when in conversation with a woman, reveal the FULL FORCE OF YOUR PERSONALITY. Enter interactions with fierce boldness, and this alone will captivate women.

❄

Bulletpoints:

5 Mindsets to not run out of things to say:

- - free association,
- - say whatever POPS into your mind,
- - talk about what you're PASSIONATE about,

- - talk about what you have a lot of KNOWLEDGE in,
- - comment about the situation, conversation, her, what she is saying, or the people around you (people watching),
- - when she talks, listen attentively and when she finishes then share your opinion on it without any social inhibitions. **Don't be afraid to disagree with her perspective; in fact, this alone can spark an interesting conversation.**

Basic Conversation Level 1 Formula:

- -> STEP 1: make an observation, provoking statement or ask a question.
- -> STEP 2: listen to her response, where she reveals personal information about herself.
- -> STEP 3: self-disclose personal information about yourself that is relatable to what she has just said, and is relatable to subjects that she values.
- -> STEP 4: repeat.

Basic Conversation Level 2 Formula:

- 1. Listen.
- 2. Identify her emotional state and understand what is being said.
- 3. Paraphrase what said in your own words; reveal empathy to her emotions.
- 4. Add insight.
- 5. Relate something from your own life that is relevant to what was just discussed.

What to talk about after the opener:

- 1. Observation about her,
- 2. Commentary about the situation (aka mutually shared reality),
- 3. Commentary about the conversation (aka going meta),
- 4. Something "crazy" that just happened to you that you can't wait to share with someone

❄

PRACTICE MAKES BETTER. 5 EXERCISES TO IMPROVE YOUR ABILITY TO NEVER RUN OUT OF THINGS TO SAY.

EXERCIZE #1

Take a dictionary and a camera. Open up to a random page and with your eyes closed choose a random word. Record yourself speaking about that subject for 5 minutes straight. **The goal is to be able to prove to yourself that you can talk about anything for as long as you want to because the ability to have a conversation is based on a state of mind and a state of emotions.** The brain wants proof – not promises.

EXERCIZE #2

Imagine spotting a beautiful woman waiting for the bus - as you are walking home from work. Imagine saying something to that woman to strike up a conversation; then think to yourself "how would she respond? How would I respond to her response?" Then "How would she respond to my response of her response?" And so on. This is similar to playing chess against yourself. The goal is to slow things down enough to understand the general dynamics of conversation, and realize that any given point you have multiple moves to play (**with some moves being more conducive to the probability of sexual success than others**) - rather than a linear path.

EXERCIZE #3

Make a list of topics that you are enjoy talking about, and have a lot of knowledge in. You can get addicted to a certain kind of misery. That is misery of the excuse of "not knowing what to say to women", so that you would have the ability to sidestep the potential pain of rejection, and having your ego attacked by the opinion of random female strangers. When you accept the possibility of rejection then women lose their power over you.

EXERCIZE #4

Make a list of at LEAST 3 affirmations to repeat every morning. Here are some really powerful ones to choose from:

- "I will speak my mind freely with women."
- **"When I am with women, I will express my opinions and share my thoughts openly with extreme confidence."**
- "When it comes to interacting with others, I will say WHATEVER THE FUCK I FEEL LIKE SAYING. What I have to say is valuable just because it came from me."
- "I have lots of things to talk about because the world is an interesting and exciting place. There is NO FUCKING LIMIT to how much there is to talk about."

- "I don't give a fuck if people disagree with my perceptions. I am an expander of consciousness and gain a lot just by talking about things that are personally meaningful to me."
- "I don't give a fuck what people think!"
- "Meeting new people is FUN and engaging in conversations has a lot of personal benefits to me!! I can gain insights about female psychology, have a good time, talk about what I love, and sharpen my social/seduction skills all at the same time! If someone doesn't like what I am doing, FUCK THEM. I DON'T GIVE A FUCK BECAUSE I AM TOO BUSY HAVING FUN!!!"

EXERCIZE #5

Set a specific time during the day when you call up some of your contacts - just to practice your conversation skills, strengthen the connections in your rotation, and follow up on potential leads. For instance this could be from 10:30PM to 11:00PM. Just call people up and schmooze. Afterwards, make notes of valuable insights that you have learned about how to interact with women successfully (also known as writing a Field Report). There is always a higher level of knowledge and skill in game. Don't settle for less just because you're the smoothest lion in your social circle. KEEP YOUR SKILLS SHARP.

❄

SEDUCTIVE POWERS HAVE BEEN WITHIN YOU THIS ENTIRE TIME. YOU JUST HAVE TO LEARN TO TAP INTO THEM.

NATURAL CONVERSATION BEATS HAVING EIGHT HOURS OF MEMORIZED LINES:

While have some memorized lines in your pocket is certainly useful for:

- (1) starting conversations with beautiful women,
- (2) case study examples to model after,
- (3) can be good "training wheels, and
- (4) having something to say just in case the mind draws on a blank,

But they should not be relied upon. Depending on having memorized lines leads to being a man with a metaphorical crutch who can't operate without the constant need of more lines.

You need to be a seducer who can generate lines from within, rather than depending on an external source to constantly feed you "what exactly to say". Give a man a fish of 100 pickup lines and he will always come back to you to buy more products because of his dependency and lack of confidence. Teach a man how to do fishing and he will operate independently.

It's imperative to learn how to always have something to say to a woman - even if you ran out of lines, or don't have memorized lines prepared. Nothing beats spontaneous natural authentic conversation that happens in the moment. **Women have an innate bullshit-senser, and can intuitively tell if a man is being REAL with them and communi-**

cating authentically OR if he is faking a personality and delivering memorized conversation scripts.

A real connection with a woman should be based on being the best version of YOU - rather than being an alternative radically different personality that you mimic. By memorizing lines that have worked for someone else, you risk:

- **being incongruent** (*something that an 22 year old college frat boy - writing field reports on the web - would say would not make a sense for a 35 year old lawyer to say; a woman's "I am being deceived" internal alarms will go off*),
- **creating something unattainable in the long-term** (*sooner or later, you'll run out of memorized pickup lines to use with the particular woman who you are interested in*),
- **sounding scripted** (*rather than creating an authentic experience for you and the woman you are interested in*), and
- **be overly concerned with "did I say the right thing that matches the script?"** (*instead of focusing on having a good time and sharing enjoyable experiences with women; if meeting women is a psychologically painful experience then you won't be that motivated to go out).*

The bottom line is this: an aspiring seducer must learn how to charm women with his own words that come from within naturally - without needing to constantly refer to his collection of conversational routines. It is better to be one who can create lines - rather than one who needs others to tach him which lines to say. **<u>When you have the right mindsets, the correct attraction-sparking things to say will come naturally to you.</u>**

WOMEN WANT TO BE FUCKED - JUST NOT BY SHY LOSERS.

---

1. Some men may need even an hour of mental conditioning to get into the right state of mind conducive to meeting and interacting with women. When you are in the right state ("feeling fucking awesome!") and have State Control skills then you'll find results improve radically.
2. Avoid songs that contain distracting lyrics - especially ones that promote oneitis (the pedestalization of women).
3. It is important to not degrade the importance and necessity of warming up. Even a veteran seducer who has thousands of approaches can feel approach anxiety and could benefit tremendously from doing a few simple short interactions with strangers as he goes about his day - to sustain macro momentum and get himself quickly into THE ZONE. Whoever says "I don't need to warmup because I'm already an expert" is either lazy, in denial, or a fucking idiot. That being said, never let "I am not in state" be an excuse for not approaching a beautiful woman or avoiding interactions entirely. In conclusion: warming up is one of the fastest ways to get into an empowered emotional state (also known as "The Indifference Threshold"). For those who want to learn more about the subject of quickly entering emotional states, I recommend researching the subject of anchoring in NLP.

ALWAYS KNOWING WHAT TO SAY TO WOMEN COMES FROM BEING IN A RESOURCEFUL, EMPOWERED EMOTIONAL STATE.

1

LAW #1: Be emotionally relevant.

LAW #1: Women are emotional creatures. Be emotionally relevant.

Technique #1: Find something that she is passionate about AND that you're passionate about; then talk about that! Look for topics of mutual interest and utilize them as "bait" for conversation.

ASK YOURSELF THREE QUESTIONS:

- -> What does she like to talk about?
- -> What do you like to talk about?
- -> Where do these overlap?

Then share insights about her favorite subjects that you actually give a fuck about. BOOM!!

THIS WORKS LIKE MAGIC. For example: women LOVE talking about relationships. If you want to turn a boring conversation around, bring up the subject of relationship dynamics and request her opinion on a hot-button issue in the subject. It is important to talk about her areas of interest, and it preferable for her areas of interest to overlap your areas of interest.

THE SWEET SPOT IS WHEN YOU FIND A SUBJECT MATTER OF MUTUAL INTEREST THAT CAN BE MILKED FOR CONVERSATION TO SUSTAIN THE INTERACTION AND BUY YOU TIME TO PHYSICALLY ESCALATE ON HER BODY.

WHEN YOU TALK about what you genuinely care about, you will feel a visceral motivating pull to keep talking. When you talk about what that particular woman enjoys, she will inspire you to keep talking by giving you positive body-language and providing juicy pieces of information for you to work with.

LAW #1

Be emotionally relevant by speaking about a subject matter that a woman genuinely cares about.

LAW #1 Clause 1

Find a way to relate that to a subject that you genuinely care about, so that your words will come from your heart and a place of effortlessly expressing passions (and self-amusement) - not from a place of being try-hard.

❄

6 CHICK CRACK **subjects of conversation:**

- - spirit animal,
- - astrology,
- - cold reading psychology,
- - her ambitions, values, and passions,
- - relationship dynamics,
- - the current news,

AN EXAMPLE OF A CONVERSATION SUBJECT THAT WOMEN LOVE:

At the risk of being slightly repetitive, I will mention this concept now (despite it being mentioned again later in the book) because is has relevancy to LAW#1. Often it is useful to hear the same concept being repeated from a different angle (for the sake of internalization purposes).

A WOMAN'S **favorite subject in the entire universe is..... (you guessed it).... Herself!** She cares more about herself than anyone and anything in the world. Don't be fooled by a woman's altruistic appearances; her primary agenda is always to serve her own unconscious or conscious biological interests because she worships the god that is her name.

THIS IS why stacking non-judgmental observations and insights about who she is will keep her hooked unto your every word. If you only learn one thing from this book then let this be the one thing that you learn: **tell women insights that you have noticed about them and they will love you for it.**

THE POSITIVITY PRINCIPLE

Don't share these insights in a condescending/judgmental, harsh way because this may discourage women from sharing openly about their lives. She might be reticent when speaking IF it frequently leads to her being attacked in an analytical manner. **As a general rule when dealing with women, being positive and enthusiastic about life is sexier than focusing on the negative and complaining.** Contrary to the behavior of certain red pill gurus, constantly complaining about how shit women are and how life "sucks because it's so unfair", does NOT lead to a healthy perspective on existence and a feel-good vibe.

DISCLAIMER: ***While the vast majority of women greatly appreciate cold-reads, there are anomalies of certain women that don't appreciate it****. A smart seducer starts with the same cookie-cutter strategy to every woman that he meets, but with time creates a more tailored mating strategy that is specifically designed and refined (on the spot) to meet the emotional needs of the woman he is dealing with that is based on the latest information in the field (such as her body-language reactions to his micro-moves and other clues that she leaves about the blueprint to seducing her). Hence, to an extent he is always in calibration-mode and "meeting her where she is at" - while simultaneously drawing her into his world and escalating the interaction.*

HOW TO CREATE **a Conversational Connection**

- Figure out what her favorite topics of conversation are [aka Elicit Values].
- Learn a lot of information about these subjects.
- Speak passionately about them.

- Use extremely powerful and dominant body-language.

BOOM! She will hold on and cling to every word that you say.

HOW TO LEARN WHAT SUBJECTS OF CONVERSATION WOMEN ARE INTERESTED IN:

When you notice that she brings a subject up on her own then take mental note of this. This is an indicator that it's a conversational topic that she is passionate about. If you notice that her eyes light up and she becomes animated as soon as a specific subject of conversation is brought up then take note of that too! Women constantly leave clues on how they desire to be seduced. Ignore what she says "she wants", and look at what she behaviorally responds to (in terms of her actions, body-language, and micro-expressions).

CONVERSATION IS NOT a blind man's game; to succeed pay attention to the ongoing dynamic between you and her, and tailor your strategies based on the current social feedback you are getting.

MAKE **a list of topics that you have a lot of knowledge in, you are passionate about, enjoy talking about, and what women will generally find interesting.** When you are in a conversation bring these subjects into the conversation. For example if you care about travel then no matter what she says then you can bring it up with a simple "That reminds me of the time I was in Florida, [...]".

. . .

A SMOOTH TRANSITION depends on relating what she just said to what you have just said; albeit, you don't always need to have a smooth transition. You can just can bring up a random subject and as long as you have the confidence and a strong frame, it will work too. **General rule of thumb: with a strong frame, you can get away with almost anything.**

WHAT YOU DON'T WANT to do is to talk about subjects that women don't find interesting. **If upon talking about a particular subject, you see that a woman is expressing disinterested body-language then that's a sign that you should switch the subject.** In contrast, if you see a woman's eyes light up (and emotional state spike) as soon as you mention a particular topic or buzzword, then that's your cue that this subject is worth talking about with her. Make a mental note in your mind to learn more about that subject, so that the next you see her: you'll be able to better engage.

THE OPTIMAL PATH is when you are interested in the same subject as she is interested in. Then when you share enthusiastic insights about that subject, then **you create a mutually beneficial and mutually enjoyable experience that is shared between the both of you.**

LAW #1 Clause 2

Be willing to learn about subject matters that women find highly interesting, and to become competent in areas that women really appreciate. It is preferable for these to be based on the type of woman that you are interested in.

. . .

AT THE SAME TIME, **don't lose your identity in the seduction game; draw women into your own world by flashing elite status, having a fiery purpose, and having your own personally meaningful hobbies that you genuinely care about and are a master of.**

ONE OF THE girlfriends that I had in college was obsessed about being a vegetarian, PETA, anime, fitness, and (ironically) video-games. I recall knowing close to nothing about most of these subjects and researching them by watching documentaries and reading articles on the web, so that I would be able to engage in conversation with **my own unique perspective on these "hot topics" that she adored**. While I did this in my formative years, I would not necessarily recommend this mating strategy unless you are already in a sexual relationship with the woman (or you are trying to break into a particular niche of women who ascribe to a certain micro culture) because researching a subject can be time consuming.

FURTHER, **it is preferable for a woman to be sucked into your world more than you are sucked into her world.** Focus on her becoming interested in your favorite subjects of conversation MORE than you becoming interested in what she is interested in. This is simply more time efficient. Further, it allows you to play the sexy role of an authority figure who guides her path (as a salsa dance instructor, college "tutor", or even a spiritual leader in some religious niches) rather than a low status follower of her world. Don't lose your personal identity in pursuit of sexual access to a specific woman, but be willing to recreate yourself and become the best version of yourself for the sake of achieving your life purpose.

A WOMAN IS ATTRACTED to a man of higher social status than her. Create this perception of status by teaching her new things about life. **After all, a teacher is of higher social status than his student.** This is more effective to do if she gets sucked into your world, and into subjects that you are a master of - rather than vice-versa.

WOMEN FUCK UP - NOT DOWN. **Women fuck men that are leaders - not followers.** You want to constantly be leading her physically, mentally and logistically. By playing the role of a leader in the dynamic between you and her, attraction levels will spike. Even a "feminist" woman, wants to be submit to a more dominant, and more competent man.

IF YOU WANT to get a woman to be sexually aroused by you then you have to frame yourself as the PRIZE and the ONE WHO IS MORE VALUABLE than her. One way of asserting yourself as the being that is of higher worth than her is by leading. **A leader is naturally given the position of being higher in relative social status than those that follow him.**

❄

HOW TO BE A LEADER

This brings the discussion to a natural question "How does one get others (whether it's men or women) to follow him?" The answer is this:

. . .

<u>A SUCCESSFUL LEADER HAS COMPETENCE, **CONFIDENCE, and DECISIVENESS.**</u>

WHEN ONE IS HIGHLY confident and decisive about a particular course of action (while having the skills to pull it off) then others will step aside to let it happen, play along, or follow him across the seven oceans. **<u>You want to get a woman used to the idea and behavioral pattern of following your lead.</u>** First she does small compliance demands (with time slowly increasing her levels of doing what you want her to do), and before you know it: she is sucking your dick.

IN CONTRAST, people are NOT going to follow someone who:

- **sucks at what they teach** ("*like a fat person giving diet advice or a broke man giving get-rich advice*"),
- **who naturally has low confidence levels** ("*because deep down he knows that he is a pretending imposter*") (a woman intuitively thinks "*if he doesn't even trust himself then why should I?*"), and
- **can't decide what to do** (a woman intuitively thinks "*don't fucking waste my time with your indecisiveness; come back to me when you have a clear plan of action and AT LEAST look like you know what you are doing*").
- **Demands too much too fast.** Don't initiate interactions with "Hey, wanna fuck?" Start with giving value, creating an enjoyable experience and fostering a man-to-woman connection. Start with

smaller compliance demands from her prior to bigger compliance demands.

- **Appears to be a loser** who can't even take care of himself - let alone those in his inner-circle.
- **Is not an effective, articulate communicator** (stutters, evasive eye-contact, fidgets, mumbles his words, looks down, touches his face due to nervousness, is too quiet, doesn't make sense, talks about things no one cares about, wastes everyones time including his own etc).

PEOPLE WILL FOLLOW SOMEONE WHO:

- **Has experience in what he is teaching, a track record of proven past successes, and positive references** (*"he's been around the block for a while; he probably knows his shit. Other people vouch for him. Lets see what this fucker has"*)
- **High levels of confidence** (*"oh snap! This motherfucker is cocky!! I wonder what he is all about?"*).
- **Knows exactly what he is doing or at least appears to know exactly what he is doing by having a clear plan of action** (*"he seems really certain about a particular path. He must be right. I don't have the time to figure all of this shit out by myself, so I'll just follow him for now."*)

TO BE A LEADER DEVELOP COMPETENCE, CONFIDENCE AND DECISIVENESS. There are other qualities such as calculated humility, being mature, being responsible, and constant reinforcement of one's blade, but these three (competence, confidence, and decisiveness) mentioned are the primary ones.

THE MOST IMPORTANT trait of being a leader is competence. Women will generally not follow a fool. **Even if that fool is extremely confident, a woman will eventually figure out that he doesn't know what the fuck he is doing, sucks at his craft, and his life is shit to begin with.** If you are a broke loser, don't expect women to follow your guidance and accept you as an authority figure in their life.

YOU NEED TO HAVE YOUR SHIT TOGETHER. This includes being good at basic self-care, having your own nice place, having a cool car, dressing like a BOSS, being financially independent, having a social life etc.

THE BEST KIND of confidence is genuine and comes from within. When you gain experience, competence, and results then you will naturally be confident. **Women can intuitively sense a man who has his life shit together and it turns them ON.**

FURTHER, I strongly encourage you to become competent in a field that women value and appreciate - particularly based on the type of women that you are interested in.

- If you are interested in young eighteen year old women, **then being competent at understanding college and career dynamics is useful.** Then work as a college tutor part time or enroll into one class for easy access to the college - while attending many of the college's social events (not Crypto Club which turned out to be a "hotdog farm").

- If you are interested in a traditional women, then **being competent at spiritual matters is paramount.** Become a member of an organization that creates events for that niche.
- If you are interested in the party type of woman then you should **become competent in traveling to different countries, knowing the best sights/places, and the coolest events in your city.**

PRACTICE EVERY STEP OF THE SEDUCTION PROCESS (INCLUDING CONVERSATION) BY MEETING WOMEN IN YOUR DAILY LIFE AS YOU GO ABOUT YOUR DAY.

GO TO WHERE THE TYPE OF WOMAN THAT YOU WANT TO MEET GOES TO. Millionaires and billionaires network at gold courses, high-end lounges, and cigar clubs. Women - straight out of high-school - that just turned 18 hang out at college freshman classes, and college prep tutoring sessions. Women who have more traditional values will be seen volunteering at organizations that have meaningful values.

IDEALLY, **you should tailor your game to a specific type of woman because one will have a higher yield of success being the "master of one than a jack of all trades".** You don't need 43 different ways to meet women and 23 different opening lines to say to women; you just need at least 1-3 reliable methods. Likewise, you don't need to know 3,423 fishing spots to catch fish (and it would be a waste of time to find all of these spots); you just need to know a handful of good spots. Life is short, so don't make things unnecessarily more complicated than they have to be, and don't spread yourself too thin.

DO YOUR MARKET RESEARCH. MASTER A NARROW PATH.

Figure out the type of woman that you desire. Describe her. Then figure out what kind of man she desires, and where you have to be in order to meet these type of women.

- What kind of traits does she have?
- What is her rough age?
- What is her body-type?
- What kind of personality does she have?
- Where does she spend time hanging out for relaxation?
- Where does she spend time being alone (hint: often a library, coffee shop, taking the bus home, on the commute to work, or relaxing at a park bench nearby her school)?
- What kind of social clubs or organizations is she a part of (such as yoga club, salsa club, or simply working part time for a college's student union)?
- What kind of subjects is she interested in?
- What kind of fields does she value?
- What kind of man is she interested in?
- What TURNS HER ON?
- What makes her go ABSOLUTELY CRAZY OVER A GUY?
- What are the top 3 things that are holding you back from succeeding with this type of woman?
- What are 3 things you can do right now to instantly turn your life around and give you a huge

seductive advantage (including moving to a new populated place that has convenient access to hotter, younger women)?

The more you learn about a target (and the sociological variables involved) the easier it will be to conquer and dominate the target.

AT THE ABSOLUTE BARE MINIMUM, **FIND AT LEAST ONE GOOD PLACE TO MEET THE TYPE OF WOMEN THAT YOU ARE INTERESTED IN. THEN FOCUS ON MASTERING THAT PARTICULAR PATH OF BANGING PUSSY. Every time you approach a woman in that place (through that particular method), you have an opportunity to practice your conversation, social and seduction skills in general. Further, every time you step outside your home: you have ample opportunities to practice your approaching skills.**

ALWAYS BE FLIRTING.

SEDUCTION IS A LIFESTYLE.

LEARN MORE about that type of woman and the kind of subjects that this type of woman is interested in (making a mental note of it). Become competent in a field that this type of woman values (whether it's travel, spirituality, cold read psychology, or college dynamics). **Know where these type of women spend time relaxing, being social, and are more receptive to being approached (note: it's not**

when she is 3 minutes late to class, and is rushing down the hallway).

AT THE SAME TIME, don't go overboard and neglect the more important aspect of bringing women into your world. While you might adopt certain values and knowledge fields to become an asset in that micro-culture, you still retain your self-identity and bring women into your world by having your own purpose in life, being enthusiastic about your own life passions and being a master in hobbies that are personally meaningful to you.

❄

2

LAW #1: SUMMARY

LAW #1: BE EMOTIONALLY RELEVANT.

UNDERSTAND WHAT HER CORE VALUES. Observe: (1) what does she value more than anything else in the world? (2) What is her Life Purpose? (3) What is personally meaningful and important to her? Then communicate those same core values back to her in conversation.

TECHNIQUE: FIND COMMON INTERESTS: UTILIZE COMMONALITIES

Find something that she is passionate about AND that you're passionate about; then talk about that! Look for topics of mutual interest and utilize them as "bait" for conversation.

3

LAW #2: THE PLEASURE PRINCIPLE; Create Desire and Leave women wanting more.

LAW #2: Women do what feels good. Create desire by leaving a woman wanting more.

TECHNIQUE **#2: End on a high note.**

When you sense a conversation is coming to an end, you be the one to end it properly first. Say something to spike her excitement and then end the interaction abruptly. This will leave her wanting you more and create artificial scarcity. This is vastly preferable to letting conversations fizzle out, die and then you eject the interaction as a result.

TV SHOWS DO this all time; they end the episode on a cliffhanger (especially on the most interesting part of the story/plot climax) to keep you hooked on waiting for the next episode to find out more.

ALL CONVERSATIONS WILL COME to their natural conclusion. This is the way of the world; nothing is permanent. Take control of this. YOU be the one to end it first (subtly rejecting her) and end it on a high point. When you sense that the conversation is coming to its organic end, be the one to end it before she does. Ironically rejecting her a bit (sometimes playfully, and sometimes seriously) makes her want you even more!

PUSHING A WOMAN AWAY, **at the right moment, makes her want you TWICE AS MUCH.** This is one of those times. By being the one to end the interaction, instead of having her end the interaction - you create this "push away" that leaves her wanting more.

WOMEN THINK that they want social power, but the moment they get it: they lose respect and attraction for the man that they are dealing with. Hence, as an Alpha Male it is imperative that you seize social power for yourself by framing yourself as the prize and sustaining that frame throughout the interaction.

AN ALPHA MALE has important life goals to attend to and a dream to chase; he has places to be, things to do, and people to meet. Hence, he increases his perceived worth through a perception of scarcity by limiting the time that women have with him. **A woman will value a man who is busy (yet still makes time for her) than a man who is always instantly available without limitations. Create perceived scarcity.**

WOMEN EXPECT **a man of high status have standards, to have things going on his life, and to be**

unavailable at times. It is not "weird" to hang up on a beautiful woman because you have more important shit to handle.

YOU ARE A PRIZE TO BE WON. YOU ARE A 10, SO FUCKING ACT LIKE IT. YOU ARE THE MAN THAT SHE HAS BEEN DREAMING ABOUT SINCE HER CHILDHOOD.

FURTHER, keeping control of the social interaction in general is paramount. If you allow a woman to control the interaction, it may not lead to sex because she may not have sex on the agenda. She may even self-sabotage the interaction and lead you to the friend zone. **Hence, ending on a high note is part of the general theme of leading a woman towards sex and being an Alpha Male who takes control of situations.** By taking control of the interaction and guiding it towards sex then you use skill to get laid - rather than relying on luck or hope.

FUCK RELYING ON CHANCE. FUCK waiting for opportunity. CREATE opportunity by taking charge of life and leading people towards mutually beneficial connections.

- YOU be the one to end the conversation first.
- END the conversation on a high-note - not when it fizzles out to death
- Be in control of the interaction from the start.

USE OPEN LOOPS

WOMEN HAVE A DEEP-NEED FOR CLOSURE. This is why cutting yourself off at the point of maximum suspense to create a cliff-hanger, is a GREAT WAY to get a woman more engaged in the conversation. This technique is known as creating open loops.

THE GAME of Thrones and other popular TV shows implement open-loops to keep its viewers hooked into watching for long periods of a time. An episode will have multiple storylines playing at the same time. The episode will start with storyline #1 with characters #1-#3. After around five minutes, that storyline will be abruptly interrupted at its most interesting point and another storyline (#2) will be introduced with characters #4-#6. Viewers will continue to watch because they want to know what happened with storyline #1 and they have a deep-need for closure.

DON'T TELL A WOMAN EVERYTHING. It is a fool who provides full closure and transparency. **You want to keep parts of yourself a mystery to keep her guessing. This will keep her thinking about you!** Imagination will spike her sexual arousal much more than seeing all the cards that you are holding. A woman may fuck you just to get the full story.

DON'T ANSWER every question that she asks you with full transparency. Don't always say "yes" to her requests. Don't always be instantly available for as long as he wants. Don't always reward her for good behavior.

. . .

WOMEN ARE LIKE CATS. If you give a cat a string, it will get bored and potentially even eject. **If you dangle a string right in front of a cat (close enough so that it can reach the string with some effort but not so far away that it's discouraging), it will be tempted to chase like crazy - losing itself in the process.** Likewise, if you tell a woman everything about yourself ("no secrets, tell-all" policy) and give her full validation then you have essentially given away the string for free.

IT IS sexier to give only bits and have her earn these as rewards with her own investments. **With time, the string can be held further and further away but the cat (read: woman) will still jump higher and higher to get it because it knows there is a possibility of getting juicy cat treats**[1] (read: more of your attention, validation, revealed secrets about who you are, and more opportunities to join you on fun adventures in your exciting lifestyle - that they see you enjoy on IG).

THE ULTIMATE REWARD is the pleasure she receives from your dick. And there are rewards that she gets that are even greater than this such as: higher levels of commitment from you. With the highest reward of all is: earning your exclusivity. Your penis is a gift, and your sperm is worth more than gold.

DON'T BE **a fool who approaches women by immediately offering them the highest tier boyfriend benefits before they have even lifted a finger to reciprocate value in return.** That doesn't sexually arouse women, and the women who do respond to do that kind of treatment are hardened, narcissistic gold-diggers with years of experience of leeching financial and psychological resources off men before discarding them once these men go broke (or lose their sanity).

WOMEN WILL UNCONSCIOUSLY troll and bait for reactions for a quick ego boost and validation fix. Drama queens live for this high. Then once they get that surge of power, they'll search for a guy who brings more challenge because women appreciate guys who are hard to get more than a guy who is a "validation slut" and sells out his attention for "cheap" the moment some exposed flesh appears.

DON'T TAKE this advice to an extreme and conclude something stupid like "NEVER show interest to women" or "NEVER compliment a woman".

JUST GIVE **out validation when it's *EARNED*. And be aware that giving it away easily "cheapens" its effect. Don't be a validation slut.**

MAXIMS:

- Cats chase dangling strings.
- Cats don't chase strings placed on their paws.

Train her to do what you want, and to please you in the way that you enjoy. This starts in subtle ways, but becomes more apparent as time goes on and the conditioning is repeatedly reinforced.

. . .

BY SEIZING **social power (being the one to end interactions first, ending interactions on a high-note, putting yourself on a pedestal and mirroring disinterest) you leave a woman wanting more because women are pulled towards being with powerful men.**

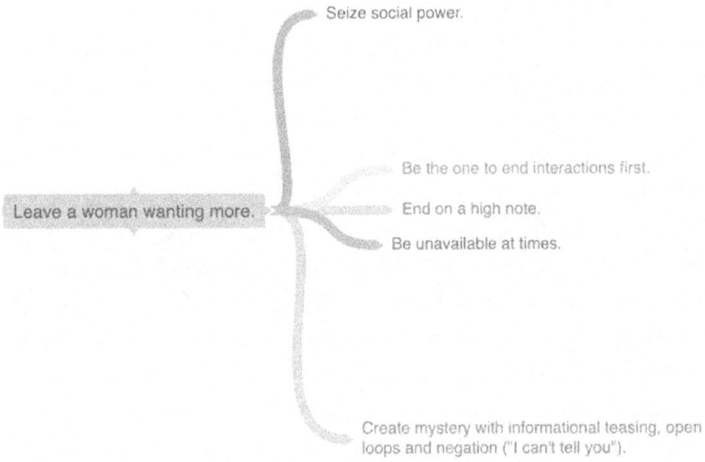
Seize social power.
Be the one to end interactions first.
Leave a woman wanting more.
End on a high note.
Be unavailable at times.
Create mystery with informational teasing, open loops and negation ("I can't tell you").

LAW SUMMARY:

Women naturally do what feels good; they gravitate towards pleasure. You want to be a source of these good emotions. Further, you want to create desire within a woman, so that craves being with you. Tactics of doing this involve leaving a woman wanting more by ending the interaction on a high note, seizing social power, the use of open loops, and negation.

---

1. Attention and approval from high status men is the currency that women accept. Hence, the removal of attention (also known as a "Freeze Out") is how negative behavior from women is effectively punished. This is the

exact opposite of some men do, which is chase harder: the moment a woman distances herself.

4

LAW #2: SUMMARY

LAW #2: THE PLEASURE PRINCIPLE

WOMEN LIVE in the emotions of the moment. They do what feels good. Create desire within a woman. Do this by leaving her wanting more. Utilize push-away, open loops, negation, mixed signals, and power vacuums.

THE PLEASURE PRINCIPLE

Above all, women care about doing what feels good. They live for these pleasurable emotions. A man who can be a provider of these enjoyable intense emotional experiences will have his fill of women.

Technique: The Push-Away

The **Push-Away** is being the first one to end interactions. This makes women desire you more. Keep in mind that you can't play hard to get if you're hard to want. So first you have to give value and spark attraction; then you can pull back and watch her chase you.

Technique: Open Loops

Open loops is teasing women by mentioning an interesting subject but not explaining the full information right away. This will keep women hooked into the interaction because they want to know the full story and get closure.

Technique: Negation

Negation is by teasing women with an interesting piece of information about yourself but refusing to give full disclosure. Simply saying "no, I can't tell you" is very powerful to women because it creates an intense level of intrigue that makes women wonder about you.

Technique: Mixed Signals

Mixed signals is switching between signs of interest and disinterest. This drives women WILD in a good way. She won't be able to stop thinking about you - wondering if you like her or not. The more a woman thinks about you, the more invested she becomes in you.

Technique: Power Vacuum

Power vacuums is seizing social power in the interaction. Women then become baited into staying in the interaction so they can get the social power back. Little do they know that in the process of interacting with you, they become more and more attracted and you're too competent to give up that social power. It's the social power that you have that makes them attracted to you in the first place. Remember: women are attracted to powerful men, so taking social power from her is imperative. Push her off the pedestal, put yourself on the pedestal and sustain the frame that YOU ARE THE PRIZE throughout the interaction.

5

LAW #3: Use psychological force - if necessary. Be ruthlessly pragmatic.

LAW #3: A woman's perception of reality is malleable. Use psychological force when necessary.

A WOMAN'S sexual selection mechanism is absolutely cruel. A woman will not mate with a man - out of pity; she will mate out of biological and psychological selfishness. To thrive in the harsh conditions of the sexual marketplace, BE RUTHLESSLY, MERCILESSLY PRACTICAL.

MATCH PSYCHOPATHY WITH PSYCHOPATHY. Outsmart a woman's mindless behaviors by always being several steps ahead. No matter what she does, it doesn't faze you because you've already predicted every common contingency in your mind and have prepared, field-tested contingency behavioral responses ready.

Technique #3: Use open-ended questions.

A question can be an excellent tool to spark a conversation - as long as it's not the generic commonly-asked question that she has heard a million times before like:

- "come to this place often?"
- "what do you do?"
- "where are you from?"[1]

AVOID generic questions that trigger the auto-pilot response of "been there, done that, another average guy, and I'm bored". If she answered that question several hundred times in the past then asking it again automatically puts her to "sleep; UHH… TRAPPED IN ANOTHER BORING CONVERSATION THAT I CAN'T ESCAPE MODE" before you even finish answering the questions.

NEWBIE: *"How are you doing during —"*

Woman: "Good."

EVEN IF SHE ANSWERS, these boring close-ended questions (that every other guy asks), the answers may be just a few words which doesn't give you a lot of fodder to work with in terms of providing ammunition for your response. **In the optimal situation, a woman's answer gives you information that you can use for the next thing that you say to her.** In contrast to close ended questions, open ended questions create more interesting responses.

CLOSE ENDED QUESTION:

Seducer: "Are you working on a passion project right now?"

Woman: yes.

OPEN ENDED QUESTION:

Seducer: "You look suspiciously happy. What is a passion project that you are working on right now?"

*Woman: *won't stop yapping**

LISTEN UP, MY SON, WHO WILL FUCK WOMEN HARD IN THE PUSSY WITH HIS MIGHTY PENIS. BE MORE FUCKING CREATIVE. **It's not hard to stand out from the average guy considering how powerful the social effect of conformity is; most guys are just basic-bitch-clones of each other.** It's called pickup-ARTISTRY because there is ART and STYLE involved with seducing women. You want to have something about you that makes you UNQIUE in an interesting manner. For instance: the concept of peacocking is the notion that a man should wear at least one interesting item that differentiates him from the hordes of other look-alike men playing the field.

THE VERY FACT that you are reading this book to gain greater levels of self-awareness, a better understanding of social dynamics and concrete actionable-intel makes you part of the 1%; you believe in yourself enough to invest in practical knowledge for a better future. **There are amazing things coming for you as long as you take daily action!!**

WHOEVER SAID **that you should never ask women a question was DEAD WRONG.** In fact, its part of the seduction community dogma that when taken out of context can ruin the game skills of young men.

HERE IS the truth once and for all:

QUESTIONS CAN BE HIGHLY effective in getting women to invest into a conversation and to frame the interaction to your seductive advantage. Contrary to standard community seduction advice, the truth is that: **sometimes a single well-thought-out non-generic question is all it takes to create an emotionally STIMULATING and ENGAGING conversation with a woman.**

THIS EXPLAINS the popularity of the opinion-opener in old school pickup theory. There was a reason why the "Who lies more - men or women?" conversational opener was so commonly used and that reason is that the right open ended question is like dropping a nuclear bomb; the effects can be remarkable to observe.

4 CONVERSATIONAL MISTAKES:

- - MISTAKE: barraging them with questions one-after-another because you're in INTERVIEW MODE. This behavior is incredibly annoying to women and can lead to them walking off in the middle of the one sided conversation. You don't want to be the guy who creates conversation with women by attacking them with list of questions without contributing something of value of your own. **A conversation is a two way street where both partners give value to each other.**
- - MISTAKE: not asking any questions at all. This is the

extreme opposite of INTERVIEW MOOD. Guys hear the advice of "don't ask women too many questions" and mistakenly assume this means "don't ask questions at all". As I have outlined numerous times, questions are an incredibly valuable tool to getting women invested into a mutually-enjoyable conversation. **Questions are absolutely essential tools.**

• - MISTAKE: only asking close-ended questions that lead to 1-2 word answers. While close ended questions may have their use in certain situations (especially to getting a woman warmed up to the idea of talking with you), they generally don't get women as involved into contributing to talking with you as an intriguing, fun-to-answer open-ended question does.

• - MISTAKE: making statements that don't provoke a response. **What gets women to respond back to what you said (thus reinforcing a behavioral pattern of taking turns in speaking) is to end your conversational gambits with an "emotional punch" that almost compels women to respond.** For instance telling a young woman attending college "When you go to college your life ends" is far more likely to get a response than telling a woman a bland statement like "College is educational." Side note: I have personally field-tested that line dozens of times and it's great at getting women emotionally engaged in talking with you because it packs a psychological punch and compromises their ego (she "HAS TO RESPOND" because her ego is at stake).

ADVANCED NOTES:

Used correctly, the tool of asking questions is vital to keep in your toolbox and will assist you in your journey towards seduction mastery. **I repeat: asking questions is a VITAL TOOL.** However, used incorrectly they will hinder you. Understand that asking questions is usually a form of taking value because you are requesting that the other person speak about a subject under your command. Asking a question is telling someone to do something (reply to your command to give information) and people don't always like to be told what to do - especially by complete strangers who they just met.

HENCE, it is better to capitalize on the principle of reciprocity by first giving value by making interesting observations and statements prior to requesting value. GIVE VALUE, FIRST; REQUEST VALUE, SECOND.

WHEN POSSIBLE, start interactions by making provoking statements and observations about her (or the situation that you share with her), that bait her to invest by talking more with you - rather than forcing her to invest with questions. Here is why: when a woman contributes to a conversation at her own initiative then she becomes more invested in you than if you force her to contribute by asking her a question.

TURN QUESTIONS INTO STATEMENTS

For example: instead of asking where she is from, verbalize your educated guess. **Instead of saying "Where are you from?" say "I can tell that you are from [XYZ]".**

IF YOU'RE CORRECT, she will be impressed. If you're wrong, she will be intrigued why you choose what you have said and will often correct you. **However, if statements fail to generate conversational investment from her then use questions to help reinforce the behavioral pattern of mutual conversation. A long pause without either side contributing can kill the interaction ("well, nice meeting you. Bye!).**

. . .

AWKWARD SILENCES KILL INTERACTIONS. Upon approaching a woman, in the first five minutes of the interaction (until the point in the interaction when a woman becomes hooked to talking with you), fill all silences yourself. If a woman is not responding to what you have said then ask a question to metaphorically take her hand and guide her to invest in you.

WHY USING PSYCHOLOGICAL FORCE IS NECESSARY.

I'm going to tell you a secret that is going to help you tremendously with women. Listen carefully.

- THE MORE A WOMAN WORKS FOR YOU, and
- THE MORE HOOPS SHE JUMPS THROUGH FOR YOU,
- THE MORE ATTRACTED and EMOTIONALLY INVESTED SHE WILL BE IN YOU.

If you literally remember and implement nothing else that I have said except this one one lesson then buying this book would be worth it.

THIS 1 PIECE of advice is absolutely essential to understand, and it will transform your sex life if you implement it.

GET **CHICKS TO DO SHIT FOR YOU.**

. . .

WHAT IS one big reason relationships fail? It is because the guy does all the work & puts in a huge amount of effort, while the girl does nothing but exist. The guy sweats for her sake, and all she does is breathe.

HENCE, the guy is super invested, but the girl doesn't give a fuck because human nature is to not value what comes easy. Condition her to jump through hoops for you because the more sweats to win you over, the more she will value you when she does finally win you over.

REMEMBER: women value what they have to work for and earn. Start with small hoops and then increase the hoop size with time. Implement this one piece of advice and you will start to see girls fall in love with you and be absolutely crazy over you.

USE PSYCHOLOGICAL FORCE WHEN NECESSARY

Sometimes a woman will do things for you simply for the sake of of making you happy and giving value; however, if this is not the case then request it.

THIS IS a book about conversation so I'll use conversation as a metaphor but the same principles that are relevant in conversation skills, also apply to general relationship skills. Here is the principle:

GIVE VALUE. **And then wait for a woman to give value back to you. If she doesn't then request it - by asking a question.**

. . .

IN CONVERSATION, this would manifest itself in the following manner:

- A seducer says something that is interesting, entertaining, relevant to the situation, and provides emotional value that uplifts the woman's spirit.
- The woman says something back that also contributes value back because of the principle of reciprocity.
- The seducer continues to say something else that is interesting and provides emotional value - thus reinforcing the behavioral pattern of conversation.
- The woman says nothing in response creating a brief silence and drops the balls. As the conversation dies, the interaction may also die.
- The seducer (sensing that the interaction may die because the woman has nothing of value to say back in response to his response) asks a question and in a way "forces" a woman to respond back. **He metaphorically picks up the ball and holds it next to her hands - making it easy to pick it up. A question applies social pressure (or psychological force) for the woman to invest back in to the conversation. After all, in most cultures it is considered rude to ignore a question.** In this case, a question was the best possible move for the seducer to play because if he would have continued to make statements then the interaction would turn into a one-sided monologue instead of an interactive dialogue. *At the risk of stating the obvious, I'll mention here* ***that long monologues***

(that lack positive social feedback from those listening-in) kill interactions because they come off as try-hard. *Hence, the goal is to have a woman engaged in a conversation with you and a conversation is a two-way street (dialogue).*

- The woman responds to the question in an enthusiastic matter (because it's not a boring question that she has answered a thousand times before).
- The seducer responds to her answer by commenting on it in a manner that is interesting, entertaining and provides emotional value. He keeps things fun by spiking her emotions with a bold statement.
- The woman returns value by also saying something that is interesting, entertaining and uplifting (implying that she is enjoying the conversation and is happy with the value-exchanges being done).
- *the cycle repeats itself through numerous rounds*
- The man makes a higher tier close by stating "Hey, it's a bit chilly here. Lets grab a coffee down the block" *pointing in the distance* This is a bit forceful because the man is taking the initiative and leading the interaction towards a greater level of intimacy - instead of waiting for the woman to take charge and make the initiatives.
- The woman concurs - thus buying into the behavioral pattern of following the man's lead
- *the compliance cycle repeats itself across multiple mediums until a fuck close is achieved, and a sexual relationship is initiated. **Even then, game skills are relevant in a 20 year relationship, just like it's relevant in a 20 second interaction.***

Perception is malleable.

ALWAYS CREATE the perception that you are a man of high social standing in society. Don't do this because you need her validation, or approval. Do this because perception management is what will get you results (e.g. sex) in the sexual marketplace.

THIS IS one of the reasons why:

- - dressing wealthy,
- - having powerful body-language (verbal and non-verbal),
- - having powerful contacts as male friends (social proof on steroids),
- - having beautiful women as contacts (preselection),
- - decent personal grooming, etc

is paramount.

---

1. At some point, the seducer does ask these basic questions of "What do you for work?" etc, but that should not be at the start of interactions because it violates the rule of: generating attraction precedes building rapport. A woman has to first become attracted to a man before she cares about learning the mundane details of his life, and sharing the mundane details of her life. First a seducer focuses on generating genuine female intrigue and then he focuses on building rapport with the female (not the other way around). Further, there are far more creative ways to learning more about a woman than asking generic questions that trigger auto-pilot negative responses because of how fucking annoying these questions can be (after all, the last 1,000 men who have said those exact words were fucking losers and have created an intense negative anchor associated with that unique combination of words). For instance, instead of saying "where you are from?" the seducer can say "You look like you're from New York."

6

LAW #3: SUMMARY

LAW #3: USE PSYCHOLOGICAL FORCE. BE RUTHLESSLY PRAGMATIC.

A WOMAN'S perception of reality is malleable. When you have a strong frame and 100% BULLETPROOF CONFIDENCE then you can say and do almost anything and it will work.

7

LAW #4: STRING THEORY;

Create a vacuum. Use silence to your advantage.

LAW #4: Women value what they work to acquire much more than what comes free. Create a Vacuum.

Technique #4: Utilize Calculated Pauses.

USE THE "PREGNANT PAUSE". When story-telling or sharing your opinion on a matter *PAUSE* at the right moments (as soon as you say something particularly edgy) to allow her to contribute back to the conversation. Create opportunities for the girl to contribute to the conversation. **Use eye-contact to reinforce the expectation that it's her turn to talk.**

IF YOU ARE the only person who is talking then it can come across as try-hard. A woman has to invest in a guy in order to value him. Women value what they work for. Hence, it's necessary for her attraction levels to jump through hoops on your behalf.

7 Conversation Sins:

- - taking too long to explain something,
- - using filler and boring fluff content,
- - repeating yourself,
- - taking too long to hit the punch line,
- - not having a punch line at the end of a small ramble,
- - not pausing at interaction points to let her talk,
- - not having an obvious ending to what you're saying, so a woman picks up on the cue that it is HER TURN to speak in the conversation,

In the initial phase of the conversation, talk in short-bursts that all have punch lines in the end. Going on a lengthy monologue, without receiving conversational feedback from her is weird and you may lose her attention span. Be self-amused. Talk about things that you enjoy.

ANTICIPATE TIMES when she is most likely to respond and pause during those moments to allow her invest into the conversation because (1) her investment in you is more important than you generating attraction, and, (2) a conversation should be a two-way street.

ADVANCED NOTES:

Time in the field will tell you proper ratios. An ideal conversation is roughly a 50/50% divide – albeit at the start of pickup it will be around 80/20% where you are doing the majority of the talking. The reason why you are doing most of the talking initially is because you approached her (hence, the burden of carrying the conversation is on you) and she may not be in a social mode yet.

THE SEQUENCE:

- The seducer says something and then ends at a provoking moment to allow a woman to contribute to the conversation.
- He holds eye-contact.
- He then waits for the woman to say something back.
- Often at this point the woman will respond (giving into the social pressure) but if she doesn't seem likely to contribute on her own initiative at this point of the interaction (providing a body-language cue such as averting her gaze) then the seducer will either move on to his next conversational point, or ask a question.

If all you do is chase a woman then you don't structure an opportunity for a woman to chase you. **By creating space, you allow a woman to invest in you!** The more she invests in you, the more she rationalize that you are worth investing in. When one creates a vacuum then women will fill it with their efforts.

8

LAW #4: SUMMARY

LAW #4: CREATE A VACUUM.

WOMEN ARE LIKE CATS. They don't chase strings they already have. They chase strings that could disappear. Women are more MOTIVATED BY FEAR OF LOSS than promise of gain. Give value; then create a vacuum, so that invests back by giving you value. For a relationship to be strong there needs to be a constant exchange of value - to the point where both members are better off together than alone.

9

LAW #5: Bring her into your world more than you are brought into her world.

LAW #5: Women want to submit to a more dominant, powerful man who has a fiery purpose. Bring her into your world. A woman should be more drawn into your reality than you are drawn into hers.

TECHNIQUE **#5: Speak with enthusiasm.**

WHEN YOU TALK with fierce conviction, excitement and enthusiasm, you will DRAW PEOPLE INTO YOUR WORLD.

BUT IF YOUR voice is robotic, monotone and flat then it will put people to sleep. Speak with enthusiasm, energy and fierce conviction to DRAW HER INTO YOUR WORLD.

GET RID of the monotone tonality, flat-line delivery style and dull energy levels.

. . .

GET EXCITED when talking about your passions and watch her get sucked into the conversation. Talk with EXCITEMENT, ENERGY, ENTHUSIASM, and PASSION. **Talking like this will SUCK PEOPLE INTO YOUR WORLD and YOUR REALITY.**

IF YOU DON'T CARE about what you are talking about then don't expect others to care either. When you talk about something that MATTERS to you, it SHOWS. In contrast, if you don't care about what you're talking about then that shows too and will lead her to not caring as well. To be interesting, be interested in what you are saying.

THE SELF TENDS **to shine through; hence, you ideally want to be the real fucking deal. Women are watching you and unconsciously soaking in everything you communicate – both verbally and nonverbally.**

HENCE, it is imperative that you show absolute strength and fearlessness. When you speak with enthusiasm, energy, passion, and conviction about your vision in life then you are sub-communicating the signal that you are a man who is on his path and purpose in life. Although she may not consciously be aware of this, a woman desires a man who has his own life and shit going on. **A woman desires to be a supplement to a man's amazing life - not be life itself. She wants to help a man succeed in his meaningful life mission - not be the mission itself.**

. . .

WOMEN ARE DISGUSTED by lost-souls who are going nowhere, have nothing going on, and have a "I don't give a fuck about anything at all" perspective. You should give a fuck about your personal goals in life and where you are heading in the next 6 months, 1 year and 5 years. If there is nothing that excites you in life then something is terribly wrong and you need to set bigger vision! Set daily, weekly and monthly goals to be aligned with that vision. Remember: you are worth fighting for!!!

WOMEN ARE LIKE TALENT SCOUTS. They're looking to emotionally support a man who has legit potential for greatness. They want to support a man on his life's journey towards greatness.

SPEAKING **with enthusiasm is part of the larger point of being a man who loves life.** If you hate getting out of bed in the morning then this is a sign that you have given up on life, your dreams and living to the fullest. Create a vision that excites you, and then take action everyday to turn that dream into a reality.

10

LAW #5: SUMMARY

LAW #5: DOMINATE COMPLETELY

BRING A WOMAN INTO YOUR WORLD, more than you are drawn into hers. Even a feminist has an innate desire to submit to a more powerful, dominant man on his life's fiery purpose.

PUSSY IS NOT the end goal. Focus on your life's purpose. Create the conditions where a woman is a help to your life's purpose - not the purpose of life itself.

11

LAW #6: THE LAW OF STATE TRANSFERENCE; Change her mood, and you'll change her mind. Be the calm anchor in her tornados.

LAW #6: Change her mood, and you'll automatically change her mind.

TECHNIQUE **#6: Add Energy and Emotion.**

WHEN YOU TAP into your emotions and speak from the heart, you will move mountains. Emotionally charged communication is far more captivating than emotionless communication styles.

SPEAK FROM THE HEART. **Words that come from the heart, enter the heart.** When you really believe in what you are saying then it will create an IMPACT WITHIN HER that will stay with her - potentially for her entire life.

DON'T TALK like a history professor reciting facts, logical discourse and dry details. Inject fucking emotion into your words. Speak with enthusiasm, energy and emotions.

The Law of State Transference

FEEL something when you are talking and she will FEEL something as well because emotions are contagious. Be in the emotional state that you want the woman to be in.

HOW YOU SAY something is more important than what you say because she cares INFINITELY MORE about energy, sensations and the transmission of good-emotions THAN she does about the gaining of new knowledge.

THIS IS COUNTER-INTUITIVE to logical thinkers such as INTJs.

INJECT EMOTION into your words to make them far more interesting. Don't talk with a monotone, flat-line voice like a fucking robot. You are a human who feels things; act like it. **Be EXPRESSIVE in communication. Being EXPRESSIVE (instead of having a flat-line delivery style) will instantly make you ten times more interesting to women .**

ONE THING that you'll notice is that women often care about emotionally-rich subjects such as animals, relationships, social dynamics, and travel THAN they care about technical, logical and emotionally-dry subjects such as day-trading analytics, and chess. Now one can make an emotionally-dry subject sound exciting by adding his own energy into it, but it's easier to do that with a subject that is inherently emotionally-rich than emotionally dry.

. . .

A SEDUCER who can captivate a woman's world by injecting emotions into his words will be able to make women feel things that they haven't felt with overly logical, deeply analytical serious men. Ultimately, a woman cares more about how she feels when she is around a man more than she cares about anything else. **She might forget what you told her specifically, but she won't forget how you made her feel.**

THE STORY TELLING TECHNIQUE

When telling stories from your personal life, take women through a range of emotions so they can LIVE VICARIOUSLY THROUGH YOUR WORDS. There is a reason why movies are a billion dollar industry; stories sell ideas, and provide an enjoyable escape from reality to the masses.

12

LAW #6: SUMMARY

LAW #6: Change her mood, and you'll change her mind.

CHANGE HER MOOD, AND YOU'LL CHANGE HER MIND. WHAT YOU FEEL IS WHAT SHE WILL FEEL. Be in the emotional state that you want a woman to be in; speak from the heart to let the inner positive emotions overflow outwards.

WOMEN ACT on emotion and then use logic to rationalize everything in post-action analysis. Women act based on how they feel, so a man who can change how a woman feels will change how she acts and views the world.

13

LAW #7: Spike her emotional state.

LAW #7: Women feed on a man's energy levels and emotional state. Be an overflowing fountain of good emotions and enthusiasm for life.

Technique #7: Have a great vibe!!!

WHEN YOU'VE GOT GAME, you can open with anything and it will still start a conversation with a cute girl. It's not the words that matter as much as the energy, vibe and vocal tonality behind the words. You want to speak from a place of high-energy, overflowing good emotions, a contagious enthusiasm for life

How you say it > what you say.

WOMEN CARE MORE about how you make them feel than anything else. Energize them, flame good emotions, provide an intense emotional experience - ignore negative vibes, and overly logical conversations.

It's not the words themselves that create the magic but the confidence from which they are said in.

<u>FOR ANYTHING **that comes out of your mouth, remember to OWN IT 100%.**</u>

WHAT KILLS THE VIBE:

- - complaining,
- - exuding sadness,
- - criticizing others,
- - bringing attention to negative emotions,

WHAT ADDS VALUE:

- - focusing on the positive,

- - exuding enthusiasm for life,
- - uplifting spirits and people's self-image.

WOMEN VIEW the world from "emotional glasses", so a man who is able to communicate in this language of emotions will resonate deeply with women. **Develop your EQ (emotional intelligence) to understand your own emotional state, be able to identify the emotional state of others, and learn how to improve the mood of those who are around you through practical behavioral techniques** (such as storytelling, pacing a woman's reality, and other techniques mentioned in this book).

WHEN YOU CONSISTENTLY IMPROVE A WOMAN'S EMOTIONAL state to one of happiness and intense excitement, then you will become an anchor that she will use to bring herself up. **Even when she's going through a storm of negative emotions and tension, you'll be there - a calm, relaxed unmoving mountain - to anchor her back to reality.**

THE GO FIRST PRINCIPLE

You must be in the emotional state that you want to take a woman into. After all, you can't give what you don't have.

14

LAW #7: SUMMARY

LAW #7: Spike Her Emotions.

BE PROACTIVE - NOT REACTIVE. Be at the cause - not at the effect. Let her play by the cards that you deal.

SUPPLEMENT A PASSIVE MATING STRATEGY, with active tactics. Take the initiative to spike a woman's emotions. Press her emotional buttons.

15

LAW #8: Provoke an emotional response. Trigger her.

LAW #8: Women are puppets of ego, emotions, primal instincts and sociological forces. Provoke a response. Be willing to be provocative.

HOW TO GET a woman committed into a conversation: provoke a response by touching a nerve and tugging on a heart-string.

BLAND STATEMENTS DON'T elicit conversation responses but bold, polarizing and controversial statements do. BE POLARIZING.

WHEN BOLD STATEMENTS WORK, they work like a BANG!!

Emotion creates motion. Get it? E+MOTION.

If she feels something then that feeing will compel her to say something. The lesson is: provoke an emotional response to provoke a conversational response. PRESS HER EMOTIONAL BUTTONS.

IF YOU ARE able to create an intense emotional state within a woman, she will not shut the fuck up. She will talk non-stop and be highly invested in continuing to talk with you. This is true even if she is "busy" and there are other guys in the scenario.[1] Here is a simple way to remember this concept: **E-motions create conversational MOTIONS.**

APATHY IS THE OPPOSITE OF LOVE. FEMALE INDIFFERENCE IS THE ENEMY.

During a conversation, when you make her feel something - anything at all - then you are drawing her into your world and making her psychologically invested in you. Emotions are addictive, create involvement and create emotional engagement.

IN CONTRAST, **if a woman feels nothing, she will say nothing.**

INCREASE THE INTENSITY OF HER EMOTIONAL STATE BY SPIKING HER EMOTIONS.

Focus on the telling of emotional information over the telling of factual information. She cares far more about the former **because inducing higher emotional arousal makes her feel more alive.**

Pump up intense emotions into her system by saying and doing things that increase emotional arousal; social scientists have confirmed that increasing emotional arousal increases enjoyment in life.

This tip is the opposite of what intellectuals tend to do. Friendly conversation is called being a bore. Don't be boring. Ensure that you sprinkle in highly-edgy, highly-emotionally-charged spikes into the conversation.

HOW TO FLIRT: CHALLENGE HER. A WOMAN'S FRUSTRATION IS A FORM OF ATTRACTION TO YOU.

When you tease, playfully challenge, or neg a woman then you are getting her engaged into the interaction on an emotional level because now her ego is at stake. When you've poked at her pride then she has to pump up her self-esteem by teasing you back; the mutual back-and-forth teasing gets a woman psychologically and emotionally invested into the interaction.

This the logic of flirting and is a far superior medium of communication to the apathetic, "I don't give a fuck" response that bland, politically correct nice guys get.

---

1. A woman in an intense emotional state is highly susceptible to being seduced because her logical mind is shut down. This is also known as High Buying Temperature and the Amygdala Hijack.

16

LAW #8: SUMMARY

LAW #8: EMOTION CREATES MOTION.

AN EMOTIONAL WOMAN is a talkative woman. Provoke an emotional response.

BE POLARIZING. Be offensive and create frustration - if necessary. Women value challenge more than the nice guy ever knew. Women will forgive the man who went too far, but they won't forgive the man who is boring. Being boring is the cardinal sin for dealing with women.

17

LAW #9: Go first; then leverage reciprocity and mirroring.

LAW #9: Reciprocity is effective for instantly getting compliance.

IMAGINE TWO DIFFERENT SITUATIONS:

- Situation #1: immediately upon entering a restaurant, a waiter asks for you for a five dollar tip. "Get the fuck outta here" would be your initial response.
- Situation #2: a waiter provides stellar prompt service throughout your meal - ensuring that you're glass of orange juice is always filled, there are plenty of napkins, there are lots of extra condiments, you have a wide selection of bagels - and then after the meal is over, the waiter requests a five dollar tip. The latter situation is more likely to get compliance because value was given upfront for free, and then value was requested secondly.

Implement the Principle of Reciprocity

Women are more likely to give value when free value has already been given to them. Hence, give emotional and conversation value FIRST. Request emotional and conversational value SECOND.

Implement the Principle of Mirroring

What you put into an interaction is what you will get out of it because women will mirror your behavioral patterns. Put into a relationship the kinds of things that you would like to get out of a relationship.

THIS CONCEPT IS relevant in having conversations with women:

- If you want a woman to invest, be a shinning example for her to role model after.
- If you want a woman to entertain you (and give value) when it's her turn to talk, lead by example and say something that is entertaining (and value-giving) to her when you are talking.

Showcase the proper model of giving value, so that a woman will reciprocate by giving the same type of value that you gave her.

SHARE DETAILS ABOUT YOUR LIFE. Talk about exciting and funny things that are currently happening in your life. Explain interesting pieces of information that you have recently learned yourself.

. . .

ASK YOURSELF:

- What is a project that I'm working on right now that I'm passionate about?
- What is something extraordinary that recently happened to me?
- What is something new that I learned recently that completely changed my perspective on the world?

Discover the answers to these questions and then share them boldly. This will encourage her to share as well because of the effect of reciprocity and mirroring. A conversation will ensue.

SOCIAL LEARNING THEORY

Share something personal about your life but make sure that it is amusing and has a funny/bold ending to it. By sharing something about your life, you are inviting her to share something about her life too. After all, according to American-Canadian psychologist Albert Bandura people learn best by role-modeling after observed behaviors. A woman is more likely to learn by seeing a demonstration of proper behavior than she is by listening to an explanation of proper behavior.

ON AN ADVANCED NOTE, sometimes you want to give sarcastic and evasive answers to women to encourage them to prod more and to spike intrigue by appearing more mysterious (See Law #2: Create desire by leaving a woman wanting more and utilizing the negation tactic).

RECIPROCITY IS REAL.

You have to value the input that you get from your conversational partner to reinforce the behavioral pattern of her responding to you. Give her intermittent reward for investing in you. Respect is gained by giving respect.

18

LAW #9: SUMMARY

LAW #9: GO FIRST. THEN LEVERAGE RECIPROCITY AND MIRRORING.

SHARE DETAILS ABOUT YOUR LIFE. Talk passionately about your life's purpose, and cool hobbies that you are engaged in. This will inspire women to open up, as well.

19

LAW #10: Don't chase; attract. Less is often more.

WOMEN VALUE what they work for, and disregard that which comes too easily. You want a woman to sweat on your behalf because that is what is going to create the emotional connection. The more a woman works to win over the prize (you), the more she will value it when it's finally won.

IN THE CONTEXT OF A CONVERSATION, **you want a woman to go out of her way for you and give conversational value - so that you are inspired to keep talking to her and entertained enough to enjoy the interaction, in general.** If you're talking non-stop when will she will get the chance to do so? Know when to shut the fuck up and utilize silence to your advantage.

IF YOU'RE the one who is doing ALL THE TALKING in a conversation then you aren't creating enough of a vacuum for a woman to invest back into the conversation. If you're the one who is doing ALL OF THE CHASING then you aren't creating space for a woman to chase you back. Hence, less effort on your behalf sometimes yields greater results.

HE WHO TRIES HARD, dies hard. Knowing when NOT to do something is just as important as knowing what you SHOULD BE DOING. Exerting less effort can ironically make you more attractive.

LAW#10 IS *relevant to those who are not struggling with running out of things to say. Someone who is still going through the struggle of learning how to talk endlessly need not apply this chapter.*

Technique #10: NXTBT.

When you get to a point where you can speak endlessly, you'll start to realize that you have approximately 3-6 ideas floating in your head that you can share with your conversational partner AT ANY POINT in the conversation. **Because you have so much that you can say, and not enough time to say it all: you inherently have to be highly selective and choose the most interesting piece of them all.**

SOME THINGS ARE MORE interesting than other things. While some things that you say, are not interesting at all. While your conversational partner is talking, LISTEN to what she is saying and simultaneously figure out what your "next best thing to say" is (NXTBT for short). Make a mental note of it. When she is done talking, deliver the NXTBT.

ONCE YOU ARE **good at assessing the NXTBT then you can create a mental list of things that you want**

to say after your conversational partner is finished talking, and prioritize them from most interesting to least interesting. Say that which is the most interesting first.

THAT BEING SAID, you don't want to be too stuck in your head thinking about the NXTBT to the point where you fail to be in the present moment and fail to listen to what she is saying. A good balance is optimal.

Who is boring? He who says EVERYTHING - even the stuff that isn't that interesting.

- **You don't want to be repetitive when talking to women. If you have already made a point, then don't repeat it.** Repeating a point is nagging and is an annoying behavior to people in general. COME UP WITH SOMETHING NEW TO SAY. If you are running out of content then this is a sign that you have to work on your improv skills, you are not in talkative state, or that you should prepare more material before meeting.
- **Aim to convey more information in less words.**
- **Cut out the boring, irrelevant details - that are not relevant to a woman's passions or your passions.**

❄

Women want men that other women want. Create Instant Social Proof

Women want men that other women want. You should always imply that you have options - even if you don't state this directly. When you are talking about other women in your life, refer to them casually as "just friends" - not former lovers.

5 ways to create instant social proof:

- - Embedding social proof into conversation: "My friends and I...".
- - Open adjacent sets. This is pickup lingo for start conversations with nearby people.
- - Mention an ex-fiancé.
- - Post photos on your social media accounts of you with attractive females doing cool things.
- - Mention times that you are busy before bringing up the times that you are available.

Display high social status via photos on your personal social media accounts such as IG, FB or even YT. It's like a "visual dating resume" that women view when looking up your name on Google. Tag successful, cool people in these photos for instant social proof.

IF YOU HAVE SUCCESSFUL FRIENDS, women will assume that you are successful - as well. Good photos (that display high status) also include traveling to foreign countries, and engaging in passions.

. . .

SOCIAL MEDIA - USED CORRECTLY (with photos that display an affluent, exciting lifestyle and being at the hottest events in your city) - can be used to generate leads and serves as a funnel for meeting local women.

20

LAW #10: SUMMARY

LAW #10: Don't chase. Attract.

SHOW INTENT, but don't be psychologically clingy. Less is often more. If you're doing ALL OF THE TALKING then you aren't creating enough opportunities for a woman to bring her own conversational value.

Who is boring?
ONE WHO SAYS EVERYTHING.
KILL THE REDUNDANT AND REPITITIVE.
OFTEN LESS IS MORE.

21

LAW #11: Don't play the game by the rules that she sets. Pattern disrupt her BS.

Technique #11: The Pattern Disrupt

LETTING a woman steer the reigns of a conversation and social interaction is just plain STUPID because I assure you that women often do not have a sexuality on their agenda. You must take control and lead things to seduction or nothing may occur but wasted time. DOMINATE THE CONVERSATION.

NOT TO MENTION, that answering boring interview questions creates BOREDOM FOR HER. She starts a boring topic of conversation, you respond with a boring answer, she gets bored and then she leaves. **Instead of playing along, answer the question that you WISH SHE WOULD HAVE ASKED.**

ONE OF THE principles of female psychology is that when women talk to men, they often don't have a sexual agenda in mind and if you let her control the conversation then it usually won't lead to sex. This is why you cannot let her lead; **YOU MUST SEIZE THE REIGNS OF CONTROL.**

DON'T LET her control the reigns of the conversation. YOU take CONTROL. Lead the conversation towards a place of mutual seduction. **Don't let girls trap you into boring, logical conversations that lead to NOWHERE.**

PATTERN DISRUPT HER SELF-SABOTAGE NARRATIVES. Alphas interrupt boring conversations or other threads that they don't want to engage in. **If she starts talking about boring things and boring herself OR if she talks about sad things then INTERRUPT HER and CHANGE THE SUBJECT.**

DON'T ANSWER **her boring questions with logical boring answers. Respond sarcastically or with humor.** This is far more entertaining than giving dull facts. Nice conversation is BORING.

DO NOT ALLOW yourself to be associated with boredom or negative emotions. Be associated with excitement & positive emotions.

YOU'LL GET MORE out of life if you stopped being a pussy, beta male, and started developing courage and TAKING CHARGE. Beta males are passive. Alpha males TAKE CHARGE OF SOCIAL AND SEXUALLY CHARGED SITUATIONS.

. . .

DON'T LIVE CONSTANTLY REACTING to things and to women. Live proactively. Don't play the game by her rules. HIJACK CONTROL. You deal the cards that she plays by. SHE ENTERS YOUR WORLD ON YOUR TERMS.

START CONVERSATIONS WITH DOMINANCE.

In NYC, if you try to start a conversation from a nervous, shy and submissive frame of mind then girls will often just ignore you entirely or pretend they didn't notice. Don't believe me? Try it. Let the lack of results speak for themselves.

IDEALLY YOU SHOULD START a conversation with a girl with:

- - SUPREME BULLETPROOF CONFIDENCE,
- - powerful body-language,
- - unshakeable frame,
- - dominant frame of mind that assumes authority,
- - coming from a feel-good place inside.
- - approach with a full cup - not from a needy, approval-seeking and reaction-seeking position.

LONELY WOMEN ARE lonely because of strong self-sabotage mechanisms. As a seducer who may encounter virgins, feminists or these type of women, instead of falling into a woman's frame and doing what she wants: have the stronger frame and lead. **Instead of playing by her self-sabotage rules and reacting to her, you set the seductive rules and have her react to you.**

22

LAW #11: SUMMARY

LAW #11: Don't play the game by the rules that she sets.

WOMEN WILL SAY stupid things and ask questions they don't really want the answer to. If you play along to her perception of how things should be, you might end up fucking yourself instead of fucking her. Ignore, and interrupt these self-sabotage behaviors with a pattern disrupt. **Introduce your own non-sequitur conversational piece with such energy that you blast right through her bullshit.**

23

LAW #12: Have a mating gameplan. Rely on battle-tested skill - not hope or luck. Play unfair.

Technique #12: The Field-Tested Line, Transitions and Routines

HAVE a few memorized lines that you can use at any moment just in case your brain can't think of anything to say to keep a conversation going. Have a default memorized line to use to start the conversation in case your brain freezes and you are lost for words.

CREATE A CHEAT-SHEET.

Be willing to write down a few topics to talk about into iOS Notes (use bulletpoints - not word-for-word scripts) and glance at them while you are in the midst of the interaction (she will think that you are just checking texts).

HAVE A GAMEPLAN.

To become more success with women, develop a conscious gameplan. Don't just leave it to chance. Figure out a step-by-step plan of action on what specifically you are going to do in order to have more beautiful women in your life.

BE ON THE LOOKOUT FOR GOOD LINES.

Every time you leave your home, you have multiple opportunities to initiate conversations with female strangers as you go about your daily life and sharpen your skills. The optimal path is to practice your social and seduction skills on a daily basis as you do simple seemingly mundane things such as shopping for groceries, or even taking out the trash. Remember: you get good at what you do frequently. **Often the best lines come from spontaneous conversations.**

THE BEST ROUTINES **come from natural spontaneous conversations.** If you have noticed that a specific line has generated results for you then remember it and add it to your pocket of lines; chances are that it will work again! **Continuously refine your arsenal of battle-tested, field-proven, non-cheesy lines.** [1]

ROUTINES

When you have a collection of field-tested lines that you can use one-after-the-other, you'll have a routine.

An experienced seducer is able to:

- stack routines one after another,
- has a short/long version of each routine,
- has different routines for different common situations, and
- has different routines (content) for different stages in the seduction process. The material that ones uses for the attraction phase (being fun, intriguing

and sometimes a bit crazy) should NOT be the kind of material used for emotionally connecting (sharing personal details about yourself).

TRANSITIONS

Phrases that allow you to bounce from subject to subject. Make some arbitrary random observation about the environment that you are in, and then say: "***Oh, this reminds me of the time that I"*** was walking on the beach in Colombia Santa Fe… While having a transition isn't essential because one can jump from topic to topic randomly without explaining himself, a transition does create a more smooth, effortless, spontaneous, natural-feeling to conversations.

---

1. Even if you have memorized effective lines, do not let them substitute for natural spontaneous conversations and natural spontaneous remarks. Memorized lines will eventually run out, but being able to generate lines by yourself will give you an infinite number of things to say at anytime, anyplace with anyone. Do you want to be a robot always putting on a mechanical performance, or a human being enjoying an authentic experiences? One must strive for an optimal balance between a reasonable amount of preparation (with ready-responses for common-contingencies) and on-the-spot improvisation (handling things as they come).

24

LAW #12: SUMMARY

LAW #12: Have a mating gameplan. Rely on battle-tested skill - not hope or luck. Play unfair.

FUCK PLAYING by the rules of society. Fuck playing by what the culture deems to be "appropriate behavior". Don't be yet another sheep amidst masses of sheep. Think for yourself.

IN THE GAME OF LIFE, the man with the plan has a massive advantage over the man who is just winging things on improvisation. Enter the sexual marketplace with clear goals - knowing what you want out of it, and the kind of bullshit you aren't willing to put up with.

HAVING field-tested lines that you know WORK (for picking up women) is a better strategy than using random unproven material that you come up with on the spot. The best lines come from burning your bridges, immersing yourself in the field, doing a ton of approaches, and recording statements that you have said that got results. When you have a collection of these statements then you have a refined, tweaked routine in your conversation toolkit that you can shoot.

KNOW WHAT YOU WANT. Have a vision. Where do you want to be 5 years from now? Describe your dream girl. CREATE A GAME-PLAN, and daily goals to get there. Stack battle-tested moves/lines (that have worked prior).

25

LAW #13: Pace her reality to break into her reality.

Technique #13: The Pace Her Reality Method

THE POWERS of observation and being assertively articulate about what you have observed will give you an abundance of sex. **The power of observation will make it rain pussy.** Get perceptive!! Use situational self-awareness to comment on what is happening in the shared experience between you and her.

IF THE ONLY **game skill that you develop is the ability to make astute observations (analytical or humorous) then you will still go far with women.**

GETTING good at making simple observations about:

- her,
- the situation,
- the dynamic between you and her, and
- other people who are present (people watching).

is a valuable ability that will lead to women spreading their legs for the pleasure that you will provide.

WHEN YOU SEE A WOMAN, stop for a moment and bring yourself fully into the present moment. LOOK AT HER. Notice at least one thing about her that is striking, or unusual. You will feel a wave of emotion. Ride that emotional wave and speak your mind about that which you have noticed.

- "I noticed you were..."
- "I couldn't help but see that you are.."
- "You look like..."

ALTERNATIVELY, notice at least one odd or interesting thing about the shared environment that you are in. Let that insight sink in; then share it excitedly with the woman that you are with.

PACING a woman's reality is a fancy way of describing the experience that she is going through in order to establish yourself as an authority in her world - a voice that dictates reality. Similar to the Yes Ladder and Compliance Momentum, saying a series of true statements leads a woman to believing everything that you say (buying into your frame more and more).

❄

PRACTICE YOUR CONVERSATION SKILLS EVERY DAY.

Get into the habit of going out of the house to a place where there are women. Approach some of them. Deliver an opening line. Start up conversations. Close the ones that have receptive body-language. You need a consistent way to bring women into your life. This is a necessity.

TAKE **a moment to observe a female stranger. Notice something that's different about her that strikes you. Make a comment about it. That alone can serve as the basis for your approach. Utilize strong conversation skills to keep the interaction alive after the initial comment.**

THE SECRET TO overcome general fears about approaching female strange and starting conversations with them is to just do it A TON OF TIMES. **It will eventually reach a point where you will be hyper-chill and hitting up random cute girls will be as chill as drinking morning coffee.**

IF YOU APPROACH women every day:

- - you will be really good at generating leads, and
- - your anxiety around starting conversations with female strangers will fade away.

You will start to wonder "What the fuss is about? Who would be retarded enough to have anxiety over this?"

. . .

IF YOU LIVE IN A CITY, you can easily have 5 conversations a day with random people as you go about your day. The skills are easily transferable. If you don't live in a populated area, then fucking move. If you want results, make pickup a PRIORITY.

CHOOSE one opening line to start conversations with women. Then verbalize it outloud ten-times. **Visualize yourself approaching women, and using that line successfully**. Then make that a motherfucking reality, motherfucker!

❄

THE SITUATIONAL OBSERVATION OPENER; HOW TO START A CONVERSATION WITH A WOMAN IN A VERY NATURAL WAY.

Situational comments are the smoothest and "most natural" type of way to start conversations with female strangers. Making an observation about her and the situation is the easiest way to start a conversation with a female stranger.

THIS IS because it taps into something that she is already used to - which is spontaneous conversation.

CREATE the illusion that she is different than all the other girls. When you noticed her, you couldn't help but say something to her because you were overwhelmed by the exotic detail that you observed.

. . .

YOU HAD to go on in a moment but she trapped you in a fun conversation. You only had a few minutes to stay with her in the fun conversation because you have shit to do, but then you found out how awesome she actually is and couldn't help yourself but invite to nearby cool events in your area.

SITUATIONAL OPENERS ARE **one of the easiest ways to start a conversation. Watch her for a moment and make an insightful observation about her or the situation.** Once opened, follow-up with something else. It's simply a matter of pacing her reality and then leading to something else.

- Pace.
- Pace.
- Lead.

26

LAW #13: SUMMARY

LAW #13: PACE HER REALITY.

BE IN THE PRESENT MOMENT. Take a moment to observe:

- \- her,
- \- the interaction between you& her,
- \- the environment that you are in,&
- \- people around you,

What stuck-out as interesting to you? Share the thought outloud.

27

LAW #14: Teach her about herself.

Technique #14: The Cold Read

MAKING a cold read (or a warm read) boils down to making an intelligent, insight about her favorite subject: herself. Tell her something about herself that she didn't know before. Give her an insight about her current life's situation that will blow her fucking mind.

COLD-READS ARE EXTREMELY effective conversation amplifiers. After all, there is no one in the world that she cares more about except herself. By revealing something about her that she didn't know before you've given her a significant amount of benefit - **one that will reciprocated by her giving conversational value of her own to benefit you!**

❄

Technique #14.2: The Dig Deeper Tactic

Listen attentively to what she says - both on an intellectual level and on an emotional level. Then paraphrase what she has already told you in your own words, and go deeper into that subject.

WHEN A WOMAN TALKS ABOUT HERSELF, read between-the-lines and understand the implications. Think to yourself:

- Why is that true?
- Why is it important?
- What are the implications and ramifications of what she said?
- What does that say about who she is?

By thinking about these questions and possible answers, you will use your mind to generate insights. Then proceed to share the most interesting of these insights with the women who you are dealing with.

❄

4 Types of Cold Reads You Can Use

- - **Comment on her energy levels.** Does she have a lot of energy or is chill and calm?
- - **Comment on her introversion or extroversion.** Is she an introvert or an extrovert?
- - Comment on her accent, and take an educated guess as to where she is from. "You have a strong accent. I can tell that you are from Russia." You can take this a step further, and take a guess about what her age is. **Regardless if you are wrong or right, she will be entertained and will wonder what lead you to come to that conclusion.**
- - Comment on her Myers Briggs personality type.

28

LAW #14: SUMMARY

LAW #14: TEACH HER ABOUT HERSELF.

A WOMAN'S favorite subject in the world is herself. And her favorite word is her own name. Share insights about her personality/lifestyle (e.g. cold-reads), and pussy will be never-ending.

29

LAW #15: Polarize. Play to a sexy stereotype.

Playing it safe is playing it boring.

A MAN **who is edgy is far more interesting and exciting to women than a man who is bland.**[1] Don't try to appeal to every woman in the world because the you will be the ultimate generic guy who doesn't have haters, but also doesn't have lovers. It is better to be loved by some, and hated by some than it is to have indifference by all. Why? Because the indifference response doesn't get you sex. But being loved by some does lead to results in the field.

FOCUS ON DEVELOPING one stereotype that is very sexy and tailoring your approaches to the specific demographic women who are into that type of value proposition. **A fisherman who specializes in a specific location is more likely to get tastier, bigger fish than a fisherman who will catch fish anywhere.** Here are some sexy stereotypes to consider:

- - a rich business man who wears slick suits and enjoys the high status perks of existence,
- - a frat-boy rockstar singer who is the life of the party and knows the hottest events in the city,
- - a spiritual guru who lives a meaningful life of fierce purpose and incredible passion,
- - a digital nomad who enjoys traveling, exotic adventures and knows the best views in the city,

Technique #15.1: The Breaking Social Norms Tactic

One way of doing this is to occasionally break social norms[2] (such as screaming, talking to random people who are nearby you, running a prank, or putting on a funny hat like Mystery's cowboy hat). Breaking social norms (doing something controversial that is anti-conforming) will instantly spike a woman's emotions. This secret "break social norms to trigger a woman's emotions" alone is worth the purchase of this book.

KEEP **in mind that when utilizing this technique of breaking conformity, it's important to be aware of a woman's comfort levels.** Take her slightly out of her comfort zone to the point where she feels the excitement of being alive, but not the point where she feels so overwhelmed and has panic attacks - ejecting from the situation as a result. Outgoing women have a higher level of endurance than shy women. If you sense that a woman is very anxious then it would be prudent to focus on building her comfort levels (through pacing reality "I know that this rather odd, and I don't usually do this, but YOLO (pace, pace, lead)" or basic "nice guy game") rather than continuing to spike excitement through the roof.

THE PSYCHOPATHIC EDGE

FUCK being a sheep brainwashed by the cultural of the times. Think for yourself. While you may look like a sheep to blend in with other sheep, deep down you are a predatory wolf who is extremely aggressive in going after what he wants in life and FUCKS ANYONE WHO GETS IN THE WAY.

BE POLARIZING.

Stating strong polarizing opinions will instantly make you more interesting. To some extent, it doesn't even matter if you speak the truth or not. What matters is that you evoked an emotional response within her, and provoked conversational investment.

DON'T PLAY it safe when you are in conversations with women. Playing it safe is playing it boring. 99/100 of guys say the same safe things that every guy says and that's what makes them boring. Playing it safe is taking the greatest risk of all: being boring. Instead of playing it safe, take calculated risks in conversation. One way of doing this is to take on a polarizing identity.

---

1. While it is true that you will lose some women in the process of having a polarizing personality, you will gain more women than you lose. This goes back to a concept mentioned earlier: figure out the type of women who you want to fuck, and tailor your game to that demographic. It is better to be loved by some, and hated by some than it is to have everyone indifferent to you. Roger Stone puts this concept nicely in one of the laws of Roget Stone "It is better to be infamous than not be famous at all." When one is able to effectively get attention then he can then utilize that attention for sexual or financial purposes. One who has a polarizing personality simply gets far more attention from women than a man who always plays it safe because he is a pussy conformist still metaphorically living in his mother's womb - terrified of claiming a unique identity. In conclusion: find a sexy

stereotype and play that role. This is a superior sexual mating strategy than just being a forgettable average guy who women have seen thousands of times prior.

2. For more information, look into the Novelty Effect on RAS

30

LAW #15: SUMMARY

LAW #15: POLARIZE.

A MAN who is EDGY is far more interesting and exciting to women than a man who is bland. Playing it safe is playing to lose because safe conversation is BORING. Take calculated risks. Speak with BOLDNESS.

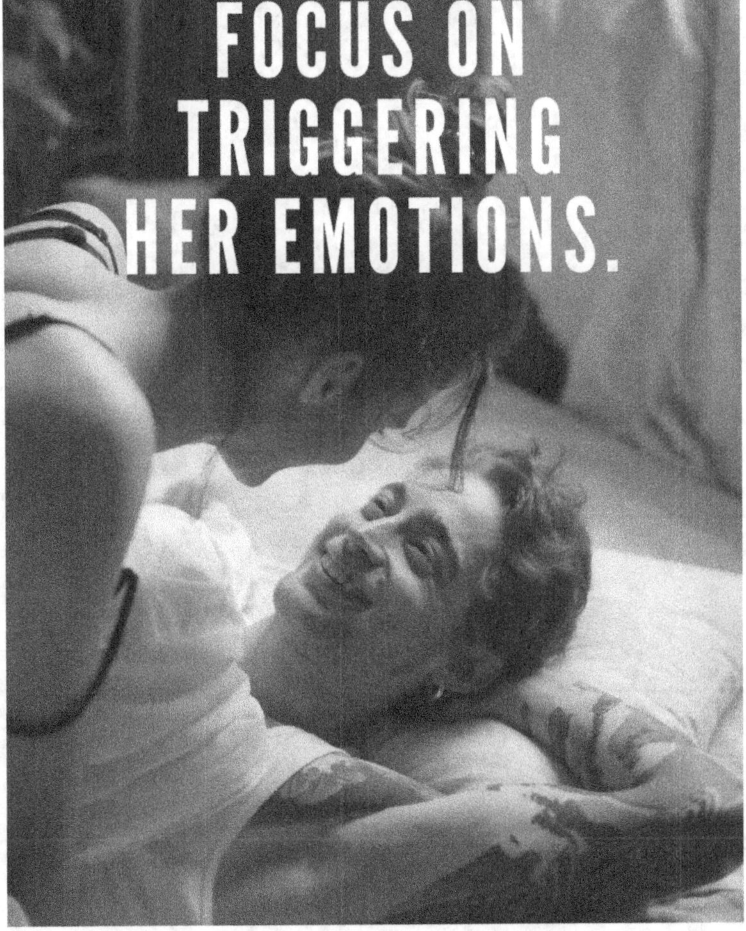
FOCUS ON
TRIGGERING
HER EMOTIONS.

31

LAW #16: Be a wolf in sheep's clothing.

Technique #16: The Prop

YOU CAN WEAR props on yourself that you can use as conversation starters. For instance: holding a book that you are reading, an extravagant necklace or even having a cute dog on a leash. This will give women an excuse to start a conversation, or she may bring it up during a conversation.

THE USE of props is similar to peacocking (attention-grabbing clothing) where you bring in items into the field for the purpose of increasing your odds of success. **Props are items that bring attention to you; once you have that attention then you can use it to your seductive advantage.**

- Bringing a dog to a park filled with young women (of legal age) is one of the oldest tricks in the book.
- Riding in an electric skateboard at a camp for older teenagers (18+) and young adults (to age 21)

will allow you to quickly work the area for social proof.

- Renting a Ferrari for dates and IG photos. This tactic in particular of flashing elite social status is incredibly powerful. Tai Lopez took this to an extreme by renting a mansion to film YouTube videos showcasing his "success" and then proceeding to make millions selling his "how to achieve success" courses.

FURTHERMORE, **the use of props is to make it seem as if you are in the middle of doing something important in your day– rather than specifically going out to the location just to meet women.**

- At a college campus, carrying around a MacBook Pro gives you the plausible deniability that you are a student who is preparing for class and has shit going on. Freshman students will simply assume this; it does not need to be explicitly stated. This makes your approaches seem more natural because they capitalize on the commonality of both being college students – rather than an outsider trying to be a part of the "in crowd".
- Another example of this, is holding something at a store – as if you are about to buy it – to appear as if you are another store shopper – even though you have specifically entered the store only to pick up women.
- Wearing religious items at a spiritual organization to meet the beautiful young women who are secretly incredibly horny, and infiltrating social

circles through consistently becoming a part of the event attendants (eventually becoming one of the highest ranking members who fucks the newcomers).

NEVER UNDERESTIMATE **the power of props.** Props have massive relevance to sociological forces at play in meeting women in social situations, and banging them in sexually charged situations.

USING props is part of a larger principle in the game of life which is to use every resource possible to your advantage. There are no "cheap shots". Use every dirty trick in the book. WIN AT ANY COSTS.

32

LAW #16: SUMMARY

LAW #16: BE A WOLF IN SHEEP'S CLOTHING. WIN AT ANY COSTS. TAKE CHEAP SHOTS. A woman makes a split-second status-assessment of a man's status before he even says anything. Dress wealthy, be well groomed, and use props."

33

LAW #17: Read the signals.

Technique #17: The Gauge

DON'T HAVE A CONVERSATION BLINDLY. Gauge her responses as you are talking to her by reading her body-language, facial micro-expressions and tonality. When she gets excited over something, you've identified a subject that interests her and you should talk more about that.

WHEN SHE GETS BORED, cut the thread and talk about something else. You can even switch subjects mid-sentence. **Keep fishing various subjects until you get a hit.**

YOU SHOULD BE able to detect from her body-language if what you are saying is boring her, or causing her anxiety. As I have mentioned numerous times, dealing with women is not a cookie-cutter, one-size-fits all; you should calibrate based on her body-language responses if you talk more about certain subjects, less about other subjects, or try an entirely new subject.

. . .

HOW TO TELL **if a woman is not interested in a particular subject matter, and it's time to alternate:**

- She will look away - diminishing eye-contact.
- She will glance at the door.
- She will give one worded responses like "cool" or her responses will be shorter than what she is used to.
- Her tonality and volume will go down (lower than her normal Baseline).
- She will take a step back.
- Her feet will start to be pointed in a different direction.
- She will make a slight turn in the opposite direction.

.

Figure out what things in life she is most passionate about. By knowing a lot about these subjects and talking about them, you will come across as far more interesting. Talking about shit she cares about is a fundamental rule towards being a good conversationalist. **RELEVANCY IS KEY.** After all, you bought this book because it was RELEVANT to an issue that has deep meaning to you; did you not?

IT IS ALSO RECOMMENDED **to mention a subject briefly before going too deeply into it.** For example: if she responds positively to a brief comment about cats then you know that it will be safe to go into a longer monologue about pets.

. . .

YOU DON'T WANT **to take this too far where you start ending statements as if they are questions,** and constantly seeking out her approval while saying anything. Do not end statements in a high pitched voice like a little bitch. Talk about a subject that you are passionate about and enjoy – without seeming like you give a fuck if she approves. If you see that she is responding positively to that then keep going. If she isn't, then alternate subjects.

IF YOU LAUNCH IMMEDIATELY **into a lengthy dialogue about a subject that she doesn't care about, and keep talking about it extensively (despite her body-language signals) then don't be surprised if the interaction ends.** Forcing women into a conversation about a subject that they don't care about and having a dull delivery style will kill interactions.

IF A WOMAN ISN'T receptive to a particular escalation move, she may choose to send subtle signals rather than outright tell you "DO NOT DO THAT!" because she wants to avoid the uncomfortable, awkward tension with direct verbal confrontation. She may be scared to deliver a direct rejection, so she'll send out subtle signals, imply a frame of "being busy", or come up with a silly excuse. A smart seducer can read these subtle indicators and adjust his game strategy - on the spot - before the situation reaches a point of "no return".

IF YOU SLIP up and make a mistake and say/do something silly, don't let it dwindle your confidence levels. It's normal to make mistakes, and women intuitively sense that. A confident man shrugs it off playfully (as if barely noticed it), and moves forward. The key is to retain calm, in-control composure at all times - even during common flinch points.

❄

THE COMPLIANCE LADDER

If you throw a frog into a boiling tea pot, it will jump off. But if you gently put a frog into a warm tea pot and slowly increase the temperature then it will eventually burn to death. Women are similar in this regard; don't come on too strong and get blown-out. Test the waters. Gauge her eagerness. If you see highly receptive body-language, then start escalating at a reasonable pace at high points in the interaction and with time you will eventually get everything.

EVEN IF A WOMAN **rejected you initially, you can still approach her at a later date - so don't take any rejection as final.** In this game, rejection is very common - even among veteran seducers - so having thick skin is paramount. Just like there is a large % of women who you wouldn't want to fuck, so too women view a large % of men as un-fuckable.

KEEP in mind that even 99 woman rejected you, but the final 100th turned out to be a fuck buddy then it was all worth it in the end - and you had 99 opportunities to sharpen your skills to be ready for the woman who is worthy. Approaching is simply a matter of finding out if a woman has a good taste. **Regardless if you get the girl or not, you still benefited by having some time to practice your conversation skills on her.**

❄

ADVANCED NOTE: **What is interesting to you may be boring to others.** Further, what is interesting to one woman may be boring to another. This is why taking in real-time social feedback and calibrating accordingly is of paramount importance. **Without reading body-language, you are essentially playing chess blindfold and hoping that a cookie-cutter plan will work on everyone in all situations.**

❄

LET'S apply the same concept to the business field…

Gauging is relevant to the business field as well.

It does not matter what your opinion is about a product. It does not matter what your dad says about it. The only thing that matters is how the marketplace responds. Let the numbers do the talking.

. . .

SOMETIMES YOU'LL SEE a product that you think is complete shit. You wonder to yourself "Why the fuck would I bother listing this on eBay (to dropship from Amazon, Sears, Kmart, HomeDepot, or Walmart) if it's worse than human feces? I would NEVER buy this in a million years?" Yet, eBay Sold Listings reveal that it's selling like hot-cakes.

SOMETHING THAT IS BORING **to you may be wildly entertaining to women, and vice-versa.**

34

LAW #17: SUMMARY

LAW #17: TEST AND READ THE SIGNALS.

PROTECT YOURSELF FROM WASTING TIME by testing a woman's receptiveness to sexual advances, relatively early on. Gauge the effectiveness of certain moves & topics before doubling down. If necessary, go fishing.

35

LAW #18: Be willing to compromise a woman's ego. Piss her off - if necessary.

Technique #18: The Neg, Tease and Push/Pull.

SOMETIMES INDIRECTLY INSULTING a woman is the best way to keep the conversation going and prevent her the girl from exiting the conversation. **When a woman's ego is on the line, she suddenly becomes highly emotionally engaged and verbally invested into a conversation with you.**

NEGS ARE INDIRECT INSULTS. They work because women are attracted to some level of psychological abuse from men. Sometimes attacking her ego is the best way to get her emotionally engaged in the conversation. A woman will want to keep her self-image positive, so she'll verbally respond so that she can fix the perception that she has of herself. **Negs are not obvious insults because that would only trigger a woman to respond with an insult of her own and then eject from the situation (unless she has low self-esteem and a verbally abusive childhood - in which case, she'll stick around).**

. . .

YOU WOULDN'T WATCH a movie where the protagonist had no problems because then it would be boring AF. You watch the movie because you want to see how the climax is resolved. A good conversation has to contain EXCITEMENT spikes. If there is not tension then there will be boredom. **When you add a bit of conflict that compromises her self-esteem, a woman will stay in the interaction to resolve the conflict and regain her self-esteem back; this buys you time to convey personality and generate attraction through the medium of conversation.**

THE PROXIMITY EFFECT

According to science, the more time a woman spends with you, the more attracted she will become.

HENCE, it is not prudent to overwhelm a woman by showing too much interest too fast and escalating too hard right away. While men are attracted to the visual and physicality, woman are more attracted to the auditory and a man's personality. The latter takes time to reveal. This is why men are instantly attracted to a woman (like a light-switch), but women necessitate a greater time period to fall in love with a man (like a volume knob). This explains the popular Russian saying "A woman falls in love with her ears."

IF YOU HAVE ACCIDENTALLY SHOWED a woman too much unreciprocated interest - creating uncomfortable tension (chasing a cat makes it run away, but slowly escalating and giving tons of value: keeps the cat intrigued), then negging will achieve the desired push/pull effect. One can balance high interest levels by flashing some disinterest. **As time expands, she will become more and more attracted to you - allowing you to increase the intensity of escalation.**

BALANCE TAKING **action with being patient and the world will be yours. How you play the seduction game, is how you play every game.**

INDIRECT GAME WILL BUY you more time to attract a woman and have her addicted to your personality than being direct. That being said, indirect game is NOT being the friend for weeks (or in some idiot's case: months). Indirect game is often just 10 minutes of having normal, fun conversation - designed to intrigue a woman into being with you - before conveying sexual/romantic intentions.

Advanced notes on Negging:

Negs and teases are flirting tactics that will create frustration in a woman, but it is the kind of frustration that works for you – rather than against you. Even if you get a verbally negative response from a woman, don't be alarmed; this is actually a positive sign because it shows that she cares enough to respond to you. A negative emotion from a woman is preferable than silence and apathy, because the former can be reversed but the latter is doomed to fail. Hence, it is better to risk being offensive and being too bold than playing it safe and walking on egg-shells with women. **When in doubt, err on the side of boldness for one can recover from an initial negative response from a woman, but one can seldom recover from being ignored entirely.**

. . .

THIS DOESN'T MEAN that you should be a complete asshole; pushing this too far will backfire and women may end up in self-sabotage mode to preserve an insecure ego. In the game of seduction it is often necessary to balance contradictory elements. For instance:

- One must balance being an action-taker with being patient.
- One must balance working on himself and living his personal life to the fullest - while finding the time to meet/be-with women.
- One must balance being bold and crazy fun, with appearing to be a mature individual.
- One must balance showing sexual intentions with not being needy. One must balance interest with disinterest.

HAVING a girlfriend does not mean you should stop developing your social and seduction skills. Nor does it mean that you should stop being social. Keep your skills sharp by approaching every day; always be flirting. Every day is an opportunity for growth. MAKE TODAY COUNT.

NICE GUYS, SHUT THE FUCK UP and be more edgy. Being politically correct and having nice conversations doesn't trigger sexual attraction; it just puts women to sleep. **Learn to tease, neg, playfully challenge and use shock humor.**

TEASING

This is poking fun of women in a funny way. If she has some eccentric or quirky behavior then make fun of her for it.

Teasing is the bedrock of flirting because it entices a woman to tease you back (creating a visceral compulsion to playfully fight for social power that almost compels her to keep interacting with you). If she punches you in the shoulder and laughs, you're doing it right.

NEGGING

This is subtly insulting a woman to compromise her ego, and get her emotionally/verbally engage into the conversation. If you go too far, be prepared to implement a good damage-recovery behavioral response. If she rushes to qualify and explain herself to you, you're doing it right. Keep in mind that NOT all personality types can pull this off successfully, as it requires a high degree of courage, confidence, and social savviness.

PUSH/PULL

This is alternating between statements of interest and disinterest. By switching back and forth between hot and cold, you keep women hooked to being with you and intensify their emotional state.

SHOCK HUMOR

This is saying something incredibly outlandish and radically bold. Then taking it back with a simple "I was just kidding" or "I was being sarcastic"; then immediately continuing the conversation - as if what just happened was not a big deal to you.

❄

WHEN NEGGING IS BEING USED ON YOU

Women can use humor, "constructive" criticism, and "positive intentions" to disguise blatant manipulation and Power Grabs. These women will make Power Grabs (such as these) to establish themselves as higher in relative social status, get their ego validated and feel important.

ONCE THESE WOMEN get relative social power, they become disgusted by the men who gave up their self-respect and power. The insight here is simple: **women desire men that are more powerful than them.** Even a savage feminist seeks out a more competent man who is higher than her in subjective social status - both relative to her and relative to society's standards of success.

TO ATTRACT beautiful women into your life it's imperative to:

- - seize social status immediately,
- - create the frame that YOU ARE THE PRIZE IN THE INTERACTION,
- - avoid exuding an apologetic or doubtful self-image,
- - ALWAYS have powerful, dominant body-language,
- - ALWAYS retain Walk Away Power by having multiple women in your orbit,
- - behave like a KING,
- - dress like you're wealthy,
- - avoid peasant and low status behaviors that indicate that you are a man of inferior social standing,

- - avoid dressing average,
- - avoid worshipping women,

THERE'S a lot more key behaviors than I'm including in this chapter, but to summarize they follow one basic guiding principle.

SEIZE SOCIAL POWER, and retain it. Women think they want social power, but quickly lose respect and attraction to a man who gives away his power.

YOU ARE A 10, SO FUCKING ACT LIKE IT.

❄

FOUR DEADLY MISTAKES TO AVOID AT ALL COSTS.

I.

Your first mistake was thinking that she was an angel of moral purity - without an agenda of her own.

II.

SECONDLY, allowing for minor behaviors of disrespect lead to major behaviors of disrespect - which ultimately killed her attraction and appreciation of your high worth.

III.

THIRDLY, you didn't know what you wanted out of the connection. You entered into a frame of friendship - instead of establishing a Rated R flirtatious frame from the start. You waited too long to make a move - playing perpetual indirect game and wasting time in the process. Women don't respect men that don't go after what they want - in a sexual medium; be physically aggressive in bed. Whip it out and fuck her HARD.

IV.

Your fourth mistake was not keeping a rotation of other beautiful women or maintaining an active social life. She was the only source of sex, and female energy in your life - which led to oneitis, and an imbalance of power. You lost "walkaway power" and she had you by the balls.

❄

WOMEN DESIRE POWERFUL MEN.

WHEN YOU YIELD power to her, you ironically self-sabotage the connection in the long-term. She might get an immediate ego-boost, but sexual attraction is compromised in the long term. Further, by developing the habits of a simp soy-boy (even for the sake of a particular woman), you compromise your general sexual market value for women in general.

WHEN YOU DON'T ALLOW a woman's pussy turn you into a beta male, you'll stop pedestalizing her, and start valuing yourself. Ironically, putting yourself FIRST attracts more women than putting a woman FIRST. Why? Because: **<u>WOMEN VALUE MEN THAT VALUE THEMSELVES.</u>**

4 EXAMPLES OF THE EASIEST TYPE OF NEG TO USE: A BACKHANDED COMPLIMENT

- You remind me of that movie star... Woody Allen.
- I think it's great that you are so confident, you can go outside in whatever you want regardless of what's in style.
- I dig the way you give up fashion for comfort.
- You're cute, in a dorky way.

36

LAW #18: SUMMARY

LAW #18: COMPROMISE A WOMAN'S EGO IF NECESSARY.

A WOMAN who feels apathetic will not be receptive to a having a conversation. Attack what is precious to her - her ego - either playfully (teasing) or seriously (negging) and she'll be hooked.

37

LAW #19: Hijack her brain. Disarm; then attack.

Technique #19: The Trance Word

WHENEVER SHE SHARES **information about herself, pay attention and remember it. It is fodder that you can use to build a conversation.** Further, by listening carefully she leaves clues on how she is to be seduced and the type of man that is interested in a sexual relationship for the long term, or sexually in the short term. If this particular woman is important to you for the long term then pay attention to create a mental blueprint of what works on her specifically.

HER VALUES, interests and beliefs are AMMUNITION that you can use to advance the interaction forward.

IF YOU NOTICE that a woman continuously uses a certain keyword or keyphrase then implement these trance words into your vocabulary for your communication to have greater resonance with her.

. . .

A TRANCE WORD is a word that puts a woman into an emotional state because of the personal meaning that she has attached to it.

FOR EXAMPLE: generally speaking the trance words "fucking awesome" and "that is incredible!" tend to put women in a positive emotional state. In contrast, the words "feces", "roaches", and "toilet" tend to trigger disgust and should be avoided.

IT GOES without saying that a seducer should not mention disgusting subjects when interacting with women - like "I need to take a shit." This shows poor social skills, lack of class, and implies that you are still a low status man. Language should be used to uplift those around you - not repel them by discussing creepy ("check out my knife collection!"), weird, socially awkward, or gross things. **A high status man networks with the educated elite, has a certain classy refined character and a level of morals.**

THE WORDS that you use have an emotional impact on others and even yourself; therefore it is wise to be selective about your choice of words. You relationship with yourself leads to a better relationship with others. If you use positive self-talk and positive word choices to be motivated in life then you are likely to do the same when interacting with others.

ADVANCED NOTES: The biggest Trance Word is her name. Her name is her favorite word in the world.

HOW TO GET A WOMAN TO TRUST YOU

Nothing will get a woman to trust you faster than by revealing that you are a G-d fearing individual who is religious - at least to a certain extent. That being said, this should not be entirely faked because women have an intuition (read: sixth sense) that will eventually detect any bullshit - especially if you enter a relationship with her (she will find out who you truly are sooner or later).

WHILE ONE CAN FAKE a certain personality long enough to have sex with a woman, it may not be sufficient to keep a woman around for a long-term relationship. For the long term, you have to be the real deal - not just a juggler filled with tricks, lines and a deceptive alter ego.

THAT BEING SAID, one should still strive to be the best version of himself every day. **A woman's purpose is to motivate a man to reach his full potential in life. The traits that women find attractive in a man - assertive, outgoing, wealthy, leader of men, traveling adventurer, fiery life purpose - happen to be things that you should want to have anyways for your own sake.**

THERE IS MORE to life than just pussy. Consider adopting a meaningful purpose to existence. When all is said and done, what do you want your life to mean?

HOW TO OVERCOME STRANGER DANGER, AND MAKE A WOMAN FEEL COMPLETELY COMFORTABLE WHEN YOU APPROACH HER - SO THAT YOU'VE ALREADY WON THE GIRL BEFORE YOU EVEN SAY ANYTHING.

The cold approach is a way to meet women but its disadvantage is that you start from scratch when you walk up to a woman. She doesn't know anything about you, and you have a limited amount of time to convey highly attractive traits/features about yourself - enough for her to want to give out her personal information for a Day Two.

THIS IS ASSUMING THAT:

- you have the game skills to overcome the initial uncomfortable experience that women feel when a strange man approaches them on these the street (with a rapid-fire series of brilliantly cunning techniques),
- the balls to disregard social norms in the first place,
- the smoothness to be seen as relatively normal,
- the charm to spark attraction, and
- the brazenness to have DOMINANT, POWERFUL BODY-LANGUAGE throughout the process.

Yes, one could get laid this way and learn a fuck ton about the game along the way, but it's not a beginner friendly method. **One doesn't get a gold medal for making things harder than they have to be - especially if there are far easier ways (and more time efficient ways) of meeting women such as joining a dance, yoga, meditation, or spiritual social club. Do you**

want ego validation points from random dudes, or do you want to get sexual ecstasy?

IF YOU SAY "YEAH, but I don't have the time for that" then GO FUCK YOURSELF BECAUSE YOUR HAND IS ALL THAT YOU WILL HAVE. This isn't your "press a button and pussy falls from the sky" kind of book. Yes, it takes WORK to have beautiful women in your life. It takes HUSTLE. **So man the FUCK UP, and EMBRACE THE GRIND LIFESTYLE.**

COMPARE street pickup to building a strong social circle in a college campus social club, or starting your own social club in a college campus. You infiltrate the group, bring a ton of value, and eventually become the highest ranking member in that group. When a cute 18 year old freshman comes in for the first time to a party that the social club is throwing, you already have built-in social proof, perceived high status, and a massive logistical advantage. You get the girl before you even say anything - as long as you don't have any kind of weird quirks or blind spots that are fucking you up (consult with peer network of successful men who get laid by showing them hidden camera footage of your interactions with women (where legal)). **The point is this: create the conditions where an approach is the most likely to succeed because sexual mating strategy is a long term play even more than it is a series of short term plays. Being the forum's most successful pickup artist is not the end goal.**

IN THE GAME OF SEDUCTION, the end goal is to create a set of conditions where you are considered to be so attractive that women will approach you. Or at the very least, when you approach a beautiful women then she will be highly receptive because your positive reputation preceded you. These conditions are created by becoming a high ranking member in a niche that women value - such as spirituality, yoga, meditation, travel. Don't be a fucking idiot starting from scratch every day; utilize prior successes to build better approach conditions for the future.

38

LAW #19: SUMMARY

LAW #19: DISARM A WOMAN FULLY. THEN ATTACK.

USE SOCIOLOGICAL, logistical factors, and trance words to maximize leverage before you even approach. Gain a woman's trust by revealing a spiritual and altruistic side to yourself. Then ATTACK.

IN THE IDEAL SCENARIO, actually be spiritual - so as using that side of you to gain the trust of women is not "fake" but rather an extension of one of the facets of your personality; after all, women can sense bullshit fakery a mile away.

USE LAW#19 with discretion and be ethically prudent. Do not reveal it to blue-pilled men or they may condemn you as evil. If positing this tactic on the internet, remain anonymous.

39

LAW #20: Leave juicy bait.

Technique #20: Use bold language.

GOOD ENTERTAINERS EMBELLISH THE TRUTH, use emotionally charged words, display personality and inject emotion into their words. They don't sound like robots citing a memorized script. Conversation is a medium to convey a sexy personality.

END EVERYTHING **you say with a bold, provoking remark to make it easy for her to respond back with her own remark then look expectantly for her to contribute to the conversation, while keeping eye-contact.** Making a bold remark, creating a vacuum with silence (because you stop talking after the bold remark is finished) and then keeping eye-contact to imply that you expect her to contribute: will lead to a woman contributing to the conversation.

- Seducer: "I can tell that you are a college freshman."

- Seducer: *stops talking and holds eye-contact - implying the frame that the conversation is still ongoing*
- Woman: "What makes you say that?"

YOU WILL NOTICE that generally speaking bolder language generates more emotions and conversational investment from women.

COMPARE SAYING:

- "this is coffee is good" with
- "this is the BEST FUCKING TASTING COFFEE that I have ever tasted in my life!"

VISUALIZE YOURSELF AS THE WOMAN; which of these remarks would get you more emotionally invested and engaged into the conversation? The latter is a superior form of communication because it generates an impulsive conversational reaction in women and is easier to respond to.

TECHNIQUE **#20.1: leave juicy bait.**

A good conversationalist makes it easy for women to respond to him by:

- **using bait** (enticing teasers that women will be tempted to inquire about; if you casually mention just coming back from London then a woman will inquire about that; if you make a mysterious cold-read about her personality that she doesn't fully understand then she'll ask you to explain it - thus falling deeper into a conversation with you),

- **talking about trending, high-demand, hot subjects** that women generally find highly interesting (discussing Algebra will most likely put women to sleep, but talking about the 2021 election clown-show debate leads to a lively verbal response),
- **triggering visceral emotions** ("No one texts faster than an angry woman.", and
- **ultra bold language** (that is triggering to the point where a woman almost can't stop herself from responding - falling into the seducer's frame in the process), and if all else fails
- **negging** (by making a statement that compromises a woman's ego - either playfully or "accidentally", she will use verbally respond to defend herself so that she can continue to feel important. Keep in mind that negs are "throw and go"; if they come across an insult then a woman will either eject from the interaction or insult you back and then eject. The incorrect use of negs can lead to a verbal harassment charge, so be smart).

BAITING.

Make having a conversation with you EASY. She shouldn't have to strain herself to come up with something to reply back to you; it should ideally flow naturally. One way to do this is to leave "tempting bait" in what you are saying.

YOU'LL FIND that when a girl likes you, it's much easier to hold down a conversation because she's contributing on her part and leaving enticing "conversation bait" - to make it tempting for you to keep talking to her.

40

LAW #21: SUMMARY

LAW #20: LEAVE JUICY BAIT.

BECOME TEMPTING. Make intriguing statements without explaining them. End each conversation piece with a bold, provoking remark; then use eye-contact to create the frame that it's her turn to talk.

BE POLARIZING
BECAUSE IT GETS
CONVERSATIONAL
ENGAGEMENT

41

LAW #21: Be the monster. Be ruthlessly pragamatic. Speak like a prophet.

Technique #21: Speak with Ultra Conviction.

HAVING INTENSE CONVICTION in what you are saying will make you twice as interesting. You want to speak as if you are a prophet and OWN EVERYTHING YOU SAY BY EXUDING 100% CERTAINTY. Talk with the frame that what you have to say holds tremendously high worth. Women can sense a man's level of confidence (or lack of) from his tone of voice.

HOW YOU VIEW **yourself is how women will view you**. If you unconsciously believe that what you are saying doesn't hold much worth then it will come across in your communications; however, if you believe that you are gold and your words are pure gold, then subtle nuances will reveal this sexy confidence.

IF YOU HAVE **strong verbal body-language then women will take what you say seriously.** However, if you start conversations with women with the body language of a weak soy-boy (timid, nervous, shy, reserved, submissive, supplicate, fearfully) then you will either be ignored or not taken seriously.

STUDY charismatic famous speakers who get on stage. When they talk, they talk as if they are 100% certain that what they are saying is absolute truth, and what they are saying holds tremendous worth. This is how they are able to sway large crowds of people. In Donald Trump's case this is how he got elected.

7 Ways to Appear More Confident:

- - **Minimize extra, unnecessary words that take up space but communicate nothing.** This is similar to the productivity tip of removing unnecessary action from your life.
- - **Get rid of filler words such as "umm..." and "uhh".** These words just take up space, but don't actually contribute any value. If anything, they remove the impact of what you are saying because they reveal the insecurity that the person you are dealing with will leave you if you pause for too long.
- - **Kill self-doubt words such as "maybe, probably, I think" that make you sound less confident**. You don't need to say things like "In my opinion" because that's already apparent. You would be better served by having a dosage of cockiness and speaking as if you are 100% certain that what you are saying is the FINAL TRUTH. This is far sexier to women than a nerd who

utilizes the words like "in the vast majority of cases, the probability of X occurring is high enough for the notion to be taken seriously."Aim for maximum emotional impact; "X is REAL!!!"

- - **Achieve maximum impact by embellishing the message and dialing it up to be polarizing.** A man who is controversial will get far more attention, and verbal engagement than the man who is too terrified to break social norms.
- - **Speak loudly, holding eye-contact, with a deep tonality, taking pauses when necessary, and touching the person on the shoulder to emphasize points.** If you don't have strong body-language, women won't take you seriously.
- - **Develop a confident, loud, dominant, deep tonality**. Study politicians who speak with absolute certainty. Women can tell if you are confident just by the way that you talk; a man's tonality reveals a lot about him.
- - **Be articulate.** Don't stutter, suddenly drop the ball or ramble incoherent gibberish. Speak clearly. If people ever have to ask you "what?" Then that's a strong sign that you aren't speaking clearly enough (which communicates low self-confidence) and it's killing the dominant frame that you should be establishing from the very start.

Confident men believe that what they have to say holds tremendous value and therefore they say it in a manner that can be easily heard by others

❋

BE THE MONSTER.

A guy who approaches a beautiful woman with nervousness and timidness has already lost before he even opens his mouth.

A woman can intuitive sense a man's confidence (or lack of). You have to be a metaphorical MONSTER - conveying absolute strength, and pure self-belief in yourself. A MONSTER is ruthlessly pragmatic.

Contrary to Hollywood movies, being nervous and shy isn't "cute"; it is absolutely repulsive to woman because it comes off as insecure. The nerd doesn't "eventually get the girl". It is the SAVAGE MONSTER who wins the game of seduction and the game of life - in general.

- BE ALPHA.
- BE ASSERTIVE.
- BE OUTGOING - NOT SHY.
- TAKE CONTROL OF SOCIAL AND SEXUAL INTERACTIONS.
- TAKE CHARGE OF YOUR LIFE, AND GO INTO SITUATIONS KNOWING WHAT YOU WANT.
- WALK AWAY FROM PEOPLE WHO WASTE YOUR TIME.

42

LAW #21: SUMMARY

LAW #21: BE RUTHLESSLY PRAGMATIC. BE A MONSTER.

HOW YOU VIEW yourself is how women will view you. If you believe what you have to say is valuable, women will fall into that frame and listen to you talk. Speak like a prophet.

43

LAW #22: Spin women like you spin plates. Keep things fresh.

Technique #22: The Multi-Thread

YOUR CONVERSATIONS with women should involve multiple subjects[1]. Instead of pursuing each subject until its very end in a linear path – like reading a single thread – it is better to implement multi-threading. Spin multiple plates of conversations, just like you spin various plates of women in your life.

THIS TECHNIQUE IS a life-savor because you will NOT run out of things to talk about with women. As soon as one subject of conversation is about to die, you still have a couple of other subjects that are still hanging in the air – waiting to be grasped again.

IF YOU ONLY HAVE ONE subject of conversation with a woman and that one subject ends then you are fucked because there is nothing else left to discuss. However, if you had 3 other topics that you were juggling then you'll just go to them instead of ending the interaction.

❄

STAYING TOO **long in a specific subject may lead to it growing stale or dead.** For instance: you can only talk about how amazing the environment is for so long before there is nothing further to say about the subject. When a subject of conversation starts to get boring, move on to the next topic to keep things fresh, and exciting.

STAYING TOO **long on a particular subject can kill the interaction because sooner or later that particular topic will become "fully mined to empty".** Then because you have nothing else being discussed on the table and nothing enticing that she can grab unto, the conversation will naturally die.

JUST LIKE YOU **spin conversational plates, spin women.** When you have multiple women in your life then you are less likely to exude neediness, desperation, or imply negative social proof.

---

1. This goes back to the concept of assuming familiarity and a level of intimacy with the woman who you are interested in. By behaving AS IF you are already close to a woman, it leads to that reality actually becoming created. People that are close to each other have conversations that span multiple subjects - not just a single subject. Replicate that behavior right off the bat.

44

LAW #22: SUMMARY

LAW #22: SPIN WOMEN LIKE YOU SPIN PLATES.

Have multiple women in your life to create an internalized perception of abundance. A man with options exudes a sexy "I DON'T GIVE A FUCK" demeanor that TURNS WOMEN ON.

Women can intuitively sense if you have no one else in your life, and nothing else going on. **If a woman senses that you have no one else in your life then it's a huge turn off because women expect successful men that have other women around them.** Men imply negative or positive social proof through their actions. When you have real options in your life, you'll unconsciously communicate this and it will spark attraction.

Internalizing abundance, by actually having other women in your life, is the optimal path because the brain wants proof not promises.

45

LAW #23: Be dynamic. Be emotionally expressive - not emotionally reactive.

Mindset #23: Have Varied Delivery.

GET RID of the formal and monotone voice. It's as painful to women as a man scratching his fingernails against a chalkboard.

HAVE A VARIED DELIVERY:

- - emphasize certain words,
- - emphasize key phrases,
- - vary your pace, tonality and volume,
- - utilize hand gestures to emphasize points,
- - implement facial expressions,

THE WAY that you say something determines if people listen eagerly or space out. Being predictable is being boring. Vary your delivery style and you'll be far more interesting to women. **You can have great content, but if**

<u>your delivery style is boring then women will be bored.</u>

IF YOU HAVE difficulty in sustaining conversations with people in general then this may be a sign that your delivery style is off. Watching TV Show hosts can be a fast way to learn how to talk in a manner that gets people hooked into your every word. Notice how certain public speakers - like Tony Robbins - can talk for hours and you'll still be entertained. It's not their words that keep you hooked, as much as their energy, and dynamic way of giving over the information.

HOW TO INSTANTLY IMPROVE YOUR COMMUNICATION STYLE WITH JUST ONE SIMPLE HACK: THE "EXPLOSIVE"

Adding emphasis on certain words makes you far more interesting as a communicator. Compare both of these ways of speaking, and see which one is more IMPACTFUL:

- "I absolutely love drinking coffee.
- I absolutely LOVE... [pause] drinking coffee."

The latter is far more entertaining to listen to. You can this a step up by polarizing it with taboo words.

- "I absolutely LOVE... [pause] drinking coffee."
- "I absolutely FUCKING... [pause] LOVE... [pause] drinking coffee."

These changes are simple and easy to implement but they can have a HUGE IMPACT. The point is this: add emphasis to certain words when talking to women - even if the words that you decide to emphasize are relatively arbitrary.

Hyperbole

Embellishing with hyperboles is also a powerful tactic to be more interesting when communicating with others. View yourself as a listener and visualize someone talking to you. Compare these two statements and ask yourself "Which one of these would spark more intrigue?":

- "I have a relatively above average size dick."
- "I have the BIGGEST DICK YOU HAVE EVER SEEN."

46

LAW #24: Enter into a Talkative State. Embrace the flow.

WHEN YOU ARE in a talkative state of mind, the right things to say will naturally come to you. This is a mental state that is conducive to being a talker. One can enter into this mental state through warming up by engaging in brief interactions with other people.

THE RECENCY PRINCIPLE

One of the important principles to master in starting conversations is the principle of RECENCY. This is where you are mention that the subject of conversation just happened to you so that it doesn't appear like you are trying too hard to start a conversation. **Using recency makes the seducer appear spontaneous.**

For example, ask yourself which one of these remarks sound smoother:

- - "*Last night*, I binge watched an entire season of The Game of Thrones" or
- - "I binge watched an entire season of The Game of Thrones."

The former appears more natural because it implements the regency principal. Cool, social guys like to talk about things that just happened to them; it's an extroverted behavior. They talk because they want to "get something off their chest", share a recent experience with someone and enjoy the present moment.

In contrast, the latter is someone who appears to be putting in a conscious effort to start up a conversation.

It's better to appear natural, spontaneous and in-the-moment. Something so awesome just happened to you that you JUST HAVE TO share it with someone! More examples:

- - "You wouldn't believe what just happened to me…"
- - "On my way here, I had the strangest realization…"
- - "Did you see the fight outside?"
- - "Last night the craziest thing happened to me."

Why is Recency Important?

It's normal to want to talk about the current exciting events in your life. **You're so excited about what you're going through that you can't help but share it with the world!** Further, describing your situation to others has a therapeutic effect, and helps one gain perspective on his life. On the other hand, starting conversations about events that have transpired years ago:[1] creates the impression that you are trying hard to entertain her. Women might be entertained by pathetic, eager-to-please clowns, but they don't fuck them.

- He who tries hard, dies hard.
- Appear effortless.

- Don't reveal knowledge of game. Reveal red pill concepts, to brainwashed blue-pilled people at your own peril.
- Don't make it seem like you prepared a lot for her. Appear natural and unplanned.
- Don't seem like you have an intense agenda. Appear like you're just having fun. This is very disarming for women.
- Don't seem like you're trying too hard to gain rapport because it comes across as needy, desperate and implies negative social proof. A high-status man who has many options with women is used to beauty and doesn't need to bend over backwards to attract one into his life; beautiful women intuitively grasp this concept and expect a high status man to have standards, have healthy expectations, and to a certain extent be psychologically aloof.

Another Reason Why You Should NOT Be a Try-Hard

BEING RAW, uncensored and having fun in the present moment and when you go out for outings is more sustainable for meeting women in the long term than excessively meticulously planning and being overly self-conscious every time that you talk to her. Introverts in particular can sometimes get to paralysis and be trapped due to overthinking. **Intelligent guys take notes: don't overcomplicate things to the point of paralysis. When you are in the field, keep it simple.**

Pickup should be fun! Have a good time! Don't make it painful by being overly self-critical, neurotic, OCD, anxious about being judged, or self-conscious.

By entering into talkative state, you'll naturally say the right things in conversation. Talkative state is a certain state of mind that is conducive to being a conversationalist. One is able to enter this state of mind by warming up and doing some socializing.

Brief note on texting:

Practical application: when you get a text from a woman, don't take 5-10 minutes to ponder the best possible response that you can send her. This is a waste of your time and psychological energy. It takes away the fun of the interaction and turns it into a chess match.

FURTHER: it can take more energy to remember to text her back than it takes to just text her back as soon as you read it. **You are far better served by just responding instantly as soon as you read her text than having to exert unconscious energy to remember in your mind to text her later and unconsciously working on the "most clever, value-giving" text back.** I advise not looking at your phone's texts until you ready to interact with women, so that you aren't put in a situation where you read texts, can't respond right away, postpone it for later, and then have your mind waste its energy.

WHEN YOU HAVE genuine fun in the field, you will be much more motivated to go out and interact with women (sustaining motivation in the long-term) than if you view it as a painful chore and a dangerous minefield.

A good approach appears like "it just happened".

A good approach appears natural and spontaneous – not planned. A good pickup should not look like a pickup. A good pickup appears as if you are in the middle of doing something important, but you happened to notice something about her that overwhelmed you so much that you "couldn't stop yourself" from sharing that thought.

AFTER ALL, you are a highly social outgoing guy. You enjoy talking to people and meeting new people - as you go about your daily life. Even if you don't "get the girl", you still got an enjoyable experience that uplifted your spirits and made your day more awesome.

AFTER TALKING to her for a bit, she ended up being so cool that you exchanged numbers so that you can invite her to fun events in the area that you are going to anyways because you have an exciting and fun lifestyle.

---

1. Remember exciting events that have happened to you - even if they happened years ago. Then share them with women as if you're going through them now. By talking passionately about something that "you're going through" you're allowing a woman to live through an adventure - just by listening to you talk. Movie entertainment is a 100 billion dollar industry for a reason; stories are powerful tools to captivate attention - whether it's male or female.

47

LAW#24: SUMMARY

LAW #24: Enter into a talkative state. Embrace the flow.

ENTER into a certain mental state of mind that is conducive to being good at conversation. This mental state of mind is achieved through warming up through simple interactions with people.

48

LAW #25: Express - not impress.

APPEAR EFFORTLESS IN YOUR CONVERSATIONS. You want to accomplish much without appearing like you are trying to accomplish anything at all. Impress without coming across as if you are trying to impress. **Speaking should come from a position of self-expression ("I'm so excited about this idea that I want to share it!) - rather than from an insecure position of trying to impress ("Hey!! Look at me!! Look at what I can do!! Do you like me now?).**

REMEMBER THE MAXIMS:

- "He who tries hard, dies hard."
- "In any social interaction, the one who is trying less has greater social power."
- "In any social interaction, the one who is reacting more to the other has less social power." Be one acts - not reacts.
- Be self-amused - not a dancing monkey entertainer.

THE IRONY IS that it takes a lot of effort to appear effortless. As mentioned in LAW #24, one way to appear effortless is to ride the waves of emotion, being spontaneous, and entering a "talkative flowing zone". When you enter the zone, you almost lose yourself and just enjoy the present moment.

Speak your train of thought - as the thoughts come into your mind - without putting in too much effort into "coming up with the perfect thing to say". This will create this sexy authentic, raw experience of connecting with the REAL YOU - rather a version of you that is carefully crafted from moment to moment.

BEAUTIFUL WOMEN ARE USED to men throwing themselves at them. Showing too much interest slots you into the category of "yet another desperate, needy guy who kisses ass", yet showing not enough interest leads to the friend-zone. The key is not start small, test the waters (seeing how receptive she is to your moves) and then escalate the vibe based on where she's at. **SHOW INTENT, but don't be needy, clingy, or show signs of desperation in conversation.**

Be self-amused; you aren't her personal slave clown born to entertain her. Talk about things that you enjoy yourself. The key mindset is: EXPRESS - NOT IMPRESS. You aren't trying to impress her by talking; your talking is simply a matter of self-expression.

49

LAW #25: SUMMARY

LAW #25: EXPRESS - NOT IMPRESS

EXPRESS - NOT IMPRESS. He who tries hard, dies hard. In any interaction, the one who is trying harder than the other has less social power. Focus on self-amusement rather than being a dancing monkey entertainer.

❄

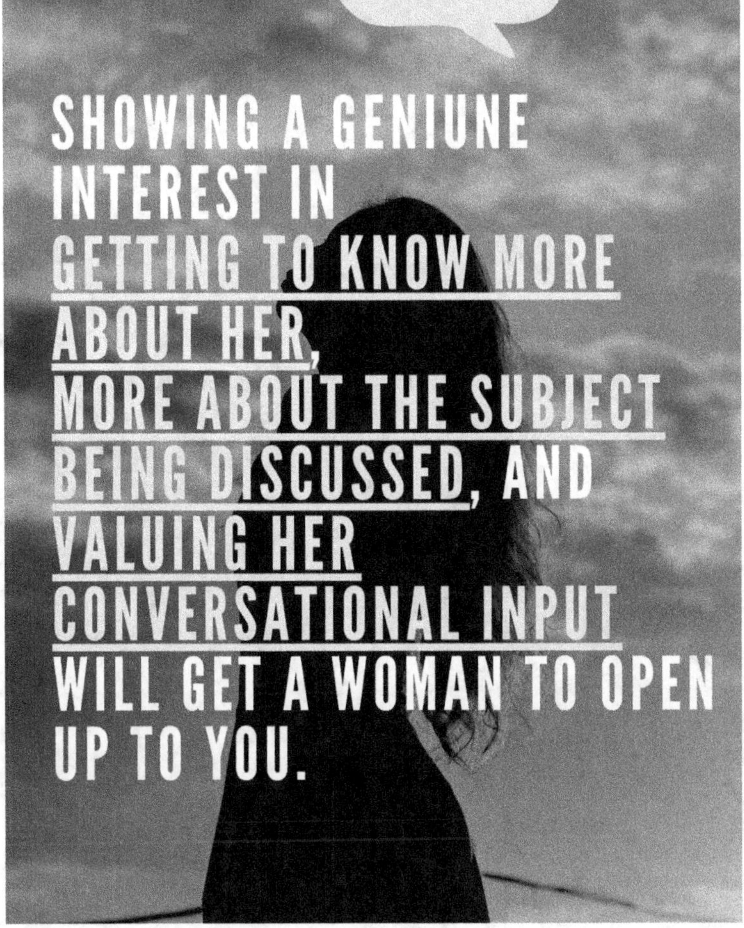
SHOWING A GENIUNE
INTEREST IN
GETTING TO KNOW MORE
ABOUT HER,
MORE ABOUT THE SUBJECT
BEING DISCUSSED, AND
VALUING HER
CONVERSATIONAL INPUT
WILL GET A WOMAN TO OPEN
UP TO YOU.

50

LAW #26: Women are disgusted by weak men. Start interactions with strength and boldness.

START INTERACTIONS WITH DOMINANCE AND STRENGTH.

HOW A RELATIONSHIP STARTS SETS the frame for the entire relationship. The same is true on a micro scale: **how an interaction starts sets the tone for the entire interaction (and eventually the ensuing sexual relationship).** Establish dominance from the very beginning. This is a superior method to engaging in the sexual marketplace than starting from a position of submission and then trying to reverse from there.

At the early phase of the pickup, you are trying to bypass the defenses that a woman may have to starting a conversation with a stranger on the street. One way of doing this is by having a strong frame ("I AM 100% CONFIDENT THAT WHAT I AM DOING IS COOL") and by having very strong, confident body-language (see the checklist below).

STARTS CONVERSATIONS WITH WOMEN LIKE A KING - NOT A PEASANT.

This can be accomplished by avoiding behavioral patterns that trigger auto-pilot rejection such as:

- speaking too quietly,
- dressing like a homeless guy, or
- opening in a submissive manner.

STARTING a conversation with a female stranger requires a certain level of assertiveness, dominance and aggression. Your first move should be one of strength and boldness.

If you attempt to start a conversation in a shy, timid manner then you may end up being ignored entirely. This is especially true in a city like NY where women are used to being hustled by beggars begging for money.

You must enter her world on a strong note.

- Be loud.
- Be dominant.
- Hold eye-contact.
- Smile.
- Be hyper relaxed.
- Dress wealthy (there is a reason why real-world pimps wore immaculate suits).

Body-language check-list:

- - Don't lean in. Lean back. Be psychologically aloof instead of being psychologically clingy.

- - Don't speak quickly like you're nervous. Take your sweet time. Take pauses.
- - Don't invade personal space on the opener, but don't stand too far away either.
- - Keep your feet apart to hold a wide stance. Take up space.
- - Don't fidget or touch your face - which are indicators of anxiety.
- - Hold eye-contact.
- - Keep your hands on the hips as a power pose.
- - Be EXPRESSIVE when communicating. This is part of being a DYNAMIC COMMUNICATOR.

51

LAW #26: SUMMARY

LAW #26: Women are disgusted by weak men. Enter interactions with strength and boldness.

HOW AN INTERACTION SETS the mutual tone, frame and micro habits for the entire interaction and eventually the following relationship. Hence, it's important to start from the right position from the very beginning.

52

LAW #27: Capture her attention like a police officer.

Technique #27: The Attention Snap

THE ATTENTION SNAP is a very important part of the opener. Sometimes girls will pretend that they didn't hear anything/didn't notice you because they are afraid of being stuck in boring conversations with guys of low social status. **In certain communities, women are constantly being hit up by random low status guys and they have developed certain "pretend like I don't hear anything" defense systems to avoid these losers.** This issue is fixed by the attention snap and being clever.

THE ART OF THE ATTENTION SNAP

- Be in her visual line of sight.
- Get physically in-front of her.
- Get eye-contact.
- Command her attention with a VERY DOMINANT "hey!"

Once she notices you, move on to the ice-breaker opening line.

THE ART OF THE FLIP

- "Which direction is the nearest library?"
- "Actually I don't care about that. You're cute and I wanted to meet you."

LAW #27: DON'T BE A PUSSY. CAPTURE HER ATTENTION LIKE A POLICE OFFICER.

Pickup is like sales. You're selling the concept of her being with you. To do that: you have invade a woman's radar. That is done by "BLASTING IN" - not by humbly knocking on a door asking for permission to talk to.

Don't ask "Hey, is it okay if I talk to you?" Don't even imply this frame with submissive body-language. Just fucking talk to her. Open like the Kool Aid man. He doesn't ask for permission by knocking on a door; he smashes through the wall and gives value.

- - Get her attention.
- - Differentiate yourself quickly from the average guy.
- - Give tons of value to spark attraction.
- - Sustain attention and her interest.
- - Always be closing.
- - Leave her wanting more.

First get her attention; then deliver the opening line. **High status men don't talk to women who aren't paying attention to them, or looking in the opposite direc-**

tion. If a woman who you are in a relationship with does this, respond with "Look at me." High-status men expect to be treated with respect.

When a woman treats you with respect, she becomes more attracted to you in the process. In contrast, if you allow a woman to treat you like a doormat, her vagina will get as dry as a desert.

53

LAW #27: SUMMARY

LAW #27: DON'T BE A P*SSY. Don't ask for permission to talk to her. Don't even imply permission-seeking with submissive body-language. Just fucking talk to her AND OWN IT 100%. Capture her attention like a police officer.

54

LAW #28: Success with women necessitates risk.

MINDSET: TAKE SOCIAL RISKS. PLAYING IT SAFE IS PLAYING IT BORING.

IF YOU WANT to be boring then play it safe, predictable and mundane. Have a nice conversation that she'll forget quickly. If you want to be interesting, take risks, be unpredictable, say the unexpected, throw curve-balls, and be edgy.

HOW TO BE BORING:

- -> Take no conversational risks.
- -> Be like all the other guys.
- -> Agree with everything that she says because you don't have a mind of your own.
- -> Be predictable.
- -> Share mundane details about irrelevant shit no one cares about with no emotion, energy, or conviction.

IF YOU ARE uncertain on what to do, do that which is BOLDER. BOLDNESS captivates the attention of women and sends ripples of vagina tingles. Be BOLD in conversations with women. Take social risks. Be willing to be different. Push social limits.

THE TIMID GUY is the boring guy. Being bolder, provoking her emotions and taking risks in conversation will make you x10 more interesting to women. STOP being the nice guy who is terrified of pissing her off, scared of disagreeing, afraid of speaking his mind freely, and engulfed in an aura of timidity. Add a dosage of "ASSHOLE" into your conversation.

MOST OF THE **guys she meets play it safe in conversations with her because they are afraid of offending her, or saying something that would lead to rejection. As a result, these men are predictable, bland and BORING AS FUCK.** To be interesting, take bold and fierce risks. Take courageous risks in conversation and you will find that you will be far more interesting to be around than ever before.

WOMEN ARE BORED of men that walk-on-eggshells around them and bored of men that treat them like they are fragile flowers. **She is not a fragile flower.**

START EXPERIMENTING with being TWICE AS BOLD in your communication style. Note the results that this experiment creates in your interactions. You will most likely find that being TWICE AS BOLD as you usually are, will make your conversations more emotionally-compelling and interesting.

. . .

BE MOTHERFUCKING BOLD, MOTHERFUCKER.

- - Take social risks. Even if it doesn't hit, you get points for taking the risk.
- - Use emotionally-charged words, phrases, and statements designed to sway emotions.
- - Say that which 99% of men don't have the balls to say.

IRONICALLY TAKING social risks and being BOLD in conversation is the safer route than not taking social risks. **When you don't take social risks with women, you are taking the greatest risk of all: being BORING and FORGETTABLE.**

PLAYING to not lose means to avoid risk. Playing to win means risking loss. **Success with women NECESSITATES risk - especially in conversation or you will be a bore.**

WHEN YOU SHOW INTENT, your ego is vulnerable. When in doubt, err on the side of boldness. **Fierce boldness captivates a woman's attention and gets her to stick around longer.** In contrast, timidity puts women to sleep. The shy, nice guy does not get women because he is not noticeable amidst the hordes of other shy, nice guys; there is nothing about him that stands out.

. . .

SHE DOESN'T WANT **to have a nice conversation. Those are boring as fuck.** She is already bombarded with nice conversations by an endless stream of nice guys. Nice guys are a dime a dozen, so nice guy conversation is as abundant as water. Be different. Be edgy. Push social boundaries. Say the things that she has never heard of before.

BE **willing to break the chains of cultural conformity that hold men prisoners, and be radically different in a positive way.**

STATE YOUR PERSPECTIVES with a certain level of aggression and absolute confidence - even at the risk social disapproval.

An Alpha Male does not care if you think he is an Alpha Male or not. He doesn't care if you disagree with his perspectives on life. He speaks his truth and expresses his personally 100% - even at the risk of social disapproval. This willingness to take risks, be his best uncensored self, and be different than average is what makes him stand out from the crowd - creating strong impressions on the minds of people that he meets; he then utilizes this attention for lead-generation purposes and runs those leads through a funnel that ends in a mutually pleasurable sexual relationship.

55

LAW #28: SUMMARY

LAW #28: TAKE CALCULATED RISKS. Success with women necessitates risk. Playing it safe is playing it boring. EVERY GUY plays it nice and safe; that's what makes him painfully predictable. ALWAYS PLAY TO WIN - NOT TO NOT LOSE.

56

LAW #29: Feel the fear and approach anyways.

IT IS normal to feel nervous before you go up and start a conversation with a cute girl. That nervousness can take the form of an uncomfortable tension and burden in your heart; don't let it stop you. Take action, anyways! Approach anxiety usually vanishes the moment you open your mouth and say something. Action is the cure to fear.

APPROACH ANXIETY or anticipatory uncomfortable tension prior to approaching or making a move on a woman is NORMAL.

THERE ARE a few keys to overcoming AA (approach anxiety):

- - disassociate your identity from that emotion; you are not defined by the feelings you experience.
- - **visualize yourself succeeding; what are you going to say to her exactly? See yourself walking up to a woman and saying the initial opening lines.**

- - utilize affirmations. Verbalize out-loud "Every approach is a success - regardless of outcome. I either get the girl or a lesson."
- - utilize a timer. Make a deal with yourself. You only have to be in "APPROACHING MODE" for 3 minutes, and then you'll initiate a break where you focus on recovering energy. As time goes on, your social stamina will increase and the "APPROACHING MODE" time will increase, as well.
- - another affirmation that is useful to say to yourself in the field is "I don't give a fuck!" Saying this mantra with feeling can make a huge difference in mitigating anxiety prior to approaching women.
- - reframe "anxiety" as excitement. Focus on amusement and learning.

Screenshot this page: if you are in the field, and every ounce of your being is telling you to quit because you are in emotional hell with overwhelming fear and a pounding heart, approach her anyways - because you are a man of courage with GIANT BALLS.

57

LAW #29: SUMMARY

LAW #29: FEEL THE FEAR AND APPROACH ANYWAYS.

ANXIETY WHEN MAKING moves on women is NORMAL. Almost everyone feels at it. The key is to not let emotional resistance stop you. Have the discipline to take action - no matter how you feel."

58

LAW #30: Kill the nice-guy conversations. Add tension.

NICE CONVERSATIONS ARE INSTANTLY FORGOTTEN in her mind. A nice conversation doesn't spark attraction.

BE willing to add a dosage of edginess to be different from the masses. Implement tactics:

- -> teasing,
- -> negging,
- -> cold-reads,
- -> role-playing,
- -> spiking intense emotional reactions,
- -> interesting storytelling,.

A NICE CONVERSATION, nice behaviors, formalities, and politically-correct mindsets, do NOT spark the feelings of attraction that would make her LUST AFTER YOU.

. . .

PREDICTABLE NICELY-BEHAVED males are a dime a dozen. The nice guy is the boring guy. He's boring because he is predictable. The nice guy is too terrified of being offensive that he avoids taking bold risks in conversation that would have made him interesting. Don't be bland, safe, predictable, and mundane. **Develop a RAZOR'S EDGE to your personality.**

NICE GUY MISTAKES:

- - purely logical conversations that don't trigger any emotions,
- - playing it safe and boring women to death with political correctness,
- - being just like every other guy instead of standing the fuck out,
- - not teasing women;(ignoring biological realities),

HOW TO BE INTERESTING:

- - Be unpredictable in conversation.
- - Say the unexpected.
- - Be willing to SHOCK her.
- - Take risks.
- - Be edgy and bold.
- - Talk about subject women actually care about.

☠ NICE GUYS are too afraid to say "the wrong thing" so they play it safe. As a result, she ends up bored and just ejects. The nice guy doesn't make her feel anything because his conversation is SO nice and makes her feel extra-comfortable. Making a woman feel *too comfortable* will land you into the friend zone. **Woman want to feel a little outside of their comfort zone because that gives them some excitement of living, and makes them feel alive.**

THE BADBOY MAKES her feel butterflies in her stomach because his conversation is SO edgy and spikes tension. Which one is more exciting? Who will she choose?

ADDING **some tension to a conversation makes women feel a dosage of the excitement that they crave.**

Nice guys make a woman feel *TOO COMFORTABLE* and as a result bore women to death. A woman is not a fragile flower; she can handle some "rocking the boat" and bloody thrill in her life. In fact, she craves it.

Get this. Nice conversation doesn't score you any points. It bores her to death. EVERY GUY is using the "nice conversation" tactic. She's seen it an endless number of times and it puts her to sleep. BE FUCKING DIFFERENT than what she has encountered her entire life.

BE **willing to disagree with what a woman says.** One of the advantages to disagreeing with a woman says it that it will stir her to invest into the conversation by wanting to "correct you". A man with a mind of his own is infinitely more interesting to women than a man who just agrees with everything that is said because he is too stupid to see a different angle to hot topic issues, or simply doesn't care enough to state an opposing viewpoint. I am not suggesting that you waste valuable time getting into debates and arguments; nor, should you suddenly become "Mr. I disagree with everything because it makes me sound cool"; but sprinkling in some disagreement on occasion to keep the conversation interesting is a useful tool to keep in your Conversation-Sparking Toolkit.

BE **willing to have a perspective of your own, and verbalize the tenets of that perspective - even if you intuitively sense these remarks will be against a woman's viewpoints.** A lot of guys are just mindless "Yes" Men that agree with everything a woman says for fear of losing sexual access. It is not having an opinion of their own that makes them incredibly boring, mundanely predictable, and men with pussies instead of dicks. HAVE YOUR OWN FRAME.

59

LAW #30: SUMMARY

LAW #30: KILL NICE GUY CONVERSATIONS.

NICE GUYS MAKE women feel excessively comfortable. This leads to platonic interactions and eventually hitting the friend-zone. Women thrive on excitement. Flirt, tease, make moves, and embrace the tension.

60

LAW #31: Avoid the logic trap. Bypass the information trap.

SHE BAITS YOU INTO A LOGICAL, boring conversation that will bore her and then she gets bored and ejects. This is a female self-sabotage mechanism. Don't take the bait. You don't have to answer mundane questions. You don't have to play along. Be a disrupter.

Frame Control 101

- Just because a woman asked you a question does NOT mean that you have to answer it.
- Just because a woman said something does NOT mean that you have to reply.
- Just because a woman introduced a subject does NOT mean you have to stick to that topic

The BIG SECRET to keeping a conversation going with a woman: GET HER EMOTIONALLY ENGAGED by provoking her emotions. Take it a step further and get her ego engaged. Doing these two things will make it far more difficult for a woman to disengage from a conversation.

WOMEN ARE SOCIAL CREATURES. They have difficulty resisting a man who is a great listener, insightful observe, conversationalist, fun and (at times) compromises her ego in a playful way (via flirting).

TWO KEY POINTS:

- **Many men are boring because they wait for women to bring up interesting topics of conversation. She often will not. You must bring the party. BE THE INITIATOR.**
- **A good frame to have is that you are the host of the conversation, and it's the host's responsibility to control the conversation to lead to a mutually sexually pleasing experience.**

A PURELY LOGICAL conversation is a BORING and DULL. Communicate to her in a language that resonates most with her: the language of emotions. Sprinkle in emotional spikes - whether negative emotions or positive ones. If she feels *NOTHING* then you're doing it wrong.

CREATE emotional spikes by pressing her emotional buttons through the power of bold language, breaking conformity, or utilizing offensive humor.

- **You can get away with saying almost anything as long as it's funny.**
- **What you are saying doesn't have to make complete logical sense in order for it to provoke her emotions.**
- **Women desire the feeling of INTENSE emotions because it makes them feel alive and excited.**

YET SOME GUYS don't know how to have emotionally-charged conversations. This is often true for intellectual who enjoy exploring the intricacies of esoteric theories. If you want to enjoy intellectual conversations, join a debate team or work as a paralegal. If a woman wanted factual information then she would read a book, but rather she is talking to you because…

WOMEN THRIVE on EMOTIONAL CONVERSATIONS that give them good emotions. Communicate with women in this distinct modality. For smart guys, this is almost an entirely new language to learn.

DON'T ALLOW a woman to trap you into a boring or super-logical conversations. You don't want to be associated with boredom and apathy. PATTERN DISRUPT HER SELF-SABOTAGE BEHAVIOR. **Be willing to interrupt her and change the subject to something more fun and emotional.** Her frame might be mighty strong but your frame should be even stronger.

. . .

SHE DOESN'T CARE about learning new concepts, and the finer points of your philosophies. She cares about feeling intense good emotions & excitement. She cares about having her ego stroked by being in the presence of a high status man. In the field being high E.Q. reigns supreme.

YOU CAN STILL TALK about philosophies but the focus should be about conveying life enthusiasm, conviction, feel-good emotions and energy through your words. Words are just a medium to get her to FEEL SOMETHING when she is with you; GET HER ADDICTED TO FEELING GOOD BECAUSE OF YOU.

DUMB IDIOTS ARE GETTING MORE girls than you because they know how to turn off their logical mind, be in the present moment and have a good time with the girl. Chicks dig those feel-good emotions and being an animal.

IN CONTRAST, high IQ low EQ guys are stuck in their head trying to think of the most brilliant thing to say, the best pickup line, and 764 step sequence. They're so busy analyzing that they forget to live in the present moment and see what's right in front of them. They're so busy living in the heads, that they never experience a moment of reality (outside their heads into the HERE and NOW of the physical tangible realm).

WOMEN WOULD RATHER HAVE **STUPID FUN than engage in deep, intellectually stimulating conversations. After all, she lives for good emotions.**

. . .

THAT'S what she cares about most - not so much for philosophical depth. As an INTJ, this is a lesson that I had to learn the hard, painful way. I would treat women as if they were rational men with vaginas and the result was less than optimal. Then I realized that women are emotional creatures who CARE ABOUT FEELING GOOD MORE THAN ANYTHING ELSE IN THE WORLD. I started using BOLD LANGUAGE and saying EXTREMELY BOLD and RADICAL STATEMENTS; my results were outstanding!

WOMEN WOULDN'T STOP TALKING **to me because I was radically different (in a positive way) than the average guy that they were used to.**

WOMEN ARE HIGHLY intrigued by a man who shares fierce opinions about controversial subjects with 100% fearlessness. **To nice guys stating an offensive opinion can be highly counter-intuitive, so it necessitates a leap of faith.** Try stating safe statements to women; mark results in terms of conversation generated. Then try saying radically bold risky statements; and mark results in terms of conversation generated.

SELF-HELP ADVICE IS HURTING you if it's causing you to be too self-conscious and overly analytical in the field. When you are in the field, focus on having fun, being bold, fully expressing yourself, and OWNING WHAT YOU SAY 100%.

WHEN YOU ARE in the field, let go of analysis mode and just enter a TALKATIVE FUN EMOTIONAL STATE that will pull women in.

. . .

SEDUCERS UNDERSTAND that women are more susceptible to seduction when they are in an intense emotional state. This is why logic is "the enemy" in conversations. Don't be too logical and deep in conversations; focus on being fun and pressing her emotional buttons.

The Information Trap

Being stuck in perpetually consuming more information, but not taking action. Don't get stuck constantly reading more theory and then not implementing anything. Skill comes from relentless practice - not relentless reading.

61

LAW #31: SUMMARY

LAW #31: AVOID THE LOGIC TRAP.

IT'S NOT what you say, but the confidence, energy and emotions behind the words. It's not the factual information that a woman craves - but as using conversation as a medium to uplift her mood.

62

LAW #32: Hijack authority. Talk about yourself, and what you enjoy, but make it about her.

WHEN SPEAKING ABOUT YOURSELF, reveal how what you are saying still has relevance to her personal life. Women unconsciously think "what does this have to do with me?"

Make conversation win/win. The most important person in the world to her is herself. This is why a good conversation makes the topic relevant to her. Talk about yourself and what you enjoy, but make it about her.

THINK:

- **"How is what I am saying relate to her and what is going on with her life?"**
- **"How is what I am going to say be relevant to the subjects that she cares most about?"**
- **"How can I make what I am about to say be connected and related to something that will personally benefit her?**

COLD-READS IS about telling her about herself, her personality and her life situation; they are very powerful. Be relevant. **Always bring the conversation back to something relevant to her personal interests.**

HAVE a unique perspective on hot topics. News, buzzwords and local events that are currently trending naturally engage women on a visceral level. Relate what you're saying to these trending popular cultural topics. Frame yourself as an authority on these subjects and use that as a starting point in conversation.

❄

HAVE **a sincere interest in getting to know her more.** This is part of exploring humanity, learning more about people and enjoying the present moment of being in the presence of beauty. **Being a good listener encourages women to invest into a conversation;** listen with the intent to listen rather than solely focusing on what you have to say next. When she says something about herself, empathize with her emotions by relating an incident where you felt the same way and/or had the same realizations.

Women are more inclined to talk when a man is in the present moment (not stuck in his head - on another planet), listens FULLY and expresses a genuine interest in learning more about the subject at hand. The interest in getting to know more about her comes from a general interest of learning more about human nature, and society - insights which can then prove to be useful for business purposes.

It is recommended that you develop a genuine interest in learning more about people, and about the world in general. **A good mindset to have is that "every person has positive qualities that I can learn from."** When you are naturally curious about human nature (and what makes people tick) then you will enjoy stacking cold-reads.

THE SAME INSIGHTS into female nature that you will clarify from making in-the-moment observations out-loud, can later prove to be useful when you are deciding on a winning-product to sell on your online store (selling $5 stuff drop-shipped from China for $20 in America and paying influencers for shoutouts to your overnight website). When you understand human nature, you can use that knowledge to profit in the business place. **The point is this: by having a genuine interest in learning more about people, you will naturally have people open-up to you and share details about their life - becoming more invested in the process of talking to you.**

63

LAW #32: SUMMARY

LAW #32: HIJACK AUTHORITY.

TALK ABOUT YOURSELF, and what you enjoy, but make it about her. Make conversations win/win. Show how what you're interested in and enjoy talking about, has relevancy to what she values.

WHEN YOU
HAVE
FEEL
GOOD
ENERGY
WOMEN
WILL BE
DRAWN
INTO YOUR
WORLD.

64

LAW #33: Flash elite status. Leverage social media. Win at any cost.

Be the different than the average guy. Flash elite status because greatness is sexy.

WEAR at least one outrageous item to help you STAND OUT from the masses and make a memorable, killer impact. This also provides women with an excuse to start a conversation with you, if they're attracted to you. If she is intrigued and wants to get to know you more, the peacocked item that you are wearing will provide that plausible deniability excuse for her.

HOW TO BE BORING: be average and do what all the other guys are doing (basic bitch mode).

WHAT YOU SAY to her shouldn't be the same boring and lame shit that all the other guys are saying. If she's heard it before then it won't spark intrigue; it will spark the "I've been there, done that already" anchor. Be different. Be a breath of fresh air.

UPGRADE YOUR PHOTO GAME.

There are men that post IG photos of themselves at a sunset and then write in the captions that they are in a foreign country. Others pay professionals to photoshop them in adventurous scenarios - such as in-front of the Eiffel Tower surrounded by beautiful women leaning into them. It's not as expensive as you would think to get flown in a helicopter, or to rent a jet-ski/Ferrari. The key is that the most recent four photos of your IG page should be dope pictures. While I'm not necessarily saying that you should engage in deception out of ethical concerns, I do advise: being creative in how you present yourself to the world.

IT SOUNDS pathetic to stoop so low to seduce women, but that is how the game is played by both genders. Since the dawn of mankind women have duped men with makeup. In the 21st century, the game has evolved and women are using plastic surgery, boob-jobs, unique camera angles, and phone filters. Why should a man not exploit the same techniques of visual manipulation? If the situation was reversed, a woman would not hesitate to win - by any means necessary.

THE GOAL IS to appear to be part of the 0.01% of society. And if that's not who you are now, work towards achieving the apex of the metaphorical human food-chain mountain. **Achieving apex social status is a longterm game.**

LEVERAGE SOCIAL MEDIA

Besides playing a religious angle, one can gain the trust of a particular woman by adding her as a FaceBook friend - provided that he has a "pimped" profile page. **When a**

woman views photos of you surrounded by successful, high-status friends (who are tagged) doing cool things, and engaging your friends in the comments then she will trust you because of the built-in digital social proof. In contrast, if your FB profile is just memes and you have weird friends (who post creepy socially-inept comments like "slay her!) then it will just be negative social proof.

THIS BOOK IS MORE about conversation skills than how to become an attractive man, so I won't get into depth here, but there is a lot to be said about having strong social media game. **Building an online presence and a positive reputation in a community that has women in it is a long term mating strategy (like farming) that might not have an immediate payoff, but it will in the future.** Don't use this as an excuse to get addicted to FB.

65

LAW #33: SUMMARY

LAW #33: LEVERAGE SOCIAL MEDIA.

WOMEN ARE ADDICTED to FB and IG. Attention is a form of currency. Develop competent photo game to showcase an exciting lifestyle, flash elite status, social proof with powerful contacts and material proof.

66

LAW #34: Flirt or be friend zoned. Sustain a man-to-woman frame interaction throughout.

Escalate the vibe to avoid falling into the friendzone.

IT LOOKS like a normal conversation to an untrained eye, but the daytime seducer is implementing a series of rapid-fire tactics, that will create an emotional connection that leads to legs being spread.

GUYS THAT GET FRIEND-ZONED:

- don't escalate the vibe,
- don't sexuality the conversation,
- don't create a man-to-woman frame, and
- don't flirt.

"TOUCH EARLY AND TOUCH OFTEN" is a maxim in the seduction community. Touch is a form of physical communication that cannot be substituted by verbal communication. Create this pattern of continuous touching from the very start of the interaction.

HOW YOU START **an interaction is how the entire interaction will continue; likewise, how one starts a relationship with a woman sets the behavioral pattern of the entire relationship. Behaviors tend to reinforce themselves overtime.** Ideally you want to start with a man-to-woman frame right away - rather than land into the friend zone and then have the hassle of changing behavioral patterns that have already been ingrained.

IF YOU DON'T TOUCH her at all for a period of 15 minutes and then suddenly start touching, it can be strange to suddenly start touching her later on.

HOW AN INTERACTION STATS is how it will continue on. You want to start with the frame that you are just a touchy guy and naturally touch everyone as you communicate with them. Physical escalation is the bridge that separates men from boys, and lovers from friends.

TOUCH HER BODY. Make a move. Shamelessly touch her body with ultra confidence - like you expect automatic compliance. Assume that it will work and often it will.

SHE DESIRES your touch but she is too restricted by social conditioning to express this outright. Slut-shaming is still a cultural phenomenon, so women tend to be more promiscuous in private than in public.

. . .

YOU HAVE to touch her body early and often because this is a vital element in the mating process. Get her hooked on the oxytocin that she feels upon skin-to-skin contact. Eventually, she will be hooked on the pleasure that your dick provides.

WHEN IT COMES to physical escalation, just make a move. Her body craves your touch. Don't rob her of this gift. Over-time increase the duration and intensity of the touch. You are having an unspoken physical conversation.

LIFE IS TOO short to take too long to make a move. GROW SOME BALLS and make a fucking move. Don't be one of those guys that needs to have endless conversations to nowhere - that span for many weeks - before you ask her out or endless dates before you physically escalate. Don't become texting penpals. She'll just use you for conversation, attention and free entertainment.

PUT A PRICE TAG ON YOURSELF. **She has to meetup at a reasonable time and make reasonable progress towards sexual intimacy or you're moving on to prospects that don't have intimacy (or logistical) impediments.**

A FEW PROPERLY PLACED AND well-timed touches can make a woman aroused. Touch her in the right area on her skin during emotionally high moments. Use conversation as misdirection while touching her; bullshit baffles brains.

. . .

DON'T JUST APPROACH to have a nice conversation to nowhere. Approach with the intention of banging her. Consistently move the interaction forward closer to sex. Your time isn't free. Always be pushing the interaction closer towards sex. Don't be one of those guys who: - has endless conversations that lead to nowhere, - becomes the penpal chatting buddy that never makes a move or - waiting around for months hoping that things will work out in the end.

OFTEN WOMEN DON'T KNOW **what they want until you show them what's possible**. LEAD. Don't ask permission to "touch her". Just touch her during the course of the conversation and watch her respond with positive EXCITEMENT.

ALWAYS BE ADVANCING the interaction towards sex. Life is too short to be spend to be trapped in an endless conversation to nowhere or going on a dozen friendly dates. **Always be moving things forward towards sex and if she resists repeatedly, NEXT HER.**

READING BODY-LANGUAGE IS CRUCIAL. She could be DOWN TO FUCK RIGHT NOW but you are still busy having a conversation trying to create more attraction and more rapport. Don't be blind. Open your eyes to the signals she is sending and tailor your game accordingly. **If she is down to fuck, don't run more attraction-generating game; just fucking close now!**

DON'T FRAME the touching as a big deal. Make it appear natural, spontaneous and smooth. Don't draw attention to it, or look at the touch while touching. The conversation will distract her from the touch being uploaded to her unconscious. Physical escalation creates excitement for women that encourages them to keep going in the interaction.

ONE OF THE best times to touch a woman is when you're making a point, or to reward her for good behavior. Start with smaller physical escalations before proceeding to bigger forms of physical escalation. *"You get a hug for that."*

67

LAW #34: SUMMARY

LAW #34: FLIRT OR BE FRIENDZONED.

SUSTAIN A MAN-TO-WOMAN FRAME INTERACTION THROUGHOUT. As a man, it's your role to create this Rated R element in the interaction.

68

LAW #35: Develop Emotional Intelligence (EQ).

HAVE A GREAT VIBE.

YOU CAN SPOT a beginner Daygamer quickly by the nervous tonality he uses when he tries to start conversations with female strangers. He feels shame, fear and places too much importance on specific approaches; the girls get turned off by his uneasiness. If he feels nervous then she will also feel nervous.

WOMEN FEED on your emotional state and energy levels.

VIBE IS about projecting good emotions outwards. When you feel happy, energetic, excited about life, enthusiastic about life goals, then she will feel these good emotions as well. But if you are sad, low-energy and devoid of purpose then she will feel that too.

. . .

HAVING **a great vibe necessitates strong emotional self-regulation skills.**

PUT SIMPLY: if you feel good, women will feel good around you; if you are in the zone, you will kill! Hence, it's worthwhile to learn how to sustain a GREAT VIBE through emotional state control tactics.

AVOID **the presence of toxic people who suck the life force out of your vibe.** Protect your mental health. Just like you avoid consuming toxic foods, avoid consuming toxic ideas that these toxic people spread. Take care of your physical and psychological well-being.

69

LAW #35: SUMMARY

LAW #35: CREATE A SEXY VIBE.

WOMEN FEED on your emotional state and energy levels. Having a great vibe necessitates strong emotional self-regulation skills. When you can pump your own emotions, you can pump a woman's emotions.

70

LAW #36: Kill formality. Assume familiarity. Set the frame with your behaviors. Lead by example.

IRONICALLY, one of the best ways to START a conversation with a beautiful woman is to assume that you ALREADY ARE in a conversation.

This is counter-intuitive. Sometimes the best way to win a battle is to bypass it entirely and assume you've already won. In business, this concept is known as "assuming the sale".

Instead of asking for permission to talk to a woman, just start talking to her! Just by the act of responding: she's already accepted the frame that it's fine to talk.

RAPPORT HACK: You want to escalate the conversation from impersonal to personal. When you act as if you've known her forever, she'll adopt the frame as well and you can hijack intimate anchors that are usually reserved for people that she is close with. **Don't be formal.** Assume intimacy.

BE one step above her in the intimacy ladder to guide her towards greater levels of intimacy with you. **By behaving as**

if you are already close to her, then you actually become close to her (because she'll start to buy-in to that frame and treat you accordingly). It is not needy to show romantic interest in a woman.

71

LAW #36: SUMMARY

LAW #36: Kill formality. Assume familiarity.

SET the frame with your behaviors. Lead by example. Don't ask for permission to escalate. Just do it. If she doesn't object, the frame has been set. Behave as if you're already intimate with her.

LAW #37: Women are value consumers. Differentiate yourself immediately. Be a giver of value.

Mindset #37: Bring the Value.

IF YOU APPROACH, you have to carry the burden of conversation. You're the one who approached; hence, you have to bring the fucking value. YOU BRING THE PARTY.

DON'T BE **one of those guys who just says "hi" and then expects her to suddenly to carry the conversation.** It can take a bit for the conversation to start but after a minute or so, you'll hit conversational momentum and it will be easy. The flow will take over.

WHEN YOU APPROACH the conversation burden is on you. **After all, she doesn't know who you are yet (so, she will naturally not invest a lot in conversation with a guy she just met)**, and she may not be in a social mode. The more you talk and give conversational value, the more attracted she will become and at some point, she will reach the social hook point and invest hard for you to stay.

. . .

THE OPENER CAN BE **solid but if that's the only thing you have to say and you have nothing to follow up with then the conversation may die soon.** At that point: ANYTHING is better than saying NOTHING. Starting conversations with strangers - beautiful females or not - has a lot to do with your general conversation skills. You have to be fun to talk to, energetic and relevant. Strangers are not necessarily in a social mode. Pump value persistently until she starts to warm up. During the 1-3 minutes of a pickup, you are essentially a live, human advertisement towards the concept of "being with you".

When you have 100% confidence, powerful dominant body-language, enthusiasm about the subject matter, and a great vibe then you can say almost ANYTHING and women will stay enjoy it tremendously.

Why? Because they feed on these positive emotions much more than the intellectual value of what is said.

That is how dumb motherfuckers get women. It's not that these dumb motherfuckers say intriguing interesting insightful gems of wisdom.

- It's that these dumb motherfuckers are genuinely happy, energetic, excited about life, and let these feel-good emotions overflow with every word that they say.
- These dumb motherfuckers speak with absolute certainty that what they just said has tremendous value. It's this conviction in their own bullshit that pulls people in.

Be the source of good emotions. Approach women with an overflowing cup of feeling good.

THIS IS superior to approaching women with an empty cup - trying to get her to give you validation and good emotions.

Maxim: DRAW STATE FROM WITHIN.

For most men, this is entirely unconscious. They might not even realize that they are needy. They might even have spent years being needy and have no idea. Then they wonder why they're so exhausting to be around with, and why they suddenly kill the vibe upon entering a room.

When you know that you have a lot to offer, that you feel excitement of life that you want to share then your approaches will be a lot smoother.

It's easier to approach from a position of an abundant giver than it is to approach from a position of a beggar living in scarcity. Think of it this way: "Would you feel nervous about approaching a girl to give her a $100 bill?" Of course, not because you expect positive reactions, you know that you're bringing value and you have worth. **Guess what: your presence and vibe are worth more than a hundred bucks.**

That's one of the reasons why you want to have a positive self-concept and follow RJ's guiding principle (which will contribute to that self-image): **"Leave women better than when you found them."** It's more for your own inner-game and benevolent intent than for the actual woman.

Bring more value than you take.

When dealing with women, don't bring your emotional baggage to the table.

- Nobody cares if you're tired.

- Nobody gives a fuck what kind of issues you're going through.

Just bring the fucking value. **Telling captivating, short stories is one of the most simple ways to bring value.** Picking up women is an art form. Another way to bring the fucking value: is to have great energy, overflowing positive emotions, and spread enthusiasm for life.

73

LAW #37: SUMMARY

LAW #37: BRING THE VALUE.

WOMEN ARE VALUE CONSUMERS; and attracted to men who are value givers. Differentiate yourself immediately by being the life of the party.

WOMEN ARE VALUE
CONSUMERS AND ARE
ATTRACTED TO MEN WHO
AR VALUE GIVERS.

74

LAW #38: Escalate the conversation.

BRING THE VALUE RIGHT AWAY

WOMEN'S ATTENTION spans are shorter than ever because this internet generation is trained to get rapid bursts of instant gratification from their phones. This relates to pickup because you have to cut out the fluff from your conversations and give a lot of value quickly.

SOME WAYS of bringing the value immediately is to:

- have an AMAZING VIBE,
- make cold-reads, and
- to dress like a boss.

WOMEN'S EGO crave the attention of a man who looks wealthy, powerful and flashes elite level social status.

. . .

GIVE **a ton of value quickly - naturally weaved into the conversation.** When the moment of decision comes, she will allow herself to be further seduced.

KEEP THE CONVERSATION GOING. If you drop the ball then as the conversation will end and so will the social interaction. The conversation is the glue that holds the social interaction together and allows you to play the game. You approached her, not the other way around. Therefore, it is your job to keep things fun until the hook-point (the moment when she wants you to stay and eventually wants to get to know you more). Carry the conversation.

THE ONE COMMON OPENER THAT SUCKS BALLS.

In case you forgot, don't start the conversation with "What's up?" This doesn't actually contribute value but rather asks for value. If you don't have an established connection prior, don't expect her to contribute value into the conversation without first getting value. Give conversational value to a woman FIRST. Then request conversational value from her SECOND.

THE "YES AND" CONVERSATION FORMAT

When a woman says something, paraphrase what she said in your own words and then add insight. The "Yes And" conversation format works well with the Dig Deeper technique.

CONVERSATION ESCALATION

Don't milk the opener! You ideally want to progress from something that is not personal to subjects that

are more of an intimate nature – such as her aspirations and learning about her deepest secrets.

IF YOU STICK to talking about the mundane with a woman then that is not a conversation that is conducive to fostering a strong genuine connection. It is smarter to find out a woman's core values are and deepest, most meaningful goals are; then connect on that.

COMMONALITIES ABOUT A WOMAN'S core values and most important aspirations is what will create a genuine, strong emotion connection.

Always move the interaction forward toward sex. If you hit a wall then cut her off. Your time and attention is worth more than money. Don't waste it on sexual-dead ends.

75

LAW #38: SUMMARY

LAW #38: ESCALATE THE CONVERSATION.

YOUR ATTENTION and time is worth more than money. Don't waste it on sexual dead-ends; focus these resources on leads with greater sexual potential. Always move forward. Frame: blow me, or blow me out.

76

LAW #39: Have swagger. Express Your Personality Freely and Fully. Put the ART into being a pickup *ART*ist.

MEN JUDGE WOMEN primarily based on physicality. Women judge men primarily based on personality. Conversation is a means to express your attractive personality - which will make a woman interested in your attractive personality, and create a connection. If you're having bland, reserved and predictable conversations with NO personality then you're missing that opportunity.

How to NOT be boring in conversations:

- - Express STRONG opinions.
- - Don't be the guy who is afraid to make waves.
- - Express your TRUE, AUTHENTIC self. Don't hide behind a mask.
- - Convey loads of personality. Don't be bland.
- - Polite is boring. Be willing to be offensive and edgy.

Confident men express themselves fully and freely. They have a personality and aren't afraid to show it. They have a certain style, swagger and art to how they interact that makes them memorable. Don't be afraid to be you. Being you is what makes you unique and interesting because there's only one version of YOU. **Showcase your personality by being highly expressive and revealing positive emotions;** In contrast, hiding or censoring of oneself stems from self-doubt. Why are you afraid?

If you heed this tip then you will start being HYPER INTERESTING in conversations. KILL SOCIAL INHIBITIONS. KILL SOCIAL FEAR. When you express yourself fully and freely, you will be a far more interesting person.

GET A FRAME.

A "yes" man is BORING AS FUCK to women because he lacks his own individual opinion. His perspective instantly becomes whatever the woman thinks. This doesn't stimulate a woman's mind - on an intellectual level. HAVE YOUR OWN INDEPENDENT PERSPECTIVE.

SIGNS YOUR FRAME IS SHIT:

- - you're a pushover,
- - you find yourself saying "yes" to things you want to say "no" to,
- - you find yourself quickly agreeing to everything someone says,
- - you're afraid of conflict and the tension that comes from disagreement,
- - you feel guilty when you say "no",
- - you lack your own independent perspective,

- - when you get into a relationship: your personality instantly changes to hers (losing yourself),
- - you're quick to trust the opinion of others without thinking things through for yourself first,

77

LAW #39: SUMMARY

LAW #39: HAVE SWAGGER.

EXPRESS YOURSELF FULLY AND FREELY. Have a style/unique way of interacting with people that is exclusive to your personal brand. Put the ART back into being a pickup - *ART*ist. Don't be the guy with no personality.

LAW #40: Don't be predictable. Be unpredictable. Utilize the Novelty Effect.

SAY SOMETHING UNEXPECTED.

A predictable guy is a boring guy. Don't be afraid to PUSH THE FUCKING LIMITS OF WHAT IS SOCIALLY ACCEPTABLE.

Rule of thumb for conversations and relationships: being predictable is being boring.

THE NOVELTY EFFECT

A woman's brain is hardwired to ignore that which is expected, and respond to the unexpected. By presenting yourself in a manner that is radically new, and inherently different than what she is used then you will be able to captivate and sustain a woman's attention.

THINK ABOUT MOVIES: if you've seen a particular plot dozens of times in movies, then you'll be remarkably bored, and won't want to even finish watching the movie because you already know how it ends. However, if a movie has a unique twist and unpredictable plots then the unpredictability will keep you hooked.

Warning:

Keep in mind that in certain situations - such as when you are dealing with police, interviews for a potential lucrative position, business discussions with business partners at networking events, at your job - it is more appropriate to use a more reserved analytical, logical calculated-mode of talking. It is not appropriate to activate "crazy fun guy" (who speaks his fucking mind freely and makes radically bold situations to stir emotions at all costs) in formal situations.

TO MEN who have strong social skills this should be commonsense, but it is worth putting in here - just in case. In an advanced note, one can use NLP and self-suggestions to quickly switch between "CRAZY FUN GUY" to " BUSINESS MODE GUY."

79

LAW #40: SUMMARY

LAW #40: DON'T BE PREDICTABLE.

PREDICTABILITY BREEDS BOREDOM. Be unpredictable. Take bold risks in conversations and interactions. Throw the occasional curve-ball. A woman's brain is hardwired to give attention to novelty.

LAW #41: Create an inner-fire. Have dominant body-language.

Technique #25: Have fierce eye-contact.

EVASIVE EYE-CONTACT IS one of the defining traits of a beta male. He is too afraid to look strangers in the eye, so he pretends not to notice them. Darting eyes betray a man with a low sense of self-worth, fear, and feelings of inferiority; he's metaphorically trying to "hide" with this defensive body-language to protect himself from "attacks".

SOCIAL FEAR IS WEAKNESS. It is not fitting for a god, such as yourself, to behave like a peasant. It is especially important to hold very strong eye-contact at the beginning of a social interaction (also known as the initial phase of a pickup).

HOLDING eye-contact makes you come across as confident, bold and it applies social pressure on the girl to acknowledge your reality. Diverting eye-contact – even for a moment – at the beginning of a pickup can be fatal. Look her in the eyes –

eyeball to eyeball – for at least a solid minute for the initial phase of the interaction.

SOMETIMES YOU WILL LOOK AROUND and notice that someone is staring at you. Don't divert your gaze downwards like a man who is terrified of others. Hold eye contact. Smile. And say "hello"; it may even lead to a conversation.

Pickup artists must thrive in social environments and are fearless.

Never be afraid to look someone in the eye. Used properly eye-contact can be a powerful medium for seducing a woman. She can tell if you are confident or not simply by your ability or inability to hold her gaze. Darting eyes reveal a nervous, insecure man; if you were approached by a nervous man how would you feel? Nervous! Emotions are contagious.

❄

THE ULTIMATE BODY-LANGUAGE HACK TO INSTANTLY BE SEXIER TO WOMEN: CREATE AN INNER-FIRE.

How you feel on the inside will directly impact the behaviors and body-language that you display on the outside. By feeling calm, confident and in-control then you will automatically convey an attractive outer-game persona.

VERBALIZE the following self-suggestions to regulate your emotional state: "I am the law. I AM THE AUTHORITY." This is MY territory."[1]

. . .

WHEN YOU FEEL RELAXED, powerful and fucking awesome then your body-language will reflect this. **Hence, one of the main keys to good body-language is emotional self-regulation. Feeling powerful leads to effortlessly displaying powerful body-language.**

---

1. As mentioned prior, different self-suggestions, mantras and affirmations work for different people. Experiment with your own choice of words. The key is to FEEL something significant when verbalizing them; if you FEEL nothing then being a tape-recorder on repeat won't make much of a difference.

81

LAW #41: SUMMARY

LAW #41: CREATE AN INNER-FLAME.

HAVE DOMINANT BODY-LANGUAGE. When you feel powerful and relaxed, you'll automatically convey high social status body-language. Command a strong presence in any room you enter.

82

LAW #42: To attract women, become attractive. Be positive, socially competent, confident, and stylish.

MEN THAT ARE positive are FAR MORE ATTRACTIVE to women than men that have pessimistic perspectives on life. Having basic social skills is necessary for dealing with people - women included. **Having an active social life will inherently lead to having strong game skills. Don't isolate yourself from society and stop developing yourself, the moment you get a girlfriend.**

IF YOU HAVE no real-world friends who you meet up with then yes, that's a red-flag that you need to socialize more. There are real benefits to having a peer support network - besides ample opportunities to sharpen your social skills. Further, one of the fastest ways to get strong social skills is to spend time with people who have strong social skills - role-modeling after them. Avoid spending time with socially inept fucking weirdos because that would only lead you to internalize their anti-game behavioral tendencies.

. . .

IT'S amazing how often basic rules of conduct are ignored like:

- - hold eye-contact,
- - articulate clearly,
- - have a strong, firm handshake,
- - keep your head held high,
- - don't look down like a beta,
- - stand straight,
- - wear clean clothes (women do notice subtle details),
- - shower daily to ensure you smell nice,
- - don't monopolize a conversation,
- - don't be clingy in conversations and "wear out your welcome",
- - don't dress like a retard,
- - don't be a downer by focusing on the negatives in life,
- - don't be bitter by speaking badly about people,
- - don't bring up strange subjects like serial killers,
- - don't bring up gross subjects like farts and feces,
- - don't be socially awkward by being fucking weird and oblivious to the unofficial rules of dealing with people,

YES, women will notice if you have:

- - greasy hair,
- - unkempt hair,
- - long nails,
- - smiling too often,
- - nodding too frequently,
- - licking your lips frequently,

- - being dressed oddly, and
- - dirty or stained clothing.

THESE SUBTLE DETAILS **reveal a lot about a man.** If you look like shit, then women will find you creepy. **Women will judge you within the first half a second of seeing you.**

DRESS IMPECCABLY. Not because you need her validation, or care what she thinks. But because you understand the importance of perception management & strong game skills when it comes to banging pussy in general.

By taking care of yourself (personal grooming, basic self-care behaviors such as good hygiene, being financially independent, etc.) you reveal the capacity to take care of others.

IF YOU ARE a LOW QUALITY MAN then even if you have 10,000 approaches don't expect significant results, and the minimal results that you acquire may be a LOW QUALITY WOMAN. By becoming a HIGH QUALITY MAN your conversion rate will be significantly higher, and women will give "invite signals" that they want to be approached. **Become an attractive man to attract attractive women; you attract based on who you are - not just based on what you want.**

ALWAYS BE WORKING TO:

- **- increase your sexual market value,**
- **- sharpen your game skills, and**

- **- expand your mental library of valuable useful knowledge.**

Getting to APEX SOCIAL STATUS is not an overnight phenomenon, but takes years of conscious self-development. Think longterm.

A HIGHER LEVEL OF APPROACHING - GAMING THE WORLD

By achieving EXCELLENCE and at the top 0.01% of men in society then women approach & make moves on you.

THIS IS ALSO TRUE IF:

- - you are the Apex Alpha Male in a social group that includes women,
- - you are a YouTuber with a huge following discussing subjects women are into etc.

MEN ARE USING social media platforms (such as IG and even YouTube) to attract women into their life by showcasing excellence in their talents, and flashing an extravagant, adventurous lifestyle. **The sexual marketplace has gone GLOBAL and DIGITAL - especially after corona hit.**

WOMEN WILL GOOGLE YOUR NAME. Be Googleable. Have a website - as "evidence" - to your exciting lifestyle. If you have an exciting lifestyle, with highlights showcased on IG she will fantasize about being your girlfriend to get some of that action. Keep this in mind.

83

LAW #42: SUMMARY

LAW #42: MAKE EVERY DAY COUNT.

PLOT YOUR PATH TO APEX STATUS. To attract women, become attractive. Every day focusing on raising your status in the sexual marketplace. Develop traits such as being positive, socially competent, and stylish.

84

LAW #43: Don't be shy, drop the ball or stale out the topic.

A CONVERSATION IS like playing a ball of catch. You say something and metaphorically throw the ball to her. She understands what you have said and catches the ball. Then she says something to you and throws the ball back at you.

This throw-and-catch dynamic has also been referred to as ping-pong. For every ping that you put out, she puts out a pong; thus, is the conversation dance.

WHEN IT'S your turn to talk, don't drop the ball. Say something that is interesting, emotionally relevant, fun-generating, **and provoking enough for her to respond to**. If you are suddenly silent then this may end the interaction.

IN THE FIRST **five minutes of meeting a woman, NOTHING KILLS INTERACTIONS MORE THAN AWKWARD SILENCES.**

. . .

THIS IS similar to you dropping the ball. Sometimes a woman will say something else or throw a question your way to resuscitate a dying conversation (metaphorically walking over to your side, picking up the ball for you and literally handing it your hands), but this should not be relied upon in the initial phase of the pickup.

IF YOU DON'T KNOW **what to say then SAY ANYTHING.**

PLAUSIBLE DENIABILITY

If a woman is sincerely interested in you then she will use what you have said and find someway to build on it. It's not the conversation that she cares about *as much as who she is talking with*; the conversation is just an excuse for her to spend time with you – without seeming like a slut who fucks random strangers she just met.

A WOMAN WILL HAVE promiscuous sex with a high status attractive man - outside of marriage or a committed relationship - even if she pretends to be prudish and "innocent".

GIVE her the excuse that she needs by not dropping the ball, and smoothly leading the interaction towards sex based on the progression that she is comfortable with. Always be escalating the interaction towards sex at a reasonable pace - not too slow, and too not too fast. It will take approximately seven hours from "hello" to "BANG BANG BANG SUCK SUCK SUCK".

85

LAW #43: SUMMARY

LAW #43: BE OUTGOING.

DON'T DROP THE BALL. Don't believe the Hollywood movie myth that the shy nervous guy eventually gets the girl because she sees through the timid persona& finds his golden heart. Have an assertive communication style.

86

LAW #44: Let go of the quest for the perfect pickup line.

THE GOAL of the opening phase is not to make her instantly attracted to you. The goal of the opening phase is simply to:

- - seize her attention,
- - break the stranger danger barrier,
- - break the icy tension,
- - make a woman feel comfortable enough to respond,
- - create the conditions for a conversation to "naturally" occur,
- - in a manner that appears natural and spontaneous,
- - not creepy or weird.

THE GOAL of an opener isn't to have the best pickup line in the world. Nor is it to get her to spike attraction - right off the bat. **The goal of the opener is to simply to grab her attention, make her comfortable enough to respond, and set the stage to start a conversation.**

. . .

SEARCHING for the best pickup-line in the world may paralyze you from taking action. You may think "The opener isn't good enough" so I won't say anything. The search for perfection is paralyzing. **Perfect is the enemy of good enough.**

YOU DON'T NEED an earth-shattering MIND-BLOWING opening line to start a conversation with a girl during the daytime. Something really super-simple will work just fine.

The Semi Direct Opener

- **At a social event: "Hey. I haven't met you yet. I'm Cory."**
- **"Hi!"**[1]
- **At a college: "Omg. You look exactly like someone else at this college!"**

The Situational Observation Opener

- **Near a bar: "Hey, did you see the fight outside?"**

Using an opening line based on what she is doing comes across as most natural. Don't be fucking weird or socially awkward by staring at a woman for a long time before approaching her. Look at her, smile, walk over and deliver an opening line.

. . .

A GOOD CONVERSATION has a flow to it. Ideally there should never be a point where you come across as "trying too hard" to keep the conversation going. Nor should there be long awkward silences in the initial pickup phase.

WHEN YOU ENJOY THE CONVERSATION, she will enjoy it as well because fun is contagious. Get into the frame of mind that you enjoy having conversations with women. You enjoy:

- talking about yourself,
- talking about your passions,
- learning about other people,
- meeting new people,
- reviewing ideas by teaching them to others
- receiving therapeutic benefits from talking about yourself.

Types of openers (mentioned in this book):

- - The opinion opener,
- - The situational observation opener,
- - The functional opener,
- - The semi-direct opener,
- - The direct opener,
- - The no-opener (just start talking),

❄

THERE IS **no substitute for actually having fun. Fun is not something that should be faked. You have to be genuinely having a good time.** Your feel-good emotions will spread unto her, and you'll be motivated to keep going out.

1. After saying "hi", it's important to immediately follow-up with something of value. Simply saying "hi" to a beautiful woman and expecting her to carry the conversation is not optimal and does not work in real life. Neither does "hey, how are you doing?" She doesn't know who the fuck you are; why would she invest effort to start a conversation with you on her own initiative? "Hi" is just the opener, but you need a strong follow-up. For instance, you can follow up with an observation "I have never seen anyone [something about her] like that before." She'll say "Oh really?" You can then say "It shows that you're a non-conformist. [Follow up with a question]."

87

LAW #44: SUMMARY

LAW #44: EVERYTHING THAT YOU SAY, OWN IT.

LET GO of the quest for the perfect pickup line. The need for perfection leads to Action Paralysis. It's not what you say, but how you say it that matters most. You can open with almost anything.

88

LAW #45: Use her imagination.

A woman's imagination does much of the seduction work for you.

HOW TO LEVERAGE **a woman's imagination to your seductive favor:**

- **Negation**
- **Open loop**
- **Push back**

I.

THE NEGATION TACTIC

Playfully letting her know that you won't tell her something because it's a secret. She'll pressure to reveal the information, but don't give in right away. Let her beg for it, and then still don't tell her.

II.

THE OPEN LOOP **TACTIC**

Give her some information as bait, but don't give her full-disclosure. YouTubers will frequently do this; at the start of their videos, they'll tell you about all of the things that they are going to cover in their video. This "teaser" keeps the viewer hooked till the end of the video because he wants to learn all of the information that was hinted at in the "trailer".

YOU WANT to hint at interesting and exciting things about your life, but when she asks about it: only reveal *some* of the information and then change the subject. She'll stay in the conversation because she wants to hear the rest.

III.

THE PUSH BACK **TACTIC**

Accuse a woman of something and watch her defend herself. When you get a woman hooked into enjoying your approval and then break rapport (by pushing her away), she'll chase hard to get it back.

89

LAW #45: SUMMARY

LEVERAGE a woman's imagination by not giving her full disclosure. Women will often ask questions that they don't want the answer to.

90

LAW #46: Exploit a woman's nurturing nature.

TACTIC #46.1 THE OPINION OPENER

THE OPINION OPENER is a massively underrated way to start conversations with female strangers; it's effective because it gets a woman to start investing into a conversation, right off the bat. Done correctly, a woman will start yapping non-stop.

"IMAGINE THIS; *someone comes up to you and offers you two pills. One is red; you'll know exactly what people will think of you - the good and the ugly. Another one is blue; which will give you blissful ignorance. Which one will you choose?"*

ONE OF THE inherent challenges of meeting women in the street is that it's not something that she is used to and it can therefore come across as weird. Hence, a sneaky way to approach women on the street is to use a 100% bullet-proof opener that is guaranteed to open.

TACTIC #46.2 THE FUNCTIONAL OPENER

Utilize props to really sell this. Have a MacBook in one hand, and an iPhone 11 Max Pro in another hand - with Google Maps open.

"HEY WHERE IS *the nearest library. I have to do some college work."*
Time passes as she responds

*"I would check Google Maps but my GPS is malfunctioning". *time passes as she responds**

"Do you think college is worth it?"

THE SPECIFIC DETAILS of this example can be altered to be more situationally relevant.

❄

UTILIZE **a woman's tendency to help others to your advantage; use every dirty trick in the book because if you don't, your competition will.** If you don't fuck her, another man will.

91

LAW #46: SUMMARY

LAW #46: EXPLOIT A WOMAN'S NURTURING NATURE.

DON'T PLAY FAIR. Use every dirty trick in the book - especially during the initial pickup process. Game is manipulation.

92

LAW #47: Seduction is a lifestyle.

Mindset #47: Embrace the Daygame Lifestyle

DAYGAME IS the art of meeting women during the daytime, and as you go about your day (in the street, coffee shop, on the commute to work, in the grocery store or the park).

THIS METHOD of meeting women saves a lot of time, has no cockblockers/competition, and allows you to meet the hottest local girls on the market. In contrast, nightclubs are packed with aggressive dudes, cockblocks, and potential distractions.

❄

YOU CAN MEET WOMEN ANYWHERE, **and ANYTIME. The only thing holding you back is MINDSET.**

When you let go of the negative beliefs:

- **- "Oh, I don't want to bother her."**
- **- "Oh, I'm too old/too young."**
- **- "It wouldn't work anyways".**

thousands of doors of opportunity will open for you.

❄

IT'S impossible to get good at a game that you don't play. The best way to learn how to meet women is to meet women every day, and then immediately (at the end of the day) reflect on the experience - asking:

- "What did I learn? How can I do it better?"
- "What did I do that worked so I can do more of that?"
- "What did I do (or lines that I said) which did NOT hit and did NOT generate results, so I can do less of that?"

AS LONG AS you put in substantial real world practice every day, and reflect on what you have learned then you will eventually get good. It's just a matter of time. Think long term.

DO 1-5 approaches a day for a year and you will be a pickup master. The way to get good at anything is to do a substantial amount of it everyday and then refine your methods overtime. You learn by doing, by thinking about what you are doing, and by improving how you are doing it by at least 1% each time.

NO ONE **ever became a master at playing the piano by reading books on the subject matter.** You learn by doing!!! To get good at talking with women, talk to a lot of women!

IF YOU WANT to have extraordinary beautiful women in your life then you have to embrace the lifestyle and the process of getting good. Initially don't obsessively worry about the results; just focus on developing a set of habits implemented daily designed to accelerate the learning curve. To get good at the game of seduction, you need COMMITMENT TO YOUR GOAL, and to ENJOY THE PROCESS.

Create a training program with a daily quota for action.

Then stick to that training program every single day - no matter how you feel - no excuses - no days off. I recommend doing AT LEAST 1 APPROACH A DAY FOR A YEAR.

IF YOU ALLOW for excuses to occur then there will always be a convenient excuse as to why "this day doesn't count" or "I need to take this day off". You will find yourself endlessly putting it off one day at a time for years. **The secret is to have a ZERO TOLERANCE for excuses.**

TALK WITH STRANGERS. This is the lifestyle of successful pickup artists. They are extremely comfortable with starting and maintaining conversations with complete strangers. Practice starting conversations with strangers.

THIS WILL TEACH you many insights relevant to the pickup process of women. **When you practice on strangers you**

don't give a fuck about, there won't be psychological pain if it doesn't work out.

APPROACHING IS ONLY scary until you do it. Once you do it, you realize that approaching ain't shit. Even a five year old can approach and utter some gibberish to open. It takes a Casanova to maintain a woman's attention and have her hooked into the conversation.

GET into the habit of making spontaneous remarks towards strangers and then transitioning off that into a full fledged conversation. This is a very important skill to master and for practice; initially do not differentiate between sets; talk to EVERYONE.

EVERY TIME YOU GO OUTSIDE, there is an opportunity to practice the art of starting conversations with strangers and accelerated emotional bonding. **Practice even on the ugly girls so that way when a pretty girl comes along, you will be ready. Have a minimum number of approaches that you do everyday.**

PICKUP SKILLS and people's skills go well together like peanut butter and jelly. If you're good at starting conversations with strangers then you will be good at picking up girls. Getting good at Daygame will teach you what it takes to get good at the game of making money and the game of life in general.

ALL YOU NEED to get results is to master one micro niche of pickup such as coffee-shop based daygame or gym based daygame. You don't have to be good EVERYTHING RIGHT AWAY. **JUST MASTER ONE PATH.**

DOING many approaches in a specific area of your city, using the same exact opener each time, will create SITUATIONAL BASED CONFIDENCE. **Once you get good at one specific model of pickup then you will gain insights and be able to expand to other models of pickup.**

IF YOUR SOCIAL skills are shit, then that's going to impact your ability to succeed with women. You want to be a SMOOTH PLAYER who can calibrate based on the situation, have instant sharp responses to any bullshit a woman may throw his way and appear effortless at the same time. Hence, it helps to have an active social life because that will naturally lead to developing strong social skills.

REMEMBER: **YOU GET GOOD AT WHAT YOU DO FREQUENTLY, so if you interact with women daily (with the intention of sharpening your skills) - as part of your lifestyle - then you will naturally have STRONG PEOPLE SKILLS.** But if you're locked in an office all day, and your only interactions are (with the store clerk) when you buy coffee at Starbucks, then don't be surprised that your people skills suck. I advise having at least 30 minutes a day dedicated to just socializing and meeting new people. You'll thank me later.

LAW #47: SUMMARY

LAW #47: SEDUCTION IS A LIFESTYLE.

YOU GET good at what you do frequently and consistently. If your idea of "getting good at game" is only reading theory then you are a fucking idiot. Skill comes from conscious relentless practice.

94

LAW #48: Immerse yourself. Build your arsenal.

READ interesting things to learn interesting things to be able to say interesting things in a conversation to become AN INTERESTING PERSON. Live an exciting lifestyle doing things worth talking about and enjoying intriguing hobbies that women are curious about - that don't involve reading comic books, jerking off, Netflix binge watching, or playing video-games.

IF YOU DON'T KNOW what to talk about then chances are that there isn't much happening in your life, you don't have that many things going for you, and you aren't reading enough. In that case, you have to quite literally GET A LIFE.

READING IS **one of the fastest ways to accumulate interesting knowledge to share with beautiful women.** Take on exciting challenge. Get a cool hobby. Embark on adventure. Do daring shit. **The more remarkable things that you have the balls to do, the more EPIC STORIES you will have to tell women.**

. . .

WHEN YOU HAVE cool hobbies and cool things going on in your life then your conversations will be much better with women because you will have exciting things to talk about, and that **gives her the ability to live vicariously through you - gaining your happiness and life passion.** When you have cool shit going on in your life then you will naturally be excited to share it with everyone - women included - making them a part of your life in the process. If there's nothing going on in your life then women will be turned off by a lack of ambition, purpose, and valuing the finite nature of existence.

TAKE **experiences from your personal life and turn them into stories.** Practice saying these stories (both the short version, and long versions) a few times to get the delivery down. Go as far as even recording yourself on video to then watch yourself afterwards to assess the entertainment quality. The litmus test: if you're bored by yourself then chances are that she is bored too.

CHANCES ARE **that there are a lot of cool things about you; you just have to learn how to convey them to women in an interesting way.** You have to learn how to talk about yourself in a way (fun, interesting, emotionally engaging, entertaining) that draws women into your world and encourages them to also reciprocate by sharing about their personal life. You can even go as far as starting a YouTube channel and shooting daily vlogs for practice.

. . .

ONE OF THE **key concepts is that you have to have ready material (stuff to talk about) just in case your brain goes blank in the midst of a conversation with a woman,** and that material is gained through research - either by reading or by throwing yourself into interesting experiences. Men with big balls succeed with women far more than men who are afraid of living a life worth sharing.

THERE IS ALWAYS something more to talk about because the world is interesting and fascinating subjects have near infinite depth. **You need to start building material that you can talk to beautiful women about.** Create a stack that can be used - because it has been field tested to create an enjoyable experience for women, sparks attraction and fosters connections.

ARE YOU REALLY LIVING OR JUST GOING THROUGH THE MOTIONS?

On your death bed, it will usually be the things that you did NOT do that, which will be cause of regret. Figure out the answer to this question:

- "What is my dream?"
- "What do I want to accomplish before I die?"
- "Where do I see myself a decade from now?"
- "What meaningful and higher purpose do I live for?"
- "What is the purpose of my existence?"

Then attack that dream with FULL FORCE. Part of being a man of high status, is being a man on a mission - chasing his dreams and living for a purpose.

❄

HERE IS the basic formula for getting good with women:

- - Getting out of the house,
- - going to a place where there are women,
- - approaching some cute ones,
- - saying an opener to break the ice,
- - starting up a conversation,
- - escalating the vibe,
- - getting her number for a date two, or fucking her on the same night.

OVERLY SIMPLIFIED MODEL OF SEDUCTION:

- **Logistics:** go to a place where there are women,
- **Find:** look for one woman to approach,
- **Approach:** walk up to her
- **Open:** start the conversation
- **Qualify:** compliment to justify greater levels of interest
- **Attract:** anchor good emotions with the concept of you; tease her
- **Connect:** build a commonality on core values, goals and interests
- **Close:** create an opportunity to continue the interaction later

THE LEARNING CURVE

- 1) take action,
- 2) get social feedback,

- 3) reflect on experience and use that feedback to refine the mating method,
- 4) review the key ideas learned every morning,
- 5) repeat cycle,

TO GET A LIFE, YOU HAVE TO KILL THE TIME SINKERS.

If you hang out with losers, you will become a loser. If you hang out with a woman who constantly creates energy-sucking drama over petty issues, nags and complains - wasting your time and psychological resources then you will become a loser.

WHEN YOU MAKE **a woman your life, you lose your own.**

TIME IS MONEY. TIME IS LIFE. YOU NEED THAT TIME TO BUILD YOURSELF UP TO BE AN APEX ALPHA

95

LAW #48: SUMMARY

LAW #48: IMMERSE YOURSELF.

THE FASTEST WAY TO learn the game is to just fucking do it. It's NOT by consuming endless amounts of theory. The best moves and lines come from spontaneous realizations in the field.

Remember which behaviors have worked for your specifically to continue to replicate them in the future. Stack these moves in a series until you have a fully developed gameplan from "hello" to sex.

ABC
ALWAYS BE CLOSING

96

8 CONVERSATION MISTAKES

CONVERSATION MISTAKE **#1:** Being a dry communicator. Being dry means not adding any emotions behind your words. Women care more about emotional content than factual content. Inject some feeling into what you are saying. Say it like you mean it!

CONVERSATION MISTAKE **#2:** Not having dynamic energy levels. Have fluctuating energy levels. Occasionally have a burst of energy and talk enthusiastically (the explosion tactic) - especially when talking about your passions. Then sometimes be lower energy (for contrast). In general, your energy levels should be substantially higher than hers, so as to be adding energy to the vibe. Women feed on the positive emotions and energetic vibe that men put out. Don't take this too far and be too high energy (because that's just fucking weird); meet her where she is at and then bring her up from there.

CONVERSATION MISTAKE **#3:** Acting like a robot. You are not a clone of everyone else. Add personality to your conversation. Be willing to INJECT the "You" Factor. The conversation is merely a vehicle to convey an attractive personality. A guy with a personality is infinitely more interesting than a guy with no personality.

CONVERSATION MISTAKE **#4:** Being formal. Formality acts like a barrier between you and her. Close friends are not formal and professional between each other. It is far better to assume a deep level of rapport and act like you've known her forever. She'll follow this frame.

CONVERSATION MISTAKE **#5:** Talking about things she doesn't care about and not being able to recognize her body-language cues that she is bored about the subject. Be RELEVANT by talking about TOPICS that matter to her. If necessary inquire about her passions to identify these (the fishing tactic).

CONVERSATION MISTAKE **#6:** Keeping your hands in your pockets, having a poker face & having a monotone delivery style. Use hand-gestures & an animated facial expressions to emphasize certain points when communicating. Emphasizing key points is part of being a captivating speaker.

CONVERSATION MISTAKE **#7:** Not holding eye-contact, looking down, talking in a timid manner, lacking conviction when speaking, talking quickly, using filler-words and talking quietly. The problem with these is by displaying weak body-language, no one will take you seriously. A guy who has weak body-language can talk but his words will fall on deaf ears.

. . .

CONVERSATION MISTAKE **#8:** Not speaking with enthusiasm. Enthusiasm is contagious. If you want her to care then you must care about what you are saying. But if you're bored then she will be bored as well. Have some fun! When you express yourself freely and enjoy yourself then she will feel at ease to do the same.

The Argument for Cold Approach

Not every woman is open to the idea of starting a conversation with a stranger and pursuing something romantic with that stranger. However, there are enough women that are open to this idea to make cold approach a legitimate method for generating leads and banging pussies. Even if 99 out of 100 women rejected you but the 1 out of 100 led to a sexual relationship with a beautiful woman, cold approach was still worth it.

Cold approach is a great way to practice conversation skills because you'll quickly learn what techniques work, and which techniques don't work.

97

14 IRON CLAD RULES FOR NAVIGATING THE SEXUAL MARKEPLACE

IF YOU DON'T KNOW who the sucker is, it's probably you. Here are 11 Iron Clad Rules to navigate the sexual marketplace without being fucked over like a soy boy. **Remember you want to fuck - not be fucked over:**

- 1// **Don't reveal knowledge of game.** Don't appear like you planned to approach her (even if you are a professional pickup-artist). Create the impression that the approach was almost an "accident" or a "spur of the moment" action while you were doing something else. Good approaches seem like natural organic conversations that "just happened" - not premeditated. Appearing to go with the flow and being completely natural has a highly disarming effect on women and makes them open up.
- 2// **Don't attach your sense of self-worth to your level of success with women.**
- 3// **Don't chase. Attract.**
- 4// **Don't depend on her approval. FUCK HER APPROVAL.** Focus on your goals.

- 5// **Don't show neediness.** If she's worth it, show interest.
- 6// **Don't be emotionally explosive around her.** Remain composed. A woman instantly loses respect for a guy if she senses that she has impacted his emotional state.
- 7// **Don't give away your social power.** Frame yourself as the prize.
- 8// **Don't compromise your sexual market value for the sake of a particular woman running "tame the Alpha" game on you**.
- 9// **Don't be afraid to lose her.** Always retain "walk away power" and have multiple women in your rotation.
- 10// **Don't neglect your own development the moment you get a girlfriend.** Keep your skills sharp with daily practice - so if the time comes and opportunities occur, you'll be ready.
- 11// **Don't be a pushover.** Be assertive. Compromising your own values may result in decrease of self-respect and is detrimental to your sexual market value. Women come and go. PUT YOURSELF AND YOUR GOALS FIRST. Women don't value men that put women first.
- 12// **Don't game for validation**. Game to get laid (or the specific end result that you want to achieve). Draw validation from within. Know what you want. Define success for yourself - without being influenced of what men view as "success".
- 13// **Have clear boundaries.** If you are not assertive then women will exploit you.

98

HOW TO BE FEARLESS

"HELP! I am intimidated by beautiful woman. I just can't get my composure around them." Have you ever heard of a fisherman who is afraid of fish?

FUCK what a woman thinks. She can take her opinion and shove it up her ass. Her perception is of no worth to you. It is meaningless. One day she will grow so that you will be absolutely disgusted by her appearance.

Repeat this affirmation multiple times: "I don't give a fuck!! I don't give a fuck!! I don't give a fuck!!" Say it out-loud. WHAT MATTER IS WHAT YOU THINK.

Approach Anxiety or anticipatory uncomfortable tension prior to approaching or making a move on a woman is NORMAL. Even veterans who have thousands of approaches can feel approach anxiety. The main thing is to train yourself to not allow emotional resistance to hold you back from taking action. Displine is the art of taking action no matter how you feel in the moment.

There are a few keys to overcoming AA (approach anxiety):

- - disassociate your identity from that emotion; you are not defined by the feelings you experience.
- - visualize yourself succeeding; what are you going to say to her exactly? See yourself walking up to a woman and saying the initial opening lines.
- - utilize affirmations.Verbalize outloud "Every approach is a success - regardless of outcome. I either get the girl or a lesson."
- - utilize a timer. Make a deal with yourself. You only have to be in "APPROACHING MODE" for 3 minutes, and then you'll initiate a break where you focus on recovering energy. As time goes on, your social stamina will increase and the "APPROACHING MODE" time will increase, as well.
- - another affirmation that is useful to say to yourself in the field is "I don't give a fuck!" Saying this mantra with feeling can make a huge difference in mitigating anxiety prior to approaching women.
- - reframe "anxiety" as excitement. Focus on amusement and learning.

If you are in the field, and every ounce of your being is telling you to quit because you are in emotional hell with overwhelming fear and a pounding heart, approach her anyways - because you are a man of courage with GIANT BALLS.

When you are determined to WIN IN THE GAME OF LIFE, NO MATTER WHAT IT TAKES, NO MATTER

HOW HARD YOU HAVE TO WORK, then the whole world will open up to you.

- VISUALIZE AN EXCITING VISION.
- SET DAILY, SHORT TERM, and LONG TERM GOALS.
- REVIEW THEM EVERY MORNING, PLAN and EXECUTE.

99.99% of men are dead men walking. There is no fire & passion in their eyes. They are just going through the motions. They've unconsciously given up on themselves, their ambitions and dreams. Part of being a SEXY attractive man is being a man who lives LIFE TO THE FULLEST. THERE IS MORE TO LIFE THAN SEX AND MONEY.

If all you do is live for others then you may be exist, but you have never truly lived. LIVE ON YOUR OWN TERMS. There is an indescribable HIGH that comes from living a life of PURPOSE, MEANING, and TURNING YOUR DREAMS INTO A REALITY.

Pussy is not the purpose of life.

WHEN YOU LIVE for your life's purpose then you live a life of passion. You wake up EXCITED TO START and CONQUER THE DAY. That enthusiasm, and energy for living is SEXY. It uplifts the spirits of anyone who encounters you - women included.

Eradicate weakness from your system. Understand that fear of women is weakness. **A fisherman who is terrified of fish probably won't catch much. Aim to be fearless in the field.**

Powerful men are sexy to women because they provide a

feeling of comfort and subjective safety that women desire. This satisfies women on a primal level.

Exude absolute strength and conviction in yourself to be able to handle ANYTHING that life throws your way.

- FUCK what she thinks.
- FUCK her opinion.
- FUCK her thoughts.

Some men have spent their entire lives just to please the thoughts of a woman that they fancy. Everything they do is managed through "but would she approve?"

- FUCK being a slave to her validation.
- FUCK trying to create a positive perception.
- FUCK caring what people think.
- It's TIME TO TAKE BACK THE POWER.
- What matters is WHAT YOU THINK.
- Put your goals FIRST AND FOREMOST.

Some men are so busy trying to please others they forget what they want out of the whole connection. Be aware of your goal. **Keep the end goal that you have with a particular woman throughout your interactions with her.**

IF SHE DOESN'T PLAY **by the terms of engagement that you set, get a new girl.** The truth is that women desire to be swept into a man's dominant reality, exciting world and lifestyle - instead of having to bring a submissive man into her world.

By entering the interaction with anxiety, you're setting the wrong kind of frame - a frame of weakness. Enter interactions as a calm relaxed man - knowing that regardless of the result: you're going to be okay.

The number one way to overcome fear of the approach is to do a lot of approaches. This conditions your mind to be desensitized to the art of meeting women anytime, anywhere.

99

HOW TO PASS SHIT TESTS

OFTEN THE BEST response to a shit test is to ignore it. **Don't reinforce the low value frame that she is projecting by giving it creditability with a logical response or show of emotion.** Instead disacknowledge the frame with silence.

If you do respond,

- then use misdirection by abruptly changing the subject, or
- humor (sarcastic agree and amplify to absurdity).

- *"Do you say this to all the women?" "You are number 1,027."*
- *"How many women have you been in a relationship with?" "3 and a half."*

THERE ARE different kinds of shit tests.

Power Play

A woman asks questions about stuff she doesn't care about to (get you to qualify yourself or defend yourself) for a quick ego boost. A Power Play can also come in the form of a woman telling you to do something for her. If a man gives up his power, she quickly loses respect and attraction for him.

Verbal Abuse

A woman says something that puts you in a negative light. If a man accepts this frame, she quickly loses respect and attraction for him.

IT'S good practice for a man's SMV to get into the habit of keeping social power to himself.

BY BEHAVING like a high status man - even around other men (friends, family or coworkers) - you create dominant attitudes and behaviors that lead to victory with women. If you spend all day being a beta male at work, don't expect to suddenly turn Alpha when there's a beautiful woman in front of you.

The Eight Key Maxims for BulletProof Frame Control:

- - Stupid questions get sarcastic answers.
- - Answer questions with questions.
- - Stupid games win stupid prizes.
- - No pussy is worth losing your peace of mind over.

- - The first rule of frame control: not every question a woman asks deserves a straight answer.
- - The second rule of frame control: not everything a woman says, merits a logical response.
- - Use silence to your advantage. A lack of verbal response is a response.
- - If you have a strong enough frame and say it without enough confidence, you can "get away with anything".

If a man took everything a woman said seriously and attributed importance to it then he might lose his sanity. Women stir-up time-wasting drama about stuff they don't understand ALL THE TIME. Learn to disregard and ignore many of the random things that she says.

If a woman gives you some shit, and you lose your shit, then you also lose the shit test. The best way to handle being given shit is to either ignore, deflect with humor and misdirection.

Don't reinforce negative behavior by rewarding with more of your attention and emotional reactions. Don't give it credibility by taking it seriously. Your attention is your time. Your time is worth more than money. Time is life itself. Don't give away all of your attention for free.

IF A WOMAN MISBEHAVES, **withdraw the amount of attention you give her.**

GOING on a rant is actually chasing her harder - which is the exact opposite of the optimal path.

- Woman misbehaves.
- Guy chases harder.
- She notices that misbehaving gets your attention, so she continues to misbehave.
- Guy chases even harder.

A negative cycle is created.

YOU HAVE **to resist the temptation to chase her harder the moment she pulls away. This would only reinforce negative behavior.**

The more disrespect you put up with initially, the more disrespect you will have to put up with in the in the future. It always start subtly.

Rule of thumb: the more disrespect you put up with, the more disrespect you will have to put up with.

IT STARTS with a shit test and if you fail, it ends with her shitting on you because she sees your value as shit. The intuitive response to a shit-test for a lot of men is to get defensive and to logically justify their behaviors.

"I DID *X because of reasons A, B, and C."*

JUSTIFYING yourself to her only creates a precedence for more justification and giving away your social power.

Here's a better frame:

"I did X because I want to do X."

and an overall implied meta-frame:

"I don't need to answer your questions, or explain myself to you, because you're not the boss of me."

THIS IS FRAME CONTROL 101, gentlemen. There's a difference between explicitly stating the reasons why she should be with you, and simply implying these reasons through your lack of words.

CONFIDENT MEN DON'T FEEL the need to compensate and convince. They simply assume the sale has already been made.

Do yourself a favor and try to limit the frequency and intensity of negative emotions being transmitted to beautiful women - ESPECIALLY women that you are just meeting and starting to get to know.

You haven't even had sex with her yet. She isn't worth losing your sanity, peace of mind, or your positive emotional center over. **She isn't worth wasting valuable psychological resources getting into an argument with.**

EVEN IF SHE does things you don't like, don't get bitter. Don't rage, lash out, get defensive or lecture her. You just fucking met her. Whatever shit she throws your way, laugh it off.

Deflect with humor, misdirection or just ignore it. She isn't important enough to take seriously, and get melodramatic over.

You're picking up and flirting with chicks - not disarming nuclear bombs. Have fun and a good time; this will help you sustain long-term motivation. If a guy gets angry over some trivial petty issue with a woman that he literally just met then it shows that he cares too much and is already highly invested before she even proved her worth.

. . .

IT'S NOT **normal for a stranger to care so quickly about another stranger. Focus on having a lot of fun, and pumping your own emotional state.** When you have actual fun (not fake fun), then the good emotions will spread on to her. This is much more effective at seducing women than throwing rational, logical lectures at emotional creatures.

100

THE 6 KEYS TO PROTECTING YOURSELF AGAINST FEMALE MANIPULATION

- DON'T WASTE valuable psychological resources on dead-ends. **Make moves relatively quickly to test and assess her potential, so you don't invest time in something that isn't an optimal lead.**

- HAVE **clear boundaries and communicate them.** If those are violated, walk away. Your energy is better spent on more promising leads, or generating new leads. ALWAYS ALWAYS ALWAYS retain "walk away" power. Ensure that you have leverage, and enough self-respect to keep your standards enforced. A woman can sense when a man is "bluffing" about leaving her if she violates his boundaries. If you don't have the ability to walk away then you just gave away your balls to her on a silver platter.

- DON'T DO **the friendship first, fucking second route.** Once a woman gets used to seeing you as friend, it can be hard for her to change those behavioral patterns. Create a dominant, Rated R, man-to-woman frame from the very start and sustain it throughout the interactions.

- IT'S imperative to know what you fucking want out of the field. **Life rewards the "specific ask" and punishes the "vague wish"**; in other words, the concrete goals should be clear in your mind. When entering pivotal situations, understand the agenda, and optimal outcome. If you don't know what you want out of the sexual marketplace and don't have a conscious plan of action then, don't expect to get it randomly. Things don't just magically fall into place as you get older; you have to consciously work towards skill to develop it, and a vision to reach it.

- RESPECT **yourself AND your time enough to walk away** from one sided "friendships" with women who you want to fuck, or being in a sexual relationship with a woman of low quality (ugly, old, lots of attitude, gold-digging tendencies, needy, non-optimal logistics etc). Your time is worth money.

- HAVE **a purpose that is more important to you than pussy.** If you stand for nothing, you fall for anything. If you live for a meaningful vision then you'll naturally be immune to female manipulation, and be too busy to get sucked into female drama designed to boost her ego.

101

HOW TO AVOID DISGUSTING WOMEN

PICKUP ARTISTRY IS SELLING yourself and the idea of "being with you" to beautiful women. I emphasize "beautiful" because it's a waste of time to learn game skills just to be with ugly, fat, old girls who have attitude and emotional baggage from past relationships.

IF YOU HAVE game skills and you're dealing with 6-7s then what the fuck are you doing, son? Why did you learn game just to sell yourself short? GROW SOME FUCKING BALLS and hit up 9s-10s. **In the game of seduction, you get what you believe you are worthy of.**

A LITTLE BIT of real confidence goes a long way. Confidence comes from:

- - competence,
- - prior success with women,
- - knowing you have real value to offer any woman,
- - knowing what you bring to the table,

- - benevolent intent, and
- - a positive self-image and self-esteem.

❄

A WOMAN'S sexual nature doesn't do pity. The world is merciless on the incompetent. If you hang out with losers, you will be a loser. Choose members of your circle carefully.

CREATE a peer network of positivity that is conducive to your growth. Those within your inner-circle have to pull their weight, or they are just dead weight wasting your attention, and emotional/psychological energy. Reject women who waste your time. Be ruthlessly pragmatic. You'll thank me later.

If you allow a woman into your inner-circle, she better be "pulling her weight" by having substantial value to offer. Simply existing is not considered "pulling her weight".

When you have status, and you have some game skills, then you will have MANY options with women. There is no reason for you to settle for a woman who doesn't have much to offer and is wasting your time.

Reject her and move on to focusing on better options. It doesn't matter how beautiful, and how "special" you think she is; she is replaceable. Don’t let your feelings trick you into thinking that she is “one of a kind”; that’s just biology creating this false illusion to get you to mate (that’s how mankind has survived for generations). You can always get another girl just like her or better. Keep that in mind, and you'll keep the power in your hands.

Be ruthless in cutting off girls who are sexual dead-ends. Believe me, she wouldn’t hesitate to block your number if she suddenly discovered that you were not as valuable as she thought she was. Don't give women an advantage that they wouldn't give you. This insight is key 🔑.

Holding on to sexual dead-ends - hoping to eventually turn things around is a HUGE WASTE OF YOUR FUCKING TIME and takes up "mental real estate". **Contrary to popular opinion, it would be wise to escalate hard and burn your bridges if things go south - instead of clinging on to vapor.**

This is a highly aggressive mentality towards playing the sexual marketplace but absolutely paramount to understand- especially for men who find themselves wasting away months (sometimes even years) just hoping that things will change on their own - perpetually knocking on a door sealed shut.

. . .

ESCALATE hard and if things go south, walk away without ever looking back. **Waiting for the perfect moment to make a move is a dead man's game because you'll grow old and die waiting**. Don't wait for opportunity to strike; CREATE OPPORTUNITIES by making moves and being ruthless.

102

HOW TO AVOID ONEITIS

YOU SPENT hours replaying moments that you have had with her in your mind and fantasizing about the future. Now you're surprised that you have oneits and can't undo your feelings for her? You created these conditions by pedestalizing her in your mind.

HERE IS *a piece of advice that is worth it's weight in gold:*

Don't feed illusions with actions because then the illusions will eventually feel so real that you wont be able to tell the difference between reality and falsehood.

AS LONG AS you live your life with integrity and based on cold logic about the best course of right action at all times then you will have order amidst chaos, secure stability and a calm eye in any storm.

The moment you feed illusions, that center becomes weakened. If you continue to pursue an irrational path based on blind emotions and arbitrary impulses, then don't be surprised if your mind starts to slip and the lapses in self-control become greater.

If you spend all your time focusing on a particular woman and neglect your own self-development then don't be surprised when other dudes get ahead of you in the game of life. **Women will always choose the coolest guy that they have available to them out of their pool of options.**

You were busy building up her SMV (sexual market value) at a cost of neglecting your own SMV; then she left you in the dust for a guy who built up his SMV to be higher than yours. The irony is REAL. Remember: put purpose first; pussy second.

103

THE 12 KEY RULES ON HOW TO BE CONFIDENT

THE KEY MINDSETS THAT CONFIDENT MEN HAVE

1// **Confident men have an intense belief that they are highly valuable, what they have to offer has substantial worth, and that women would be fortunate to be with them.** These mindsets aren't a gimmick or tactic, but real belief.

Confident men believe in themselves truly and sincerely from the bottom of their heart. They don't pretend they believe they deserve her. They authentically believe it.

REMEMBER THIS: in the game of seduction, one often gets what he believes he deserves. If you think she is out of your league, she will be. If you think she in your league, she will be. Confidence quickly becomes a self-fulfilling prophecy.

Women use a man's confidence levels as a mental shortcut to assess his social status in society. Hence, it is imperative to exude EXTREME CONFIDENCE when you are in the field.

. . .

2// **Seize social power.** By simply assuming a position of high-status - by acting "AS IF" you are already in authority, it will be given to you. Put simply: you are a 10, so fucking act like it!!

And if you are a 10, but behave like an 11 then people will simply assume that you are an 11. Women take cues on how treat you based on your self-image, and behaviors.

3// **Exude powerful body-language.** Dominant body language is a short-cut to communicate to her primal side. THE WORLD IS YOUR HOME. When a woman interacts with you, she is a guest and you are the host. Hence, have interactions occur on your terms. Have her play by the cards that you deal because you are at the cause - pulling strings; this is superior to always being in reaction mode.

4// **BE EXTREMELY AGGRESSIVE in going after what you want in life - whether its girls, business deals or any ideal that you set your mind upon.** Confident men have a fierce belief in their ability to TACKLE ANYTHING that life throws at them. It's this belief that inspires women. Some men have been beta their entire lives.

THEY HAVE BEEN BRAINWASHED to be chronic people-pleasers - always putting everyone's needs and goals above their own; then they get surprised "why the fuck did I get nowhere in life?" FUCK BEING NICE. Be a predator - not a prey.

5// **Confident men have enough self-respect and self-esteem to walk away from a connection with a**

woman that is no longer serving them. They'll walk away without looking back. Why? Because they recognize their worth enough to have REAL STANDARDS and be SELECTIVE IN CHOOSING.

6// **Confidence comes from competence and clarity.** When you know what it is that you want then you are far more likely to get it. This is a simple truth but is often not applied. Know what you want out of the marketplace. Sharpen your skills consistently and you will be sharp.

7// **Confident men have assertive communication styles.** Stand up for yourself. When you aren't willing to walk away from a woman (and you have no clear boundaries) then she intuitively senses that she has you by the balls, and loses respect. When respect fades, so does attraction. Always retain "walk away power".

8// **Confident men are confident in their ability to win in the game of life and this turns women ON.** And that comes from winning. When one wins a lot, he starts to believe that he is a winner and that he can achieve anything that he sets his mind to. He starts to believe in himself and develops a sexy aura of "I HAVE GOT MY SHIT TOGETHER" that women find irresistible.

In contrast, someone who has his entire life falling apart because he is a broke loser with a dead-end job, no marketable skills and no plan for the future.....leaks the perception of incompetence.

When one is good at the game of life, he exudes a sexy confidence that communicates to others "I'VE GOT THIS. I CAN TAKE CARE OF MYSELF. And I CAN potentially

TAKE CARE of ANYONE IN MY INNER-CIRCLE." It's this frame that women find sexy.

9// **CONFIDENT MEN ARE SOCIALLY FEARLESS.** Make moves to metaphorically take what you want in the sexual market place. Social inhibitions, hesitations and insecurities undermine confidence. Let go of being stuck in your head when interacting with women. Express yourself fully and boldly.

10// **Confident men are comfortable with social tension.** They don't rush to make others feel extra comfortable. Nor do they rush to appease with bribes, try extra hard, or go out of their way to impress: to compensate for them "not being enough". Instead, they confident men assume attraction. They take the frame that *she already likes them*, and that *he is enough as is*. He doesn't have to go over-the-top to compensate for insecurities, or to keep selling to someone who is already sold. IT IS ON. JUST FUCKING CLOSE.

11// Confident men are extremely comfortable in their own skin. They are absolutely "hyper relaxed" - almost appearing to be "too relaxed". REMEMBER THIS: Calmness shows confidence; nervousness shows self-doubt. When you know you're gold, you don't feel shy or nervous.

12// **Confident men are not in approval-seeking or reaction-seeking mode.** Why? Because they already have approval from themselves. They don't give a fuck what you think, or if you approve because they approve themselves and that's all that matters.

You won't find a confident man asking:

- - "Do you like me?"
- - "Are you having fun?"
- - "Is it okay if I do XYZ?"

Because they have a strong sense of self-importance. "Of course, she likes me! Of course, she's having fun because she's with me!" Here is a useful psychological tactic to condition your mind:

Ask yourself: "How would I act if I was 100% certain that she liked me? How would I behave if I knew I was the sexiest man alive?" Imagine and visualize it. Now behave like it was true starting THIS MOMENT!

104

PLATE THEORY

ALWAYS JUGGLE MULTIPLE girls to prevent yourself from living in scarcity mode, developing oneitis and turning desperate. When you have other girls in your life, you have "fuck you sex". You know that you can walk away from any particular girl at any moment because you've got sex from multiple sources anyways. Having something is better than knowing that you can get it "in theory".

The brain wants proof - not just promises. Seeing is believing.

When you actually have other girls in your life, you're sexier than when you know that you can get other girls theoretically. Social proof is often implied. When you have other beautiful women in your life, you'll unconsciously imply it and she'll be even more attracted to you.

When you only have 1 beautiful woman in your life (and no social life), it shows. Always retain "walk away power".

It is incredibly empowering to know that you can walk away at any moment if you wanted to whether:

- your boundaries were violated,
- she fails to meet your standards, or

- you find a hotter and higher quality woman.

This advice is not necessarily ethical, or politically correct. But FUCK political correctness. Don't be a slave to the culture of the times. Political correctness is meant to serve society as a whole - but not you specifically.

DEVELOP THE UNFAIR ADVANTAGE.

FUCK playing by the rules of society. Women are RUTHLESS in the field - mercilessly rejecting guys they deem to be of low worth. Don't give a woman an advantage that she wouldn't give you. Remember: Alpha males are extremely aggressive in going after what they want in life.

105

THE IMPORTANCE OF STYLE; WHY DOES IT FUCKING MATTER?

WOMEN ARE objects of beauty and sexuality. Men are objects of success, high status and live fashion accessories to show off to her peers.

This sounds dark.

- "Isn't there more to a human being than these superficial qualities?"
- "I might appear like shit on the outside, but I'm amazing on the inside. Isn't that what counts most?"

Answer: yes, but the masses are shallow.

YOU CAN COMPLAIN about how it's unfair that people care so much about these things that they shouldn't care about, or you can play the game by its rules. Women don't have the time to get to know every guy they cross paths with, and to give every a guy a "full chance".

They rely heavily on these instant assessments as short-cuts to see if they want to invest further. Hence, your outer presentation to the world MATTERS. There's a reason why real world pimps wore flamboyant suits.

Yes, it can cost a pretty coin to dress like a boss, but it's fucking worth it. If you can't afford it then develop high-income earning skills. Further, dressing like a boss has an indirect impact of improving your confidence skills.

106

22 STEPS ON HOW TO UNFUCK YOURSELF IF YOUR LIFE IS FUCKED.

GUYS:

- - binge-sleep,
- - waste away tons of time playing video-games, Netflix, or watching random YouTube videos,
- - hang around toxic losers who have no ambitions and talk about unproductive topics,
- - don't take care of their own body, mind, or spirit,
- - lack mentors,
- - don't have a vision of where they want to be 5 years from now,
- - don't take daily substantial action to getting there,
- - don't have a set of daily positive habits,
- - don't take the time to reflect on their journey to refine their methods,
- - don't have a way to refuel energy

And then wonder: "Why the fuck am I broke, depressed and have no cute girls in my life? **Answer: you let yourself go.You haven't heavily invested time, and effort to develop yourself.**

. . .

YOU ARE where you are in the present because of the choices that you have made in the past. Your past behaviors has brought you to the present. And your present behaviors will bring you to the future. It doesn't matter how badly you have fucked up. You can pickup yourself up from the ground RIGHT NOW, and START OVER.

BELIEVE **in the beauty of your future.**

HOW TO UNFUCK YOUR LIFE

- 1. Kill time-sinks.
- 2. Utilize the mornings, and evenings.
- 3. Habit stack. A habit stack is a series of positive habits that you do every morning, and evening.
- 4. Capitalize on the commute. Fully utilize traveling time.
- 5. Avoid toxic people. These are people that take up a lot of your psychological energy but give little in return.
- 6. MENTOR UP. Find someone who is already successful in what you want to do, and learn from them.
- 7. Reflect daily.
- 8. Review your goals, and principles frequently.
- 9. Take daily, substantial action towards your vision.
- 10. Continue to learn high-ROI (high return on investment) subjects.
- 11. Sharpen your marketable skills.
- 12. Take good care of your body.

- 13. Don't neglect your spirit and mental health.
- 14. Cultivate social alliances with powerful and useful contacts.
- 15. Let go of excuses, limiting beliefs and the past.
- 16. Utilize the power of affirmations, mantras and self-suggestion to condition the unconscious mind.
- 17. Invest in improvement of thy self. Invest in yourself by getting better every day.
- 18. Keep a learning journal.
- 19. Don't waste time in dead-end relationships.
- 20. Approach.
- 21. Develop your will-power. Have the ability to take action - even when you don't feel like it and your emotions tell you to do nothing.
- 22. When will-power fails, you will fall to the level of your system of habits. Develop a set of good lifestyle habits ("automated success").

Exude powerful body-language.

- - Be loud.
- - Take up space.
- - Have fierce eye-contact.
- - Take a comfortable position.
- - Use power-postures.
- - Don't lean in.
- - Keep head straight.

107

FUCK CORONA

THE SECRET **to having a high quality life is to have high quality thoughts.** Changing how you think, changes how you feel, which changes how you behave. **By thinking positively, you will feel positively and that will help you take positive constructive action.**

• FOCUS on the positive of life, feeling gratitude for your strengths/talents, and the light at the end of the tunnel ("Where will you be 5 years from now based on the current rate of progression?").

• DON'T FOCUS on the negative, dwelling on the unchangeable past, and complaining bitterly about the present. **THINK INSPIRATIONAL THOUGHTS TO BE IN A PERPETUAL STATE OF INSPIRATION TO TAKE RADICAL BOLD ACTION AND CONQUER LIFE!**

WHERE YOU ARE RIGHT NOW in life does not reflect where you will be in life in the future. While you may be dissatisfied with what where you are now, contemplate the idea that in a few years, months, weeks - or even a few days - everything can change for the positive. Where you are now in the present is based on the actions that you have taken in the past, and where you will be in the future depends on the actions that you are taking right now in the present. **PUSH YOURSELF HARD EVERY DAY BECAUSE EVERY TINY AMOUNTS OF PROGRESS ACCUMULATE FAST.**

THE CORONA VIRUS is an interesting time period that in many ways is unprecedented. Many men are staying at home. Here's an important key to understanding this crisis: life is what you make it. Experiences are based on how you perceive reality and the effort that you put into living your best life. **5% OF LIFE IS WHAT HAPPENS TO YOU AND 95% OF LIFE IS HOW YOU RESPOND TO WHAT HAPPENS TO YOU.**

Life deals you a set of cards. It is your mission to use these cards to the best of your ability.

One can take this time to mourn over the fact that 2020 started in an atrocious manner, or to worry about the non-controllable, but that would be a waste of valuable mental energy. Understand this mindset: if you can't change something, accept it! It is futile to worry about something that you have no control over. You can't do undo this pandemic, so why suffer the agony of being excessively fearful and worried.

Sure, take basic precautions such as:

- avoid touching your face (eyes, mouth, and nose), or food with unwashed hands that may have been exposed to Corona,
- avoid areas that have a large gathering of people,
- wear a mask in public areas,

But outside these basic precautions, use this time to develop yourself!

Use this time (until a vaccine is out) to focus on your mid-game skills that involve:

- texting,
- calling, and
- video-chatting girls.

You can be extremely good at approaching women, striking up conversations, sparking attraction, but if you don't know how to follow up on the phone to set up a second date then you will get nowhere!!

The phone is the bridge between the first encounter to the second meeting. Use this time to improve your phone related skill-sets.

This is also a good time to sharpen online-game by messaging women on different dating sites and apps. While this is not a permanent substitute to daygame, it is a temporary one for the time being while the world's health heals (and a vaccine becomes accessible). You can sit at home and mourn, or you can use this valuable time to increase practical knowledge, sharpen valuable skills, accumulate experience and take on-screen action.

Covid 19 is a storm that will pass, and when it does if you used this time to grow then you will be in an optimal position to DOMINATE.

108

CONCLUDING THOUGHTS

LISTEN TO ME, my dear son. Come closer because I want to tell you something important. I give you permission to let go of the past, and start over. Right now - this exact moment - is a NEW CHAPTER in your life. You can write in this chapter ANYTHING that you want.

I don't just give you permission. I command it. FUCK THE PAST!!! It's over. Don't dwell on something that that is long gone because dwelling on the past, does not help the present.

The past doesn't matter. The only thing that matters is WHAT YOU DO TODAY. FOCUS ON NOW. You could have been a beta male your entire life. Your past identity does not have to define the present. Burn the past to the ground.

Make a fierce resolution to be a dominant Alpha - starring this exact moment. As the old weaker version of you dies, the new one emerges. **BE THE MOST DOMINANT MAN IN THE ROOM.**

Men on the Asperger spectrum have serious difficulty reading the body-language of others, basic human social skills and even having normal male friendships.

They can't even tell if the pickup tactics are working due to difficulty in detecting social cues.

Yet they expect an overpriced $500 five hour course (+30 page pamphlet) on the internet from someone with dubious credentials and intentions to suddenly transform them into a Casanova overnight so they can approach women on the street and achieve same day lays. HA.

Buying a product will not suddenly give you pickup skills. Even if you consume the entire product from start to finish you will still not suddenly have pickup skills.

Knowledge is only half the battle. It takes tons and tons of practice to develop real skills. It takes months (and sometimes years) of conscious mental conditioning to undo years of beta male programming. **YOU HAVE TO BE PERSISTENT IN APPLYING THE STUFF THAT YOU HAVE LEARNED IN THIS BOOK!! CONSCIOUS IMPLEMENTATION OF THE TECHNIQUES AND REVIEWING THE MINDSETS IS SUPER KEY.**

STOP looking for a quick fix. There are shortcuts, but you have to think long term. Life is a marathon. You have to pay your dues by putting in daily practice to get good conversation and the seduction game in general.

AVOID THE INFORMATION TRAP

You don't need to read 494 pages on how to approach a girl before approaching a girl. Just fucking do it!! Just fucking walk up to her and say something!!!

You don't need to watch a 7 hour video course to learn how to wipe the shit off your ass. Likewise, you don't need to watch a course on how to use your feet to move closer to something that you like and then open your mouth to create words that sparks an interaction.

It's super simple. Learning too much advice can actually paralyze someone instead of helping them.

. . .

METAPHOR: instead of simply wiping their ass they start thinking "what's the best angle to wipe? What are the top 10 best toilet papers? How many wipes?"

Overthinking = stuck.

Don't get stuck in a state of perpetual over-analysis and overthinking. There comes a think when one has to shut off his mind and just act.

MAKE MOVES TO WIN IN THE GAME OF LIFE & SEDUCTION. ✅

And you can't win if you're too busy thinking about the moves instead of doing them.

CONVERSATION IS NOT THE END GAME.

Conversation should not be an endless end unto itself. The goal is continuously progress forward in the mating process. Conversation is simply that which takes up the space in between the physical moves and escalation. The purpose of conversation is to hold her attention long enough to showcase your charming and attractive personality that win over her heart, and to **distract her conscious mind while you physically escalate.**

WHEN YOU TALK about things that you sincerely care about, you gain greater insights into them and come to understand yourself better. While you can say "all the right things", knowing how to say those things is x10 more important. How you say something is much, much, much more important than what you are actually saying. **When speaking it is of paramount importance to have strong body-language (both verbal and non-verbal), a great vibe, energy, extreme confidence and to have a dynamic delivery.**

You can talk to anyone, at anytime and anywhere. All it takes is confidence and the willingness to take bold action.

FROM THIS VERY **moment and forward, unlimit yourself from limiting beliefs. NOW.** You have finished this book and you have all the knowledge that you need to take action with women. Start immediately. The next time you see a cute girl, walk up to her and say something to strike up a conversation.

EVERYTIME YOU STEP FOOT OUTSIDE YOUR DOOR,. **START NOTICING OPPORTUNITIES TO PRACTICE YOUR GAME SKILLS AND CAPITALIZE ON THEM.**

109

TAKE ACTION EVERY DAY

MOTHERFUCKER
STOP
EVERYTHING
THAT YOU ARE DOING RIGHT NOW AND LISTEN TO ME, MOTHERFUCKER.

I'M GOING to ask you to do something that is going to make you feel uncomfortable. If you do this exercise properly it might just change your life right now. This is worth your time, bitch!

Take a small step outside your comfort zone **at this exact moment** and ponder these potentially disturbing questions:

- **"What do you truly truly truly desire with women?"**
- **"If you could have anything in the world with women then what would you like?"**

- **"If you could live out your wildest fantasy with a woman - without any chance of failure than what would it be?"**

BE BRUTALLY HONEST WITH YOURSELF. Visualize that reality in your mind. Picture it CLEARLY. Listen to me my son, if you can visualize it then you can achieve it!!!!!!!

YOU CAN ACHIEVE ALMOST ANYTHING WITH WOMEN THAT YOU SET YOUR MIND TO ACHIEVE. 99.99% of the limitations that you perceive are merely illusions created by social conditioning. Society brainwashed you to be a conforming sheep; unlearn that which you have learned. **I hearby give you permission to be an ALPHA PREDATOR STARTING NOW.**

I am going to teach you how to achieve lustful physical intimacy with women. HERE IS LESSON #1, SEXY PLAYER. The secret to getting good with women is really the secret to getting good at anything: you have to do a lot of it. Humans get good at what they do frequently, BITCH!!! FUCK YOU if you disagree with this advice.

I don't care how much pickup theories you know, how many books you've read, or how many hours you've spent on YouTube. **If you don't actually go out, and practice the skills of meeting women EVERY DAY then your skills will remain stagnant and your results will be ZERO. Taking daily action is ABSOLUTELY PARAMOUNT**.

- Repeat after me: I will make it a top tier priority to take action with women everyday!!!!
- Verbalize this right now: I will make it a top tier priority to take action with women everyday!!!!

- SAY IT!! I will make it a priority to take action with women everyday!!!!

This means YOU. And this means TODAY.

Let these self-suggestions and affirmations sink into your unconscious mind.

- Do you want to settle with old, ugly, fat, broke girls who gives you attitude , drain your bank account, and then have the audacity to treat you like shit? FUCK NO!!! You don't have to settle for low quality garbage when you have the skills to meet new women!!!!!
- Do you ever want to be in a situation where you see cute girls, but are paralyzed from taking action because you're too much of an ignorant pussy? FUCK NO!!!!! Invest in the knowledge of practical pickup, and sharpen your skills on the daily.

Here's the truth: YOU can meet women ANYTIME and ANYWHERE. If you don't truly believe this then it's because you have been brainwashed by angry, hypersensitive #MeToo feminists. FUCK what they think. It's WHAT YOU THINK THAT MATTERS. Having the skills to go out TODAY and meet cute girls - who desire you - is a fucking superpower power. Learn these skills and reap the sexually charged benefits to years to come.

Guys stay in shitty, toxic-as-fuck relationships because they're afraid of leaving the girl because they think: "oh no!!!!!! If this relationship doesn't work out then it would take FOREVER for me to find another girl like her." When you know you've got SOLID GAME SKILLS to approach, meet and attract new women into your life then you will be fearless in existing relationships because you retain that sexy "walkaway power" and you will have tons of options to choose a *crème de* la crème if you're single.

INVEST IN YOURSELF by training high ROI skills every day. You'll thank me later. **"In a year, you would have wished that you had started today!" So start TODAY.**

TAKE
ACTION
EVERYDAY

110

THE END GAME

<u>IF YOU DON'T KNOW **where you are going, you will get nowhere.**</u> Take a moment to visualize your ideal self with girls.

- What kind of man do you want to be?
- What kind of high-demand skills do you want to develop?
- What kind of lifestyle do you want to have?
- What kind of beautiful girls do you want to have in your life?
- What kind of responses do you want to elicit from women?
- KNOW WHAT YOU WANT. Are you interested in being a player who gets laid with a new girl every week every time his week, or do you want to have a relationship with a single beautiful women (but have the sharp skills to get new beautiful women if you want to)?

<u>EVEN IF YOU KNOW WHERE YOU ARE GOING, YOU STILL WON'T GET THERE IF YOU DON'T</u>

WORK ON IT CONSISTENTLY. Work towards your vision every day!

Let go of the need to learn pickup-skills to impress other guys. Don't game for validation. Game to achieve a specific result that is personally valuable to you. Know what the end goal is.

AGAIN: if you don't know what you want, don't expect to suddenly get it. You have to know what you want out of this game, create a game-plan to get it, and consciously work on a daily basis to reach this vision.

TAKE ACTION EVERY DAY! **WIN AT ANY COST.**

Sincerely,

Cory Smith

P.S. Also see the other books in the series, "The Sexcalation System", and "Womenese 101" which discuss different aspects of seduction.

How you play the game of seduction is how you play the game of life. Dominate EVERYTHING and DOMINATE WOMEN COMPLETELY. While having strong game skills is essential to a man's path to power, it is not sufficient in itself. You must have a game plan. It's all about the lifestyle and the long term. On your current rate of progress where are you going to be five years from now?

Womanese 101

HOW TO TALK AND FLIRT WITH WOMEN, MAKE GIRLS ADDICTED TO BEING WITH YOU

Cory Smith
@PUA_DATING_TIPS

Introduction

THE 5 PRIMARY COMPONENTS OF THE MINDSET OF A SUCCESSFUL SEDUCER

I. BE RUTHLESS

Life is a short, and then you die.

Your life is composed of a certain amount of TIME TOKENS (a series of moments) and when these TIME TOKENS are gone, then you cease to exist on earth.

Your days are numbered, bitch.

You have a limited amount of this INCREDIBLY VALUABLE RESOURCE, so it's essential that you don't give out your TIME TOKENS for free and without much thought. **Be highly selective** about who you give these TIME TOKENS to. **If a woman is taking up your hours, then she better be fucking worth it.**[1]

Here in New York City, a dentist will charge $120 for just a 10 minute consultation. It doesn't matter how much pain you're in, the dentist doesn't have a "savior complex" and won't give away his time to your for free because of your entitlement. The Dentist will tell freeloaders to "FUCK OFF" because his business is not a charity. Even if the Dentist doesn't say "I don't give a fuck about your problems if I'm not being paid" **it will be implied with his actions** - e.g. not being available to freeloaders, and having lots of excuses as to why he simply "can't" be available to you (See Law #53: Action Reveals All).

Some men waste years of their life running a Time and Psychological Energy Charity for low quality unworthy women - instead of running a ruthlessly efficient clear GAME PLAN for GETTING SEX.[2]

- **Be clear about what you want out** of the sexual marketplace to make the most out of your finite time.
- **Be clear about what you <u>don't</u> want,** so you can assertively communicate clear boundaries, and have the ability to say "no".

Be highly selective about those who you allow within your inner-circle.

Learn this right now and right here: **if a low quality woman is taking up a lot of your time (without giving a substantial amount of value in return), dump her and never look back. Period. Bottom line.**

Having the ability to walk away from connections don't serve you: is a fundamentally crucial aspect of manhood. Simply knowing that you have the ability to walk away: will give you a sense of real confidence, and will come across in your interactions with women - giving you a competitive sexy edge.

You are constantly sending signals out to women - consciously and unconsciously. Some signals are seductive and lead to sex occurring (such as signals that convey that you are THE PRIZE, THE SELECTOR, and A HIGH STATUS AMAZING CATCH). Other signals are anti-seductive (such as putting up with bullshit, weak body-language, being overly available, making her your Life Purpose etc).

What you believe about yourself (you hold yourself in high esteem; you have the belief that "ANY WOMAN IN MY INNER-CIRCLE IS FORTUNATE TO HAVE ME; I AM A WOMAN'S BEST OPTION") **and what you believe about what you have to offer women** (your competitive value proposition in the sexual marketplace) **is intuitively sensed by women.**

This bears repeating: what you believe about yourself and what you have to offer women will intuitively be sensed by women. A high status self-image leads to sexy high status behaviors.

- For instance: women intuitively know that that an ELITE HIGH STATUS MAN (a man who is in the top 1% of society) has REAL OPTIONS with other women and has HIGH STANDARDS. Hence, she intuitively senses that he won't put up with bullshit (low quality behaviors) for too long; there will come a point when he will just be fed up and walk away. **If a man allows himself to be treated like a doormat, then women will start to view him as having the same worth as a doormat.**[3]
- **In contrast, if you believe you're gold then this will come across in how you conduct yourself and be intuitively sensed by those around you.**
- If you believed you were GOLD and what you have to offer is GOLD, then you wouldn't stay in a situation where other people were treating you like shit, because you would know that it would be easy for you find new relationships with new people (after all, you are offering GOLD). You would naturally have higher standards, and convey a willingness to walk away - which ironically will make women like you even more.

A key fundamental in learning to speak Womense is to condition your mind that you are GOLD, what you have to offer is metaphorical GOLD, and your time is GOLD; when you truly believe this then you'll unconsciously communicate this through your body-language, actions, and words. For instance: simply feeling powerful leads to exuding powerful body-language.[4] As I explain in a later chapter in this book, behaviors stem from beliefs.

It's also worth noting that **beliefs are contagious. By changing your beliefs about yourself, you'll change women's beliefs about you.**[5]

ASK YOURSELF THESE 6 QUESTIONS TO GIVE YOURSELF A REALITY CHECK:

- #1) How much is your time really worth?
- #2) **Put a price-tag on your time** to gain a better perspective. If a magical potion would take away a year of your life in exchange for $10,000 would you agree? If someone paid you an hourly rate to stare at a wall and do nothing; what would your price be?
- #3) Your time is worth a fucking lot, so why do you give it away like it's cheap by being overly available to anyone who asks? **Why do you feel inclined to say "yes" to things when you really want to say "no, I am busy"?**
- #4) Why do you waste psychological energy on things/people that are unworthy of you? Why do you allow yourself to be swept up into a woman's bullshit drama over petty issues - instead of focusing on your own personal development and goals?
- #5) You are a biological ticking time bomb headed towards an irreversible end. Do you make every day count? Do you use every hour of the day? Do you use every minute of every hour?
- #6) The Corona Virus Pandemic has made it ultra clear that life is fragile. Do you live with the

awareness that one day the life force within you will be gone? If so, what do you want to accomplish before the Final End? **Make a Final Bucket list titled "Things that I want to GET DONE Before I Go Away Forever."**

THE WOMENESE PARADOX

While it is true that this entire book is dedicated to understanding the secret language of women: Womenese, it is also true that you don't want to waste away your valuable time getting caught up in a woman's silly bullshit and pointless drama (created because she is starving for attention).

THE 7th QUESTION

Every minute you spend obsessing over "What did she really mean when she said X" could have been a minute that you spent investing in yourself, executing daily goals, or meeting new girls. **While you're thinking about her, do you think she is thinking about you?**

THE KEY TO SOLVING THE PARADOX

Always focus on the primary goal of understanding and speaking Womenese; **the primary goal is to efficiently and effectively have sex with a beautiful woman - which leads to a long term mutually beneficial sexual relationship that includes countless additional nights of sex.** You want to accomplish this primary goal with Bullshit Encountered Counter at null (or as close to null as possible), and not getting sucked into time-wasting drama.

The secondary goal is to develop GAME SKILLS, so that you can go out, meet and seduce a new woman - if the necessity arrives. Don't wait for a breakup to start developing GAME SKILLS. Develop GAME SKILLS SHARP and KEEP THEM SHARP - even if you currently are in a relationship right now.[6]In the event of the relationship ending, you want to still have the essential skills necessary to meet women and generate the value that women feed on, ON-THE-READY.

It's important to keep this always keep the primary and secondary goals in mind at all times when dealing with women, so you don't lose the forest for the trees and you don't waste psychological energy on a lot of the stupid petty bullshit that women talk about. You want to enter The Womanverse so you can get practical knowledge that leads you to FUCK HER IN THE PUSSY - not so you can get lost in an endless blackhole of abstract theory.

I will be guide on this educational journey and hit you with various game-changing epiphanies. Let's get started with this introduction by talking:

- about common traps in the sexual marketplace,
- the overall mindset that you should have when dealing with women,
- the goals of speaking Womenese,
- the cardinal rules of seduction,
- how to be a badass Alpha Who FUCKS, and
- how to communicate the sexy irresistible trait of confidence.

❄

FIVE COMMON SEXUAL MARKETPLACE TRAPS THAT MEN FALL INTO

- **#1) THE FRIEND ZONE TRAP** Think about how guys are stuck in one-sided friend-zone "relationships" with women that are not sexually receptive. The solution is: MAKE A MOVE. **Making a move will force a woman to either get involved with you on a sexual level, or fuck off.** A key concept in speaking Womenese is to understand that a woman's actions reveal more about her than her words. Thus, it's prudent to force a woman into making a behavioral choice, so that you can make an accurate assessment of the situation.

- **#2) THE TOXIC RELATIONSHIP TRAP** Think about guys stuck in dead-end toxic relationships where they are treated like shit, and stepped over like they're doormats. They treat the woman like a goddess, while allowing themselves to be treated like trash. They've idealized this woman in their mind, developed feelings for her, and rationalize her bad behavior as "love doesn't come easy; it must be earned". Don't let a woman treat you like shit; **have enough self-respect to walk away from a woman who isn't pulling her weight in a "relationship".** When you know you have GAME SKILLS, you won't be afraid to walk away because a better higher-quality woman is right around the corner.
- **#3) THE ENDLESS DATES TO NOWHERE TRAP** Think about guys spending months fantasizing about a woman who they're too pussy to make a move on. She might not even be aware of their existence. In the process of waiting for months, they lose their own self-esteem and confidence level. **If a woman makes you wait for months, in the vast *vast* majority of cases: her pussy isn't worth the wait.** Opportunity Cost is the price of lost opportunities. You are so

obsessed with one particular pussy, you didn't even notice the dozens of other pussies that were available. Don't have endless dates to nowhere, or be the perpetual texting penpal. You have to be constantly making reasonable progress (at a reasonable pace) towards sex, or she needs to fuck off.

- **#4) THE OBSESSION TRAP** Think about guys obsessed over one particular woman. They'll spend all of their time, and mental energy thinking about her constantly. **They're so busy obsessing over one particular woman, they'll stop developing their sexual market-value, miss out on opportunities with other women, and even lose valuable male friendships with cool guys.** You might find a relatively high quality woman to be in a relationship with, but this doesn't mean that you should stop developing yourself, stop focusing on your Life Mission, start losing your competitive edge in the sexual marketplace, and start losing valued male friendships.
- **#5) THE LOW QUALITY WOMAN TRAP** Think about how much of a person's life and psychological health is wasted by spending time with low quality women who infect his mind with negative emotions and petty energy-draining drama. If you are a high status man, you shouldn't need to settle down with a woman who has severe issues; aim higher. Your psychological resources are finite, so if a woman is taking them then she better be fucking worth it. Focus on high quality women; cut out low quality women.

Falling into one of these traps is months (sometimes years) of valuable TIME TOKENS being poured down the toilet. Spending time on a woman who is a good sexual potential is like watering a seed that turns into a plant that bears fruits, but spending time on:

- a toxic woman (with severe emotional baggage) ,
- on a woman who has friend zoned,
- on a woman who has low interest (and unavailable for in-person meetups),
- on a woman who is perpetually in a bad mood and always finds things to complain about,
- on a woman who has perpetual problems that she needs saving from because she is incredibly incompetent,

you is like watering a rock. Pouring more water is not going to magically change the rock into a plant; if you keep doing what you're doing then you'll keep getting what you're getting. You have to kick the rock to the curb, go find time-worthy seeds and **never look back**. Next level behaviors lead to next level results.

In the case of a toxic woman who is a relationship dead-end, it's better to move on with your life, **because no pussy is worth your peace of mind.** Even if you fuck her, the psychological toll is not worth it, because that's psychological energy that you could have spent developing better leads that are of healthier connections.

No pussy is worth your self-respect , and sexual market-value. Even if you fuck her in the end, think about how you've lost opportunities with other girls in the process.

I'm about to say something that is incredibly politically incorrect (and should not be shared with blue-pilled male associates): **women have different levels of quality in sexual relationships.** Not every woman that you can fuck is worth fucking. Some low quality garbage should be left in the garbage.

In contrast, there are higher quality women out there that are worth getting into a long-term sexual relationship with.

THE GOALS OF SPEAKING, SIGNALING, UNDERSTANDING, AND OBSERVING THE SECRET LANGUAGE KNOWN AS WOMENESE.

When you meet a beautiful woman who is worthy of your time, you want to be fluent in Womenese to be able to:

- Truly understand her thoughts, feelings, and actions, so that you can behave in a manner that resonates positively. **Do more of what is seductively impactful, and less of what is seductively repulsive.**
- Understand what she means when she says specific things, so that you can calibrate your strategy accordingly. A key principle of this book is: **a woman's words reveal the mechanism of her psych.**
- Understand the signals that she is sending out with her body language and what they mean, so you can capitalize on "DOWN TO FUCK RIGHT NOW" signals. **If you miss the DTF Signals, you won't fuck her at the moment that she is sexually available.** Be aware of the signals that a woman unconsciously (or consciously) sends out when she wants to fuck, so that you'll be able to notice them when they occur in real time, and you'll act on them. When opportunity meets a man who is ready, sex happens.
- Understand the truth behind the male-to-female dynamic, so that you can leverage the variables in

this dynamic to your seductive advantage. A woman wants you to play the dominant masculine role in the relationship, so she can play the submissive feminine role. **Treat a woman like a woman, so she can feel sexy.** Submission within a woman unleashes her sexual side.

- Understand what you have to do specifically to solidify a physical connection. **It is your responsibility as a man to physically escalate the interaction towards sex because a woman's ego prevents her from doing this that will make her feel slutty.**

Womenese boils down to these 6 mediums that give off signals:

- **#1) Thoughts**
- **#2) Feelings**
- **#3) Words**
- **#4) Actions**
- **#5) Body Language**
- **#6) Social Media**

The first 5 factors tend to feed off each other. For instance: thoughts lead to feelings lead to words lead to actions and vice versa.

The 6th factor is a woman's social media lifestyle which are quite revealing about her and sometimes can reveal what her thoughts are about you.

INDICATORS TO GAUGE A WOMAN'S QUALITY, SO YOU DON'T WASTE YOUR TIME LOOKING THROUGH METAPHORICAL GARBAGE.

A HIGHER-QUALITY WOMAN WILL:

- **#1) inspire you to be your best** (doesn't bring out your worst),
- **#2) bring value to your life** (your life is better with her than without her in it),
- **#3) is frugal when making decisions that impact your wallet** (is conscious about your wellbeing when making decisions that could impact you),
- **#4) respect you -** fostering confidence levels/building your self-image (a woman's respect is essential for sexual attraction to stay high), and
- **#5) create a positive vibe** (creating a feel-good environment that is conducive to your personal development).

IN CONTRAST, A LOWER-QUALITY WOMAN WILL:

- **#6) constantly complain** (something is always "wrong"),
- **#7) criticize** (it seems to be her life mission to find out what is missing within who you are, instead of being grateful for your strengths)**,**
- **#8) seems to always be in a bad mood** (a key aspect in learning to speak Womenese is being able to identify the emotional states of others and the variables that influence these emotional states)**,**
- **#9) create drama/chaos -** making it more difficult for you to be successful in your life purpose

(because the drama takes up a lot of your time and psychological resources),
- **#10) only cares about what she can get out of you and what you stand for** (rather than your personality and who you actually are),
- **#11) isn't kind to strangers** (because she is obsessed with her own self-gain and can't see past her own sense of self-centeredness),
- **#12) tends to talk negatively about other people** (including her past relationships and the people that are presently in her life), and
- **#13) post semi-clad IG photos** because she's consciously (or unconsciously) fishing for other guys.

Some female characteristics are more important to some men than than others because preferences are subjective. As I discussed in "The Sexcalation System" *(2nd Edition)* it's important for you to know what you want out of the Sexual Marketplace through the exercise of:

- "Precise Visualization",
- verbalizing your goals/visualizing your vision every morning, and
- writing down what you want.

The most important indicator of a high quality woman is sexual availability towards you. Sex is an incredibly important aspect of a relationship for both partners involved. No, that is not being petty; it's being hyper realistic and practical. **A woman becomes emotionally invested to the man that she has sex with and is physically intimate with** - unless she is a prostitute and has learned to detach herself.[7]

Likewise, **a man values a woman and is inspired to**

invest into the relationship when he is fucking her (with orgasams included). This is why sex occurring is essential for the health of the relationship for both partners.[8]

THE CARDINAL RULE OF SEDUCTION #1: FUCK ME, OR FUCK OFF.

In the case of a woman who has friend-zoned you, you have to start making moves that will lead to sex occurring - adopting the mindsets of:

- **"blow me, or blow me out"**
- **"fuck me, or fuck off"**, and
- **"FUCK or BOUNCE**."

By being overtly sexual, you're forcing a woman to make a choice - (option 1) either fall into your frame, or (option 2) walk away.

Regardless of her choice: you win.

- **OPTION 1:** if she falls into your frame by allowing you to make sexual advances, then you'll eventually have sex with her.
- **OPTION 2:** if she walks away, then you stop wasting time and psychological energy on a sexual dead-end.

Express sexual intent. If she responds on a sexual level then good *(you got what you wanted)*. If she rejects you then that's also good *(because now she'll stop wasting your time and you can focus on better leads)*. By making sexual advances, you can't lose regardless of the outcome, so there is no reason to be anxious over sexual escalation.

THE NICE GUY DELUSION

- **The nice guy will rationalize spending hours upon hours with a woman who is not sexually available** by giving into her frame of entitlement, and being mislead by his Savior Complex.
- He was brought up to be a "gentleman" and mistakenly assumes that being a "gentleman" always being available to **help women (without getting value in return) because it's "the right thing to do" - regardless of how psychological energy or personal time it costs him.**

His actions of wasting time and putting up with bullshit communicate volumes (to women who notice these subtle signals) about his worth. It communicates that he doesn't value his time, and thus women don't really value him. The moment they get all of the value that they can from him, they're gone. After all, the entire relationship was based on a one sided platonic providership.

The nice guy should learn three things immediately:

- **(1) he doesn't owe women anything,**
- **(2) a woman has to be sexually available for her to even warrant his time** (or at least allow for physical escalation to occur at a reasonable pace, so that it eventually does lead to sex within a reasonable time frame)[9], and
- (3) **to be worthy of a relationship, the woman has to reciprocate by providing substantial value of her own** (other than just

having a hole in between her legs; remember: women only value what they work for).

THE CARDINAL RULE OF SEDUCTION #2: WHEN IT COMES TO SEX, PAY MORE ATTENTION TO WHAT SHE DOES THAN WHAT SHE SAYS.

This is a book about understanding the Womenese language. Understand this right now and right here: women speak the loudest with their actions. You've heard the phrase "A picture is worth a thousand words." **A single action reveals more about a woman than 10,000 words.** A woman could verbally bullshit you from morning to night, but her actions and body-language reveal the truth about the situation.

IF SHE:

- allows physical escalation to occur on an intimate level,
- initiates touching by herself,
- qualifies herself to you (e.g. gives you reasons why you should be with her by explaining different ways that she is awesome),
- moves with you to an isolated spot,
- brings up the subject of sex by herself, or
- initiates interactions first AND makes time to see you on one-on-one dates:

then she is into you, and there is sexual potential. This is true even if she is verbally dismissive and says "the wrong things". I repeat: this is true even if on the surface the words that she uses seem to portray you in a negative light. **When actions differ from words, trust the former.**

Words convey what a woman wants to be. Actions convey who she is now. The smart seducer behaves according to how women are - not how they wish to be. He pays attention to their actions and body-language to ascertain the truth. **Much of Womenese is unspoken**.

THE CARDINAL RULE OF SEDUCTION #3: ALWAYS RETAIN YOUR LEVERAGE.

Be acutely aware of the value that you are giving her that she needs, and values. Retain that leverage.

THE CARDINAL RULE OF SEDUCTION #4: ALWAYS RETAIN WALK-AWAY POWER.

Time is life itself. To give it out to a woman, she must be WORTHY. If she isn't worthy or proves to be unworthy later on in the relationship, then walk away. **Always always always retain leverage and the ability to walk away.** Women are like children, and need to be dealt with by having a firm hand.

Women have the irrational emotions of a child. This inner-child is always within her but masked because she has learned to appear adultish for the sake of her professional life. Smart seducers know to look past the fake facade of her appearing like a mature adult, and communicate to the inner-child that is within her; this style of communication is known as flirting. One key concept of flirting is to be high status, and a high status man's power is in his ability to walk way because he has other options and the game skills to generate more options.

You have to be ruthless in cutting out women who are wasting your fucking time. Be merciless when rejecting women who are unworthy. I assure you that a woman is incredibly ruthless when it comes to rejecting men that she sees to be of low worth, so why should you be different? Don't give women an advantage they wouldn't give you.

A master seducer is efficient. When he meets a woman, he thinks her through a live funnel. This funnel involves constantly leading the interaction towards sex. Life is too short to play indirect game that spans months. You have to consistently be moving the connection towards physical intimacy by doing a series of moves. If you spend 5 time tokens achieving something that should have only taken 1 time token then you're just inefficient; don't spend 5 dates to fuck her if you could have fucked her on the first day.

SPEAK WITH YOUR ACTIONS

Women are in abundance - with more turning 18 years of age every minute - but your time is not. Treat your time with respect because time is life itself. [10]

If you don't even respect your time, women won't either. A key concept in speaking Womenese is that you are communicating to women through your actions. YOUR ACTIONS SEND A MESSAGE. By not always being available, you are training the woman to value your time in a language that she truly understands: consequences.

OPERANT CONDITIONING; HOW TO CONDITION A WOMAN TO DO WHAT YOU WANT

Women are like cute puppies. **Attention is the currency.** They are being trained by how you consciously or unconsciously reward them with attention and expressions of emotions.

- **RULE #1:** Female behavior (whether it's good, or bad behavior) that you reward with **attention** will be repeated.
- **RULE #2:** Female behavior (whether it's good, or bad behavior) that you reward with an **emotional reaction** will be repeated.
- **RULE #3:** Female behavior that is completely ignored and that you are "emotionally numb to" will subside. Hence**, withdrawing attention and emotions** is an effective strategy for punishing bad behavior, to ensure that the bad behavior does not repeat itself.

.A key concept in speaking Womenese is to understand that Women should be trained like an animal master trains adorable, cuddly puppies - with a firm hand and being careful to **give much more attention for positive behavior than negative behavior.**

Within her is a child that never matured. This inner-child craves attention. Communicate directly to this child by giving attention (and emotionally expressions) when she does what you want, and withdrawing attention (and emotional expressions) when she doesn't. Remember: attention, fun, and ego validation are forms of value that plays as the currency of the night.

Create the conditions for it be more fun and emotionally enticing for a woman to go along the seduction process than for her to against it. Women just do what feels good and uplifts their spirits, while avoiding that which feels bad and dampens their spirits. Being with you and doing what you want, should be a clear emotional win.

- **Practical example of operatnt conditioning in action:** In the context of physical escalation, the moment a woman doesn't allow for an advancement of physical escalation to occur should be the moment that you temporarily withdraw attention, emotion, fun, and the value that you have been providing her. This way she'll miss what she used to have, and realize that it's more fun to just comply with what you want.

❄

II. BE THE PREDATOR.

Don't wait to be saved. No one is coming to save you.[11] You have to be your own savior. It is your duty to be a fighter for yourself - just like you would be a fighter for your best friend. **Be your own best friend and take care of yourself.**

You see, everyone is too busy obsessing over themselves to prioritize you. You have only yourself to rely upon. If you don't fight for yourself then you will be lost. It's imperative that you PUT YOURSELF FIRST, take value, and ensure that your goals are met. **Just like a woman looks out for herself - you must look out for your own interests.**[12]

As mentioned a moment ago, a key concept in speaking Womense is sending a message with your actions. You can lecture a woman for 10 minutes straight, or you can say nothing and communicate all of that in a single 5 second action. By being a man who is on his mission in life and takes action to achieve his daily goals, you are non-verbally communicating to women that you value yourself. **Women value men that value themselves because they are biologically designed to feed off a guy's vibe, self-image, and perspective.**

Even in a relationship, continue to run attraction-generating game and develop your sexual market-value. Game is as relevant in a ten year relationship as it is relevant when you first meet a woman. This is why there is no such thing as retiring from game; you are always playing the game - whether you realize it or not. **The game never sleeps. Hence, it's essential that you increase your sexual market value on a consistent basis (over a long period of time) to be head and shoulders above the competition.**

Don't you get it? A woman is constantly on the lookout to trade up. She can't help but follow her hypergamous nature and crave to capture the highest value man that she can. **A woman will always go for the best option available to her.** In the digital age, women have greater ability to have access to top-tier men because of apps like IG, Snapchat and TikTok. Hence, it's imperative that YOU BE THE HIGHEST VALUE MAN. By being at the APEX, even if she decides to act upon her inner-instincts to trade up: there is no one else to trade up to because you are "the most up" option. BE THE CREME DE LA CREME.

Improve yourself by at least 1% every single day. Even marginal consistent improvements ADD UP FAST, and over the aggregate add up to something very substantial. **Self-development is a long-term game.** One does not transform into a Casanova overnight, but rather its a process of conscious self-improvement that spans years. Power does not randomly fall upon a man, but it is SEIZED. Excellence of character is forged.

Power is a game and if you're not at the field being a player - you're usually the one who is being played by an actual player. In life there are two types of people:

- **TYPE #1:** A Wolf (🐺 Predator), and
- **TYPE #2:** A Sheep (🐑 Prey).

The wolf use the sheep for their own personal gain - just like employers use employees for their own personal gain, or how Alpha Males tool Beta Males. **In the game of life, strong men control the weak, but the clever and skilled control the strong.** If you are not part of the predator crowd then you're by default part of the prey crowd. **In life, you have to be a predator. <u>You have to be extremely aggressive in going after what you want.</u>**

III. BE AN APEX ALPHA.

ALPHA TRAITS

- One of the defining traits of the Alpha Male is that he TAKES WHAT HE WANTS. **While the beta male is drowning in "What ifs" and perpetual analysis, <u>the Alpha Male TAKES ACTION TO GET WHAT HE WANTS.</u>**
- **The Alpha Male cultivates the proactive behavioral tendencies of taking consistent, daily, focused, MASSIVE action to bring himself closer to his goals.**
- **The Alpha Male values himself and his own personal agenda more than anything else in the world.** That is why he is able to advance forward in life at incredible speeds - leaving people-pleasing suck-ups in the dust. While soy boys are wasting their valuable life force slaving away to please a pussy they've pedestalized, the Alpha Male is busy GETTING SHIT DONE and CLIMBING THE PATH TO POWER IN SOCIETY.

BETA TRAITS

- The Beta Males cultivates passivity tendencies. The Beta male waits for sexual opportunities to find him, while the Alpha male creates them.
- The Beta Male is stuck in a perpetual procrastination trap that spans years (and sometimes his entire pathetic existence).
- The Beta is constantly "getting ready to take radical action" but never actually hits the "take radical action NOW" phase. He is "too smart for his own good" - stuck in never-ending overthinking.

THE ALPHA VERSUS BETA SPECTRUM:

Whether your skin is thick or thin determines your success with women. The Beta male doesn't act upon on sexual opportunities because he is terrified of rejection (his fragile ego can't handle the burn), but the Alpha Male acts upon sexual opportunities immediately because he knows that occasional rejection is part of the game; **the Alpha Male doesn't give a fuck if a woman rejects him because he knows that he can get another.** He who fears rejection has already granted women too much power over him; he who retains "Walk Away Power" saves himself from misery and being dragged into toxic and one-sided relationships.

Always retain Walk Away Power and that's done by having other options in your life, having sharp game (so you know that you can go out on any day and get a woman), and continuously raising your sexual market value and sharpening your skills. MAKE EVERY DAY COUNT.

The Beta Male is plagued with self-doubt, but the Alpha Male makes decisions with confidence and decisiveness -

making him a natural leader. **How you behave in life, is how you behave with women.** If you find yourself constantly doubting yourself then this kind of behavioral tendencies will be relevant when dealing with women as well. This is why it is important that you DOMINATE EVERYTHING.

HOLD NOTHING BACK. YOU ARE THE CHAOS. YOU ATTACK LIFE WITH FULL FORCE, AND GET SHIT HANDLED. NO MATTER WHAT LIFE THROWS AT YOU, YOU FUCKING HANDLE IT.

Being an Alpha Male communicates volumes to women simply by the way that you live your life, and the values you stand for. Being an Alpha Male makes women WANT to follow your lead - creating a river trickling down their panties. Remember: **a worthy Dom creates a willing Submissive.**

❄

IV. YOU BECOME WHAT YOU THINK, SO THINK POSITIVE.

8 MORE COMMON TRAPS IN THE SEXUAL MARKETPLACE

- **#6) THE TIME SINKS TRAP** spending countless hours binge watching TV shows instead of **developing and sharpening high demand skills**,
- **#7) THE SMALL POND TRAP** Wasting incredibly valuable time hanging out with loser friends instead of **cultivating a tribe of HIGHLY DRIVEN KILLERS**,

- **#8) LIVING IN THE PAST TRAP** Engaging in emotional suicide by endlessly thinking about prior rejections, past mistakes and futile pointless thinking ("what if I would have done ____?" or "If only I would have avoided ___") instead of **having a VISION, creating GOALS for that VISION, TAKING ACTION DAILY, and EXECUTING LIKE THE TERMINATOR.**
- **#9)BEING A PEOPLE-PLEASER TRAP** Being obsessed over low-quality women who don't care about them in, who treat them like shit and don't have much to offer besides a used-pussy instead of focusing on further **developing yourself to BECOME AN APEX PREDATOR.** When you're focusing on other people (by endlessly scrolling through their social media feed) then you aren't focusing on yourself. **Self-development requires a significant level of selfishness because it takes a ton of fucking time, and energy;** if you're busy running favors for other people then you won't have leftover time/energy for yourself for your own development.
- **#10) THE NEGATIVE MIND TRAP** Constantly repeating negative thoughts such as "the situation is hopeless", "I am so disgusting that no women will want me", or "learning self-help theories is useless because it never leads to anywhere" instead of focusing on your strengths, talents and creating a **HIGHLY PRACTICAL PLAN OF SPECIFIC BEHAVIORS THAT LEAD TO RESULTS.**

Why do guys FUCK THEMSELVES UP by engaging in self-sabotage behavior?

#11) TAKING THE BRIBE OF THE DARK SIDE TRAP

Don't you get it motherfucker? **There is a certain kind of addiction to misery.** Guys engage in self-sabotage behavior because there is a hidden emotional-pay off.

- By saying things like "I am worthless. No women will want me - no matter how hard I try" you are able to create justification for being lazy.
- By thinking self-sabotage negative thoughts such as "There is no point in approaching beautiful women because I know that it won't work anyways" then you release the responsibility off your shoulders, and you get to waste away valuable evenings playing video-games without feeling guilty.
- By focusing on past mistakes you can procrastinate and avoid confronting challenges in the present.

If you look closely there is always some hidden benefit to engaging in a self-sabotage behavior that is FUCKING YOU UP. If you can identify the hidden payoff then you can bribe yourself by counteracting it. Create a bigger incentive for doing what's right and living a life that leads to COMPLETELY DOMINATING EVERYTHING THAT YOU DO.

SEDUCTION IS A LIFESTYLE.

#12: "THE PLEASURE HABITS DIE HARD" TRAP

You'll know where you will be in 5 years based on your current rate of daily progress. You have to kill bad negative habits (that are addictive because they provide a sort of pleasure) by replacing them with *positive habits* that you have personally engineered to give a greater amount of pleasure than the *negative habits*. **A successful seducer has a set of lifestyle habits that lead to him meeting and having sex with beautiful women - almost on autopilot. Hence, seduction is a lifestyle - living these daily habits day in and day out.**

The Stacker Method for Getting Laid

- For instance: create a daily habit of getting work done or hanging out in areas where there is a high traffic of beautiful women who are receptive to meeting strangers. These places include but are not limited to coffee shops, the library, Yoga club, a local park, or various social clubs at your local college campus. Then set a personal goal to talk to at least one girl at this location every single day. Don't be a lazy ass motherfucking bitch ass motherfucker cunt soy boy bastard who is afraid to leave the house; if that's you then close this book right now and live under the bed at your mama's house (still suckling her warm milk). **This book isn't for BIIIIIATCHE PUSSIES.**
- Another example: create a daily habit of following up on the leads that you have acquired. This is simple as having a set time each day (perhaps 10:00-10:30pm) where you call up the girls on your phone to flirt, and sustain the connection.
- Finally, have a weekly habit of inviting women out for cool events in the city during the weekend.

First you create your lifestyle habits and then these lifestyle habits create you. The problem is that some guys have lifestyle habits that are destroying them (sleeping in late, hanging out with the wrong crowd of people, being in a micro environment that is toxic, being addicted to fapping etc) and they are having difficulty overcoming these behavioral tendencies because the behaviors happen automatically - on autopilot - without their conscious awareness. The goal is to consciously create a set of positive habits that replace the negative ones and then stack positive habits until you **BECOME A FORCE TO BE RECKONED WITH.**

❄

V. EXUDE EXTREME CONFIDENCE. YOU ARE THE GREAT PRIZE TO BE WON.

#13: The Being Afraid-to-Make-a-Move Trap

MAKING MOVES ON A WOMAN AND GETTING REJECTED IS INFINITELY BETTER than not making moves on a woman and not getting rejected. In Pook's words "Rejection is better than regret."

Every time you advance (do something specific on a particular woman in order to lead the interaction to sex), you learn something in the process. This is true - even if you are met with a harsh blowout. He who keeps advancing will eventually learn enough to be a master.

In contrast, someone who has a fragile ego won't escalate (and won't even try) because he is too terrified of getting blown-out: will learn NOTHING. Someone who doesn't even attempt to make moves on women sends a signal to his unconscious mind that he is UNWORTHY. He rejected himself because he allowed his limiting beliefs of his self-worth win over.

Old belief:

- *"I am too unattractive for any woman to like me, so I won't even try because it won't work anyways."*

- *"I don't want to approach because it will be cringe, and I'll feel like shit."*

REFRAME:

- *"I have a lot to offer women. Being with me is one of THE BEST CHOICES SHE CAN MAKE."*
- *"Regardless of the output of this particular approach, I am going to have fun and learn something from it. Even the worst rejections, make the best stories."*

Be acutely aware of your strengths and talents. Write them down. By being aware of what you're good at then you have it ready-at-hand to be used to help you in life. Women find excellence in almost any particular field to be incredibly attractive. Know what you're exceptional in, and then go to venues that where people gather (women included) who value that which you're exceptional in. A key in speaking Womenese is to show the best parts of yourself.

MY DEAR SON, I ASK OF YOU ONLY ONE THING THAT YOU SHOULD REMEMBER. REMEMBER THAT: HE WHO HESITATES IS LOST.

Why is confidence the ultimate sex appeal?

Just like you are attracted to slim women (because slimness is an indicator of fertility), women are attracted to CONFIDENCE (because confidence is a solid indicator of competence). Generally speaking: confident men are KILLING IT IN LIFE which is why they are confident in the first place.

Women don't have the time to give each guy a FULL CHANCE and to LEARN EVERYTHING ABOUT HIM, so they use shortcuts such as looking at a man's level of confidence, style, and his status within society, to ascertain if he is worth getting to know. These shortcuts save them a lot of time.[13]

Confidence and status will get you in the door; conversation, escalation and giving value will get you into the bedroom.

4 ESSENTIAL KEYS TO HAVING CONFIDENCE AND HOW TO CONVEY IT IN A MANNER THAT TURNS WOMEN ON

- 1// Be extremely confident when you are around women. Don't just be a little confident around women; **be extremely confident.**
- 2// **It is better to be irrationally confident than rationally insecure.** Even if you have plenty of reasons to be insecure, focus on the reasons why you are THE BOSS. Show confidence - even if "it doesn't make sense". **Be extremely confident - even if it's on an irrational level.**
- 3// If you aren't feeling confident, take some time to **verbalize your strengths,** talents, skills and the type of value that you have to offer women. Meditate on your strong points, and leverage them in interactions with women. **If you aren't using what you're really good at then you missed the fucking point, bitch motherfucker.**
- 4// **Stand up for yourself.** Spend time with people that bring you up, and inspire you to be your best. Don't spend time with people that put you down - compromising your self-esteem in the process. Have standards, boundaries, and a healthy sense of independence. Further, don't ascertain

your level of worth based on your results with women, or the opinion of other people.

Just like confidence is sexy, self-doubt is repulsive to women. Hesitation is a show of self-doubt. Hesitation comes from being unsure of yourself, and delaying taking action, so that you can confirm your own worth in your mind. Even if you have legitimate questions about yourself and what you are doing, when you are in the field **EXUDE 100% STRENGTH AND A BULLETPROOF FRAME.**

Make decisions with certainty and decisiveness. Women will follow a leader who believes in his path. **BE A WARRIOR ON HIS LIFE PURPOSE.**

SEND A MESSAGE WITH YOUR ACTIONS, WHAT YOU STAND FOR, AND THE WAY THAT YOU LIVE YOUR LIFE

Simply by the way that you live your life, you are sending signals to women about your worth (or lack of it). Understand this right now and right here: **most of Womenese is non-verbal.** This is why guys often fuck themselves up by sending low-worth signals to women without even being aware that they are sending out these signals.

By living the life of an Alpha Warrior who

- knows what he wants out of life,
- has clearly defined goals that are reviewed daily,
- goes after what he wants aggressively,
- values his time,
- respects himself enough to retain Walk Away Power,
- lives in accordance with his values,
- doesn't waste time with petty drama,
- doesn't put but with second class behavior,

- doesn't dwell around negative unambitious people, and
- doesn't waste time going on endless conversations and dates to nowhere .

you'll unconsciously send "I AM SEXY" signals to women.

---

1. Every woman has a vagina. Some women have something of more substantial value to offer. You have to have an acute understanding what you bring to the table in a relationship because that is going to be a source of tremendous confidence. Then look at what the particular woman you are with is bringing to the table. A relationship is simply a constant value-exchange over a long period of time. If you're doing all of the giving and none of the taking then that is a serious problem. First of all, by not taking any value from the woman who you are dealing with: you won't be that motivated to keep going and keep investing in her. Second of all, a woman is biologically designed to only value what she works for. If she isn't working on your behalf and sweating to jump through hoops to win you over, then she won't really appreciate you. A woman needs to put in effort for you in order to value you. This is why it is not petty to ask "What is doing for me?" and "What does she have to offer besides a used-vagina that guys have used within 24 hours of meeting her?" but rather these questions are practical in nature. Create a pathway for a woman to sweat for you, and she'll appreciate you a thousandfold. In contrast, play easy to get and easy to keep and she'll take you for granted. In this specific issue, you are the same: you're more likely to value and apply the information presented in this book because you paid for it. It's human nature to cherish investments, but disregard the free/easily acquired. Don't hate women for their dark nature; just play the fucking game and WIN.
2. If you don't even have a plan then you are leaving everything to chance and hope. Hope and chance are not effective strategies. **Some plan is better than no plan.** Not bothering to prepare by having a specific strategy for your sex life is plain stupid.
3. Actions create beliefs just like beliefs create actions. The mind is always listening. If you behave like you are a 10, you will come to believe that you are a 10. If you allow a woman to treat you like shit, she will eventually come to believe that you are shit.
4. You become what you think. Thoughts literally shape your emotions, character and decisions. Everything you see around you was once a thought . By thinking positively about yourself, and holding yourself in high esteem in your mind then you foster sexy confidence. **Attack the behaviors, and not the person.** This is a key concept in learning self-help

material. Learning self-help content doesn't mean that you suck with women, or that you are awful. It means that you are good, and want to be great!

5. The unconscious mind is more powerful than the conscious mind. Most of your behaviors are on auto-pilot directed by your unconscious mind.
6. It's pathetic to see a high status man get into a relationship and suddenly lose his own identity in the process of creating rapport. It will go as far as his losing male friendships, personal goals and compromising his life mission. A sexual relationship is a beautiful thing, but NEVER NEVER NEVER let it be at the cost of your soul. There are more things in life than just pussy. Know what your purpose is in life. Create a vision. Have daily goals that you review every day. Pussy is not the end goal. While you are delving into the world of Womenese, don't get lost in it; just gain enough practical knowledge to be effective in dealing with women, but don't get drowned in abstract theories that are irrelevant or non-actionable.
7. A woman who has had many sexual partners compromises her ability to form close bonds.
8. The smart female seducer will use sex as a way to gain power in the relationship.
9. Sex should occur within approximately seven hours accumulated over the span of 1-3 dates.
10. Time is the currency that life runs on. The older you get the less of it you have. The young are the richest, while the old are the poorest.
11. Even if you read every seduction book ever written, you won't get results until you apply what you've learned in the field. What you get out of this book is determined by the extent that you apply the principles in real world situations, and consciously practice the techniques mentioned.
12. Just like a woman goes out of her way to consume value from the man she is with, it's important for you to be clear about what you want in the relationship and TAKE IT. Having a strong sense of purpose and being decisive about what you want out of life are core Alpha Male Traits that TURN WOMEN ON.
13. Women are often better players of the game than men are. Don't be tricked by a pretty face and a facade of submissive ignorance.

1

FAST START: HOW TO TALK TO GIRLS, 6 FUNDAMENTALS

BE INTERESTING 🔪.

1. **Add energy, enthusiasm, and passion to your words.** If you don't even care about what you have to say, then don't expect others to care. In contrast, if you think what you have to say is interesting and you're naturally excited about it, then women will be more inclined to listen to you.

Talk about what is interesting to you, and exciting events that have happened to you. When you discuss your life's passions then you'll naturally be enthusiastic. Women feed on the positive energy that you exude when you talk passionately about your Life's Mission.

This is why having a vision that is more important than her is critical. It has been said: "*The best way to get a woman is not be out to get a woman.*" A woman wants to be a helper to your Life Mission - not the Life Mission itself. She yearns to be a part of your ambitious journey to success. Know your purpose. Know the answer to this question "Where do you see yourself five years from now?"

POWER IS THE ULTIMATE SEX APPEAL.

2. Have powerful body-language when communicating with women. Often how you say something is more important than what you are actually saying; hence, your delivery skills are crucial. **You can have the best pickup lines in the world, but if the delivery is off then the pickup lines won't hit.** If you body-language is weak then women won't take you seriously. Here is a checklist for good body-language when communicating with women. Each one of these is incredibly important.

- ✅ #1) Be **LOUD.**
- ✅ #2) Have a **DEEP TONALITY.**
- ✅ #3) Hold **STRONG EYE-CONTACT.**
- ✅ #4) Take your time when talking. Talk slower at times to emphasize key points. **GOOD PACING** is vital. 🔑
- ✅ #5) Use **PAUSES** to build anticipation.
- ✅ #6) **TOUCH** to emphasize key points.
- ✅ #7) Use **GESTURES** to emphasize key points.
- ✅ #8) **TAKE UP SPACE** when talking to women. Keep your feet apart. Have a Power-Posture.
- ✅ #9) **HAVE VARIETY** in your tonality, temp and volume.
- ✅ #10) Communicate with NON-VERBAL body-language such as your posture, and practiced **FACIAL EXPRESSIONS.**
- ✅ #11) Practice emotional regulation techniques and meditation skills to communicate from a position of having a **RESOURCEFUL EMOTIONAL STATE**, and peace of mind. Being relaxed will help you avoid nervous ticks, facial flinches, or signaling stress.

- ✅ #12) Keep your head up, and chest out. Keep your back straight. Lean back. **OWN THE SPACE.**
- ✅ #12) Feel good. Enjoy the experience in the present moment. Flash a **GENUINE SMILE.**
- ✅ #13) Amplify your volume and **SPEAK CLEARLY.** Articulate yourself well.
- ✅ #14) Sit down, lean against the wall, or get into a comfortable position. This is known as **LOCKING IN.** Confident men don't position themselves in an uncomfortable position when communicating.
- ✅ #15) Command the environment. Move things around. Control and adjust things in the environment. Behave like **THE PLACE YOU ARE IN IS YOUR HOME.**
- 🛑 #16) DON'T 🛑 Talk quietly. Talking quietly is the most effective way to have women ignore you. If you don't even take yourself seriously then why should women?
- 🛑 #17) DON'T 🛑 Have a high pitched tonality. Research done on studying high pitched tonality versus low pitched tonality revealed that the latter is more influential towards impacting people, and is more attractive to women.
- 🛑 #18) DON'T 🛑 Have evasive eye-contact and darting eyes. Eye-contact is one way that close connections are formed. It's especially important to hold eye-contact when leading her logistically; take her hand and fucking lead.
- 🛑 #19) DON'T 🛑 Use fast moving gestures that reveal nervousness - instead of slow moving gestures. **High status body-language is like moving through water.** Fast jerky movements reveal nervousness and overcompensating due to

insecurities. Another example: when a woman calls you from a different direction, don't quickly move your head like rapid fire, but rather slowly move and acknowledge her presence.

- #20) DON'T Not take up any space at all - which is submissive body-language and reveals weakness. **Women want to mate with the Apex Alpha which is why it's imperative that you exude dominant, powerful, and strong body-language. <u>Be the most dominant man in the room.</u>**
- #21) DON'T Having monotone delivery and only using 1 type of tone the entire time. A predictable tonality makes one boring to listen to. **Variety is the spice of life.**
- #22) DON'T Keep a poker-face during the entire interaction - which is part of a larger problem of being too serious and intense instead of being playful and flirtatious. Generally speaking, women at parties would prefer to relax and have light fun banter instead of engaging in intense conversations about the meaning of the universe. **Light conversations precede deep conversations.**
- #23) DON'T Be in a non-resourceful emotional state which doesn't lead to effective communication. Remember: the emotions that you feel within yourself, manifest themselves in your body-language. **By managing your inner-emotional state, you automatically manage your outer-body-language.**
- #24) DON'T Keep your head down, and look down. Don't Lean in and be hunching. Stop sitting with bad posture when you're in front of a computer for hours at a day.

- 🔘 #25) DON'T 🔘 Mumble, or stutter your words. Don't speak in a manner that is difficult to understand. If people have to say "what?" That's a strong sign that you aren't communicating clearly.
- 🔘 #26) DON'T 🔘 Touch your face during communications, or pace back and forth (both behaviors reveal nervousness). When approaching a woman, if you feel nervous then just imagine how she must feel.
- 🔘 #27) DON'T 🔘 Speak quickly like you're rushing to get through your message because otherwise people will stop listening. **Play the pauses.**
- 🔘 #28) DON'T 🔘 Always keep a Resting Bitch Face on, and forget to smile. If you're suffering, other people around you will feel those negative emotions and be turned off. This is especially true if you have a anti-seductive habit of complaining and focusing on the negative in life. **Smile from a place of overflowing positive emotions.**
- 🔘 #29) 🔘 DON'T 🔘 Use meaningless filler words that take up time, but don't actually contribute any sort of value. Examples include: "Umm..", "Uhh…", "Like…" **Use pauses instead of filler words.**
- 🔘#30) 🔘 DON'T 🔘 When engaging in a lengthy conversation, be standing while the girl is sitting down. The fact that she is relaxed, but you're putting yourself in a relatively uncomfortable position just to talk to her is giving away subjective social status. **Alpha males don't make themselves uncomfortable just to talk to girls.**

It's your delivery of the content and belief that the content is worth listening to that carries it enough for women to WANT TO LISTEN TO.

3. Learn to communicate with non-verbals. In fact, most of communication occurs non-verbally. Practice communicating with your body-language (including having good facial expressions, posture, and gestures that are congruent to the content) to emphases important points. For instance, when approaching a female stranger on the opening line: it's a good idea to open over the shoulder and to appear like you're about to leave because it has a disarming effect.

BE A LIFELONG LEARNER ✏️.

4. Learn about what's new in the world, and learn more about subjects that are interesting to women. Travel. Do crazy bold shit, so that you can talk about it later. Expand your interests by taking on cool hobbies.

One of the reasons why guys have difficulty talking to girls is because they don't have enough knowledge about subjects that women are actually interested in. Being interesting is simply a matter about sharing insights that bring depth to specific subjects that women care about.

Simply by reading up on subjects such as Yoga, Meditation, Astrology, or Spirituality then you'll infinitely be more interesting to women. Become a relative "expert" in at least one subject that women find interesting by reading at least 3 books on it. This it will put you in a position to be a teacher who can show women the world, and take them on amazing experiences. Teaching her is a technique to establish dominance and get her used to following your lead.

A woman's favorite subject is herself, and a woman is absolutely fascinated by how she is perceived by the world. Hence, making clever observations about who she is and how she presents herself is effective conversation fodder. Become an authority in her world by being knowledgable in the fields of knowledge that she is fascinated by - first and foremost: herself. This is why cold reads (which are statements about who she is as a person) are considered to be chick-crack.

ESTABLISH COMMONALITY ✗.

5. Look for what you have in common with the woman. **Feelings of (emotional connection) rapport comes from having common interests, goals, and values.** Identify a woman's interests and see if your interests match hers. Discuss insights on topics of shared interest.

When you're introducing a new subject of conversation, pay really close attention to her non-verbals. Her non-verbals will reveal if that subject of conversation is actually interesting to her, or if she is just being polite.[1] Know the subjects that you enjoy talking about, and that you're knowledgable in. Test different subjects until you get a hit.

It's also important to keep a mental note of the subjects of conversation that a woman brings up on her own initiative. These are are strong clues that she finds them fascinating. **In general, aim to be a detective in figuring out which subjects of conversation excite the woman who you are dealing with.**

BUILD YOUR ARSENAL OF SOUND BITES ✗.

6. Keep a player's black notebook. Jot down good lines that have worked for you in the past, and thus empirically shown to generate results for you in the field. The best lines comes from natural spontaneous conversations that you've had with women; the best conversational content is that which is most congruent with your personality and makes sense in the situation that you are in (which is why using memorized

pickup lines or routines that you've read off the internet isn't as effective as developing your own content).

Study comedians and stand-up improvisational comedy to learn the speech patterns and verbal structure that they use to make themselves interesting enough to get millions of people to listen to them. Write down interesting quotes, phrases or expressions that you have heard that you would like to start using in your own personal conversations. The goal isn't to become someone else (even someone who you really admire), but to **adopt their effective communication elements for your OWN PERSONAL STYLE.**

---

1. Establish a woman's baseline (the norm) of body-language behavior to be able to differentiate between a mere Polite Response versus Attraction Response. Women will often give you a Polite Response to avoid hurting your feelings. **You want to focus on the elements and mindsets behind the behaviors that you did which evoked an Attraction Response within the woman.**

2

MEN AND WOMEN ARE DIFFERENT PLANETS AND THIS IS WHY IT MATTERS.

MEN AND WOMEN **are VERY different.** You have to let go of the bullshit feminist propaganda, feminists want to brainwash you into believing, that men and women "are the same" and "equal". Men and women are VERY different;

- **THOUGHT**. They *think* differently.
- **BEHAVIOR**. They *behave* differently.
- **ACTION.** They make *decisions* differently.
- **PHILOSOPHY**. The process of how they look at the world (and *interpret* events) is different.
- **SPEECH**. And most importantly: they *communicate* differently.

This is crucial for you to understand because viewing a woman as "a man with a vagina" leads is the equivalent of playing chess with a blindfold on. If you treat a woman in the same exact way that you treat a man then YOUR GAME IS FUCKED.

Don't treat a woman like she is a man - who just happens to have a vagina. Treat a woman differently than you would treat a man because the woman operates on Feminine OS and speaks Womenese, while a man operates on Masculine OS and speaks Manese.

THE TRUTH: WOMEN LIVE ON A DIFFERENT PLANET, AND COMMUNICATE WITH A DIFFERENT LANGUAGE.

FUCK political correctness. This is the truth (be willing to verbalize this 5 times over for the concept to sink in):

Men communicate in the masculine style 🔪, and women communicate in the feminine style 🍑.

It's problematic when newbie seducers think women ALSO communicate in the masculine style. These clueless guys will interpret a woman's words incorrectly because they fail to realize that she is communicating in the FEMININE which is an entirely **divergent language** and operates based on a different set of variables (e.g. emotion, ego, primal imperatives etc).

The core of problems in long-term sexual relationships is using Manese Tools to understand Womenese.

These clueless guys use the rules of masculine communication ("Manese") to interpret feminine communication and then are left scratching their heads when her actions are misaligned to her words. **They're trying to interpret Womenese with the tools of Manese** (e.g. they think women mean what they say literally, say what mean literally, and uphold their word as honor dictates).

These guys are projecting themselves unto others - erroneously concluding that women are just like them and think just like them. Don't project your own mind unto women because women don't see the world as you do, and don't operate based on the same rules as you operate in. **Don't assume women think a certain way - just because you think that way.**

It's important that we establish the truth immediately that women might as well live on a different planet because of how different they are from men. **Women speak womenese, motherfucker.**

- **The way that a woman shows love to a man** is different than the way a man shows love to a woman.
- **The way that a woman navigates through the world** and makes decisions is entirely different than the way a man operates.
- **The way that a woman communicates** is entirely different than the way a man communicates.

Women communicate in a secret language that is understand by other women and by men who fuck women. My goal with this book is to teach you how to decipher this secret language so that you can understand the meaning behind her words, and if you wanted to, could communicate to her in Womanese so she could TRULY UNDERSTAND YOUR THOUGHTS.

Remember: woman want to fuck guys who "just get IT". If she has to explain what she means then inherently the guy "is a loser who doesn't get IT". Being a guy who "JUST GETS IT" implies social proof, social intelligence, and status. Be that guy.[1]

The irony is that women expect a guy to just "get it" without explaining what "it" is. They'll shame men for reading seduction self-help books like this one that reveals the truth about women, while simultaneously reading advice columns in popular female magazine.

WHY DECODING A WOMAN'S LANGUAGE MATTERS

Sun Tzu once said "If you know the enemy and know yourself, you need not fear the result of a hundred battles." Practical knowledge is potential power; applying practical knowledge in the field leads to actual power.

It's a tremendous help to have an acute understanding of "Female OS" operating system to be able to seduce her mind, and unlock her legs. Understand this well: dominating a woman's mind leads to dominating her body.

Mind fuck her, body fuck her and then you OWN HER SOUL. To mind fuck her, you have to understand her mind. **A woman's communication is the window into seeing how her mind operates** - so being able to decipher the truth behind her words is essential.

If you know how a woman thinks, her value system, her belief system, and her emotional-buttons then you'll be able predict how she will behave in response to your sequence of behaviors. **When you understand female nature on a deep level, then women's behaviors become pathetically predictable.** You should understand a woman (and her emotional, psychological, primitive and physical needs) better than she understands herself.

Breakdown on why Womenese Matters:

- **<u>If you understand a woman's deep desires then you will be able to give her that which she values and that will MAKE YOU INCREDIBLY VALUABLE TO HER.</u>** If you don't understand WHAT her primal needs ARE, then your value offerings will be disregarded as useless. Remember: women are value-consumers and are attracted to men who value-givers. **<u>You can't be a value-giver if you don't speak enough Womanese to understand what type of value she deems valuable in the first place.</u>**
- If you understand the true meaning behind a woman's communications to you and you're able to acutely read her like a book, then you will be able play her like a violin, and eventually bang the shit out of her. The goal is to constantly progress TOWARDS FUCKING HER IN THE PUSSY - without ever being in the friendzone, wasting time on pointless "going nowhere" perpetual texts, or spending endless dates "getting to know each other". **Put simply: if you know what a woman is thinking and feeling then you'll**

be able to calibrate your strategy accordingly.

- **A woman is constantly leaving clues on how to effectively seduce her, and these clues can be picked up by a man who is fluent in Womanese.** A woman is constantly sending out signals on what you have to do to FUCK HER, but most men are unable to decipher these clues and as a result of this the sexual opportunity is left uncapitalized.
- **A woman's body-language will betray the truth.** If you simply pay attention to her body-language, you'll be able to identify if what you just did TURNED HER ON 🔥 (so you can do more of that behavior), or turned her OFF (so you can do less of that behavior).

❄

I'M NOT GOING to sugarcoat the truth. Knowing how to have successful sexual relationships with women is an important part of being a man. The moves you make to advance the connection towards sex is based on how you read the woman, and how you read the situation. So it's important that you learn Fluent Womenese **to accurately read the signals that a woman is sending out (while cutting out the noise) to paint an accurate map of reality.**

Nice guys have difficulty exciting women on a primal level because their speech patterns are overly friendly. They fail to understand that women enjoy being teased and appreciate a man who is a challenge. Playing easy-to-get, being a "Yes" Man, being overly available, being safe/predictable, being a push-over bores women to death. **A woman's perception of the world is based entirely on how she is feeling at in the moment, which is why her perception of reality is volatile and likely to change from day to day.** If you make her excited then by being anti-nice and having an EDGE to your communication style then she'll form perspectives about you that are positive to rationalize having guilt-free sex. If you bore half to death by being every other average guy then she'll feel anti-climactic and form perspectives about who you are based on those emotions. Remember: a man forms his perception of reality based on logic and empirical evidence, but a woman forms her perspective entirely based on what she feels is the truth based on her current emotional state.

---

1. It's worth noting that a guy who just "gets it", doesn't have to verbalize what "it" is to women. Just because you understand the dynamics of what is happening, doesn't mean that you have to announce them. On the contrary, it is better to feign ignorance and appear effortless, natural and spontaneous. After all, women would prefer sex being something that "just happens" rather than meticulously planned for. That being said, don't let this become a limiting belief. You can absolutely tell a woman that you want to fuck her, and then fuck her. In fact, you can break many rules of

the game and still get the girl in the end, as long as you have confidence, balls, and you're a value-giver.

3

WHY SHE DOESN'T ALWAYS MEAN WHAT SHE SAYS, AND SAY WHAT SHE MEANS

Memes like these depict women as "impossible" to understand and perpetuate the problem. LET GO OF THIS LIMITING BELIEF. While it's not possible to understand a woman 100%, using maxims and general principles depicted in this book: you'll understand enough about women to radically increase your effectiveness in banging pussy.

Why doesn't a woman just say what she mean?

A MAN'S thoughts and intentions are aligned with his words. A man will communicate DIRECTLY. He means what he says, and says what he means. If he has an issue with you, he will confront you directly. A man who communicates indirectly and uses passive aggressiveness is a feminized soy boy.

In contrast, a woman often communicates indirectly. They will say one thing, but mean something entirely different. They will mean to say one thing, but actually say something entirely different. If a woman has an issue with you, she will often be passive aggressive instead of blurting out what the core of the problem is.

- **MASCULINE STYLE OF COMMUNICATION:** **Meaning = words.**
- **FEMININE STYLE OF COMMUNICATION:** **Meaning =/= words.**

A woman is often NOT able to accurately represent her thoughts, perspective, intentions and feelings with the words that she uses. What a woman says to you can be COMPLETELY DIFFERENT than the true meaning behind the words. This is due to multiple Distortion Factors such as ego, conformity, peer pressure, anti-slut-defense, fear of confrontation, fear of social discomfort etc. These Distortion Factors will lead to her bending (distorting) the truth

Her words (if taken literally) actually grossly misrepresent her inner-world.

- She'll tell you the truth is "A" but by using your female-decoding intel (because you speak fluent in Womanese) you will see that the truth is NOT "A" but rather: "B".
- She'll tell you the truth is "A, B, and C" but by using your female decoding intel, you'll recognize the truth is NOT "A", or "C", but rather a harder version of "B".

To the untrained eye, a woman's words are quite misleading. Hence, it's vital to take a woman's words through a decoding filter to cut out the bullshit, untangle the misleading statements, and find the truth. A woman's words are more clues about reality (mixed in with a lot of misleading statements) rather than reality itself.

KEY: Train yourself to NOT be bullshitted by a smooth-talker, and to see the RAW REALITY/TRUE MEANING of the SITUATION. This is a general principle of communication that goes beyond just dealing with women, and extends to dealing with people in general. Don't believe everything you hear. Nor should you believe everything you read.

By swallowing the metaphorical Red Pill and being determined the truth - no matter how painful - you will be in the best position to succeed. Learning to understand the language women speak - Womanese - will enable you to decipher the situation and accurately read the beautiful women in your life. This way you won't get hit with curve balls, and unexpected surprises; for everything a woman does, you would have already anticipated it. **Always be a few steps ahead.**

THE DON QUIXOTE EFFECT

- **MASCULINE STYLE OF COMMUNICATION: Words = actions.**
- **FEMININE STYLE OF COMMUNICATION: Words =/=actions.**

Women can say ONE THING, but then DO something ENTIRELY DIFFERENT.

THE DON QUIXOTE EFFECT: women will often

say things based on how they wish the world was - instead of saying things based on how the world actually is. For instance, a woman may tell you things that encourage you to be a nice guy to her, even though those exact behaviors lower her sexual attraction for you. This is because she WISHES that she was attracted to a nice guy, and she'll go as far to even pretend that she is attracted to him; however, she truly fails to understand that she is **disgusted** by NIGE GUYS and NICE GUY BEHAVIORS.

More examples:

- A woman will claim that she likes nice guys, but then spend all of her time chasing bad boys.
- A woman can claim that she is being confused and frustrated by her boyfriend, but the truth is that his behavior TURNS HER ON. Hence, she can't stop talking about him.
- She says that she really wants you to be sweet to her, but immediately gets COLD the moment you are: then you know that she is TURNED ON by challenging behavior.

If you hear a woman say one thing, but do something completely different: believe the latter. Actions speak much louder than words ever could.

Talk is cheap. Actions show substance. **What women claim they want is often different than what they actually respond to on a behavioral level.** What women claim they want is often just theoretical and based on fantasies (unrealistic unattainable personal goals), but what they actually respond to on a behavioral level is based on what's practical and the current reality.

Women will often "white lie" to avoid uncomfortable confrontations. It his body-language, micro-

expressions, and actions that betray her by revealing THE TRUTH. Learn to not take a woman's words at the surface level, but look to see the implied frames that she is trying to set, the overall meaning of the interaction, and messages communicated by her body-language.

There is saying "people vote with their feet"; this means that a woman's behaviors speaks louder than words ever could. By studying a woman's actions and body-language, you'll quickly assess her true feelings about you. She can be verbally sweet, but if her actions reveal a different story then don't waste your time. **OR she can be verbally repulsive but if she's still talking with you and her body-language is receptive then you can still fuck her on that day.**

Do more of what works based on a woman's behaviors, and less of what she says she wants (but doesn't respond to on a behavioral level). Live life according to empirical evidence - not according to unproven theories said by women.

THE FIVE FACTORS TO PAY ATTENTION TO ASCERTAIN THE TRUTH WHEN DEALING WITH WOMEN:

- #1) General Body-Language
- #2) Micro Expressions
- #3) Actions
- #4) Honest Signals
- #5) Google her Name, and Look into her Social Media Accounts (to see what kind of person she presents herself to the public - which will reveal who is striving to be)[1]

❄

FUCK FEMINIST PROPAGANDA. As mentioned multiple times, men and women are different, and part of that is: DIFFERENT COMMUNICATION STYLES.

By understanding the feminine style of communication, you'll be able to communicate to her in her own language for maximum impact. Hence, one of the goals is to understand Womenese and be able to speak it back to women.

The Masculine Communication Style

Men say what's on their mind. They are direct. Their words have weight to them because there is a code of honor. Men's verbalized thoughts have consistency because logic is consistent. Hence, a man's words are usually aligned to their surface level meaning.

The Feminine Communication Style

Women say what's on their heart. They talk based on how they feel at the moment.

Their words often don't have weight to them because women don't follow a code of honor. Women's verbalized thoughts don't have consistency because emotions are volatile. **She can say that she loves you today, but a few days later break up with you.** What she really meant is that she loves what you represent, the feelings that you make her feel, the value that you give (not you per se) and she'll continue to love you - as long as you continue to give her those things.

4 DISRUPTION FACTORS

It can be hard to decipher the true meaning behind a woman's words because:

- **even the woman herself doesn't understand** half the vomit that comes out of her mouth,
- **women buy into their own bullshit** and can have strong frames themselves,
- **the woman herself will often say things that if taken at face-value are very misleading,**
- **her words are based on how she feels at the moment and how she feels is liable to change.**

A woman actions and words are based on how she is feeling at the moment; just like her feelings are liable to change, so are her actions and words liable to quickly change from extreme to extreme. **Women mean what they say but only at that moment - when she feels what she feels then. After all, women live entirely on the emotions of the moment.** A woman's opinions and behaviors can change as soon as her feelings change.

In post breakups, women will often rewrite history in a manner that conveniently forgets the positive things that their ex-boyfriend did, and embellishes the negative things that were done.

The key to understanding how women communicate is to understand that women live in the emotions of the moment.

- According to her, if something feels true then it is true.
- If doing something feels good then she will do it.

To communicate on a woman's level then show how being with you is the most enjoyable and fun option for her; demonstrate, don't just explain.

To speak Womenese, minimize logical lectures and instead

communicate in a manner that is emotionally expressive. Touch a woman's emotional buttons through good story-telling, taboo words MOTHERFUCKER, and a style of communication designed for emotional impactfulness. **Women perceive the world through their feelings, so a style of communication designed to trigger a woman's emotions will be more impactful than a style of communication that is logical and emotionally dry.** This can be hard for high IQ men to implement because they are used to communicating solely on a logical plane, and completely disregard the emotional plane; to go from one world, to another world can be quite challenging for them.

---

1. When looking into a woman's social media account, only casually skim it for a maximum of five minutes - just to get a sense of what her core values are, what her hobbies are, what her ambitions are and so on. It's extremely unhealthy behavior to constantly be checking a woman's social media accounts and to comment with pedestalizing comments like the hordes of other thirsty men. By pedestalizing a woman with your behaviors, you end up pedestalizing her in your heart and mind. Female influencers don't respect their followers and certainly won't respect a thirsty guy writing thirsty comments. Don't waste your life living through the social media posts of someone else. Skim through casually for 5 minutes to gather some actionable-intel (about a woman who you are already communicating with in person in real life) but don't spend any more time than that.

4

What is verbal communication? Why does it matter

COMMUNICATION IS **the act of sending the selected ideas that are on your mind and the emotions that are in your heart, unto someone else.** Likewise, it is the process of receiving the ideas that are on the minds of other people, and accurately reading their emotional state.

Communication is a a two-way street. You are constantly sending out and receiving signals from women.

Womenese is the art of understanding the language of women, and being able to read the language of Women. You should have the ability to send out signals (either verbally or non-verbally) in a way that TURNS HER ON, and also understand the signals that she sends out to you in a manner that you are able to accurately read her emotional state, intent, and current sexual interest level in you.

The goal of Seductive Communication is to send out **Sexy Signals** (also known as **Attraction Spikes**) that amplify attraction and avoid sending out **Repulsive Signals** (also known as **Repulsion Spikes**) that decrease attraction.

- E.g. when you casually mention female friends in an entertaining story (where the punchline of the

story is something other than the fact that you have female friends), then you'll have effectively sent out Sexy Signals and spiked attraction.
- In contrast when you talk about how lonely you are, and that you haven't been on a date in a while then you've effectively sent out Repulsive Signals and decreased attraction.

Effective communication is important because it is medium of which connections are formed, value is exchanged, and interpersonal goals are achieved. **When you give a lot of value to someone, eventually you become valuable.** After value is exchanged in a mutually beneficial connection over a long period of time, sometimes a relationship is formed. For our purposes, this relationship is of a sexual nature. She feeds on your emotions, attention, and physical pleasure.

Fortunately for her, you're a man of abundance and you have plenty of that which she see desires. You are The Great Prize that she has been born to seek.

Women are value-consumers, and attracted to value givers. **By becoming an effective communicator, you'll be able to generate value from scratch.** I repeat: when you have the right communication skills, you'll be able to create on-command the value that women feed on.

Communication is a medium of giving value.

- Fun is a form of value. You can use communication to entertain, and improve the mood of others - achieving a therapeutic effect.
- Intrigue is a form of value. You can use communication to teach her fascinating facts about her (cold reading, astrology, palmistry, personality

type etc.) or her favorite subjects (yoga, meditation, spirituality, her ambitions).

DARK COMMUNICATION

Women are naturally manipulative (and are driven to achieve their personal agenda that benefits them directly - as is human nature in general), **so often the ideas that are they transmitting to you do not reflect reality.**[1]

- 1// Some men have been manipulated by a shitstorm of lies for so long that they've started to believe these lies as reality. This manipulation tactic used by women is known as Normalization.
- 2// Another dark communication tactic used by women, Gaslighting (making a man question his ability to form accurate perspectives of reality) is a tactic that is sometimes implemented by cunning women to take the man a notch down, so he becomes more easy to manipulate.

In Law #1, I discuss one of the primary fundamental concepts to speaking and understanding Womenese: don't always interpret a woman's words literally; ascertain the truth for yourself by using critical thinking skills, and looking at the hard evidence.

---

1. Womenese behavior can be difficult for men to grasp because in the world of men, one's word actually means something substantial. **A man can rely on another man's word because both men abide by honor to keep their word.** Women do not have this notion of honor; they only "honor" their ruthless opportunistic tendencies. The Truth in a woman's eyes is simply that which supports her personal agenda, that which she feels is true, and that which will help her form connections in the social circle that she finds herself within. In contrast, The Truth in the eyes of a man is based on empirical evidence, and cold logic - without being influenced by the peer pressure of conformity to the same extent.

5

An introduction to female psychology

Women see what they want to see.

SHE SEES the world through her own personal filter. She'll interpret events based on her own subjective point of view - seeing evidence that confirms with her prior beliefs and ignoring contradictory evidence.

The words that come out of her mouth are merely opinions - even if they sound like convincing facts. Fortunate is the man who doesn't believe everything he hears a woman say, but is skeptical; have your own independent opinion based on:

- critical thinking,
- empirical evidence,
- clusters (multiple pieces of evidence) and
- the assessment of independent unbiased third-party observers.[1]

Frame is your perspective of reality. When your frame is strong, a woman will accept your perspective of reality as her perspective of reality - resulting in a mutual understanding.

Even a dominant woman desires to submit to a more dominant and competent man than her. Even if a woman's frame is very, very strong, your frame must be even stronger. Sometimes it can seem like a woman is extremely certain about her view of reality and it can be tempting to give in to her perspective; even in this moment, your frame should be stronger. Her frame might be IRON STRONG, but your frame should be TITANIUM STRONG.

A woman finds it difficult to respect a man with minimal belief in his perception of reality. The liberal perspective of "everyone is right in their own way" is an ideological virus; **in any interaction, there can be only one version of the truth that is mutually acknowledged, and that version of the truth should be yours. He who controls the frame, controls the game.**

A woman will unconsciously misinterpret events so that it fits in with her prior understanding of reality.

- When a woman is attracted to you then (1) she'll ignore your faults, (2) find excuses for negative behaviors from you, and (3) go as far as breaking her own personal rules for you. She'll be (4) readily available for communication (responding almost instantly to texts), and always down to meetup.
- When she is repelled by you then she'll amplify the nitpicks that she has for you, find ways to reframe even positive behaviors as negative behaviors, and create rules for you to follow - assuming she's still even spending time with you in the first place.

It is silly to follow a woman's lead in life. She simply lacks the ability to reason with cold logic (uninfluenced by emotion), and execute accordingly. **Her actions are based on impulses, what feels good in the moment, and what**

feels good to believe. Establish a behavioral pattern of dominance from the very start. Take control and lead - physically, psychologically, and logistically.

A woman sees the world based on who she is - not so much based on how the world actually is.

Hence, how she describes other people is actually quite revealing about who is as a person. If she constantly focuses on the negatives about other people then this reveals that she is actually quite bitter, and will one day discuss negatives about you. In fact, the words that she uses to describe men in past relationships will eventually be the words that she uses to describe you. **As a side note, inquiring about her past relationships will also reveal the sorts of behaviors and character traits lead her to forming an emotional attachment.**

The words that a woman uses to describe the male/female friendships that she currently has in her life reveal more about her than they do about the people that she is describing.

- She'll discuss traits that she admires and wants to emulate. From this you'll be able to give her solid **<u>specific compliments</u> (based on the person who she wants to be)**, and encourage her to pursue her life dreams.
- She'll mention activities that she has done, and experiences that she's experienced that have helped her form an emotional bond with her friends. From this you can get **<u>exceptional date ideas</u> (based on things that she actually really enjoys).**
- She'll reveal seemingly negative behaviors that her close friends have done that has caused her to form a strong bond with them. If she mentions having a

verbally abusive ex boyfriend for several years then **she's dropping hints that she bonds through trauma (also called <u>Trauma Bonding</u>) created through specific negative behaviors.**

Further, the people that she associates with are actually quite revealing. Women like people that are like them, or who are like who they want to be. **If she has no female friends at all, then you should 🏃 RUN AWAY, before you develop feelings for her.** Lacking female friends is a strong sign that she doesn't have anything of value to contribute to the world, lacks the basic social skills essential to getting along with others, and hence doesn't have people around her.

Every woman has a vagina, but not every woman has something of real value to offer. **If she has female friends then this is a strong sign that she actually has real value to offer to the world - enough for other people to want to be around her.** If she only has male friends then this isn't evidence that she has substantial value to offer (other than her body) because the male friends could just be with her for access to a loose pussy.

A woman will rewrite her past history based on how she feels like in the moment.

99.99% of relationships are temporary in nature. This phenomenon is largely due to the prevalence of the internet, social media, dating apps, and dating sites, that has made it easier than ever before for women to meet men (and hit the "Next!" Button the moment something goes wrong in their current relationship).

Even if you get married and raise a family with a particular woman, divorce or death may occur. Alternatively even in a marriage, the relationship can be severed in everything but the legalities. Having the status of being in a relationship does not necessitate that there is a healthy mutually beneficial connection.

Women will use the status of being in a relationship with a high status man as a way to show off to their peers, and boost their ego; it's not just who you are that matters to her, but what you stand for. **You have to recognize when you are merely a pawn in a woman's game, or the king in her life. Then prioritize her accordingly.**

The savage reality of life is that it is made of a series of creating, and breaking connections. Someone who meant everything to you one day, can suddenly mean nothing to you on the next day. This phenomenon is especially true for women who are biologically hardwired to be able to branch swing to a higher status man - given the opportunity. Hypergamy is a bitch. **One day she loves you, the next day she doesn't care if you're dead.**

Women come and go, but you are with yourself forever. This is why it's important:

- (a) to focus on developing yourself to the fullest,
- (b) use a woman as a practice dummy for the next one, and
- (c) not reveal sensitive information about yourself which can then be used as unconscious blackmail leverage.

Even if the relationship is strong at the moment, your secrets are not actually safe with a woman (including nude photos) because the relationship may fall apart later and then the secrets could be potentially exposed to the world. Don't text something that you wouldn't want to be screen-shotted and sent out to populated FB groups/Whatsapp groups. To keep a secret truly secret: tell no one. Having yourself as an audience should be more than sufficient.

- Your own approval is the only approval that truly matters.
- Draw a sense of happiness from within - without needing to depend on external unreliable factors such as the approval of others.

A woman's word does not mean much because there she does not have the notion of keeping her word for the sake of honor.

While she may say things "I love you", or promise things "We are going to have sex on [specific location]" she may rewrite what has transpired based on how she is feeling like at the moment. This is because women (unlike men) do not have a notion of keeping their word of honor. Their words simply reflect their current emotional state at the time of verbalization. Emotions in general are highly volatile and often based on irrationalities, so they generally should not be relied upon to stay consistent.

Instead of relying on a woman's words to ascertain the future, focus on using her past behaviors to predict future behaviors and creating lifestyle habits that are tailored around quality spending time with you. You want to become an enjoyable habit in her life because that will eventually lead to you becoming an addiction.

PLEASURE HABITS.

Pleasure Habits are some of the strongest psychological forces in the universe; a pleasure related habit can be extremely difficult to break.

- They can be used for the negative (such as smoking habits, drug use habits) that eventually form unhealthy addictions.

- They can be used for the positives (the habit of spending every weekend with you etc) that eventually forms seductive addictions.

THE FAST GIRLFRIEND METHOD

This concept forms the basis of The Fast Girlfriend Method. **The more quality time a woman spends with you, the more emotionally attached she will become.** In the field of psychology, psychologists refer to this phenomenon as The Mere Exposure Effect. To capitalize on The Mere Exposure Effect: the smart seducer will create a Lifestyle Habit for a woman to spend that time with them.

- **Set a time for each day that you will talk to her on the phone.** Create a reason for this such as reading 3 pages of a specific book together. Or talking about how your day went.
- **Set a specific day during the week that you will see her**. The reason for this could be to be Gym Buddies, or to catch local events in the city.

The key is to be consistent and not miss any days - without coming across as needy. If for whatever reason, something comes up and you/her can't make the weekly meetup then be relaxed about it - with a simple "Next week".

- Assume the sale and it will happen.
- Assume that she doesn't like you, and it will often be a self-fulfilling prophecy.

Your assumptions about the degree of your worth, and the degree that she will comply to your requests often become true because ideas are highly contagious.

QT -> Quality Time

Remember: one of the primary goals of communications is to have both parties feel good in the end. When you ensure that the time spent together is of quality - where both of you end up feeling good and both of you have uplifted spirits as a result of the meetup - then a pleasure habit will eventually be formed through enough repetitions.

Pleasure habits eventually form into addictions. **One day when she's expecting you to do your usual meetup, you'll suddenly disappear for a few hours - without explanation - and it will be at that moment that she'll realize that she can't live without you.**

---

1. Don't be afraid to ask for the perspective of male friends. They are emotionally unattached from the situation and thus can give a sharp perspective on the situation.

6

Law #49: Communicate strategically. When entering into interactions, know what your goal is.

Enter interactions with a purpose in mind.

Strategic communication > mindless communication.

STRATEGIC COMMUNICATION IS ENTERING interactions with a *specific goal* in mind, and communicating with the purpose of achieving that specific goal.

- (1) Knowing what you want,
- (2) being conscious of it while engaging in the field (interacting with women), and
- (3) going out of your way to getting what you want (doing specific behaviors designed towards generating results).

are the three most important aspects in getting it. Don't just talk simply to talk. That's a massive time-sink. When you have a goal in mind when interacting with women, you'll communicate with purpose and get more done in less time (maximizing efficiency).

This way you get what you want out of the person who you are dealing with. You'll emerge from situations victorious much better than you were before you even entered them.

Create mutually beneficial situations - where both partners involved get what they want.

- Identify the goal.
- Understand the person's values.
- Show how you can offer the person that which he values.
- Take action to take what you want.
- Both persons involved benefit from the association.

It's worth mentioning that being too outcome dependent can turn women off. Neediness is repulsive to women just like it is repulsive in business interactions. Learn to balance going after what you want, with having fun and enjoying the present moment. Time in field will teach you how to find the correct level of balance.

7

Summary of Law #49

LAW **#49: COMMUNICATE STRATEGICALLY**

- **Enter interactions with a purpose in mind.**
- **Strategic communication > mindless communication.**

8

LAW #50: Don't be a sponge.

Don't believe everything she says; think for yourself. Women will say one thing, mean another thing, and the truth itself can be something entirely different. Don't take her words at face value; look deeper.

SEXUAL RELATIONSHIP PROBLEMS **are caused by miscommunication problems.**

You misread the situation, and you misread the meaning behind a woman's communication to you. She said "X" and the meaning behind what she said was "Y", but you interpreted the meaning to be "X" and behaviorally responded to "X". You failed to see the actual reality of the situation, and as a result: acted based on an inaccurate map of reality.

HOW MEN SPEAK: X -> X
HOW WOMEN SPEAK: X -> Y
YOU UNDERSTOOD: X -> X

As a man, you will be the most successful when you operate on an accurate perception of reality -

rather than believing in misleading statements women tell you. Knowing the truth is empowering; allowing a woman to put the wool over your eyes is disempowering.[1]

- **1. Don't believe everything you hear.** Look at the evidence including but not limited to: her past behaviors, her present behaviors, her lifestyle, her body language, who her friends are, what other people are saying about her, and micro-expressions. Do these elements confirm her statements, or do they contradict them?
- **2. Don't take a woman's words at face value and interpret them literally.** Only a fool will trust a woman's words as the final truth.
- **3. Use critical thinking skills to separate fact from opinion.** Your mind is one of the most powerful tools in your arsenal for personal advancement, yet most men would rather numb themselves with endless hours of Netflix than think about critical issues currently relevant in their life.
- **4. Learn to be particularly skeptical about information that women give you if they have a personal stake at the matter.** Ask "Does she have something to gain by bending the truth?", "What does she have to gain?" , and "What caused her to say what she told me?" If she has a personal incentive for you to believe something in particular then take it with a serious grain of salt.
- **5. If you are horny, or emotionally invested, then the chances are that the thinking being used at that exact moment is clouded.** The bias can be too high for you to make a rational logical decision. Be willing to take

a walk to emotionally detach from the situation, achieve a clear state of mind, and then make a decision based on that clear state of mind.

Critical thinking skills are your most powerful weapon for filtering out bullshit from entering your mind, and only allowing the truth to enter. When a woman loses her ability to trick you into believing a set of fantasies and illusions (designed to maximize the resource extraction that she can get from you), you gain the ability to think for yourself and **always take the smartest course of action in the given situation that you find yourself within.**

Life is like chess. You have to be able to read the board accurately because then you'll be in the optimal position to make the best move. In life, you always have to be making moves to advance your position.

Understand this right now and right here: the sharper and clearer your understanding of the situation that you are in, the better your decision making will be. This is why it's important for you to not be easily bulshitted and intake false information about the reality that you are in. Being fed false information leads to false actions.

You become what you read. You become what your mind intakes as the truth.

Women are masters of unconscious and accidental deception, simply by the vast number of misleading statements that they make. Making a move on a woman[2] that forces her to take an action will reveal the truth in the situation, for actions, micro-expressions, and body-language reveal all. Testing a woman by acting upon her is a huge time savor because it lets you quickly read the situation.

A lot of psychological energy is wasted trying to figure a

specific woman out. This process of "trying to figure her out" and "see if she likes me or not" can span weeks, months, and in some pathetic cases for years.

It's just smarter to simply make a move.

- Text her.
- After a series of back and forth texts, video call her.[3]
- Invite her out to a local event in the city.
- In the in-person meetup, read her body-language.
- Physically escalate all the way to sex.

By taking action you'll know exactly where you stand, and won't have to waste mental energy doing guesswork.

A woman's operating system follows two codes: "Do what I mean, not what I say", and "Give me what I need, not just want I want."

1. Women will often state partial truths to help make lies easier to swallow.
2. Give her a call. Invite her out to a date (local event in the city). Physically escalate on her body. There is a clear binary "yes, it worked" or "no, it didn't work" response to you making a move. "Yes it worked" lets you know that she IS INTERESTED and you should proceed forward in smoothly escalating the interaction towards sex. One of the key concepts in dealing with women is to eject from a state of limbo; force her to make a clear decision towards you, so you aren't wasting psychological energy thinking/planning towards a girl who isn't even sexually available. There's a lot girls out there who are down to fuck you right now as you are. If you're busy staring at closed doors then you can just miss out on walking through the open doors.

3. FaceTime/Facebook video calls are preferable to just sending out texts because they allow you to see a woman's facial expressions (as well as, signaling with your own facial expressions) during the communication process.

9

Summary of Law #50

LAW **#50: DON'T BE A SPONGE.**

- **Don't believe everything she says; think for yourself.**
- **Women will say one thing, mean another thing, and the truth itself can be something entirely different.**
- **Don't take her words at face value; look deeper.**

10

LAW #51: See the meta-frame that her words carry.

Understand the implications behind a woman's words.
Words are windows into the mind.

UNDERSTAND **the frame that she is attempting to set up. Don't play the game by her rules. Pattern disrupt. She should play by the cards that you deal - rather than the other way around.**

Womenese skills is about cutting through the bullshit, ignoring the noises, and using Critical Thinking Skills to decipher the actual truth of the situation. **IT'S NOT ENOUGH TO HEAR JUST THE WORDS THAT SHE SAYS; <u>YOU HAVE TO UNDERSTAND THE DEEPER MEANING BEHIND THE WORDS.</u>**

A woman's belief system will bring about her behaviors. Her words reveal the truth behind her belief system. By changing her beliefs, you'll be able to change the behaviors that stem from these beliefs.

4 questions to ask yourself to ascertain the truth of the situation:

- **Perception lead to thoughts which generates words.** #1) "What do her words reveal about her perception of the situation?"
- **Beliefs lead to behaviors.** #2) "What do her actions reveal about the current state of her belief system?"
- **Actions follow ingrained habits and expectations. A woman is collection of her habits.**#3) "If I allow her to behave in this current matter, what precedent am I setting and is this habitual precedent sustainable in the long-term?"
- **Character creates choices.** #4) Ask "Why did she behave in this manner and what does that say about the kind of person that she is?"

One powerful question that will help you form a clear perspective of the situation is: "Will this matter a year from now?"

The frame that a woman sets about the interaction (through implications of her words) sets the stage for future behavior. For instance: if she says "buy me a drink" she is setting the frame that you are so low-value that you have to pay for her time. If you give into that frame then you're likely to keep paying in the future.

11

Summary of Law #51:

LAW **#51: SEE THE META-FRAME.**

- **Look at the implications that a woman's words have.**
- **It's not just what she says. It's the frame that is being set.**
- **It’s not just what she says. It’s how she is saying it.**

12

LAW #52: Leverage silence.

Learn to use silence to your advantage. What you don't say is as important as what you do say. Silence itself is a response. Learn to leverage silence.

KEEP **in mind that NOT everything a woman says is worth deciphering.** Often a woman will vomit an entire series of random nonsense that doesn't matter at all and doesn't have any deeper meaning. Never underestimate the incredible effectiveness of ignoring a woman, as a frame control tactic.

Using silence as a communication weapon will save you from a lot of time-wasting drama. Simply ignoring a woman at the right times will save you a lot of unnecessary pain-in-the-asses. The use of silence is especially golden during shit-tests; when a woman says some stupid drama-creating bullshit then just ignore it, and misdirect her attention to something else - to save yourself the headache.

Ignoring female bullshit will save you a lot of headaches.

What you reward with your attention tends to be reinforced. So it's important to bring attention to positive behaviors, and disregard negative behaviors (even avoid mentioning them entirely. **Attention is the currency that women crave**, and what you give attention to: will be repeated. This is why it is best to not give credibility to negative behaviors by discussing them .

There are certain specific moments in your communication with a woman where it will be of tremendous benefit for you to be able to understand the true meaning behind the signals that women send out. The key is to pay attention to what matters, and disregard the irrelevant bullshit that doesn't matter.

The 5 Key Rules of Frame Control

- #1) Not everything a woman says is worth acknowledging.
- #2) You don't owe a woman anything - not even closure.
- #3) Not everything a woman says is worth responding to verbally or emotionally.
- #4) Not every question a woman asks is worth answering.
- #5) You can redirect a woman's stupid questions with either a sarcastic answer, or a question of your own.

❄

Learning to say "no" and just ignoring her shit, will save you from tons of female drama and bullshit.

13

Summary of Law #52:

LAW **#52: LEVERAGE SILENCE AS A PSYCHOLOGICAL WEAPON.**

- **What you don't say is just as important as what you do say.**
- **Being silent will save you tremendous time and energy from being sucked into petty drama.**
- **Attention is the currency that women crave.**
- **What you reward with your attention tends to be reinforced.**
- **Bring attention to positive behaviors, and disregard negative behaviors (even avoid mentioning them entirely).**

14

Law #53: Action reveals all.

A woman reveals who she is by her actions. Look at what she does, not what she says she will do; what she does is who she is now, while what she says she will do is who she is striving to be.

WOMEN ARE predictable if you know to look at the right **Predictive Indicators.** Most men are clueless because they're using a woman's words as a way to try to predict what she will do - instead of realizing that a woman's words are as cheap as sand on a beach. They merely offer a glimpse into the conflicts of her ever-changing mind. It is action that is king - both in terms of you taking action to achieve your goals, and in terms of predicting a woman's future moves.

The best predictors of a woman's future actions is her past actions, her lifestyle, and her peer-group.

ACTION REVEALS ALL

When seeking to understand women, focus on what she does. Her behaviors are very revealing about who she is. Disregard what she has said, and the reasons that she uses to justify her actions. **Women will say almost anything to get what they want; they won't lose any sleep over using flattery and deception to set you up in the best position to exploit resources from.**

Don't be gullible. Don't trust a woman's words just because she has a pretty face. **Look at the behaviors to see if what she is doing is in accordance with what she is saying.** If you notice a contradiction between what she says and what she does (also known as a Hotspot) then draw conclusions about reality and how she actually feels about you based on what she does.

A fool and his money are quickly separated. If you convey yourself to be a provider then women will use you for resources - even going as far as getting married for that purpose (rather than being with you out of a sincere interest in your personality and physicality). **Look to see if she is behaviorally responsive to spending time with you - even if money doesn't play a role in the dynamic.**

Women will often say one thing, and then do something entirely different. When there's a Hotspot like this, trust the latter for actions speak much louder than words.

Be in the present moment. Observe what is going on, and learn the truth of the situation. Most guys don't even pay attention to what is happening right in front of them because they're stuck in their head thinking about irrelevant concepts (living in their head), and then wonder they don't have an accurate understanding of the sexual marketplace.

15

Summary of Law #53:

LAW 53: **ACTION REVEALS ALL.**

- **A woman reveals who she is by her behaviors. Look at what she does, not what she says she will do; what she does is who she is now, while what she says she will do is who she is striving to be.**

16

LAW #54: The body doesn't lie.

Look at her body-language to see the truth about what she feels about you.

WOMEN COMMUNICATE **and process information inherently differently than men.**

By understanding basic fundamental concepts of how:

- women communicate,
- how they understand what is communicated to them, and
- what changes their mind:

you can utilize this information to control the process. You can manipulate the variables and **hijack the communication process** to your seductive advantage - making a woman emotionally addicted to being with you, as a result of the techniques mentioned in this program

The goal of learning to be fluent in womanese is to:

- be able to decipher the true meaning behind a woman's words,

- to be able to accurately read a woman like a book,
- to be able to speed read situations,
- to be able speak womense yourself to maximize the impact of your communications, and
- to learn to recognize down-to-fuck signals when they occur, so that you can capitalize on opportunities when they appear.

HOW TO DECODE WOMANESE

Don't believe the egalitarian concept that women are just like men. Women operate differently than men.

Women communicate and process information inherently differently than men.

- 1) Men talk in a masculine style of communication. Women talk in a feminine style of communication. Don't judge a woman's feminine style of communication with the rules of masculine style of communication.
- 2) Men talk to achieve a specific purpose. Women talk just to boost their mood.
- 3) Men will talk to achieve a to exchange ideas related to achieving a specific goal. Women will talk to achieve an emotional high, and to boost their ego. For women: talking is a form of therapeutic catharsis.
- 4) Men meet up to do and get shit done.Women meet up just to talk and experience a good time.
- 5) Men talk to solve problems - talking is a means to an end. Women talk just to talk - talking is an end unto itself.

Don't talk to a woman the same way that you would talk to a guy. Don't treat a woman like a man with an attached vagina. Use the right tools for the right situation.

- 6) Men are direct in their communication style. Women are indirect in their communication style.
- 7) Men state their intentions blatantly and overtly. Women state their intentions subtly and covertly.

Flirting involves showing interest in a woman in subtle ways that keep her guessing. Women get turned OFF and bored if a man gives full validation immediately because it removes the thrill of the chase, and the excitement of figuring him out. Women are TURNED ON by mystery, push/pull (cycling between validation and devalidation), and mixed signals; they get bored when full-disclosure is given. Remember: women value what they work for. The more time a woman invests in thinking about a guy and solving the mystery, the more she becomes hooked.

- 8) Men say what they mean, and mean what they say. Women say one thing, but can mean something entirely different.
- 9) Men talk to convey logical information. Women talk to convey emotions.
- 10) Men talk to exchange facts with one another. Women talk to exchange feelings with one another.

THE EVOLVING CULTURE

The new generation of women is being raised by the internet (TikTok, FB, IG, OnlyFans etc), and this is impacting their ability to effectively socialize with men in a traditional relationship context. A beautiful women who posts photos of revealing clothing for a quick ego boost and is constantly being hit up by men through her IG feed: compromises her ability to pairbond in the long-term. Hookup culture has cheapened the traditional long-term relationship, and has made it easier for women to "hit the next button" the moment something goes wrong in a relationship - instead of trying to fix it.

❄

SUB COMMUNICATION

Don't always take what a woman says at face value. Don't always interpret her words literally. There is more than what meets the eye. Learn to see past the shallow surface level, and uncover the deeper truths of the situation. Learn to see past her behaviors, and into the beliefs that drive her behaviors.

What a woman says, and the true meaning of the situation are often polar opposites. Be a stickler for finding the truth of the situation. Don't be an idiot "Yes Man" agreeing with everything she says just because she has a vagina.

Learning to see the truth behind situations isn't just relevant to dealing with women. It is relevant to how you approach life in general. Don't be gullible and believe everything that you hear - just because it comes from someone who is well-spoken, or has a pretty face. Think for yourself.

WHAT IS SUBCOMMUNICATION?

Subcommunication is the implications behind what a woman is saying[1]. For instance: if a woman asks "How many women have you slept with?" The subcommunication is that: she is interested enough in you to shit-test you. she is testing your composure. she is trying to set the frame that she is THE BOSS of the interaction, and it's your responsibility to answer her directly.

The correct response to a shit test is to agree with the negative and amplify to set the frame that you're a man who *GETS IT* and keeps his social power. After all, women are attracted to POWERFUL men - not men that give away their power. Hence, you respond with a cocky and funny line (instead of getting defensive and justifying yourself to her) like: "You mean only today?" OR "Only 34.5." The key is to always communicate with extreme levels of confidence. Whatever you say, you have to own it 100%.

NOTEWORTHY MAXIM

Deaf men are the best at understanding women because they aren't distracted by a woman's words. A woman's body-language will betray her true feelings, and intentions, but often men are too busy thinking about the bullshit that came out of her mouth to even notice the signals being sent by her body.

THE PRINCIPLES OF FRAME CONTROL (Continued)

- #6) Frame is the mutual acknowledged perspective of the dynamic between you and her. It is the perceived context of the interaction. He who controls the frame, controls the game. You want to be the one who controls the frame, but don't appear like you're like actively trying to do so.
- #7) The stronger frame absorbs the weaker frame; the one who believes more: wins.
- The one who controls the frame, controls the relationship.
- #8) Dominating her mentally leads to dominating her physically. Fucking her mind leads to fucking her body.

- #9) Not everything a woman says warrants a response - or even an acknowledgement.
- #10) Not every question a woman asks warrants a direct answer - or even an answer at all.
- #11) Don't just look at the words she uses, but the frame that she is trying to set.
- #12) Arguing with a woman is falling into her frame. Don't waste time on her petty drama. Win with actions - not debates.
- #13) Being bitter and negative is falling into a woman's frame. Be positive.
- #14) Set the frame with your actions. Touch her body early on, and frequently. Consistently lead the interaction towards sex.
- #15) A woman should be more invested in you than you are in her; this way she is in your frame.
- #16) A woman should be emotionally reacting to you more than you are emotionally reacting to her; this way she is in your frame.

---

1. Generally speaking: the more adept a woman is in sub communicating, the higher the level of social skills she has, and the more Social Capital she has. Subcommunicating is similar to the Law of Say More with Less words. **It's important because one should aim to set the frame of the interaction - without looking like he is trying to set the frame.** It's easier to manipulate a woman if she doesn't see the puppet-strings that she is being pulled by because she can't resist what she doesn't even know exists. **Aim to have your puppet-strings invisible.** Win through actions - not logical debates. **Often by simply assuming that a woman will behave in a sexual manner (or the specific set of behaviors that you want) and acting in accordance with that belief, she'll just fall into that frame;** in fact, you can get "can get away with" almost anything if you have enough confidence in your perception of reality.

17

Summary of Law #54

LAW 54: **THE BODY DOESN'T LIE.**

- **Look at her body-language to see the truth about how she feels about you.**
- **LEAKAGE explained: Women will bend the truth verbally, but their emotions cause the truth to leak-out through unconscious Body Signals.**

18

LAW #55: Test her.

TESTING **a woman lets you quickly ascertain the truth,** without having to put in tons of effort making educated guesses and looking at empirical evidence. This way you won't be wasting time on sexual duds, and won't have to wait for the truth to spill out on its own.

When it comes to compatibility, it's better to find out earlier than letting things drag out. Further, in the context of men seeking a long term sexual partner: it's important to find out if a woman is low quality, or high quality BEFORE you develop any sort of feelings for her and BEFORE you invest a significant amount of time into her.

There are specific things that you can do to test a woman that are mentioned in this book, such as making a specific move on her. She can either go along with your physical advance/accept your date to an invite (which is HARD EVIDENCE) that she is interested in you, or deny it (also which is HARD EVIDENCE). Her actions are binary: it's either a "yes" or a "no", so you'll know exactly how she feels about you through her actions.

Don't fall for the bullshit of a woman saying that she "doesn't have the time" or other excuses that she gives. Busy people make time for things that are important to them. That's why they are busy in the first place. The extent to which a woman goes out of her way to make time for you shows you the extent that you're important to her (psychologically and emotionally).

If Brad Pitt wanted to see her, I assure you that she would suddenly have a lot of time available.

It's worth mentioning that even if a woman is legitimately busy, if she is interested in you then she will respond by telling you a time that she is available. If she doesn't, inquire about her schedule and create a time based on that.

Understand this: women find time for men that matter to them. If she doesn't make time for you then you are not a priority in her life - to the extent of the high priority that other tasks have. It's time to move on to a woman who values you enough to go out of her way to find time.

On a different note, touching is a key test. **If a woman is responsive to intimate touches then she likes you - even if she appears to be verbally dismissive.** Learn to trust the touching and her actions above all else.

19

Summary of Law #55

LAW **#55: TEST HER.**

- **Women lie, so men test. When it comes to compatibility, it's better to find out earlier than letting things drag out - wasting your valuable psychological energy in the process.**

20

LAW #56: Ignore the noise. Read the signals.

Read the signals that paint the map, and calibrate your strategy accordingly.

<u>THE GAME **of seduction is a continual process of reading the signals that a woman is sending out and adjusting your mating strategy accordingly.**</u>

- This means being able to accurately decipher a woman's true thoughts, feelings and intentions - without being mislead by a woman's white-lies, subtle deceptions, and misleading statements. By knowing what a woman is thinking, feeling and what her belief system is then you put yourself in the best situation to seduce her.
- This means being able to accurately understand a woman's true communication to you - beyond what was said on the surface level.

AS A SEDUCER YOU HAVE TO BE ABLE TO READ THE WOMAN LIKE YOU CAN READ A CHESSBOARD - BASED ON MANY SIGNALS THAT

SHE IS SENDING OUT (to paint a map of what types of moves work on her versus the types of moves that don't work on her) - AND THEN CONSISTENTLY MAKE MOVES THAT LEAD TO SEX.

"YOU SEE, BUT YOU DO NOT OBSERVE." SHERLOCK HOLMES

A good seducer is able to observe the accurate reality of the situation, and is able to read a woman's feelings and intentions like he reads a book - by deciphering signals and correctly interpreting the true meaning behind a woman's words.

Use the information that a woman sends out, as a way to learn what works on her (so you can do more of that). For instance:

- If you notice that when you talk about spirituality (astrology, life after death, the butterfly effect, palmistry, PETA etc), she gives POSITIVE BODY-LANGUAGE INDICATORS then this is a clear sign that you should keep using that particular move to form a genuine connection with her. *GREEN LIGHT! GO!*
- If you talk about the technical aspect of your business, and she gives one-worded responses (and other NEGATIVE BODY-LANGUAGE INDICATORS) then you know that, it's time to switch up subjects of conversation. *RED LIGHT! SWITCH IT UP!*

POSITIVE BODY-LANGUAGE INDICATORS

(signals that what your'e doing is working and you should double-down on that particulate move) INCLUDE:

- #1) her eyes light up (including pupil dilation),
- #2) her eyebrows have a brief raise,
- #3) her tonality has a sharp increase (more high pitches),
- #4) she moves closer to you,
- #5) she moves very close to you (past the social zone and into the intimate zone)
- #6) she touches you,
- #7) she positions the direction of her feet/torso towards you,
- #8) she becomes more physically animated,
- #9) she invests more into the conversation (doesn't give merely a polite response to be friendly, and doesn't just give a one-worded response), and
- #10) she is preening (fixing herself up to look more pretty for you),
- #11) she has sustained eye-contact over a long period of time,
- #12) she stops what she is doing in order to pay attention to you,
- #13) when you move somewhere, she'll automatically follow you without saying anything,
- #14) if you tell her to do something, she complies instantly - without hesitation,
- #15) if you ask her out, she says "yes" immediately,

❄

21

Summary of Law #56

LAW **#56: IGNORE THE NOISE. READ THE SIGNALS.**

- **The game of seduction is a continual process of reading the signals that a woman is sending out and adjusting your mating strategy accordingly.**

22

Law #57: Identify Honest Signals, Leakage, and Hotspots

The harder it is to fake something, the more reliable of a truth indicator it is. Look for Honest Signals, signals that are hard to fake (like micro-expressions, leakage, and micro-actions).

WORDS ARE easy to fake because lying doesn't take much effort. However, actions are much harder to fake because they require a far greater level of conscious effort. This is why a woman's actions are more accurate indicators than a woman's words. Body-language is the hardest to fake of all.

Don't you fucking get it? A woman's body is constantly unconsciously sending out the truth. She can't help it but LEAK THE TRUTH - past her polite filters - through her body-language signals that her body is constantly transmitting.

EMOTIONAL LEAKAGE

Sometimes a woman will try to put on a show for the sake of politeness, but her emotions (are so overwhelming) that they still leak the truth - even if the truth is flashed only for a fraction of the second via a facial expression. This is because the emotions within her are so strong that she's not able to hide them entirely.

HOTSPOT

If you notice a **HOTSPOT (or a contradiction between her verbal communication versus her non-verbal communication) than trust the latter.** A woman's verbal communication is what she wants you to believe and it's within her conscious realm of control (manipulatable). A woman's non-verbal communication is what she actually believes, and for the most part is outside of her realm of control to direct (involuntary).

23

Summary of Law #57

LAW **#57: IDENTIFY HONEST SIGNALS**

- **The harder it is to fake something, the more reliable of a truth indicator it is. Look for Honest Signals, signals that are hard to fake (like micro-expressions, leakage, and micro-actions).**

24

LAW #58: Conclude Based on Clusters.

Identify Clusters.

WOMEN ARE CONSTANTLY LEAVING clues (signals) on what turns them ON. They're communicating these signals on different mediums - NOT just the words that she says on a surface level. DON'T ACCEPT HER WORDS AT FACE VALUE AS THE FINAL TRUTH.

Look to see if what she says is aligned to the multiple channels of communications that she is sending out. A single indicator pointing towards a particular direction may not be sufficient to form a conclusive conclusion about the woman; however, multiple indicators (CLUSTER) pointing towards the same direction leads to a more decisive conclusive conclusion.

When you are looking to determine the truth about a situation, look for multiple pieces of evidence (CLUSTERS).

11 DIFFERENT CHANNELS THAT WOMEN COMMUNICATE:

- #1) what she is saying,
- #2) what she is doing,
- #3) how she treats you in public,
- #4) how she describes you to her friends,
- #5) how she poses on photos with you,
- #6) the way that she dresses when she is with you,,
- #7) the implications of what she is saying,
- #8) the frame that she is trying to set, and
- #9) the signals being sent with her body-language (including facial expressions, posture, tonality etc),
- #10) how she texts you[1], and
- #11) what she posts about you on social media (if anything at all).

ACCUMULATING INDICATORS TO USE IN CLUSTERS

The digital age has completely changed the way that people communicate. Studying a woman's digital footprint by Googling her name will be quite revealing about her character.

- For instance, if she claims that you're in a relationship with her, but all of her Facebook photos are of her being "alone" (or even worse: you're cropped out) then she is still fishing for a higher status man to come along.
- Another example, if you see that she has dating apps on her phone, then she is still uncertain about a long term future with you.

If a woman rejects you just once then you don't have enough evidence that she isn't interested. She could have just not been in the mood at that specific point in time. Look for multiple pieces of evidence (cluster) to create a conclusion that is worth acting upon. Put simply: don't make mating decisions based on snap judgments and insufficient evidence.

---

1. If she responds to your text messages FAST and leaves detailed responses then she is INTO YOU. However, if it takes a long time to respond to your texts and they are low-effort texts (one word, or a canned response) then she is not that into you. In general: don't get trapped into becoming a woman's texting penpal. The goal is to always be moving the interaction closer to sex at a reasonable pace. Invite her to a date to an event in the city; then take her home and fuck her.

25

LAW #59: Simply observe.

The Map is Not the Territory

THIS NLP MAXIM means is that there is no person on the planet that has a 100% exact perspective on what REALITY ACTUALLY IS. We're all operating based on rough estimations, and that's fine - as long as you don't mistakenly think a woman wants to say "X" when she really meant "Y" because that's a recipe for disaster. You can never see the truth with 20/20 vision, but 18/20 is enough to be hyper-successful with women.

You can't know the exact truth, but you can know enough of the truth to take action successfully. When interpreting a woman's signals, be aware that your interpretation can always have more clarity but you don't need 100% perfect clarity to act. What you don't want to do is fall into The Information Trap of saying, "I can't do anything until I know everything."

OPEN YOUR EYES 👁 👁.

You don't need to be an expert detective in order to ascertain the truth. Nor, do you need to be super high IQ in order to figure out what a woman is thinking and feeling. You simply need to pay attention to what she is doing, tap into your intuition, and look at her body-language (including her tone of voice, pace of speaking, facial expressions and other signaling modalities). **If all you did was simply pay attention then you'll be able to make insightful observations about what** specific strategies work on her, and which ones don't. Ask yourself "What can I learn from this situation to help me in future interactions with this sexy creature?"The problem is that many guys are stuck in their head, and are not even in the present moment to notice what is happening right in front of them.

26

LAW #60: Calibrate, pilot.

PAY ATTENTION TO A WOMAN'S SPECIFIC SET OF BUTTONS.

EVERY WOMAN HAS a specific blueprint on how to seduce her, and its your responsibility to pay attention to her body-language, micro-expressions and clues as to what specific moves work on her. While there are cues that are universally attractive, there are also specific cues that are attractive to specific women; a woman who frequents bars and night clubs will be as responsive to certain as buttons as a career focused women who stays up late studying at libraries to achieve a 4.0 GPA.

When you make a move on her, pay attention to her feedback and use that information to refine your tailored sexual mating strategy towards her. Take the feedback that a woman is giving you and calibrate accordingly.

Learn her buttons. Let go of what isn't getting results, double down on what's working, and be willing to experiment with new tactics to increase the number of effective field-proven tools in your toolkit. Keep a black-book of specific notes about what works with best for each woman in your rotation. On your phone under the contact info, write some basic notes about who the girl is, where you've met her, her favorite topics of conversations, her core values, and places that she likes (for date ideas).

27

Law #61: The truth is always showing.

THE TRUTH ALWAYS SHINES THROUGH.

THE TRUTH IS OUT THERE in front of you. You just have to pay attention to notice it.

If you pay attention you will be able to see the truth. LOOK AT THE SIGNALS and SIGNS; read them and you'll know WHAT THE FUCK IS GOING ON - instead of playing chess blind.

A man who is skilled at reading a woman's body-language can ascertain the truth of what she is feeling at the moment, the level of interest that she has towards him, her intentions, and whether or not she is lying to him.

- **Further, he can take specific actions that will force a woman to reveal more information about herself and the situation.** For instance, he can come physically close to her. If she pulls back then she's not interested; however, if she stays the same then this is an indicator that she is physically receptive. If a woman is receptive to lower levels of physical escalation (like a 2 minute handhold) then this is a strong sign that she's receptive to being kissed.

- Another example is if a woman is receptive to drinking from your cup of coffee then she is fine with being kissed (because it reveals a relaxed attitude about sharing your saliva). When you've done this enough times, you'll be able to intuitively sense when the seductive situation is in your favor and you can increase the level of physical intimacy to a more intimate level.

A woman is constantly sending out signals about how she feels at the moment through her body-language (facial expressions, micro-expressions, tonality, body-posture etc), actions, and key phrases. **THE TRUTH IS ALWAYS SHINNING THROUGH.** [1]

Even if she tries to manipulate the presentation of herself, her body and/or emotions will betray her (known as LEAKAGE), and still reveal the truth.

- For instance, she might consciously smile with her eyes, but her feet are pointed at the direction of the door,
- she might be rude verbally (on the surface), but she's letting you massage her butt, OR
- she might be unresponsive to emails/voice messages, but highly responsive to Snapchat DMs, calls and meeting-up.[2]

While a specific signal is subject to different interpretations, when multiple signals (known as a CLUSTER) point to the same conclusion then you form a conclusive insight about her and the situation.

---

1. The truth is always shining through, so how come men don't capitalize on this? Well first of all: many do. But for those that don't: it's because they don't pay attention to the signals that women send out. Simply by paying attention to the truth that is being sent out all the time then you'll have the practical information that you'll need to seduce her.
2. Guys in their late 20s, early 30s might still be used to ancient ways of communicating such as emails, and leaving voice messages. Younger women are communicating on newer mediums such as Snapchat DMs (sometimes to protect their own reputation in the case of having you only as a temporary sexual partner), Facebook Messenger, or IG DMs. If you want to hookup with younger women then get with the times, motherfucker! When you get a woman's personal information I recommend being connected with her on multiple platforms - including FB (where you can see her personal history over the last couple of years). If a woman gives you a throw-away FB account (you can tell that it's fake by the limited number of posts on it) then in the case of men seeking long-term relationships: that's a HUGE RED FLAG.

28

LAW #62: It's not just what she said; it's HOW she said it.

Words are cheap.

ACTIONS SPEAK LOUDER THAN WORDS. Her actions speak volumes. If there's a contradiction between what she says, and what she does: trust the latter. Words are cheap. Look to see if she walks the talk. Look at what she does - not just what she says.

Pay attention and you'll be rewarded. Don't pay attention and you could miss out on sexual opportunities that are right in front of you.

SIGNS SHE IS DOWN TO FUCK

Major indicators:

- #1) She touches herself in a seductive manner, in front of you.
- #2) She brings up the subject of sex first.
- #3) She brings up "condoms" and/or asks if you have one.
- #4) Mentions that's she's home alone now.

- #5) She takes off any of her clothes.

Minor indicators:

- #1) She shows off her body, and flashes part of her body - making sure that you see it.
- #2) She walks in a way that accentuates her hips and butt.
- #3) She compliments your body, or how you smell.
- #4) Dresses provocatively (more than usual).
- #5) When you touch her body, she doesn't take a step back. When you move in close (past the social space) into the intimate space, she doesn't flinch and doesn't say "what are you doing?"
- #6) She touches you first.

To know for sure, just make a move. Making a move will force a woman to show you the cards that she is holding.

29

LAW #63: Be a Truth Seeker.

CONDITION YOURSELF TO WANT THE TRUTH AT ALL COSTS.

SEEK **the Truth - even if it's extremely painful.**

While this rule sounds obviously, you would be surprised to find that not all men actually want the truth. As mentioned prior, some men prefer to live in a world of pleasant illusions rather than confront painful truths. Red pills may be empowering, but blue pills taste better.[1]

Men conquer worlds. Women conquer the men who conquer worlds. Don't underestimate a woman's capacity for bullshitting you. Don't accept what a woman says as the truth just because she said it with conviction and confidence. As a man, you have to be able to see past the noise, the distractions, the lies, the bullshit, the temper tantrums and SEE THE TRUTH FOR WHAT IT IS - EVEN IF IT IS DARK AND TERRIFYINGLY UNCOMFORTABLE.

All of Red Pill philosophy is based on the idea of having the truth at all costs - even if the truth is incredibly painful for you to realize and even if the truth shatters your fantasizes of an idealized world. Some men CLING to the hope that their girlfriend is a pure angel because this illusion is erotic, and will deny the truth of the situation to avoid breaking their emotional addiction to having pleasurable feelings towards her. **To be good at speaking Womanese, you must be a good detective about deciphering the truth of a situation - even if a woman is spitting lies into your face.**

ALL MEN CAN HEAR AND SEE WHAT A WOMAN SAYS AND DOES, BUT MOST MEN FAIL TO OBSERVE AND DECIPHER THE TRUE MEANING BEHIND WHAT THEY HEAR AND SEE.

Women will lie at the drop of a hat just to make themselves feel comfortable, and to gain your trust - so as to disarm you - before she exploits you for financial resources. **Some lies can be incredibly convincing because women believe in their own bullshit, and the lies are a long-term play.**

Some lies can be incredibly convincing because society has brainwashed you to "be a gentlemen" and believing "what women say is inherently true". When a man thinks with his dick, he becomes gullible; his lust turns his brain to mush and he becomes easily to manipulate. To be a player you have to always be ALERT and SHARP. DON'T LET YOUR LUST FOR SEX CLOUD YOUR LOGICAL THINKING AND OBSERVATION SKILLS.

Thinking with your dick can ruin your life.

Verbalize the affirmation: "I want the entire truth - no matter how unpleasant the emotional aftermath will be. I WANT THE TRUTH BECAUSE I CAN HANDLE THE TRUTH." While verbalizing affirmations like this may seem a bit "cheesy" and "silly", understand that the unconscious mind is susceptible to self-suggestions. Have a list of personally written affirmations based on sticking points that you want to work on, and read them every single morning. Be willing to change the wording to these affirmations in a manner that emotionally resonates with you the most.

YOU HAVE TO WANT THE TRUTH - AT ALL COSTS. The issue is that some men engage in denial because it makes life more pleasant for them.

MORE TRAPS THAT MEN FALL INTO THE SEXUAL MARKETPLACE (on the theme of COMMON SELF-DECEPTION TRAPS that cause men to misunderstand women)

- **14//**They would rather **pretend that a woman is an angel** because it makes falling in love with her easier and the sex much hotter.
- **15//They would rather ignore their own flaws than deal with the unbearable pain of realizing that they SUCK in certain areas of life.** If a date didn't go well, they'll blame it on the girl rather than themselves (disallowing self-development to occur). It's only when you accept blame upon yourself and take the responsibility of the outcome that you will learn from the situation.
- **16//They would rather pretend that a woman is really into-them** because their ego can't handle the realization that she isn't interested and it would be a waste of time to pursue this dead-end lead.
- **17//They would rather pretend that a woman is NOT into them at all,** so they can avoid the uncomfortable fear of escalating. Accept the possibility of rejection when you play the game. When you are fearless of rejection then you will be at your best position to succeed.

- **18//They would rather imagine that they have no potential,** so they don't have to push themselves outside their comfort-zone of binge-watching TV shows while eating junk-food at 3am in the morning.
- **19// THE HALO EFFECT:** They find it difficult to believe that someone who is so beautiful can be so damaged on the inside. They think that outer-beauty necessitates inner-beauty.

---

1. Denial is not just the Nile in Egypt.

30

LAW #64: Persistence shows confidence.

DON'T TAKE A WOMAN'S FIRST RESPONSE AS SET IN STONE.

BEING **able to see past what a woman says on the surface level, and understanding the implications is KEY to being able to decipher her words.** What a woman says and what a woman actually means are often two entirely different things. What she says is based on how she feels and her own understanding of her thoughts, both of which are volatile factors. How she feels can easily change from moment to moment, and her own understanding of her thoughts can change too - as she begins to develop a better perspective of how sexy you actually are. This is why a wise man once said, "Don't take a woman's first response as set in stone."[1]

For instance: when a woman says the words "Are you a player?" you misinterpreted the meaning behind her communication to mean "I hate players!! STOP doing the things that are driving me crazy!!" Then you acted in accordance to what she requested, and became the ultimate nice guy: boring her to death. You can be many things to women, but boring is not one of them; being boring is the cardinal sin in a relationships.

You should have accurately read her words "Are you a player?" to mean "What you just did TURNED ME ON!!!" so I naturally followed up with wondering if it was "too good to be true" and "too effective to be accidental". **If you accurately deciphered the true meaning behind her words then you would have doubled down on the behavior that spiked her attraction and continued to press that specific button.**

Often a woman's first response to your move is just an auto-pilot response that is more based on habit than an actual true response to what you've done. By persisting a bit, you'll convey high levels of confidence and can turn things around. A confidant man doesn't suddenly lose his cool the moment he gets a bit of disinterest from a woman.

A confident man isn't fazed by a bit of disinterest. He'll keep going because he knows that he has a TON to offer women, and he can't even understand that a rejection from her is possible. That's the kind of mindset that he takes with himself to the field, but deep down he knows the score to not waste his time on sexual dead-ends.

---

1. According to science, the more positive time a woman spends with you, the more attracted she becomes to you. This is known as "The Mere Exposure Effect". Hence, by dis-acknowledging a woman's first response and continuing to spend time with her, you can eventually win her over. A confident man isn't fazed by a bit of initial disinterest. Take this advice with a grain of salt. This doesn't mean that you show go full-on verbal harassment situations and get arrested for plowing too hard.

31

Law #65: Capitalize immediately while the iron is still hot.

When a woman really likes a guy, it is blatantly obvious. If she likes you, you'll know.

THIS IS the answer to the age old question "Does she like me?" You don't need tor read a 300 page book on how to tell if a woman is into you, if she is really into you. The signs are as clear as daylight.

A guy would have to be really insecure to miss them; an insecure guy will generally misinterpret signs of interest as somehow being signs of disinterest because he can't possibly fathom how a beautiful women could possibly be INTO HIM. All that is left is for him to capitalize on the situation, and make something out of it. ONE NEEDS TO ACT ON OPPORTUNITY.

If a woman really likes you, it would be obvious and you wouldn't even ask the question: "Does she like me?" A woman's body-language will reveal the truth; she can't control the signals her body is constantly sending out.

Even if a woman really likes you, if you do nothing then the lead will die. Women have been raised to be passive (although feminists are trying hard to change that). Even if a woman likes a guy, she'll still wait for him to make the move - even if it means losing him in the process. Some women have an ego that is too sensitive, and fragile to risk handling getting rejected, so they won't even try to make a move on a guy (even a guy who they really like). This is why if you wait for sexual opportunities to come to you then you might die waiting. The responsibility for making things happen, and escalation is ON YOU. Don't wait for opportunities. CREATE THEM.

You're the man with a dick, so don't be a fucking pussy. MAKE THE MOVES ON HER. THIS IS YOUR DUTY AS A DICK OWNER.

If a woman gives you bullshit like:

- #1) one worded text replies,
- #2) significant long delays when texting you back (even when you text her back right away),
- #3) doesn't put in significant effort in conversation with you,
- #4) glances away when talking with you,
- #5) doesn't hold eye-contact while talking with you,
- #6) seems easily distracted when interacting with you,
- #7) has a much higher tonality pitch when talking to others,
- #8) spends excessive time on her phone when she is with you,
- #9) is in a relationship with you, but also posts semi-clad photos on IG, texts a lot of male "friends", and has Tinder on her phone,
- #10) is using you as a texting penpal but won't get on a video-call and won't meet up in real life,
- #11) is only interested in spending time with you when you go on fancy expensive dates and doesn't

enjoy basic one-on-one time with you in a simple "free date" (like a date at Washington Square Park)
- #12) keeps digging for info in regards to how wealthy you are (by asking things like "Do you live in a house?")

then she is NOT that into you. Time spent with you is based on what she can get from you, but not because she is actually into your personalty per se. She views you as "he is only good for his money" or "he is only goof for that one thing I can get from him".

Don't take it personally. Just cut your losses and move on to another lead; don't throw more good money after bad money. Don't fall into the Sunk Cost Fallacy of continuing to invest into a losing hand, and continuing to dig a deeper hole. JUST WALK AWAY.

The best way to get over a former lover is to get a better lover, and focus on your personal development. When you find yourself thinking about a former lover, just acknowledge that and without rendering negative judgement about yourself, redirect your thoughts.

32

Law #66: Be as cold as ice.

Don't take it personally. In fact, don't take anything a woman says personally. Be as cold as ice when calculating and executing decisions.

WOMEN ARE LIKE CHILDREN. They say all sorts of random stupid bullshit that they don't understand. Don't take it personally. Life is too short to obsess what someone else thinks. Focus on what you think. Focus on your life goals, and mission.

In the early stages of a relationship, a woman's rejection is meaningless because she doesn't even know you. She isn't rejecting you per se, but she is rejecting the way that you treat her and your specific approach towards her. This is even more reason to not take a woman's words or actions personally.

Seeking a woman's approval is a never-ending blackhole. One day you'll learn that the only approval that really matters is your own. When you give zero fucks about what other people think, you will finally be free to behave as you wish. Truly not giving a fuck is a superpower.

33

Law #67: Don't project your own insecurities.

REMOVE THE BLINDERS of PROJECTION

THE ISSUE IS **that sometimes a guy will be incredibly into a particular woman and projects his own feelings/thoughts unto her;** he thinks that just like he has strong feelings for her, she has strong feelings for him. The guy thinks that she thinks just like him, and feels the way that he feels.

As a result of this blatant misreading of the situation, a guy is likely to waste tons of energy and time pursuing a dead-end lead because he sees potential when there is none. Don't water a rock because you'll waste away that precious water; focus on watering seeds that can sprout into flowers. YOUR ENERGY IS INCREDIBLY VALUABLE; WHY WASTE IT ON NONSENSE? **You wouldn't invest in a stock that is going down, then why invest in a dead-end woman who lacks real potential?** Your time is better spent investing into leads that could lead to something amazing.

Don't play roulette with your life. Your time is more precious than gold. Some guys waste months of their life on an ungrateful selfish woman - who ends up trading up. Invest in women who are "FUCK YES" towards you; don't invest in women who are lukewarm. Life is too short to waste it on women who don't really like you, instead of spending time on women who are crazy about you.

Don't make lots of assumptions about the women and the dynamic between you and her, without taking the time to look at the evidence. When you have multiple pieces of hard evidence pointing towards a single conclusion (also known as a CLUSTER: see Law #4) then trust that conclusion - even if your emotions and feelings are painting a different picture entirely. **No matter how you feel, trust the cold hard evidence.**

Nice guys have the tendency to make lots of assumptions about their low self-worth and lack of options; these assumptions tend to become a self-fulling prophecy. If a guy thinks he can't get girls, he won't. If he thinks his situation is hopeless, it will be. YOU HAVE OPTIONS, MOTHERFUCKER; JUST OPEN YOUR EYES.

TRUST EVIDENCE OVER EMOTION. THINK WITH COLD HARD LOGIC UTILIZING FACTS AND STACKING OBSERVATIONS; DON'T THINK WITH YOUR DICK AND MAKE IMPORTANT LIFE DECISIONS BASED ON THE ARBITRARY WHIMS OF EMOTION.

❄

OVERCONFIDENCE CAN LEAD TO SELF-SABOTAGE. If a guy thinks every single girl is down to fuck then he will waste a lot of time pursuing girls who aren't excited about picking up what he is putting down (value exchange compatibility) instead of pursuing girls who are excited about what he has to offer. Filter for women who are picking up what you are putting down - buying what you are selling.

IF YOU HAD TO ASK THE QUESTION "Does she like me?", YOU ALREADY KNOW THE ANSWER.

Seducer: "Hey, lets head out and meetup on Sunday for Coffee. I know this great place in XYZ location."

Woman: "I have to think about it" or "I'll get back to you on that!"

If a woman says anything but a certain "yes!!" then she's not into it. When a woman is DOWN then it is clear that she is DOWN. If you're missing those signs then the answer is an acute "I'm holding on to you - just in case I can't find another guy. You're my backup guy" or has your name saved as "free food" on her phone.

34

Law #68: Maybe is no.

Anything that is not an enthusiastic immediate "yes" (such a 1-2 worded verbal response that beats around the bush) is a lukewarm "no".

WHILE IT'S CERTAINLY possible that you can eventually turn a woman's mind around - considering how susceptible women are to having their mind changed - it should be noted that not every woman who you can get, is worth getting. Some women are too much of a hassle (carry too much emotional baggage) to be worth the effort to fuck, when instead you could have just focused on women who are a lot more interested in you (your effort would have a more bang per unit of sweat). Instead of trying to win over a disinterested woman, wouldn't it be a better use of your time to focus developing stronger connections with interested women?

35

Law #69: Silence is NO.

Not saying something is saying something. Silence means "no".

A WOMAN DOESN'T WANT to be seen as a bitch, so instead of confronting you directly (like a real man would), she'll use a passive-aggressive approach and simply ignore the issue entirely. Understand that no response is a response in itself. **<u>In other words, not saying anything is saying something; silence communicates a signal.</u>**

Understand that when a woman is crazy about a guy, she can't stop talking about him. If she really likes something, she won't shut up about it. The passion is overwhelming for her, and she wants to share it with the whole world! The fact that she is able to stay silent about the matter simply reveals that she doesn't care for it.

Guys will sometimes fall for the Polite Response Fallacy thinking that if a woman is simply friendly to them then she is interested in a romantic manner. The truth is that the woman was just being friendly because she was raised to get along with others. Simply experiencing friendliness is not sufficient enough evidence to conclude that a woman is into you; look for enthusiasm, excitement and eagerness (Ask "Is she really into the interaction?" or "Are these elements missing?"). Does she light-up when she is with you, or are her responses "forced" monotone - almost robotic?

❄

HOW TO SCREEN FOR HIGH INTEREST

Life is short and then you die. Choose who you allow into your inner-circle carefully.

YOUR TIME IS WORTH MONEY. A lot of womenese is about being able to decode which women are really interested in you (and to what extent), so that you can continue to invest in them and not waste time/psychological energy on women who are not interested in you. Run tests on women to gauge physical devotion, and then prioritize them accordingly.

An important concept to understand in regards to speaking womenese is that women have been conditioned to be polite. Even if a woman doesn't like you in a sexual way, she'll still be friendly because this is how she was raised. Guys can read too much into a woman's friendliness and misinterpret it as signs of attraction. **This is why you want to MAN THE FUCK UP, and MAKE A MOVE to force a woman to show the cards that she is holding.** Touching a woman in an intimate matter is the fastest way to test sexual receptiveness. A woman being conditioned to being friendly, and a woman's desire to ease social tension/uncomfortable confrontations is what leads her to using softeners - white lies that are there to make the guy feel better about himself and to minimize the chances of aggressive intimidation.

THE SPECTRUM OF HONEST SIGNALS

While this is a book about speaking womenese, it's worth pointing out that a woman's words ultimately can't be trusted. They are merely a glimpse to a woman's emotions and intentions AT THAT EXACT MOMENT IN TIME but these can change quickly. More reliable indicators of a woman's behavior are her past behaviors, her character, her body-language and her present actions. Women will lie at the drop of a hat, so the truth is best deciphered through more than just a woman's words - such as looking at what SHE DOES, and the clues dropped by her body.

36

LAW #70: Passivity is YES.

A WOMAN IS BRAINWASHED by society to be acted upon - more than to act on a man. Hence, she spends most of her life just waiting for men to make moves on her. The most she can do is send clues and signals that she wants to be acted upon (for instance she can "accidentally" expose parts of her body for you to notice her, she can "accidentally" brush up against you, or she can "accidentally" say something overtly sexual), but her ego is too fragile to being the one who does the acting.

If a woman isn't saying "no" (in terms of her body-language, her actions, and words) then the answer is "yes" and you should keep advancing the interaction towards sex.

If she is still showing up on dates and spending time with you (despite the sexual frames that you set and frequent touching that is happening) then assume that is interested in being with you.

An absence of a "No" is a "yes" because if a woman wasn't interested in you then she wouldn't even be responding to you at all. She would just ghost, block, or tell you to leave her the fuck alone.[1]

---

1. The exception to this rule is in a work environment where a woman may be just being friendly to create a pleasant vibe. In that particular case, look to see if she goes beyond basic friendliness and her basic obligation to being polite into doing something "extra" for you. If she does then she is interested.

37

LAW #71: Identify her core values, and then feed it back to her.

Identify a woman's core values and communicate them back to her. Establish commonalities of interest.

- Learn to identify the feeling that is valuable to her that is behind her words. Reflect that type of feeling back to her.
- Learn to identify specific trance words that she uses. These are specific words that have special meaning to her. If you use these same words, you'll maximize impact.
- Identify her specific body-language and feed it back to her through Mirroring and Matching.

Look for what is valuable to her. Then show her that you've got plenty of that in your life. By being a part of your life, she'll get access to more of which she values.

38

LAW #72: She should be sucked into your world, more than you are sucked into her world.

Speak her language, but don't be sucked into a woman's world. Bring her into your world.

WHILE YOU WILL OCCASIONALLY SPEAK Womense to have a maximum impact on her, you want the woman to be more drawn into your world than you are drawn into her world for the sake of sustaining attraction. A woman should be pulled into your perception of reality more than you are pulled into her perception of reality. **Even a dominant woman wants to submit to a more dominant and competent man.** For instance: in religious circles, this would mean being a spiritual leader that will guide a woman towards living a life of greater meaning based on shared values and shared philosophies.

Don't spend too much time deciphering the true meaning behind a specific woman's words for the sake of gaining access to her pussy. If you pedestalize a woman in your mind, you will pedestalize her with your actions. Needy behaviors are very unattractive to women. Being more invested in her than she is in you leads to low status behaviors. The goal is to improve your skills with women in general - not just to get a specific woman that you want.

HOW TO SPEAK WOMANESE

- Men talk about abstract concepts and philosophy. Women talk about gossip, food, and shopping - down-to-earth concepts. A woman's favorite subject of conversation is herself, and about things that directly benefit her. When talking show how what you're saying relates back to her - even if you're talking about yourself.
- Men care about how what you say teaches them something new - the educational value of your communicational content. Women care about how what you say makes them feel something - the emotional value of your communicational content.

39

LAW #73: Stack value.

Attention from high status men, good emotions from a positive vibe, and fun from enjoyable experiences are forms of currency that women value. Bring the value.

WOMEN LIVE FOR GOOD EMOTIONS. What she cares more about than anything else is how you make her feel. She feels what you feel because of mirror neurons. When you feel AMAZING, then she will feel AMAZING. Feel joy and enthusiasm for life; let that joy overflow in your words.

Communicate to women from a place of overflowing positive emotions, benevolence, and high energy. Focus on uplifting her mood, and pumping up your emotional state. Press her emotional buttons. When y0u understand the maxim that girls just want to have fun, then a lot of what a woman says/does will start to make sense.

- Men focus on the content and the rational arguments behind issues. Women focus on the context and how issues make them feel.

- Men are moved by solid logical arguments - that are backed by evidence. Women are moved by stories, and appeals to emotion.

Be a giver of value. Stack it.

40

Law #74: Play along the fantasy she desires to see. Leverage sexy stereotypes and her imagination.

ADOPT A SEXY STEREOTYPE THAT IS BASED ON THE DESIRES AND WANTS OF THE DEMOGRAPHIC OF THE WOMAN THAT YOU ARE INTERESTED IN. Understand that women respond to their imagination of you more than the objective reality of who you are.

AS A MAN, **YOU CAN BE MANY THINGS TO WOMEN, BUT YOU CANNOT BE BORING.** Being boring is the cardinal sin of dealing with women. Playing it safe, predictable, and nice is playing it boring. You need to START TAKING RISKS in interactions with women. Be edgy. Polarize. START DRIPPING WITH PERSONALITY. Bare your naked soul. Express yourself freely and fully. Take on intriguing hobbies and develop an identity that women will find interesting.

Womenese isn't just about what you say directly to women. It is also about who you are as a person. Your identity and behaviors communicate signals to women that speak louder than words. For instance: if you live a spiritual life dedicated to a Higher Purpose then those set of behaviors communicate waves of messages to women about who you are, and the values that you stand for (much more than words could possibly articulate). In stark contrast, if you live a fast life of cracking the code to beating casinos at their own game and drive a Ferrari, then you're likewise communicating on a medium that sends shockwaves to a woman's system - even without speaking a single word. The key is this: your clothes, accessories, body-language, facial expressions, actions and life-style are sending messages to women in a silent language that creates IMPACT in their minds.

A woman who is attracted to you is unconsciously visualizing herself as part of your life. Her fantasies feel very real to her. A woman's imagination leveraged properly can be a powerful seductive weapon. Hence, posting exciting photos that showcase your lifestyle will have a woman imagining what it would be like to spend time with you.

I'm going to take a moment to reveal an extremely powerful tool to make a female friend desire to go on a date with you. Don't underestimate the power of this. Describe in detail a date that you took a woman to. Make it exciting. Have it include emotionally intensely fun activities. Hype it up to the moon. Paint a vivid picture of an enjoyable experience. After a couple of days break up with this "woman" (it's better for her to be a real woman who you want to date a long time ago, so the details of the date will be real - instead of made up). Invite the girl you like on a date and she'll say "yes" because she's already been pre-seeded into the idea that dates with you are fun. Using stories and third-person framing are powerful ways to subtly set the right ideas into a woman's mind.

❄

3 SPECIFIC EXAMPLES ABOUT PREEMPTING WOMEN'S BEHAVIORS WITH COUNTER MEASURES DESIGNED TO AMPLIFY HER LEVELS OF SEXUAL ATTRACTION FOR YOU

1// For instance: if you know that asking a woman for permission before doing something will lead to her losing respect for your authority and ultimately resulting in lackluster sex, then you'll immediately cease this beta male behavior. Be a leader - not an approval seeking simp. Be a decisive warrior - not a soy boy. A woman wants to look up to her man and be challenged (she resents being able to control a man like she controls a dog on a leash), so put yourself on a pedestal and don't ask her permission to do what you have to do.

2// Another example: if you know that saying "sorry" sets a precedent for more simp like behavior, then you'll avoid unnecessarily apologizing for your existence. Apologizing is beta male behavior that comes from insecurity and self-doubt (the exact opposite of confidence). Expressions of self-doubt and weakness absolutely disgust women - just like men are disgusted by expressions of obesity. Stop saying "sorry" (a word that kills the vibe), and start OWNING IT. For every word that comes out of your mouth, own it 100%. When dealing with women, exude extreme confidence. YOU ARE A FUCKING 10, SO ACT LIKE IT. YOU ARE THE PRIZE TO BE WON, SO BEHAVE ACCORDINGLY.

3// Final example: if you know that giving into a woman's Boundary Pushes, only reinforces her negative behavior and will embolden her to progressive violate even more of your boundaries, you won't stand for her bullshit. The more disrespect you put up with, the more she will disrespect you in the future. Here is a savage truth about women: they don't respect men that they walk all over - like a doormat. If a woman treats a man like shit, she will start to believe that he is shit. Don't be a fucking pushover. Don't put up with bullshit. Call women out on their BS behavior. Communicate boundaries clearly, and be willing to walk if they're violated.

STAND UP FOR YOURSELF. LOOK OUT FOR YOURSELF. This is a job that only you can do for yourself because women are too busy obsessing over themselves. Everyone is out for his own skin. It's imperative that you look out for YOUR SKIN

Women see the world through emotional lenses. Feeling something is true is enough for it "to be true" - to a certain extent. Women use their emotions as a guiding system to navigate their behaviors, and to "perceive the world with". Men that are able to express themselves on an emotional level will be able to communicate in a manner that really resonates with women.

41

LAW #75: A woman's view of the world reveals who she is.

A woman sees the world as she is - not as the world is. This is true for you, as well.

YOU SEE the world as you are. How you interpret a woman's communication shows a lot about who you are. An insecure guy will interpret everything a woman does in the negative, but a confident guy will see everything as signs of interest. Ironically: having the habit of confidently reframing of a woman's actions is a self-fulling prophecy. If you convey the frame that she likes you, she will often fall into that frame.

THE SIX LAYERS OF COMMUNICATION

- **1. The first layer is the truth of the situation (also known as The True Meaning).** This includes: the truth about her wants, the truth about her desires, and the truth about her feelings towards you. *Example: The truth of the situation is that her body craves sex, she enjoys the* *sexual pleasure of clit stimulation, but she can't actually verbalize these truths directly because society will judge her for it (and her fragile ego won't let her). You can decipher the true meaning of the interaction by judging her actions. If she is spending a lot of time with you, SHE LIKES YOU. If she followed you into the bathroom, she is DOWN TO FUCK RIGHT NOW. If she got on your bed, she is DOWN TO FUCK RIGHT NOW.*

- **2. The second layer is a woman's perspective of the truth;** what she believes is the truth (a subjective diluted understanding of the true meaning). Most women do not have a well-developed understanding of their nature, so their perspective can be very off. This is especially true if a woman is stupid because she relied heavily on her looks to get by in life (and thus her perspectives can be remarkably off). *Example: the woman engaged in self-denial that she enjoyed being FUCKED HARD in the bathroom because this would make her feel very guilty. She REALLY BELIEVES THAT SHE IS AN INNOCENT PURE ANGEL because her ego wanted to feel important and she buys her own bullshit. She wants to have sex but she can't admit this to herself because it would maker her feel slutty.*
- **3. The third layer is a woman's intention and purpose of communicating her perspective (The answer to "why did she this?).** Sometimes a woman will have the intention of just talking to improve her own mood and meet her social needs ("talking for the sake of talking" - a stark contrast to men who talk for a specific purpose). She aims to convey her beliefs - either partially or entirely (what she means to say) - as a means of self-expression. Other times: it's for a

specific unconscious goal such as mating, unloading her feelings, or virtue signaling. *Example: she said "I thought we weren't going to have sex" so as to take the blame off herself and then be able to justify things to herself as "it just happened".*

- **4. The fourth layer are words that she uses to convey what she meant to say**. The words she uses can be very misleading to what she means to say, her perspective and to the actual true meaning. *Example: she said "I thought we weren't going to have sex" taken as face value implies that she doesn't want to have sex with you. Her words are not good at conveying her intentions and desires, so this leaves guys confused.*
- **5. The fifth layer is what she didn't say.** Guys can be so focused on what she DID say that they fail to pay attention to what was NOT said - which leaves clues to the reality of the situation. *Imagine this: her pants are down, and you took out a condom. She says "I thought we weren't going to have sex". She didn't say "NO!" You should have put on the condom and fucked her hard because complaining about getting FUCKED is not the same as saying "I don't want to have sex with you." Sometimes women give token resistance because they get TURNED ON by the man being aggressive. Needless to say, if she did explicitly says "no" or "stop" then don't proceed and get a rape charge.*
- **6. The final layer is that which you understand her words meant about her intention, her perspective of the True Meaning, and what you concluded the true meaning was based on observations/deductions.** For clueless guys playing a broken game of telephone, it's no wonder that they misinterpret the true meaning of

the situation and behave in ineffective ways towards women. *Example: the guy thought her words meant "I don't want to have sex with you", so he ended the sexual interaction - without tapping into his killer instinct to fuck close and seal the deal.*

SUMMARY OF THE 6 LAYERS OF COMMUNICATION

- **Layer 1:** She desires to fuck. This is clear by her actions. She went into the bathroom and took off her pants.
- **Layer 2:** She mistakenly thinks she doesn't desire a good fuck because her self-denial is preventing her from seeing the truth. However, even if she thinks sex with you is "wrong" or "sinful", she still went into the bathroom with you and isn't walking away because HER BODY CRAVES THE EXCITEMENT/PLEASURE YOUR DICK PROVIDES - hijacking control of her actions.
- **Layer 3:** Her intention is to say something to make herself feel less slutty/guilty by taking away (from herself) the responsibility about what is going to happen.
- **Layer 4:** She complains by saying "I thought we weren't going to have sex" - giving herself catharsis in the process.
- **Layer 5:** She didn't say "NO", "Lets not have sex", or "Stop". This gives passive permission. This also conveys an unconscious desire to be "swept away" in the moment by Alpha Male Leader.
- **Layer 6:** The guy takes her words at face value and doesn't give her the physical value that her

body craved. An opportunity is lost because he didn't understand womanese, and didn't read the overwhelming series of "DOWN TO FUCK" signals.

❄

42

LAW #76: Most of communication is unspoken.

Control the controllers.

A WOMAN'S words reveal a window of insight into her belief system and character - which ultimately drive her behaviors. It is prudent to look past the surface level of her words, and aim to see deeper meaning behind what she said (or didn't say). Likewise, don't just look at her key actions (or lack of) but the decode the reasons that motivated these actions. When you understand the variables behind the drivers that drive her behavior then you'll be able to manipulate these variables to influence her behaviors.

A woman's communication style and behaviors are influenced by multiple variables. When you gain an understanding of these Influential Variables, then you will be able to manipulate these variables and redirect the outcome to an outcome that you seek. Control the controllers.

What are the variables that direct a woman's behaviors?

- Her ego

- Her emotions
- Her unconscious mind (and set of beliefs within there)
- Her conscious mind (and set of beliefs that she is aware of)

Game is manipulation and manipulation is game; if you have a problem with that then this book isn't for you. OWN YOUR IDENTITY AS A PLAYER OF THE GAME - or get played by other people in the network of game players that is the world. You are in the game of life - whether you want to acknowledge it or not. STOP FUCKING DENYING the fact that life is a game and one is far more likely to win in this game by being proactive, being aggressive in executing goals, implementing conscious strategies, and following a plan of action than if he takes on a passive approach merely hoping to get lucky.

❄

SUMMARY OF KEY POINTS:

Men and women are VERY different physically and psychologically. As a man, it is a grave error to project yourself unto women; just because you think and operate in a certain way does not mean that women share your sentiment. Just like men and women are VERY different physically and psychologically, they are VERY different in their communication styles - both in regards to how they transfer over information to others, and how they process information from others.

In fact, the difference is so vast that women might as well be speaking in a different language - namely Womenese and the subject matter of this book.

I. LOGIC VERSUS EMOTION

- **Men focus primarily on communicating logical information.** He says what he believes to be true based on facts, evidence, careful thought, and logical deduction. Just like logic is consistent, a man's word tends to be consistent.
- **Women focus on communicating emotional information.** She says what she feels like is true. Just like emotion is volatile and tends to embellish reality, a woman's word tends to be volatile and inaccurate.

II. DIRECT VERSUS INDIRECT

- **Men tend to be more direct and confrontation.** They aren't afraid of social awkwardness and tension, so they'll generally have no issue with saying something negative straight to your face. Hence, they will say what they mean and mean what they say.
- **Women tend to be more indirect and passive aggressive.** They actively seek to avoid social awkwardness and tension, so they'll say something negative to others about you through gossip (also known as SOCIAL AGGRESSION). When talking to you, they will sometimes say what they mean, and sometimes NOT say what they mean. Instead of saying what they mean, women will use white lies to bend the truth, and leave clues about what they mean. Women expect men to "just get it" without blatant explanations - even when she can be quite misleading.

III. PRACTICAL VERSUS MERELY CHATARSIS

Men are inherent problem solvers, achievers, and focus on communication as a medium to GET SHIT DONE. In contrast, women aren't thrown in to the world with a stark need to build their sexual market value, so their communications are focused on talking just to talk, and to uplift each other's spirits. Men earn their sexual market value; women are born into their sexual market value. Men generate value; women protect their value. Men focus on achievement; women focus on enjoyment.

❄

IT IS **worth noting that generalizations such as this are not binary and should not be interpreted into extremes.** We are dealing with spectrums. There is some feminine in the masculine and vice-versa. For instance: men are not cold machines executing based on 100% logic and 0% emotion; men's judgement is influenced by emotion just like women but to a lesser extent than women. These are generalizations, and like generalizations there will be anomalies and different people will be on different ends of the spectrum.

In general, women are far more emotional than they are logical, but a woman's upbringing will influence her psychology. In certain cultures such as the western culture in the U.S., individualism and achievement are heavily promoted as valued ideals; thus, women in this demographic will be more focused on achievement than traditional cultures that hold traditional values as sacred: women stay at home to take care of the children, clean and cook - while a man is the breadwinner. Context and a woman's upbringing should be taken into account when decoding Womenese.

❄

THERE ARE three primary goals of learning to speak Womenese:

- **1) To create an immediate feedback loop.** A man who is able to decipher a woman's body-language will know instantly if what he is doing is working by reading her positive body-language. Likewise, he will know instantly if what he is saying is NOT working by reading her negative body-language. This immediate feedback loop is valuable information to improve your game. The problem is that men that can't speak Womense can't decipher the clues constantly leave on how they desire to be seduced.
- **2) To understand what a woman value,** so as to be able to give them that specific form of value and become a valuable emotional commodity in her life.
- **3) To be able to quickly read the signals that a woman is sending out that she is DOWN TO FUCK, so that you can capitalize on the opportunity immediately.** Likewise, it's important to read the signals that a woman is not sexually open, so that you can stop wasting your time. It is more efficient to focus on fucking women that are more promiscuous in nature than it is to attempt to emotionally and physically persuade a virgin into intercourse. As a man, don't take the role of savior; unless you're married to her and in a mutually beneficial long term relationship, it is not your responsibility to save her from herself. Women use a man's Savior Complex as a means to exploit him for his financial resources.

43

LAW #77: Thinking and making decisions with your dick can destroy your life.

Don't think with your dick.

NOT MATTER WHAT A WOMAN SAYS, or does: remain calm, composed, and unaffected. Getting emotionally attached to what a woman says makes you susceptible to making stupid decisions. Lust turns a brain to mush; when you are horny, your thinking is clouded. Thinking and making important life decisions with your dick can destroy your life. If you have to make an important decision, take a walk around the block to clear your mind and think from a position of clarity - rather than giving in to the heat of the moment.

While not everything a woman says is worth your time to decipher, there are key moments which will be quite revealing about who she is as a person, what she finds valuable, and what turns her on, that is worth your time to pay attention to. **Everyone sees what women do, and everyone hears what women say, but not every man observes.** When you know what to look for and have a refined process of observation then women's bullshitting doesn't stand a chance; you'll come out with the truth every time.

Women are not "pure angels"; they "smart girls"

and they have an agenda. Don't underestimate a woman's capacity to bullshitting and manipulating you - especially if you are a man with resources. While you can take time to understand what she said versus what she means to say, understand that the truth of the situation may be entirely different. Always confront the truth regardless of how painful it is for you to acknowledge because a man as it his best with an accurate map of reality - rather than a map of reality based on self-denial and pleasant illusions. In fact, the entire premise of the Red Pill is to accept the reality for what it is NO MATTER HOW PAINFUL THAT REALITY IS and act accordingly.

THE GAME **of seduction is like flying an airplane. The smart seducer is able to read a woman's signals and then make micro-adjustments to his seduction plan based on the signals that he is getting.** Double down on behaviors that get excited positive body-language, while minimizing behaviors that get a flatline negative (or null) body-language response. It is not prudent to play the game of chess with a blindfold on. It's worth your time to pay attention, read the woman, read the situation, and make CALIBRATED MOVES that make sense in the context. A tailored seduction approach based on a woman's specific blueprint on how to be seduced will work much more than a cookie-cutter "same thing for everyone" approach.

WHAT A WOMAN SAYS, **and what she meant to say can be entirely different.** She might not have the word power to accurately articulate the thoughts that her on her mind. Even if she was more articulate, she might not understand the situation and herself enough to be able to portray an accurate perspective about what is happening. Further, what a woman says is often entirely based on how she feels at that exact moment which is subject to change; hence, the classic maxim "Change her mood to change her mind." The conclusion behind these truisms is that a man it's your responsibility to have your own unbiased independent opinion about her, the situation that you're in with her, and the dynamic between the both of you. While a woman's words provide clues about the reality, they should not be taken at face value - especially if it is her first response to your move.

44

LAW #78: Women are indirect creatures.

Women will go to far lengths to avoid social awkwardness, and to generate good emotions for themselves. Billionaire dollar industries are built on a woman's need to feel important, and filling that need with physical possessions.

MOST WOMEN HAVE BEEN CONDITIONED to be polite. They'll avoid direct confrontation for fear of retaliation from men, and being perceived as a "bitch". In general, women will go to far lengths to avoid feeling socially uncomfortable around people they just met. I'm going to repeat this again because it is an incredibly important principle in understanding how women communicate; **women will speak in a manner to create good emotions for themselves and will go to far lengths to avoid social awkwardness.** Hence, women will communicate rejection in subtle ways - nicknamed Soft Rejections - to preserve a man's ego and the feel-good vibe. These Soft Rejections can take the form of made-up excuses that shift the blame on to her.

. . .

AS JUST MENTIONED, most women have been raised to be friendly to others. In the case of a woman seeking revenge, she'll use indirect social aggression such as gossip, spreading lies, or reporting a man to authorities with false/greatly exaggerated accusations (behavior encouraged by the #MeToo movement). Fortunately for men in the U.S., rape is incredibly difficult to prove in a court of law (just save the texts and don't write self-incriminating field-reports on the internet); however, unfortunately for men, even a false accusation is enough to smear one's good name and reputation in work circles.

In the case of men, direct confrontation clears the air; however, in the case of women, passive aggressiveness for former perceived wrongs can span years and generate a toxic vibe. In the case of the latter, it is much more efficient to start a new relationship with a new woman than to invest mountains of effort to healing a woman's emotional baggage; when you have game skills, women become as abundant as sand on a beach. Instead of wasting days upon days trying to fix things with a damaged woman and a broken past with you, it's more efficient to just meet a new woman to start afresh.

❄

COMMUNICATION IS the art of transferring the thoughts that are on your mind, and the feelings that are in your heart to someone else. **The meaning of communication is how what you said was interpreted.**

It's not just just the content of what you said that matters, but the overall implications and frame that was set through a verbal medium. A frame is the mutually acknowledged perspective of the situation. The seducer's goal is to set frames that are conducive to sex occurring; it is beneficial for the seducer to learn how women process information, so that he can be effective in setting seductive frames.

45

LAW #79: Create a mutual understanding that sex will happen.

Set frames that are conducive to sex occurring. The mutually acknowledged perception of reality sets the stage for the actions that will occur.

FOR INSTANCE, the frames:

- #1) Sex is normal."
- #2) "Sex is healthy."
- #3) "We enjoy the pleasure our bodies give."
- #4) "I am the authority and dominant leader in the interaction."
- #5) "Meeting new people is fun, and engaging in physically intimate acts is fun too."
- #6) "It is not our role to negatively judge others. Why people engage in "nasty" sex is not our business."
- #7) "Life is short. It's important to enjoy momentarily pleasures while we're still alive."

are far more conducive to sex occurring than "Sex is dirty.

Sex is sinful. I feel shame and guilt for feeling sexual gratification. You (the woman) are just as much of an authority as what we are going to do as I am." To speak Womenese, take a few moments to deeply reflect on how a woman's mind operates.

46

LAW #80: BE AN INSIDER.

BE THE GUY WHO "JUST GETS IT".

IRONICALLY, women expect a man to "just gets it" - without it being directly explained to him. For a woman to explain the seduction and communication process to a man, would ruin the experience for her and takes the man out of the category of "just gets it" and into the category of "socially inept incel who "is too stupid to be worth my time. Don't take it personally; this is just the brutality of nature at work. **A woman's sexual nature can be incredibly sexually ruthless and efficient;** this is why women resent men reading books like this that attempt to inflate a man's sexual market value.

As a man, you want to "just get it" without explaining the dynamics of the situations to the woman because that would take away from the natural spontaneous feel of the conversation. Behave from a position of effortlessness - even if you are carefully executing a plan that leads to intercourse. Just because you understand what is happening doesn't mean that you should explain it to her; men that "just get it" don't feel the need to tell the entire world about it.

47

LAW #81: A woman's mind has ambivalence.

Why do women say one thing, but mean something else?

THERE IS someone within you who is seeking to sabotage you - all the time. This person lives with you, and knows everything about you because... *drum roll* he is YOU. This is the weaker version of you that is always present. Life is a constant struggle between the weaker version of you, and the stronger version of you. This battle is ongoing 24/7. It is the version of you that you FEED WITH ACTION that grows stronger with time. If you keep taking POSITIVE ACTION in the direction of your goals and vision, then you'll naturally create a POWERFUL MOTIVATIONAL MOMENTUM THAT INSPIRES MORE ACTION.

Eventually, you'll reach a point where all you do is WIN ALL DAY LONG. You become addicted to the high that you feel that comes from WINNING.

The weaker version of you feeds an endless supply of excuses and reasons why you should be easy on yourself. "Sleep in because it's cold outside" it whispers in your mind. "Don't work out today because you need a break. You've had a long day" it continues to tell you. "There is no point in approaching and making moves on women because you are disgusting" it whispers in your ear - baiting you to go easy on yourself. When a man believes in these limiting beliefs and excuses, they have greater power over him. The more one believes in a limiting belief, the more it limits him. The key is to not identify with the weaker version of you, but to identify with the stronger version of yourself.

You can recognize this internal struggle by differentiating between what you feel like doing and what you actually want to do. You FEEL like binge watching a show on Netflix, but you WANT to read a book on business. You FEEL like not approaching and making a move on the beautiful woman that you like because it's scary (and your ego can get hurt in the process of playing the game), but you WANT to develop the TAKE ACTION HABIT and a fiery momentum, so you approach anyways. You FEEL like emotionally exploding to a verbally insulting comment a woman says to you (shit-test), but you WANT to stay composed and not waste your time on her petty drama. The aim is to develop enough self-control to be able to do that which you WANT TO DO, and that which is aligned to your GOALS - rather than what you FEEL LIKE DOING in the present moment and that which gives into your desires for instant gratification. SELF-CONTROL IS CHOOSING TO DO THAT WHICH IS YOUR HIGHEST PRIORITY - even when you really don't feel like it.

Psychologists refer to this as the battle between the ego, and the super-ego. The ego is about having instant pleasure at all costs with complete disregard to the consequences. The super ego is about having a higher purpose and keeping your actions attuned to that which is beneficial for you in the LONG TERM. It is the ID (namely YOU) who decides between the two sides: good versus evil - or in this case, beneficial versus self-sabotage.

I'm bringing down these concepts to make a few vital reasons:

I.

Firstly, I want to emphasize the fact that YOU ARE AT WAR. Don't you understand that power isn't handed out for free? It is SEIZED. It is TAKEN. Don't you get it? One doesn't magically land on the APEX OF THE SOCIAL STATUS HIERARCHY by accident, or luck. It takes years of conscious self-development, overcoming inner-weaknesses, internalizing WINNING MINDSETS, and creating sets of lifestyle habits that lead to results - such as the TAKE ACTION EVERY DAY HABIT. You have to be your own best friend and coach to constantly inspire yourself to get the fuck outside of your comfort zone, and take EXTREME RADICAL ACTION TO GET MOTHERFUCKING RESULTS TODAY!!!

II.

Secondly, within here is a key concept in understanding how women communicate. It is **ambivalence**.

Women can hold contradictory ideas and have mixed feelings and issues about people.

This is why women will often say one thing, but do something entirely different. This is why women seem to consistently shift their perspectives and change their mind from one extreme to another extreme. This is the answer to the age old question: "Why do women say ONE THING, but actually mean something ENTIRELY DIFFERENT?"

The answer is: even women don't fully understand themselves. They are plagued with confusion. They are often torn themselves between doing what their super-ego wants versus doing what their ID wants.

One of the reasons why women will have contradictory ideas in their mind is because of an unconscious need to keep their options open. They don't want to give a HARD NO, because that can burn bridges, but they also don't want to give a HARD YES because of reservations. A woman is a flawed creature that is still trying to get by in life - in anyway that she knows how.

You sit down deep in your couch scratching your head pondering hard "WHY did she say XYZ, but later say ABC? Why did she promise she would do XYZ, but later completely flipped to ABC? Why is there no consistency in what a woman says, to what she actually believes and does on the next day?" It is because there is a significant inner-conflict within a woman that includes confusion. Put simply: she hasn't figured herself out, and she doesn't even know what she truly means.

You're probably thinking "Okay, so I can't trust what a woman says to be the final truth because what she says may not be aligned to her beliefs, and even if what she said is aligned to her beliefs, those beliefs can change. If I can't trust what she says then what am I supposed to do? How can I predict a woman's behaviors enough to not lose my mind in dealing with her? How can I play the game if I can't see the chess board, and have some consistent expectation about how my opponent will move his chess pieces?"

The secret is to understand that women are actually predictable, but not in the way of looking at their words and expecting women to keep their promises. Talk is cheap - even among men. Talk is even cheaper amongst women who will promise the world, and then do nothing. Women will say almost anything to avoid uncomfortable tension that comes from social confrontation, and this is why they can't be trusted; a woman's talk is the cheapest of cheap because she will easily bend the truth to avoid feeling uncomfortable in the situation (and then do something entirely different when you're not around, or flip her perspective by 180 degrees when she feels differently). The way to predict women is to look at that which is far more consistent and predictable: a woman's habits, lifestyle habits, and character.

If you understand human nature, you'll understand women and will come to realize that women are pathetically predictable.

48

LAW #82: In her mind: if it feels true, it is true.

Women think with their emotions.

DON'T TAKE anything a woman says personally. If a woman says something insulting to you: don't take it to heart, because she is just expressing how she feels at the moment, and her feelings are subject to change. Change her mood to easily change her mind. Women "think" with their emotions; feeling something to be true is enough to make it true.

Don't accept a woman's first response to you to be set in stone. As she gets to know you more, her attraction levels can spike, her mood will change, and behavioral response can shift radically in a positive direction.

❄

- Men care about the truth. They have an open mind to accepting the truth - as long as sufficient evidence and a strong argument is presented. Women care about believing what feels good. They see what they want to see, and believe what they want to believe.

- Men process the world based on facts. Women process the world based on how they feel.

MISCOMMUNICATION HAPPENS when a man uses his information based perspective of understanding the world to interpret and attempt to understand a woman's emotional way of communication. Miscommunication happens when men use their manese language to understand womanese.

- Men make their decisions based on what they want and cold logic (which stays the same). Women make their decisions based on what they desire and how they feel at the moment (which can change).

WOMANESE IN RELATIONSHIPS

- Masculine men have a stronger frame (perception) and lead a woman - mentally, logistically, and physically. Submissive women have a weaker frame, and submit to a man's view of the world - following his lead. Even if a woman's frame is very strong, your frame must be STRONGER. A confident man has a bullet-proof frame. He inspires women to follow his lead. A submissive woman is a sexual woman.

- When expressing a problem, men want solutions. When expressing a problem, women want empathy.

49

LAW #83: A woman's mind is malleable.

A WOMAN'S PERCEPTION IF MALLEABLE. If a man has intense conviction in his beliefs then his belief system will overtake a woman's belief system.

A MAN with in intense conviction in his high worth, and the high worth of what he has to offer will create a positive emotional experience for women.

By changing a woman's perception of your worth, you'll directly impact whether she says your sexual advances are "cute", or "creepy". If she sees you as an APEX ALPHA MALE at the top of the social hierarchy and socially proofed (other women want to fuck you, and men want to be you) then she'll use language patterns that are suggestive of you guys getting together. But if she sees you as a broke loser living with his mom with no future, ambition and no friends then she'll use language patterns that are suggestive of you not being with her. It's the difference between her saying "us" or "you". While a woman's language patterns offer a glimpse into her world, it is prudent to take them in context with other signals that a woman sends out such as her body-language, facial expressions, present actions, past actions, the actions of her close associates, social media presence, her reputation, and the enthusiastic (or lackluster) recommendations of her references.

SOFT REJECTIONS

Women use socially acceptable ways of rejecting men like:

- "I need space",
- "I have to think about it",
- “I need some time",
- "I'm not ready for dating right now",
- "I have to figure things out for myself right now",

because they want to avoid being seen as a bitch, and they want to bypass burning bridges. Understand this other Red Pill Truths about Women:

- 1. A WOMAN WILL GO FAR TO AVOID FEELING SOCIALLY UNCOMFORTABLE.
- 2. A WOMAN WANTS TO KEEP HER OPTIONS OPEN.
- 3. WOMEN ARE SOCIAL CREATURES AND CARE GREATLY ABOUT THEIR POSITION IN THEIR SOCIAL CIRCLE.
- 4. A WOMAN USES A MAN IN HER ORBIT, LIKE A MAN USES A TOOL IN HIS TOOLBOX.

Hence, women will say things that are intentionally ambiguous and non-committal, so as to not say "yes", but also not give a definite "no". This way you'll stick around just in case she needs to use you in the future. While men stick to values such as HONOR and doing the right thing, women stick to solipsism and being ruthlessly efficient. It's more ruthlessly efficient to lead a guy on with false hope, so as to use him in the meantime for his resources than it is to give a HARD REJECTION and burn the bridge. For some guys who are conditioned to pedestalize women, these hard truths to accept as reality, but you must UNDERSTAND THEM TO BE THE PAINFUL TRUTH, so that you can free yourself from enslavement to pussy. Pimp - don't simp.

The problem with SOFT REJECTIONS is that they are incredibly misleading for the vast majority of men who don't speak womenese. They also prevent guys from learning from their mistakes because a woman puts the blame of sex not occurring on herself. Finally, soft rejections lead guys to waste more time on a sexual dead-end instead of using their incredibly valuable time to generate more leads, or to invest in women who are actually worth it.

The key Red Pill Truth to understand is: DON'T BLAME A WOMAN FOR WHERE YOU ARE IN LIFE. Where you are in the present moment is based on the actions that you have done in the past. Where you will be in the future is based on the actions that you are doing in the present. You have to understand this incredibly important concept: YOU ARE THE ONE TO BLAME FOR YOUR CURRENT POSITION IN LIFE. If you wasted thousands of dollars on a woman who never really care about you, and only cared about the financial resources that she could extract from you then that's your fault. No one told you to believe her lies. No one told you to believe affectionate words such as "baby" meant that she really likes you. No one put a gun to your head and told you to spend your valuable resources on an ungrateful women would would trade-up the moment opportunity presented itself and conveniently rewrite history. YOU ARE THE ONE RESPONSIBLE FOR YOUR ACTIONS.

Likewise, if a date didn't go well then it's YOUR FAULT. And it's on you to figure out what set of behaviors or things that you said implied low social status, so that you can learn the lessons from the experience and implement a refined mating strategy in the future. The problem with soft rejections is that guys might not view them as rejections, but rather actually believe the woman when she puts the wool over the guy's eyes with "You're an amazing guy, and you'll find someone! I'm just not dating right now." This advice is misleading. It is more efficient to tell the guy exactly which specific set of behaviors he has to work on to improve his dating strategies in the future, but women won't reveal this because of their general principle of avoiding confrontation.

50

Law #84: A woman is a slave to her personality.

A woman is a slave to her personality.

SHE DOESN'T EXERCISE her freedom of choice and willpower to break out of human nature. If you understand a woman's character you'll be able to predict her behaviors. For instance: a woman of low social economic status is more likely to do drugs, steal, and have questionable morals than a woman of higher social economic status.

THE 4 KEYS TO BEING ABLE TO JUDGE A WOMAN'S CHARACTER

- 👉**To ascertain a woman's future behaviors look at her previous behaviors.** To see a woman's future, look at her past. To predict what she will do, look at what she has done.
- 👉**To ascertain a woman's character look at how she treats people who can't do anything back to her**. It is easy to be nice and friendly when it is convenient, but look to see how

she behaves when it is not convenient to do "the right thing".

- 👉**To see what kind of person she is, look to see how she treats her father because this is how she will come to treat you.** A woman has been conditioned to treat her dad - the authority figure - in a specific way, and she will come to treat you in the same manner. Likewise, pay attention to how she treats people who are close to her because if you become close to her (through being engaged in a long-term relationship with her) then chances are that she'll treat you in the same way.
- 👉**To ascertain a woman's level of promiscuity, gauge how many other instant gratification behaviors she engages in.** If you notice that she's engaging in instant gratification behaviors such as tattoos, piercings, weed, alcohol, mild altering drugs, revealing clothing, petty theft then these are signs that she has the kind of adventurous

51

LAW #85: A woman can't be trusted with your life.

A woman's words can't be trusted because of a woman's inherent biases to knowing the actual truth of the situation.

PEOPLE ENGAGE in self-denial because fantasies are more pleasant than truth. Even if you accurately interpret what a woman meant to say, and her view of the world, you still have not uncovered the true reality of the situation. How a woman views the world and the actual True Reality of the situation are different things. A woman's perspective can vary from 10/20 to negative 10/20 (what she believes can be the exact opposite of the reality) because there are psychological barriers (self-denial, confirmation bias, emotions, ego, distractions, etc) that prevent a woman from seeing things clearly.

Women are highly emotional creatures. Their perspective of how the world works is heavily subjective and based on their emotions; her judgement is clouded by her desires. **A woman will behave according to the world she WISHES she lived in - rather than confront the incredibly painful reality that the world is much more grim than she imagines.** This is similar to the story of Don Quixote; an aspiring knight would so emotionally attached to a perspective of reality that gave an emotional high that he convinced himself that the world was according to how he felt like - instead of looking at the RAW HARD COLD FACTS. It is painful to acknowledge certain truths about the situation, so women will just ignore those truths and pretend everything is sunshine; denial isn't just a Nile in Egypt. Denial of the truth is a psychological phenomenon women use to protect their emotional state and egos; it happens more often than you realize.

52

Law #86: Don't fall into the Halo Effect Trap.

Don't be fooled into thinking a woman is an angel of purity.

WOMEN HAVE an agenda - even if that agenda is unconscious. If a beautiful woman is with a guy then you better believe that she is getting some sort of value from him. Understand this very clearly in your mind: the moment a woman stops getting value from a guy is the moment that she vanishes from the face of the earth and focuses on other guys. Women are value-consumers, and will stay with you as long as you are a value-giver; fortunately for them, you are A MAN OF ABUNDANCE and have tons and tons of value to offer. You have a TON TO OFFER to any woman who enters into a sexual relationship with you. BE A GIVER OF VALUE.

It is crucial to be able to know the type of things that women value, so as to be able to give women value consistently and thus have them around in your life. It takes an understanding of Womenese to be able to provide the type of value that women find valuable; after all, what is valuable to you as a man, is not necessarily what is valuable to a woman. BURN THIS INTO YOUR BRAIN. Women value three things more than anything else in world and these three things are: good experiences, good emotions, and happiness. As a man, you are essentially a drug dealer dispensing the chemical high of good feelings to women - over a long period of time. She is using you for good emotions.

Guys misunderstand women because they take what they say through a literal medium, instead of reading the vast number of other signals that women are constantly sending out (such as facial expressions, body-language, tonality, a woman's past actions, and current actions). Womenese is ultimately understanding what a woman means to communicate, the truth of situation, and being able to communicate effectively. To truly understand what a woman means, you have to look at the entire CONTEXT of the situation (this means being aware of where you are in the environment, the dynamics of the situation, and key signals that a woman is sending out); likewise, to speak womenese effectively, you should take the CONTEXT of the situation to account.

53

Law #87: Control the Controllers part 1

TREAT WOMEN **as they are - not as you wish them to be.**

You have a conscious mind, and an unconscious mind - with the unconscious mind being far more powerful. Most of your daily decisions are run by the unconscious mind that is operating in the background. By changing the unconscious mind, you'll be able to change thousands of micro decisions and behaviors that happen on auto-pilot throughout the day. **A woman's unconscious mind is a primary driver of everything that she does in life.**

Another factor that influences a woman's decisions is her emotional state. Women are highly emotional creatures. They'll make important life-changing decisions based simply on how they feel at the moment. Women live in the emotions of the moment. This goes so far as women deciding certain things about the world are true simply because it feels true.

- By changing how she feels, you'll change how she views the world and how she will behave.
- By changing her unconscious mind, you'll likewise change how she behaves.

54

Law #87: Control the Controllers part 2

YOU ARE **A COMMODITY**

Create the frame that you are The Prize to be won. This frame is set by your actions, words, and body-language. You are the one who screens women to see if they're worth your time - not so much, the other way around. You are "VALUABLE ASSET" in the interaction. When this frame is set, then women will be uncontrollably attracted to you.

So what is the great secret to spiking your perception of high worth - to the point that women are dripping wet?

The secret is: SELF-PERCEPTION.

What does self-perception have to do with attracting women?

EVERYTHING.

Self-image influences external behaviors, body-language, and signals.

Women will view you based on how you view yourself. If you think you are a shit women will see you as a shit. If you see yourself as THE SHIT then women will likewise see you as THE SHIT. Know that you are GOLD, and that what you have to offer women is GOLD.

It's female nature to use a man's level of confidence as a shortcut to assess his competence in the game of life, because a woman's lifespan is too finite to give each man a full chance. A woman's time is too limited to give each guy a complete try, so she relies on Honest Signals and other indicators to see if the guy has "got the goods" that she is unconsciously and consciously looking for.

When you have an intense conviction of your high worth then it shows!

The body is always communicating by sending out external signals. Women automatically decode these signals that you are sending out about your worth, and then either get TURNED ON (by Displays of High Status) or turned off by displays of low status. The key is exude Sexy Signals, and avoid sending out Loser Signals. It's not just about hyping yourself up; it's also about not talking yourself down - even with self-deprecating humor.

You're wondering "Okay so I have to come across as IMPORTANT. I have to send out signals that show me as IMPORTANT, and avoid sending signals that make me seem IRRELEVANT. But how does one go about doing so? Does one memorize a list of 100 different sexy signals and then consciously send out all 100 - a nearly impossibly overwhelming task?"

There is one incredibly powerful shortcut that is the equivalent of consciously implementing 100 seductive behaviors. This self-development technique can be quite literally LIFE CHANGING.

By changing your beliefs to "I am THE GREAT CATCH", then you'll automatically have the behaviors that reflect this mentality. Beliefs = behaviors. Merely having the self-perception that you are a high-status man leads to behaving like a high-status man; likewise, having the self-perception that you are a fucking loser leads to behaving like a low-status man. Changing 1 internal belief leads to automatically changing 100s of behaviors associated with that belief.

The same is true in regards to controlling a woman's behaviors. By changing her belief system, you change the behaviors that go along with that.

1 BELIEF = 100+ BEHAVIORS

For instance: imagine knowing that you have a million dollars in your bank account. Simply that knowledge automatically changes the course of hundreds of micro behaviors. You don't need to read a list of 43 techniques in a hypothetical "How to Have Rich Man Energy to Make Accelerate the Networking Process" ebook, because you'll automatically have Rich Man Energy. When you have the belief system of a man who is naturally confident with women then you'll effortlessly do sexy confident behaviors. Being extremely confident won't just attract women into your life; it will also attract rich men into your life - effectively allowing you to network and create mutually beneficial business arrangements. Game skills are transferable, motherfucker!

Women naturally gravitate towards men they see as being of ultra high worth, so by creating this perception that you are high worth then you'll be able to fuck an ocean of pussy. Confidence is incredibly sexy to women. While you look for a young fertile body, a woman looks for high levels of confidence; she's screening for your level of self-belief, and using that as a shortcut to assess your worth in the culture and society she's born into.

High worth means different things to different types of women. Being a spiritual guru will open an ocean of pussy.

DEVELOPING TRUE CONFIDENCE

This self-perception of high worth comes from:

- - having self-respect,
- - having standards,
- - being willing to walk away,
- - being able to set clear boundaries,
- - standing up for yourself,
- - being assertive,
- - having competence in skills valued in society, and
- - having your life shit together.

IT GOES WITHOUT SAYING THAT: if you are an unemployed broke guy who:

- - lacks grooming,
- - dresses like shit,
- - doesn't have a future,
- - doesn't have an established peer network tribe of winners,
- - lacks a basic self-care routine,
- - smells,

then your confidence levels won't be significant. Confidence comes from life competence. If your life is falling apart, then consider taking a break from pickup, cutting off losers, cutting off low ROI activities, cutting off time-sinks (social obligations) and putting an extremely concentrated intense effort GETTING YOUR SHIT TOGETHER NOW!!

Allowing yourself to be treated like shit lowers your own confidence levels. Likewise, giving into social inhibitions compromises confidence. When you don't approach and make moves on a beautiful woman that you like then you are sending signals to your unconscious mind that you are UNWORTHY.

THE UNCONSCIOUS MIND WANTS PROOF - NOT JUST PROMISES

The unconscious mind is always listening. If you treat yourself like a priority then self-esteem will develop. If you treat yourself like trash the insecurities will develop. Behaviors are more influential in creating your personality than affirmations, self-suggestions, pep-talks, and research. You create your personality with every choice that you make.

The perception of high-worth is created by being dominant in interactions. Lead, lead, and do more leading. Being dominant creates a perception of status and confidence. Lead a woman towards a path of victory. According to researchers, simply behaving in a dominant manner makes people (women included) believe that you have greater levels of competence.

You don't need to compensate with money to make a woman like you. In fact, using money to attract a woman has the opposite of its intended effect. You'll end up attracting gold-diggers who don't give a fuck about you; they just care about the money that they get from you. The emerging sex (if any at all) will be lackluster or fake at best. The goal is not to have sex with a beautiful woman at all costs. The end goal is to have sex with a beautiful woman who is interested in you for you (your personality). There are levels to the game.

While men are attracted to physicality, women are attracted to personality and status. Unfortunately for women, their beauty is locked by whether or not they have won a genetic lottery of looking pretty. There is a limited flexibility that a woman can do about her own beauty - outside of plastic surgery. In stark contrast, through intense conscious consistent development, a man can raise his status within society, improve his game skills, and improve his abilities to generate value that is valued by women.

55

Law #87: Control the Controllers part 3

PROJECTION

WOMEN THINK that other people are just like them. Hence, how she describes and talks about other people is actually quite revealing about her own character. If she says that all of her friends are sluts then she probably has a promiscuous nature too. If she mentions that all of her boyfriends (sexual relationships) are assholes then you know what you have to do. ;-)

THREE MORE WAYS TO KNOW HER CHARACTER

Keep in mind that you can tell a lot about a woman by the places that she visits, the company that she keeps, and what she talks about.

1// For instance: if she's a student in the New York Police Academy then understand that it takes a certain kind of person to choose that kind of career path; for whatever reason, there's a lot of cuties going down this path (speaking from personal experience as one who attended New York Police Academy meetings). Another example: if she's a studious college student then it's clear that politically correct success is a value in her belief system. In general, you're more likely to meet higher quality relationship material young women in a college campuses than in bars and clubs; the former is focused on long-term success, while the latter is sunk in a lifestyle of perpetual instant gratification.

2// Likewise a woman's choice of friends reveals a lot about her character because it is human nature to become just like the people that you hang out with. If all of her friends are males then she probably doesn't have much to offer besides a used vagina. If she did have something of more substance to offer then she would actually have female friends. People with similar interests, goals and value CONNECT together. Hence, finding commonalities with the woman that you're interested in is an essential strategy in seduction. The value system of her friends is likely to be her value system too because of Group Think; women are like sheep following what other sheep do.

This is why having markers of success is an extremely effective strategy for seducing women. Women are influenced by the prevalent views of popular culture. And that prevalent view in popular culture is that success is "god". Dress like you are a successful man. Behave as if you shit gold. Act like you've got all of your shit together 100%.

Everyone doesn't know what the fuck is going on in this revolving earth that they suddenly found themselves in. For all we know, there could be a nuclear war in the next hour and we will all be dead. Yet, those who have learned to feign extreme confidence and act as if they've got it all together have been able to achieve far more success and generate more results than the rational "life is doom and gloom" losers. Positivity attract success.

SUBJECTIVE BIAS

It's a mistake to take a woman's words as the final truth because a woman doesn't see the world as it is; a woman sees the world as she is. A woman's own personal bias means that she has a subjective interpretation of reality - not an objective interpretation of reality. It would be foolish to take a woman's words as more than just clues about what the actual reality is. BE YOUR OWN SOURCE OF REFERENCE; DRAW THE TRUTH FROM WITHIN. In other words, have your own fucking opinion. Being a Yes Man and outsourcing your thinking to a woman is absolutely pathetic behavior.

EGO PROTECTION

A woman has a significant need to feel important. Women crave validation and approval from high status men for this very reason; it makes them feel valuable and fulfills a deep need for ego validation. A woman won't flat out say "I need to feel appreciated!" because this will make her look weak; instead she shows her need for approval with her behaviors. Even a "confident" woman craves your approval, attention and ego validation - even if she doesn't say this outright.

Understand the role of ego in communications is absolutely essential. A lot of what women say is just there to boost their own ego and feel important. When she talks its sometimes a matter of saying the kinds of things that will uplift her mood, and bolster her ego.

As a man, it's important that you have women work hard to win you over, and you have women jump through hoops on your behalf. Why? Because women value what they work for, and then to disregard that which is free and easily acquired. If a woman works hard to earn you, you better believe that she will appreciate you when she finally has earned you - much more than if you handed your heart and soul to her on a silver platter the moment you meet. WOMEN VALUE WHAT THEY WORK FOR is a maxim that you should burn into your mind, similar to the other maxims:

- **(1) WOMEN VALUE MEN THAT VALUE THEMSELVES.**
- **(2) WOMEN MEN THAT OTHER WOMEN WANT.**
- **(3) WOMEN WILL VIEW YOU AS YOU VIEW YOURSELF.**

EVEN IF YOU "FELL IN LOVE" with her the moment you saw her, don't let this be known and don't make grand confessions declaring your love. A woman is like a cat. Cats chase what is within their reach but not fully acquired; cats don't chase strings that they already have. You have play easy to be with, but hard to acquire. Don't give full validation because the full validation is exactly what keeps her chasing you. Use what you have as bait to keep women working hard for you (falling in love with you in the process); don't give away the bait for free.

It's imperative to understand that a woman has a deep need to feel important. Many of her actions stem from this basis of boosting her ego, and avoiding ego downfalls. For instance: a woman will buy expensive clothing she doesn't really need because it makes her feel valued and important. A woman won't make a move on a guy she likes because she is terrified of getting blown out and having her ego smitten. A woman is a slave to her ego - just like she is a slave to her personality. If you understand human nature, you'll be able to predict a woman's moves before they even happen - to an astonishingly shocking degree.

Men are very ego-centric. The right type of compliment

can be very disarming and the start of a great mutually beneficial connection. That being said, understand that sucking up to men is detrimental - just like kissing a woman's ass is. No one respects the kiss ass; don't pedestalize mere mortals who were born - outside of their own choice - and will then one die with nothing. Even someone who is wealthy is unworthy of being worshipped; one day they will rot and perish from the earth that is not their own. Everything in this world is temporary. We are mere passerby making the most out of a bizarre situation of being born in a world that we didn't choose to be born in, and don't fully understand. Ultra successful people aren't inherently smarter or more talented than you. They just think differently. They just have different kinds of experience. They shouldn't be worshipped. Use them merely as case studies to learn from, and believe that you can surpass them. I pity the man who worships a woman just because she won a genetic lottery and was a born with a hole at the bottom of her body.

CONFIRMATION BIAS

A woman's tendency to only see evidence that supports her prior views of the world, and disregard contrary evidence that conflicts with her prior views of the world. Bait a woman to work hard towards winning you love. She'll then backwards rationalize her behaviors as evidence that she does indeed like you - solidifying her attraction for you. Further events will be interpreted as more evidence.

WOMEN'S BELIEFS FOLLOW THEIR BEHAVIORS

Before sex, a woman might have a 100 reasons why she doesn't want to sleep with you; however, after sex a woman will have a 100 reasons why you're worth sleeping with . A woman's line of reasoning simply follow their behaviors. She'll rationalize away everything she does to avoid feeling guilty; then continue to find evidence for her prior decisions and prior conclusions because of a confirmation bias. This is how people in cults stay in cults; they've invested so much into the cult that it would be heart-breaking for them to admit that their entire life was a lie, and that they are stupid as fuck for falling for the confirmation bias fallacy. My intention with this writing isn't to make women look like shit, but to teach you how they operate so that you can condition her mind to serve your dick.

56

LAW #88: Be good at telling your story.

Story-telling is a vital aspect of communication. Have good stories.

HE WHO CONTROLS THE NARRATIVE, controls the relationship. Have the stronger frame. Be an effective story-teller and use stories to embed important values that you want her to internalize. Use stories that are emotionally relevant, integrate trending buzz-words, and a woman's personal trance words. Stories are incredibly effective tools of persuasion - even more so than logical lectures.

Know how to tell the most important story of all: your story. Be the master of that story. Spin it in a way that presents you in the best light.

57

Law #89: Communicate from a position of benelovence.

Don't hate women. It's simply a matter of understanding female nature and playing accordingly.

FEMALE NATURE ISN'T INHERENTLY bad, or good. It just is - just like a snake won't be blamed for biting an ankle. The key is to use your understanding of female nature to your seductive advantage - NOT letting female nature use you. If you aren't a player of the game, then you are being played. STOP being a bystander. START PLAYING THE FIELD.

Don't hate the game. Don't hate the player. Just accept them for what they are, and play the game accordingly. Hating women unconsciously impacts your game by compromising your vibe. Women can sense inner-resentment[1], and will mirror it back (look up "Mirror Neurons" on Google for more info on that). It is more seductive to have a benevolent intent and leave women better than when you first found them.

❄

1. Being bitter is a sign of a weak frame.

Law #90: Say more with less words.

Communicate more with less words.

APPEAR TO BE EFFORTLESS AND "MINDLESS" - even if you're executing a well thought-out plan. Being spontaneous is disarming to women and puts them at ease. Women will often discuss sex as occurring in a manner that "just happened". A woman wants to "be swept in the moment" and fall into an enjoyable experience where "one thing led to another" ending in sexual pleasure. MEN JUST WANT THE END RESULT; women enjoy the process. While you're ready to fuck within minutes, a woman will want to be taken through an emotional rollercoaster ride that accumulates in sexual intimacy. Foreplay isn't just physical, but emotional, logistical and verbal.

He who tries hard, dies hard. Even if you're putting in a lot of effort into the interaction, appear to be effortless - like you're just going with the flow and riding the emotional waves.

Womenese is an art form. Take a moment to think about how you talk to girls.

- Do you always say what is expected of you?
- Are you speech patterns predictable?

- Do you say that which is safe?
- Are your conversations nice?
- Are you overly concerned with making women feel comfortable?

If you answered yes to 4/6+ more of these questions then you have a fucking problem, and that is that you're boring as fuck. If you learn anything from this book then let it be this incredibly important Womense concept: say more with less words.

59

LAW #91: See the world from her perspective.

When talking to a woman, make what you are saying RELEVANT to the core values that she believes in, and the core topics that she is interested in. Always relate it back to these things.

TALKING from a position of situational relevance will ensure that your communications are SMOOTH and not weird. Be a wolf dressed in sheep clothing. Whatever you say to a woman, relate it back to what is emotionally valuable to her because a woman is always listening to the "What's in it for me?" Channel.

❄

"WHY DO I need to learn to speak Womanese in order to understand Women? Why don't women just say what they mean and what they say? Why don't women just articulate clearly in their mind - instead of playing games?"

Reason #1: Women can very inarticulate. Even if a woman WANTS to accurately explain her perspectives she may be unable to do so because she is not good at putting her thoughts into words. Put simply: **women suck at communicating effectively and instead just leave hints about what's on their mind.**

Reason #2: Women will go to far lengths to avoid feeling socially awkward - even blatantly lying to your face. Women are physically more fragile than men and thus, since the caveman era: have used their social skills (instead of direct aggression) to gain power and exert influence. In other words, women will prefer to avoid awkward social confrontation if possible, and will use white lies to bend the truth to help them avoid these social confrontations. To a narcissistic female liar, lying is a way of life; the truth is simply a matter of how she feels like at that exact moment in time. A narcissistic female liar doesn't even feel guilty for lying because how desensitized she is to it; nor, would she even admit that her white lies are lies in the first place.

Reason #3: Women are not good at deciphering the truth themselves. A woman's strong emotions makes her susceptible to self-denial and self-deception. **A woman is not in touch with the deeper side of her nature**, and thus she can't say the truth even to herself. This is why asking women for dating advice is not prudent; her own intense emotional bias prevents her from assessing the situation in a clear light.

Reason #4: Certain dark truths are too ego-damaging, stigmatized and humiliating for a woman to confess to, so she'll lie to cover it up. The classic example of this is a woman's desire for sex. Women really do enjoy sex and crave it; however, they can't verbalize this explicitly because society (and religious men will judge them for it). If a woman is 18 and comes from a traditional family with spiritual values, she might be shamed by her social circle for engaging in "sinful lust". She doesn't want to feel slutty because the guilt is painful. So a woman with a traditional background will either deny her lust for men (even from herself and even if she engages in sex), or she will admit this lust for men for herself but will hide it from others - even as going as far saying that she is a "virgin". Women will easily bend the truth intentionally if they think it makes them look better; this is a woman's words can't be trusted and a man is forced to use tests/look for other indicators to ascertain the truth of the situation.

While you have purchased this book on womenese, understand that ultimately it doesn't matter what a woman really meant to say. What matters is TRUTH OF THE SITUATION. A woman meant to say something that would only have shed light to the truth of the situation, but not explained it entirely; its up to your detection skills to be able to use to clues to put together a puzzle piece that shows an accurate map of the reality.

60

Law #92: Don't get sucked into her world.

Don't spend too much time trying to figure a woman out. Pedestalizing a woman in your mind, leads to pedestalizing her with your behaviors. Ask yourself this question: "While I am spending my time thinking about her, is she spending time thinking about me?"

DON'T GET CARRIED AWAY THINKING about a particular woman because thinking too much about a woman leads to developing oneitis and strong feelings - which then leads to needy behavior. The more you think about her, the more emotionally invested you become in her - eventually developing feelings for her. Instead of obsessively thinking about a particular woman (causing yourself to fall deeper into clutches) bait her to think about you by sending mixed signals.

Focus on sharpening your game skills - instead of getting a specific woman. You're learning game **NOT** to get a specific woman in general but to be good with women in general.

Law #93: Fuck or bounce.

Change her mind, change her experience.

HOW SHE SEES **THE WORLD IS HOW SHE WILL EXPERIENCE IT. A positive outlook leads to a positive emotional experience. Hence, it is helpful to be positive when dealing with women to encourage them to focus on what's about good in life, and to experience the good emotions that comes from gratitude.**

FUCK, OR BOUNCE. Don't be the friend.

NEWSFLASH: If you are knee-deep in the friend-zone with a particular woman then you're giving away the relationship benefits of being with you for free. You are giving away the best parts of yourself FOR FREE**. It's much smarter to have a "cost" of being with you, and that "cost" is that women within your inner-circle need to "pay" is sexual access to their bodies - as well as an acceptance of specific frames that are conducive to that sex continuing to occur.** These frames include accepting you as "THE AUTHORITY" in the dynamic between you and her, accepting your role as the leader who makes decisions for the both of you, and accepting you as THE PRIZE.

She "takes one for the team" by submitting to overtly sexual frames that you set up, and blatant physical advances - even if she isn't in the mood for sex right now. That being said, if you're good at touching a woman's body in specific areas (and using a correct sequence of motions), then she will WANT to have sex with you; she will become physically addicted to you, hooked on the chemicals released in her brain that come with your physical touch, and the pleasurable habits will overtake her. Women WANT TO HAVE SEX - just not with fucking socially-inept losers living in their mom's basement playing video-games all day long lacking in any cool hobbies/passions. BE THE APEX ALPHA WARRIOR.

It's essential for you to understand that YOUR TIME IS WORTH REAL MONEY. Your psychological energy is WORTH REAL MONEY. Are you giving it away FOR FREE to a woman who won't even reciprocate by allowing sexual advances to occur, and to allow the interaction progress at a reasonable pace towards sex? Well STOP.

A high status man wouldn't waste his time on bullshit, and women intuitively know this. They quickly lose respect for a man who puts up with bullshit.

You have enough friends in your life right now as it is, and you don't need more. You have to be clear about what you want out of her. Fuzzy goals lead to fuzzy results. Be willing to admit that you desire "dirty" sex with her; acknowledge this and then make moves to realize this goal. Continually progress the interaction towards sex; increase the level of physical intimacy at a reasonable pace until you BANG THE SHIT OUT OF HER. Making a move will force a woman to show you the cards that she is holding; if she keeps putting ON the breaks then it's time to kick her to the curb and stop wasting your time.

Kicking her to the curb means letting go of the illusions that you have developed in your mind that she is somehow "one of a kind" and "special". You need to BREAK YOURSELF - in regards to that false deception. She is NOT special. She is NOT one of a kind. She is NOT a unique goddess. These inaccurate perceptions are your feelings tricking you into mating; it's this psychological and emotional bonding process that has ensured the survival of the human race. You have to snap out of it and stop clinging on to the time-wasting narrative "that one day you will get her".

Don't you get it? If you're sinking in your time with a female friend that doesn't value you enough to see you in a sexual light then you are WASTING TIME that you could have spent on a woman who would value you in a sexual light, finding one that would, or developing your skills to have a higher level of worth in the sexual marketplace. OPEN YOUR EYES TO THE TRUTH: If you are too pussy to make a move on a woman that you like the you are pathetic. Your ancestors fought in WW1-WW2 - risking their lives in the battle-field - and you can't even show sexual intent? Yes, that's a fucking problem. And yes, you need to MAN THE FUCK UP SON!!! THIS MEANS YOU. THIS MEANS TODAY. THIS MEANS NOW.

Women are much smarter and more cunning than you realize. In fact, the average women is superior to a man in understanding dynamics in game. While men are busy talking about sports, video-games, working out and making money, women love gossiping and discussing relationships.They'll spend hours upon hours chatting over the phones over different issues encountered in man-to-woman interactions/relationships. This is why a lot of old-school set of memorized lines (known as routines) are centered around stories of couples; it's because next to cold reads, relationships are the second biggest chick crack subject. All of this talk about relationships has led to women having an acute understanding of the subject matter, and you should never underestimate the level of a woman's cunning - even if she's operating on an unconscious strategies. Men conquer worlds; women conquer the conquerers of worlds.

Women know what they are doing: when they string men along with false hope that one day the guy might have sexual access to her body. They'll keep the guy hooked, so that he will continue to do free favors for her in the meantime. Women like two different types of guys: providers, and lovers. On one extreme is the APEX ALPHA LOVER who turns her WET, and the other extreme is a BETA SIMP PROVIDER. If you aren't the lover then you are by default: the provider, and she is stringing you along with false hope of sexuality in the super distant future that may never happen.

YOUR TIME IS YOUR MOST VALUABLE RESOURCE and you're going to throw it down the toilet (!) with a woman who is playing waiting games with you? HA! When a woman friend-zones you, what she is really saying is that she doesn't consider you to be high status enough to be sexually-worthy, but she'll still use your resources in the meantime. She wants you to orbit around her so she can continue to exploit your imaginary relationship and false idealization of her - brought on by unreciprocated feelings. In the meantime, she'll continue her search for a better guy.

Women continue their cock carousal with Apex Alphas until they start sensing that their looks are fading and they need to lock-down a wealthy provider before their sexual market value plummets. It's not the guy that she's attracted to but his wallet and her performance in bed will reflect this - as she'll rush the guy to cum, so she can move on with her life. Women are not attracted to beta simp providers, but will still spend time with them for the sake of pragmatic purposes. Don't get bitter; GET BETTER.

<u>The first thing you can do to instantly raise your sexual market value is to get better at being a</u>

producer of emotions that women value - specifically fun, intrigue, and good emotions. Learn to generate these emotions from scratch with specific techniques that I mention in my first masterpiece book "Conversation Casanova Mastery". When you give tons of value (NOT the financial kind), you become valuable and eventually she becomes emotionally addicted to you.

You aren't asking the right questions. You are only asking "How do I please her?" instead of focusing on "How can she please me?" Alpha Males TAKE WHAT THEY WANT. TAKE VALUE by touching her body from the very start of the interaction, keeping the touching frequency, and escalating the level of intimacy in the touching. TAKE ACTION EVERY DAY MOTHERFUCKER!!!!

❄

WHEN A WOMAN SAYS "I NEED SPACE" what she really means is that she needs your dick to move further away from her, so that another dick can enter inside. If you're taking up her time, then she has less time to invest in men perceived to be of higher worth in her eyes. Understand this Red Pill Truth about Women: A WOMAN WILL ALWAYS GO FOR THE BEST POSSIBLE OPTION AVAILABLE TO HER.

A woman's level of sexuality depends on the guy that she is with. An Apex Alpha male - running unconscious lover game - unleashes a woman's wild sexual side. The woman will behave like a sexual ANIMAL - enough to make a nice guy blush. A Wimpy Beta Male - who judges women negatively on their promiscuous nature, and runs predictable provider game - gets a woman's starfish position (if he even gets sex at all). When it comes to Beta Males women just stick around for pragmatic purposes such as resource extraction - rather than a lust for the guy's physicality and a genuine attraction to his personality.

The relevant Red Pill Truth here is: **ALPHA FUCKS, BETA BUCKS.** Alphas get lustful sex with women because women are with them due to their personality and physicality; in contrast, betas get starfish sex with women (if any sex at all) because women are with them due to their financial resources and other practical purposes. Not every woman marries for love; some women marry for practicality.

What is considered "disgusting" versus "dangerously SEXY" depends on a man's level of attractiveness. A man who is clearly high in sexual market value is perceived as "cute" and his advances will be "cute; the same advances by a man who is low in sexual market value is perceived as "creepy" and "verbal harassment”.

62

Law #94: Bypass emotional bias. Execute coldly.

As a man, learn to ignore your feelings and trust the evidence.

UNDERSTAND this about how women understand the reality of the situation: A WOMAN WILL SEE THINGS ACCORDING TO WHAT GIVES THEM THE GREATEST EMOTIONAL PAYOFF. For instance: if a woman breaks up with a former lover then it gives her greater emotional payoff to say things like "I broke up with him because he was an asshole and a loser!! He had no future!" This gives her a greater emotional-payoff than to say something along the lines of "If everyone who I date is an asshole then maybe I am the asshole. There's something about me that makes men do crazy things that are against their best interest. I seem to feed off the attention that I get from generating drama and some men don't have time to deal with this pettiness. The guy is a pretty good guy, but he lacked the composure to deal with the nuclear shit-tests that I threw his way when I lost self-control and threw one of my classical temper tantrums."

Further, a woman's susceptibility to confirmation bias only

confirms her prior world views; in other words, women see the world as they are - not as the world actually is. This is why how a woman describes her friends and other people in her life reveals a lot about her personality. You can tell a lot about a woman about how she describes her prior associates. If she describes her prior associates in negative terms then be aware that you are dealing with a hypersensitive woman with poor conflict management skills and will generate negative vibes the second something goes wrong; however, if she describes her prior associates in positive terms then you'll know that she prioritizes positive vibes, and has good conflict management skills. Not all good fucks are good long term relationship material; when it comes to long term relationships, or the type of woman you would like to build a family with, there's a wide range of competency found in women and a woman's words provide a glimpse into her skill level of dealing with inherent challenges common in long term relationships.

Women are often too busy pursuing instant gratification and meaningless distractions such as the latest hype on Netflix, to invest time in figuring themselves out, and creating a realistic mature perspective in the reality that they live in; this is why women's perspective on life has a lot of inaccuracies, and why your masculine frame is the more competent one and should also be the dominant one in the relationship.

Remember: a submissive woman is a sexual woman; as a man, you should lead from the very start. By behaving like a dominant masculine man, you'll unleash her submissive feminine side and thus her sexual side.

63

LAW #95: Listen to understand - not just to reply.

Use a woman's personal language, valued beliefs, and worldview when communicating with her.

"SO WHAT'S the point of deciphering what a woman means to say and her view of the world?" the aspiring seducer ponders. The point is that it will allow you to speak to her in a way that is in her Personal Language. You want to answer a woman based on HER perspective of the world because this will resonate the most with her - rather than talking to a woman based on YOUR (more accurate) perspective of the world which will fall on deaf ears.

Let's say that you are suddenly teleported to Planet Homogobins. You're surrounded by green aliens with lizards living on their heads and long earrings that touch the ground. In this planet, these aliens stay awake from 12am-4am and spend the rest of the day deeply staring into the cosmos. These aliens speak in a different language than you, have different values, dress differently, and have an entirely different way of living (culture).

Normally you would do your own thing and give zero fucks about green aliens and their irrelevant bullshit. You're too busy pursuing your own goals than to care about what green aliens care about. However, in this particular situation you realize that: (1) you need food to survive, and (2) you're horny as fuck and want to fuck green aliens that are legal. Therefore, you have to figure out (1) what is considered valuable on this planet so that you can trade it for food, and (2) what is considered to be high sexual market value and high social status in this culture, so that you can become that type of person.

The problem is that if you speak English to them, they won't even understand what you're saying. You need to learn a different language (Alien Womenese) to be able to communicate with them, and to be able to understand what they are saying/the signals they are sending out. Then in the process of reciprocal communication, you discover what is valuable to these green aliens on the planet and how you can give that sort of value as a form of currency in exchange for food. Then you discover the type of man that these green 18 year old female aliens find attractive and become that type of man - which (you guessed it) is communicated to you and you are able to learn, because you understand Alien Womense.

Women are not always aligned with their true nature. To ask a woman point-blank what do you find attractive in a man can lead to misleading answers. To figure out what a woman is actually attracted to, you have to look at THE TYPE OF MEN THAT SHE HAS HAD RELATIONSHIPS WITH IN THE PAST, WHAT SHE TALKS ABOUT, and HER BODY LANGUAGE RESPONSES. These are clues about which sort of behaviors and embodiment of traits will turn her on.

Each women has several (or one) sexy stereotype that she is attracted to - whether it's successful business man, spiritual guru, Bad Boy Rebel, The Party Guy, or corporate lawyer who fucks. Once you figure out which sexy stereotype is best aligned with your personality and the type of girl that you want to fuck, then the next step is to hang out in places where women are attracted to that type of guy. Develop a social circle and become the number one guy in that social circle because women fuck the APEX ALPHA MALE - not the #2. In the game of seduction, it's winner TAKES ALL and losers TAKE NOTHING. You have to be AT THE APEX.

KEY POINTS TO REMEMBER FROM PRIOR CHAPTERS:

- Don't just see what she said - look at what was NOT said.
- Don't just view what her words mean on the surface level; look for a deeper meaning.
- Much of what women do say is just random nonsense that isn't worth deciphering, but sometimes there are noteworthy remarks that will leave clues on how to seduce her - if you pay attention.
- Be a good detecting at deciphering the truth.
- Operate on a map of reality - instead of a map of illusions and self-denial.
- Listen to understand - not just to reply.

64

Law #96: Be aware of your awareness.

YOU COULD BE DEALING with a female narcissist and not even know it!

Awareness is absolutely essential to protecting yourself from common exploitations used by aggressive women. If you thought women were stupid, think again; they often have a cunning agenda. This agenda can be so covert that even the manipulator may not be consciously aware of it. Even a woman's submission is a ruse to make you feel relaxed, let your guard down, and to gain your trust.

Men conquer worlds; women conquer men. Don't underestimate a woman's capacity for bullshitting you, and utilizing covert manipulation tactics for you to do her bidding.

How can you protect yourself from something that you don't even see!!?

> Simply being aware of common female manipulation tactics will give you greater levels of immunity against them. Acute self-awareness = improvement.

When you become acutely conscious of covert manipulation tactics used by women then you'll be able to identify them in real-time when they occur, and STOP BEING AN EASY TARGET SUCKERED INTO THEIR TRAPS.

Here's the truth: female narcissists use people in the same manner that men use tools. The'll use the tool for all that it's worth and then discard it; cancel culture encourages women in hitting the "NEXT!!!" button and jumping on to a new dick the moment there is some conflict over a silly, petty issue.

When a psychopath is finished milking the cow until it bleeds, she will discard the target into the trash. She doesn't "love you" per se; she only "loves" what she gets out of you, and the idealization that you represent in her mind. If you are in a relationship with a narcissist, understand that they are with you for as long as they keep getting something out of you. The moment the value ceases to be available then they will disappear. Their "affection" is conditional.

Don't take it personally. It's just built into their nature. You wouldn't blame a wolf for eating a sheep; don't blame a predatory narcissist for going after someone she perceives as prey. It's important that you get what you want out of a relationship with a woman - just like she's ensuring that she's getting her needs met. THE FIRST KEY FOR DEALING WITH WOMEN IS TO KNOW WHAT YOU WANT. After all, if you aren't clear about what you want out of this whole connection then how do you expect to randomly get it?

The sense of loyalty that you feel is misguided. It isn't your responsibility to save her from herself, or to fix by playing the role of a therapist. Don't get attached because of your inner Savior Complex; playing the "Victim Card" is exactly what these narcissistic predators do to entrap you into their clutches and exploit you for psychological/emotional resources. Don't continue to drain time, energy, and money into a woman with emotional baggage and issues - hoping that she will magically change.

You would just waste months (sometimes years) of psychological energy trying to get a woman to change and still get barely move the bottom line forward. As a result, you'll miss out on other opportunities in the sexual marketplace. Realize that energy wasted on a sexual dead-end was vital energy you could have spent in developing yourself to reach your own full potential!

Female narcissists brainwash men into being servants, and these guys fall for it because:

- (1) they are desperate for some pussy,
- (2) they lack other options,
- (3) they don't have the game to generate new options,
- (4) they fail to recognize their tremendous potential, and
- (5) they have been brainwashed by society to pedestalize women with "the woman is always right" bullshit.

Getting into a sexual relationship with a beautiful woman at all costs - including selling out your soul - is not a "win". Don't sell out your life purpose and life goals just because you want some sex, and want the empty-ego-validation status of "lay+1" or "in a relationship". Making important life decisions with emotions and thinking with a dick has ruined the lives of many men.

BE A MAN ON YOUR LIFE PURPOSE. Have an amazing life. A woman is just a supplement to that. PUT YOURSELF FIRST. Never compromise your life purpose or peace of mind for the sake of pussy; you'll lose self-respect, and she'll (unconsciously or consciously) lose respect for you too.

Narcissistic women are absolutely obsessed with themselves. They have difficulty seeing outside their own personal world. Empathy shown is fake. Altruism exuded is merely a ploy to gain your trust with virtue signaling before making a move for significant resource extraction.

If she's hanging around she's certainly getting something out of it. While every healthy relationship has a mutual exchange of value that is win/win, in the case of having a relationship with a toxic narcissist the relationship is often one-sided. There is a massive power-imbalance where one partner takes significantly more value than the other partner.

Men get trapped into one-sided imaginary relationships where they do all of the giving, and almost none of the taking. The woman tricks them into thinking that they just have to comply with their demands even more, so they can get access to a prior state of sexual access and physical intimacy. At this point, the man's feelings are so intense and he is so emotionally attached, that he continues to cling on to her and doing whatever she wants in the hopes of "winning" over her affection.

Unfortunately for him, she becomes disgusted with being worshipped in this matter and views his pedestalizations as proof that he is weak/inferior in the sexual marketplace. The more power he gives away by chasing her (without her reciprocating), the more disgusted she becomes; ironically, by trying harder to win her over, he actually loses her. Intuitively a woman knows that a high status man would LEAD and DOMINATE. A high-status man wouldn't beg, give up his social power, and make her the center of his life. By valuing yourself and putting yourself FIRST, women become more attracted to you.

Leveraged correctly, a woman can be a helper in helping you achieve your life mission. Leveraged incorrectly, a woman can destroy you. Never underestimate the potential cruelty of women; their sexual nature is ruthless in easily discarding men perceived to be of low worth and trading up when the opportunity presents itself.

BE THE FUCKING BEST. When you're at the apex of

the mountain, you don't have to worry about the competition. Be a predator. When you are skilled at manipulation tactics yourself, you'll be able to recognize when manipulation tactics are being used on you and properly counteract them. It takes game to recognize game. Learn the fucking rules of the game, and play them better than anyone.

65

Law #97: Think ahead.

Always be a few steps ahead.

WOMENESE IS the ability to understand female communication on a deep level, and being able to effectively communicate in a manner that is understood by females. Put simply: Womense is the art of being able to decode, and encode Female OS. When you can speak Womense fluently then you'll have ample insight into how a woman operates, and you'll able to predict her moves several moves in advance; when you know ahead of time how a woman will behave, you'll be able to have calculated moves ahead of time that preemptively disarm her. ALWAYS BE AT LEAST ONE STEP AHEAD OF HER.

And if you're really skilled at the game, you're several moves ahead of her - yet you come across as unscripted and in the present moment. No matter what a woman says, or does, you would have already anticipated it and have a prepared a counter-response.

One of the key strategies to effective game is to create a system designed to get you laid and sticking to that system every single day. By doing the same key behaviors over and over, you'll eventually get mastery over them. **After all, repetition is the mother of skill.**

- For instance, if you just have one opening line to start conversations with women and you focus on one area of meeting women then eventually you'll master both of them. You'll know the natural follow-ups that occur from that opening line. You'll know the nooks and crannies of that specific location (including the best specific times that women come out).
- In contrast, if you do something new each time then you won't actually master any thing. It's like someone who "trains" by trying 1 new instrument every week; the jack of all trades is the master of none, and it is mastery that gets you sexual results. Stick to one game-plan until it succeeds.

66

Law #98: Stay true to your values.

WHEN YOU STAND FOR NOTHING, you fall for anything. Don't compromise yourself.

THE DANGER OF SPEAKING WOMENSE

While this is a book that talks about learning to understand and speak Womense, there is an inherent danger that is worth mentioning, and that danger is being pulled too far into this blackhole of caring too much what women think. As an Alpha Male man, it is imperative that you have your own life purpose and goals that you're busy focusing on; don't take Womense too far and start obsessing with thoughts like:

- "What did she really mean when she said THAT?!"
- "How did she interpret my words?!"
- "How did she interpret my interoperation of her words?"
- "What was running through her mind when I responded this way to her?!"

- "What did I say that caused her to behave in THIS WAY?"
- How will I be perceived if I behave in this specific way?"

These thoughts are conducive to the Analysis Paralysis Trap, Excuseitis Trap and the Information Trap. These traps are incredibly common and they stop men dead in the tracks from succeeding with women. Highly intelligent men are especially susceptible to having their sharpened intellect work against them.

I. ANALYSIS PARALYSIS TRAP

In the Analysis Paralysis Trap, the man is too busy thinking about the situation to act. While The Thinker is busy thinking, the Man of Action runs laps around The Thinker. The key is to set a limit to how much time one spends in analyzing the situation, and then when that limit is reached: FOCUS ON RAW, PURE ACTION IN THE FIELD.

II. EXECUSEITIS TRAP

In The Excuseitis Trap the aspiring seducer uses his high IQ to come up with different reasons why today is not a good day to take action - landing from "I'm too old and unattractive" to "She probably has a boyfriend." As soon as one allows for excuses then he will easily become frozen because there is always a "VERY LEGITIMATE" excuse readily available to avoid taking action. The higher the IQ one is, the smarter and more sophisticated the excuses will sound. The key is to take it upon yourself to have a "NO EXCUSES ALLOWED POLICY!!!"

III. THE INFORMATION TRAP

Finally in the Information Trap, the aspiring seducer doesn't take action because he perceives himself having a lack of necessary information; he's fallen into the mistaken belief of "I can't do anything, until I know everything." The aspiring seducer mistakenly tries to come up with a PERFECT PLAN based on ALL OF THE INFORMATION and then take PERFECT ACTION. The problem with this is that there is such thing as the perfect pickup. Pickup is messy. In the process of seducing women, mistakes will be made, and that's okay. The key is to keep going with confidence and hold a confident frame of "It's ALWAYS ON. Everything is going according to plan."

DON'T GROW A VAGINA. Spending a little bit of time seeing the world from a woman's perspective does have its practical uses. See the world from a woman's eyes, and you'll be able to better understand her needs, AND how her needs and your needs aligned - creating a win/win connection with the beautiful woman (a mutually beneficial exchange of value). However, spend too much time seeing the world from a woman's eyes, and you'll start losing your own identity and sense of personal priorities.

Spend too much time trying to understand how a woman thinks, and you'll develop a vagina; while a little of a good thing is beneficial, too much of it is harmful. Just because you're reading a book to understand how women THINK, doesn't mean you should spend all of your time pondering how women think because that would result in you becoming feminine and pedestalizing pussy. Spend a bit of time each day researching seduction-self-help topics, but don't spend more than an hour on the subject matter; it's better to prioritize taking action in the field and reaching your full potential than delving deeper into research. FOCUS ON YOUR PERSONAL DEVELOPMENT.

Remember that one of the primary Alpha Male Rules of Life is: PUT YOURSELF FIRST. Women are too busy obsessing over themselves to care too much about you. If you don't care about yourself then you will be lost. YOU HAVE TO BE A FIGHTER FOR YOURSELF! That's a job no one can do but you! Take care of yourself just like you would take of a best friend; push yourself just like a coach would push a client.

SEE A WOMAN'S WORLD, BUT DON'T GET SUCKED INTO IT You'll notice that women will often embellish details in their narratives because they would rather live in an imaginary, pleasant fantasy than confront a harsh, painful reality. Spending too much time thinking about what a woman is thinking is a waste of psychological energy because the opportunity costs are significant. You spent so much time thinking about a particular woman ("What did she mean when she did THAT? What was the deeper meaning behind what she said that day?") that you failed to develop yourself further and failed to pursue other women. When one's emotions become engaged it can be VERY EASY to spend hours replaying scenes in your mind thinking about what it all means, instead of focusing on high priority tasks and your life's purpose.

Further, women's inner-worlds are not built on objective truth but rather pleasant lies. When you discover the deep truths about how women understand the world, you'll also get the rude awakening that women's perspective on the world is pathetic, inaccurate and dark. While it is beneficial for your sake to understand what women VALUE, so you can deliver that form of value to them and BECOME VALUABLE, it's also important to not be too pulled into a woman's frame. While it's beneficial for your sake to having a working knowledge of how women view the world, so you can understand how they operate, don't be swept into their perspective and start behaving like a woman yourself; you want to look into the darkness, but not be pulled into it. HAVE THE STRONGER FRAME. Even if a woman's frame is incredibly strong, your frame must be even stronger!!!

There is an extremely important concept to understand: PSYCHOLOGICAL IMMUNITY. Women exploit mentally-weak men for their resources. If a woman recognizes that a man with money is mentally weak then she will put her hooks on him; she'll send sexy photos, use endearing language like "babe", and make (empty) "promises" to snare him into his world. Once the man becomes emotionally and psychologically addicted to her pussy, she'll suddenly withdraw her attention, affection and access to her pussy. The man will then do whatever she wants to get back what he became used to.

WHEN A MAN STANDS FOR NOTHING, HE FALLS FOR ANYTHING. When a man in a relationship doesn't have a life purpose, and life goals: then a woman easily takes over his life, and her frame becomes his frame. Her thoughts and values becomes his thoughts and values. He loses his own identity and becomes just like her - turning her into the center of his universe. The man grows a vagina. Women find this simp type of behavior incredibly repulsive.

WHEN A MAN STANDS FOR SOMETHING, HE HAS PSYCHOLOGICAL IMMUNITY. As a man, it's important to have your own goals, and life purpose that you are striving for every single day. Make each day count! It has been said in the seduction community: "The best way to get women is to have something better to do than to get women." Women can sense when a man has nothing going on his life, and its very unattractive.

In contrast, when a man has an exciting lifestyle and an exciting life mission then the woman gets swept into his world. She accepts the man's thoughts and perspectives as her own. She changes her personality to help the man on his life's mission. This is where you want to be. BE A DECISIVE WARRIOR who inspires followers,

Women want to follow and submit to a more dominant man, but they won't follow a loser who can't get his shit together. Get your shit together. Become a leader. And watch women follow your lead - psychologically, logistically, and of course most importantly: physically. Dominate completely. Own her soul.

67

SPECIFIC EXAMPLES

WHAT SHE SAYS **VERSUS WHAT IS REALLY HAPPENING**

CHECKING OUT YOUR AVAILABILITY

- **1 "Do you have a girlfriend?"**
- **2 "Are you Single?"**
- **3 "Is anyone home with you?"**
- **4 "I'm sure your girlfriend would enjoy that." [Or mentions your girlfriend at all] to bait you into saying "I don't have a girlfriend".**
- **5 "Are you seeing anyone?"**

She is assessing your level of social proof, and your availability in the sexual marketplace. This can be because she interested in you for her personal self, or potentially she wants to hook you up with a female friend that has in mind.

Assuming that this is a serious question and not a sarcastic question (based on her body-language) respond by mentioning that you had a prior ex-fiancé in the very distant past, but you're single in the present. While you do have "female friends", you are still searching for "the right one".

BINGO 🔥 If a woman is asking these type of questions (in combination with positive body-language) then it's a strong sign that she interested in you.

💧 CHECKING OUT YOUR LEVEL OF INVESTMENT

- **6 "Do you love me?"**
- **7 "Did you miss me?"**
- **8 "To what extent do you love me?"**
- **9 "Is she more pretty than I am?"**
- **10 "Are you free now?"**

She is setting you up to be susceptible to a big ask. By saying that you love her, it will naturally follow that you'll agree to do whatever she asks afterwards. Women want loyal soldiers in their army. These questions are designed to see if you're a loyal soldier in her personal army, and thus how much she can take from you.

She wants to see how much power she holds over you, so that she can unconsciously decide how much bullshit she can get away with in the future. She is going to do some stupid shit, and have you put up with because of your "love".

This is a cocky question because it assumes that you're already in love with her. It lets you know that you may be dealing with an overly arrogant woman who assumes that she has more worth in the sexual marketplace than she actually does.

These type of questions could also mean that she is feeling insecure and wants to get some quick ego validation by affirming that at least she has you in her life. It's important to look at the context to properly interpret her words.

Keep in mind that a woman who is feeling insecure is easier to seduce than a woman who is arrogant. Combine giving a compliment with physical escalation at the same time; say "You have sexy legs" as you massage her leg. Verbally framing the interaction as having a sexual charge sets the stage for further smooth physical escalation.

FISHING FOR COMPLIMENTS

- **12 "I'm so fat."**
- **13 "I'm so ugly."**
- **14 "This dress doesn't look good on me."**
- **15 "You don't even like me."**
- **16 *flashes a part of her body to you***

The woman is feeling insecure, and wants you to validate her ego by correcting her. When she says that she's fat, she wants you to confirm that she is still attractive. When she says she is ugly, she wants you to tell her that she is pretty.

When she flashes a part of her body to you "accidentally", it's because she wants you to physically escalate on her.

PLAYING BUILD A BETTER BETA

- **17 "We aren't communicating that well."**
- **18 "We need to talk."**
- **19 "You should do [xyz]."**
- **20 "You should stop doing [abc]."**
- **21 "You should apologize to me."**

What she means to say is *"You aren't listening to me me explain why my needs are important."* In these instances, the women wants to continue the relationship and is working towards building you into the type of person that she thinks she is more compatible with in the long term.

Unfortunately, often women don't give good advice when they tell you to behave a specific way. They'll tell you who they think they are attracted to, but they actually aren't attracted to the ultimate nice guy that they're preaching you to become. Remember: when seeking advice on how to catch fish, ask a fisherman - not a fish.

ATTEMPTING TO PUT YOU INTO THE FRIENDZONE

- **22 "I don't want to ruin our friendship."**
- **23 "I see you as just a friend."**
- **24 "I'm not going to have sex with you."**
- **25 "I'm going to go to your place, but we're not having sex."**
- **26 "I thought we weren't going to have sex!"**
- **27 "We shouldn't be doing this."**

When a woman mentions the fact that she wants you to only be friends with her then this is because she isn't attracted to you in the moment, and **sees your genes as inferior.** Keep in mind that for men attraction is a light-bulb switch, but for women **attraction is a volume knob**.

While it is true that she doesn't feel attraction for you right now at this exact moment which is why she says some bullshit like "we are not going to have sex!", it is also true that women live in the emotions of the moment and her feelings about you can change.

She might mean what she is saying at that exact moment, but the situation can change and she can suddenly become sexually aroused later. The appropriate response to these kind of statements is to explain to the female is "We'll see. I'm quite charming."

THE MOST CUNNING GAME THAT WOMEN PLAY IS PRETENDING THAT THEY AREN'T PLAYING ANY GAMES

- **28" I want honesty. Don't play any games."**
- **29 "I hate games."**
- **30 "Tell me the truth."**
- **31 "You know you can tell me anything, right?"**
- **32 "I won't judge you. Just spill the beans."**

What a woman really means when she says these things is *"I want to see the cards that you're holding, so that I can better manipulate you."* A woman is a player of the game, but she'll pretend that she isn't playing any games - sometimes even to herself - to disarm you into revealing all of the cards that you are holding.

Here is the truth: women appreciate challenge. It excites them. The moment you confess your full love to her is the moment that her pussy dries up because it means that she will be bored out of her mind, and she'll seek to chase someone else. Confessing your feelings might make you feel better because you experience catharsis, but it removes the exciting challenge and thrill of the chase that women want to experience.

A woman isn't control of herself enough to be above human nature. It's within human nature to value things that are scarce and hard to get more than things that are overly available and easy to get. This is why it's important to not give a woman full disclosure. **A bit of mystery keeps her thinking about you.** You wouldn't watch a movie if you knew the ending because it is the not-knowing that keeps you hooked.

HERE COME THE EXCUSES TO PULL THE WOOL OVER YOUR EYES

- **33 "I'm busy right now with my career."**
- **34 "I have homework to do."**
- **35 "My cat can't be alone right now."**
- **36 "I'm in the middle of an emergency."**
- **37 "It's late and I have to go to sleep."**

If a woman uses her career as an excuse then what she is really saying *"My career is more important and fun than you. This is true even though my career is boring and tedious."*

Here is the truth about excuses: **when there is a will, there is a way.** This bears repeating: **WHEN THERE IS A WILL, THERE IS WAY.**

When a woman wants to spend time with you then SHE WILL MAKE TIME FOR YOU - even if she is busy. She will find a way to make it happen.

- She'll cancel her other plans.
- She'll say "no" to other people, so that she can make time for you.
- She'll reschedule at at time when she's available.
- She'll do certain things faster, so time can be made.

No one really has time for anything. Time is "created" by being planned for. Inquire about her schedule and then give her a specific meetup time to meet up with her.

In contrast, if she isn't interested in you then she'll find lots of excuses to let you down easily - without hurting your feelings. The excuses are just there to avoid bruising your ego.

The truth is that if she keeps giving you excuses, she is really saying that there are lots of things that have a greater priority than you.

A woman's availability (or lack of) shows how much she is sexually interested in you. If she seems to always be busy, without a very strong good reason, and she doesn't suggest other times to meet-up then she just ins't interested in you. In contrast, if she suggests other times to meet up, then she is interested in you. It's important to gauge a woman's interest level in you to filter out women who are too low interest to be worth your time.

THE FAKE YES

- **38 "Fine."**
- **39 "K" (in texting)**
- **40 "Do what you want."**
- **41 "Whatever."**
- **42 "You can do whatever you want because I don't care!"**

These statements in the context of a relationship are actually quite misleading. On one hand, she is saying that you can do what you want, but on the other hand she is doing it in a bitter way. What does she really mean?

What she really means to say is *"I'll pretend to not care for my ego, but I'll extract vengeance later by being passive aggressive and emotionally abusive."* In other words, **SHE DOES CARE** (based on the fact that she said what she said in a butt-hurt type of way), but she is pretending that she doesn't care in order to feed her ego the message *"I am important. I don't need anything from anyone."* It hurts a woman's ego to admit that she needs something, and to admit that she cares, so she pretends that she doesn't.

THE FAVOR DIGGER

- **43 "Lets build a bookshelf."**

What she really means to say is *"You do the work. I'll help out by watching and giving suggestions."*

- **44 "This thing that I have to do is very hard."**

She wants to bait you into helping her, but her ego is too fragile to admit that she can use your help. If you try to help her, she could say "no" (even though she wants you to help her) so that she doesn't feel like she is imposing a burden on you.

THE PLEASE CHANGE THE SUBJECT CRY FOR HELP

- **45 "Uh huh"**

I don't really care about what you just said, but I'm trying to be polite so I'll respond with a one-word. Please change the subject to something is more aligned to my core values.

- **46 *one worded response***
- ***47 (in person body-language) looks in the other direction while you're talking to her***

I don't really care about what you said, but I have to be nice, so I'll say something.

- **48 On FB gives you a thumbs up 👍 response to your long message (or she**

takes a really long time to respond to your message)

I don't care about what you just said and the topic that you just brought up is boring, but I don't want to look like a bitch and completely severe our connection, so here is a droplet of ego validation.

68

MORE SPECIFIC EXAMPLES

49 "I WANT A STABLE FUTURE"

I want you to pay for everything, while I relax at home.

50 "You won't understand."

I don't even understand it, so I can't explain it to anyone.

51 "Why did you break up with your last ex girlfriend?"

Do you have any serious problems that I should be concerned about?

52 "This guy asked me out today."

I want to make you jealous, so you would finally ask me out already.

53 "What do you think of Jenny?"

Is she someone who I should be concerned about? Is there competition that I should be worried about? Are you going to badmouth her and thus badmouth me too?

54 "Come here."

55 "Hold this for me."

"Help me with this homework."

I want to see if you're a little bitch who will do whatever I want like a little doggie.

56 *Mentions her ex-boyfriend*

I am still in love with him. I'll tell you that he doesn't mean anything to me, but the truth is that he means the world to me.

57 "You're cool and I like you, but..."

She doesn't really like you, but she's bringing the compliments to avoid hurting your feelings. Notice the "but" which is a way of retracting the prior statement.

58 "I am not upset."

She is upset but she is saying that she is NOT upset to calm herself down, and avoid losing her temper.

59 "I don't want to talk about it."

I don't have enough evidence to bring a compelling argument yet. **OR** *I want you to figure out why I'm upset by yourself.*

60 "I am very caring."

I am controlling. I use my "caring" as a guise to get what I want.

61" I want to be friends first."

You don't turn me ON. If you were hot then i would be all over you.

62 "I'm open-minded and non-judgmental."

I am desperate. I use these politically correct words to disguise my neediness.

63 "I'm outgoing."

I will talk your ear off. I'm LOUD..

64 "Are you gay?"

Why haven't you made a move on me already? I desire to feel desired.

65 "I'm not looking for a relationship right now."

I am not looking for a relationship with you.

66 "You're just like a brother to me."

In my eyes, you're a sexual dud.

67 "I like adventure and meeting new people"

I'm telling you now that I'm promiscuous, so as to soften the blow and so you won't come raging at me later

68 "You should enjoy the pleasures of life."

She's into you, and hinting that you show become more passionate towards her.

69 "The guy thought you were hot."

I think you're hot, and I'm projecting my own perspective on to the situation.

70 "I don't remember the price."

It's expensive, and I don't want to tell you because I'm trying to being the bringer of negative emotions.

71 "I want new furniture."

I want a complete home reconstruction. I'll just be starting with this, but as time goes on: I'll have a lot more things on the list.

72 "It's a girl's night out."

Tonight I will do whatever I want. I'm creating the justification for it now, so as I can use that as a defense "I already told you that it's a girl's night out) in the case that you try to use it against me. I'm also justifying it for myself now, so I don't feel guilty later about all the stupid shit that I'm going to do.

73 "Did you get a chance to do the thing I asked about?"

Hey!!! GET IT DONE!!! I mean now!

74 "Sure, I don't mind paying."

Yes, I do mind. But I'll say that I don't mind, so that I can avoid feeling like a bitch. Secretly, I wish you will insist.

75 "Now is not a good time."

I have other priorities which are more important than you.

76 "You give me your number."

I'm not planning on calling you, but I want to avoid an uncomfortable confrontation; therefore, I'm going to use a socially acceptable white lie and imply that I'll call you even though I won't.

77 "I'm upset."

This one means exactly what she said.

78 "I'm not going to have sex with you."

I am not going to have sex with your right now, but maybe later if I get TURNED ON.

79 "Am I fat?"

I am baiting for compliments. Tell me I'm pretty, so I can feel better about myself.

80 "We need to talk; don't get mad."

I'm just saying that to avoid triggering you when I bring out the "big guns". I'm going to use that conversation as a way to complain.

81 "I need to think about it."

I'll just say that to avoid looking like a bitch, but if I had balls like a man then I would be direct and just say NO.

82 "I feel like I've known you forever."

I really like you.

83 "You never listen!!"

You listen sometimes but at this moment, I feel like you never listen. I'm just saying what I FEEL like the truth is.

GOLD DIGGING QUESTIONS

- **84 "What job do you have?"**
- **85 "Are you in college?"**
- **86 "Hey, is this your car?"**

I'm curious to your potential as a provider.

87 "What are you doing this weekend?"

She wants you to ask her out.

88 "Tell me about yourself."

Tell me things about yourself that showcase what makes you attractive.

69

DEEPER EXPLAINATIONS

"Do you have a girlfriend?"

SHE IS ASSESSING:

- your level of social proof,
- your availability in the sexual marketplace, and
- your level of confidence.

Assuming that this is a serious question, and not a sarcastic one (you'll be able to tell based on her body-language, the amount of interest that she has given you in the mutual past history) respond by mentioning that you had a prior ex-fiancé in the very distant past, but you're single in the present.

Bringing up an ex-fiancé will take away the "fuck boy" persona:

- get her drunk on your personality,
- fuck her in the pussy,
- take photos for underground FB groups and forums,
- discard like she is nothing but leftover trash,

- repeat cycle,
- lose your soul in the process of chasing temporal sensual pleasures,

but also signal that you're sexy enough for OTHER women to be interested in. Remember: women want a man that other women want. A high status man who doesn't have beautiful women as "friends" in his life and never had any prior lovers sets off unconscious Red Flags that there must be something wrong with him (he has no women in his life because he is fucking socially inept dork).

Saying that you are currently single will show her that you're AVAILABLE in the sexual marketplace. Further, if you have an ex-girlfriend just randomly show up around the house or at your work place, then this could be a significant annoying turn-off for other women.

In regards to these lessons that I am writing to you now: I paid for these lessons with incredible pain. I paid for them by going through fiery trial and error. Experience is one hell of a motherfucking teacher - absolutely brutal but effective. Become a lifelong student of the game of life and seduction; there's always more to learn, and a higher level of skill to achieve. One can't achieve perfection, but one CAN achieve an impressive level of competency to stay competitive in the sexual marketplace.

"Do you love me?"

In the context of a relationship: this could also mean that she's had a tough day at work, and is feeling insecure. Your words of validation will give her a boost of morale. She's implying that she has an emotional and psychological need to feel important and she wants you to fill that need with your words.

She is setting you up to be susceptible to a big ask. By saying that you love her, it will naturally follow that you'll agree to do whatever she asks afterwards. She's conditioning you to be a personal butler. These behaviors are relatively normal; it is human nature for one to go after what they want - especially for beautiful women who have become used to getting what they want from men since a young age.

It goes without saying that what a woman says at the pickup phase can have a different meaning than what she says at the relationship phase. Saying "Do you love me?" at the pickup phase would be a power-grab and a power-assessment. This is true even if it said with a smile and playfully to disguise its true intentions.

- -> Firstly, she wants an ego rush of knowing that she has a high-status man such as yourself, who is in love with her.
- -> Secondly, she's assessing how much power she has over you, and will then use that knowledge to gauge how much she can take from you. If she senses that you're really into her then she'll know that she has a lot of "social capital" and can take whatever the fuck she wants - making unreasonably large requests. If she senses that you're somewhat of a challenge, then she'll be on her best behavior to keep giving you value so that you'll stick around and allow her to keep extracting value.

Women won't necessarily admit this, but they appreciate challenge. They detest a man who is too easy to get. If a man is too easy to acquire, she'll assume that he lacks options. She intuitively expects a high-status man to have options.

Don't use the L word too early on in the connection, unless you want to get rid off her because you're sick of her bullshit. Confessing your feelings to a woman too early will remove the level of challenge that makes her want to invest in you because why chase a string if you already have it?

This is why it is best to not give a woman full validation, so that she will be like a cat who keeps chasing string. Dread game (implying that you have options) will make a woman anxious enough to keep fighting to keep you.

Give a woman a specific compliment and observe her reaction. If she immediately responds with a conscious/unconscious signal of disinterest then this is a sign that she doesn't like compliments from men, and you should follow up with a tease 😈 to release the tension ("too bad you're such a dork"). As I mentioned multiple times in this book, a woman's body-language will betray the truth even if a woman will try to verbally disguise it because the truth always shines through. Ignore her words; look at what she does and the signals her body is sending out.

"To what extent do you love me?"

She is going to do some stupid shit, and have you put up with because of your "love". This question is similar to "Do you love me?" but it said with different words. The key is to understand that it is not the words verbatim that matters, but the idea behind the words. "To what extent do you love me" is the same as if she said "how much do you love me?"

"We aren't communicating that well."

You aren't listening to me me explain why my needs are important.

She really wanted to say "You are not communicating that well", but she is using the words "we" as a softener (so your feelings don't get hurt), and as an insidious method to get you to accept her idea as your own.

Women are naturally manipulative because they don't say

the truth straight the way that it is. Don't take it personally. These women don't even know that they're being manipulative; they see it as a normal way of life. A fish born in water - spending a lifetime in water - doesn't even recognize there is such as a thing as "air".

The key here is not to be angry with women. Nor is to explain what they truly mean when they say all sorts of random bullshit. If you explain to a woman what the secret signals are that she is sending out then she'll become self-conscious and stop sending them out. Don't reveal your source of information, or it will become contaminated. Just acknowledge the reality and play the game accordingly.

There's a saying: "Don't hate the player. Hate the game." It's more accurately to say, don't hate both. Make peace with the dark reality of what works in the game, and what doesn't. Accept the world for what it is, and play accordingly. Respect the rules of nature.

"I don't want to ruin our friendship."

Your genes are inferior. Your personality and physicality don't turn me ON.

At this point, in the vast vast majority of cases you should make a move, and let the cards fall where they will because you have enough friends as it is.

"I want honesty. Don't play any games."

I want to see the cards that you're holding, so that I can better manipulate you. I want full disclosure and transparency because I want full control over you, and the resources that I can extract. In return, I may or may not engage in selective honesty.

A relationship is a hidden negotiation table. You bring something of value to the table, and she brings something of value to the table. There's a mutually beneficial exchange of value. You appreciate the value proposition that she has to offer, and it works the other way around too! She pickups up the contribution that you put down, and vice-versa.

If she wants full transparency and honesty in a relationship then expect her to the same, because this type of communication works both ways; if you're the one who is putting in all the effort and she is barely putting in any effort then you're in an "imaginary" one-sided relationship that is doomed to fail (because women only value what they work for).

The truth is that women don't want full disclosure because it makes you boring. Think of going to a movie that you already know the ending to. It would be incredibly boring to watch that movie because it's spoiled; there's no mystery, intrigue, or hidden surprises

70

SILENT COMMUNICATION

WOMEN ARE FICKLE CREATURES.

- You're spending time trying to understand them, when they don't even understand themselves. And when you can barely understand yourself.
- You expect women to keep their promises to you, when they don't even keep promises to themselves. Nor do you keep promises to yourself.
- You expect women to be honorable and not cheat with higher status men, when they often lack the self-control to keep themselves from eating a fattening chocolate donut. Women are not honorable; they are ruthlessly opportunistic.

Get your expectations straight.

- You expect to manage women, yet you barely can manage yourself.
- You expect women to be submissive, respect your decisions, and follow your lead, yet you haven't achieved much in your life and your competency is

close to null - so who says you are worth following?
- You expect to be a Casanova with women, but you barely clock in one hour of practice a week?

Everything comes down to being the best option that a woman can choose at her given time. The cold truth is that a woman is inherently selfish. Her primary agenda is to serve herself. Being with you should be a clear win for her, just like it is a clear win for you.

The key to dealing with women is to convey the message that you are a lover by the behaviors that you do when you're around her. Treat her like a lover, and you'll create a romantic sexualized frame. Treat her like a friend, and don't be surprised that you're knee-deep in the friend zone. Understand that you are communicating messages to women simply by your choice of actions.

DON'T DO:

- #1) Behave like a man without a dick = friend-zone.
- #2) Hide your dick = friend-zone.
- #3) Never express any sexual interest = friend-zone.
- #4) Don't flirt with women = friend-zone.
- #5) Don't tease, touch, role-play, or use future-projections = friend-zone.
- #6) Never make a woman jealous by flirting with other beautiful women = friend-zone.
- #7) Appearing to be lonely and without close contacts = friendzone.
- #8) Believing that women are innocent angels who are disgusted by sex = friendzone.

DO:

- #9) Owning your dick and sexuality = lover-zone.
- #10) Whip out your dick = lover zone.
- #11) Conveying sexual intent = lover zone.
- #12) Being flirtatious = lover zone.
- #13) Using attraction amplifying tactics = lover zone.
- #14) Using the nuclear bomb of making a woman jealous = lover-zone.
- #15) Implying social proof and appearing popular = loverzone.
- #18) Understanding that women are sexual creatures who enjoy sex and desire to be desired = lover zone.

Your actions convey your belief system which then influences her belief system. What you do is a form of silent communication.

- For instance: if a woman calls you and you don't pickup the phone then you are silently communicating that you are a man of ambition, action and you have shit going on - thereby spiking your perceived worth through scarcity.
- In contrast, if you're always available then women will simply assume that you don't have a lot going on in your life; she's thinking "Why else is he available every day of the week for dates? Why else does he respond instantly whenever I reach out to him?" Women might not say this outright but they crave a man who has his own shit going on, and his own life mission that he is focusing on. These are

sexy traits that you are communicating indirectly by how you behave.

Don't always attach true meaning to what a woman says. She might not even understand what she just said and will forget about it later. **Constantly spending time figuring out what she means will put you into reaction mode. Live life in proactive mode - not in reactive mode.**

Sometimes a woman will enter an intense emotional state and say some random bullshit that she doesn't mean in order to get emotions and thoughts out of her system - as a form of catharsis. You don't need to waste valuable energy responding to what she just said. Ignore and misdirect to a different subject. OR you can deflect what she said with humor through the agree and amplify to absurdity technique. Just let her empty words pass through, and move on with your life.

Understand that although a woman is an adult, she is still like a child on an emotional level. While you are communicating to her mind, understand that you are simultaneously communicating to this inner-child.

This is why it's important to not be overly sensitive by pedestalizing her too high with too many compliments, supplications, begging, or excessively being defensive. If you treat a woman like a superior, she'll start viewing you as an inferior and become disgusted. WOMEN WANT TO BE WITH POWERFUL MEN. HENCE, YOU MUST SEIZE THE SOCIAL POWER IN INTERACTIONS.

- Don't talk badly about yourself - even in a self-deprecating humorous manner.
- Don't put her on a pedestal or she will look down on you.

- Don’t talk negatively about your friends because that only comes to reflect negatively on you for spending time with those friends.

On the other side of this extreme, don't treat a woman too harshly. Women appreciate ego validation and attention from high status man. A WOMAN VALUES HER EGO MORE THAN SHE VALUES MONEY. Give respect to get respect; what you put into a relationship is what you will get out of it. That being said, keep mutual flirting ongoing to spike her excitement levels, and keep her emotionally engaged.

Being boring is the cardinal sin of dealing with women. Use an edgy, polarizing communication style and be a man of adventure to keep women hooked to being with you.

71

LAW #99: Trust female nature.

- **Don't trust so much what a woman says she will do.** Women say all sorts of random bullshit that they don't understand.
- **Don't trust a woman's sense of honor, and doing "what's right'**. Women are hardened to do that which feels the best in the given situation that they are in, and that which is the most advantageous to them.

TRUST FEMALE NATURE. Trust that a woman will do that which is within her nature to do because her capacity to exercise her freedom of will (to act against her nature) is very limited.

Don't think she is different.

LAW #100: A bulletproof frame will change her mind.

A LOT of guys fuck up because they don't have an independent mind. Their identity changes based on the woman who they are with. They turn into "Yes Men" who just agree with everything a woman says for the sake of rapport.

The truth is that women are sexually attracted to men who are leaders. Lead with competence, confidence - psychologically, physically and logistically.

A woman can have an intensely strong frame (conviction in her belief about reality and what the best plan of action in a situation is) but your frame should be EVEN STRONGER. You need to believe in yourself more than she believes in herself. By having extremely intense conviction and confidence in what you're doing, women end up falling into your frame, your world, and your dick.

Remember: the strongest frame wins.

73

CONCLUSION

KEY POINTS FROM THIS BOOK

#1) WOMEN MAKE decisions and perceive the world through the medium of how they feel. By changing a woman's mood, you'll be able to change a woman's mind and behaviors. 🔑 **Control her emotions = control her perspective of the situation = control what she does.**

#2) A lot of guys try to communicate with women through logical persuasion which falls on deaf ears on women who are emotional creatures. You have to learn to press a woman's emotional buttons. 🔑 **Control her emotions = control her behaviors.**

#3) A lot of guys can't even manage their own emotions yet they expect to manage a woman's emotions. Mastery starts from within. By learning how to lead yourself, you'll learn how to lead other people - women and men included. 🔑 **By improving your own emotional state, you'll improve the emotional state of those around you.**

#4) **Even the most dominant of women, wants to be dominated by a stronger and more competent man.** Lead the men and the women will follow. Lead a woman and she'll get TURNED ON 🔥. Learn to be an effective leader by being competence, and leading with confidence. 🔑 **STRONG DOMINANCE CONVEYS INTENSE CONFIDENCE.**

#5) What a woman says is not what she truly means because what she said was based on her current emotional state. As her current emotional state is subject to change, so does her thoughts on the subject matter. Don't take anything a woman says too seriously, or attribute it too much importance. **Understand that a woman easily changes her mind, as easily as she changes her mood.** 🔑 **DON'T TAKE A WOMAN'S WORDS AS PERMANENT.**

END NOTE 🔪

Congratulations on finishing this book. I commend you on investing in yourself to get the practical knowledge that will lead you to success with women. Be willing to review key lessons in this book multiple times to have the lessons really sink in. Go out and conquer!

The Sexcalation Method

A STEP BY STEP SYSTEM TO SMOOTHLY ESCALATE THE INTERACTION TO SEX

Cory Smith
@PUA_DATING_TIPS

1

INTRODUCTION 🔪

EVERY SINGLE DAY do at least 1 thing that terrifies the shit out of you, to train yourself to be fearless in the sexual marketplace. Keep track of that 1 thing in a special journal made specifically for this purpose.

Show yourself what is possible at one key moment during the day, and it will inspire you for the rest of the day. You will absolutely shock yourself about the kinds of things that you can do when you aren't afraid of the consequences, and aren't held back by what people think of you.

You have been conditioned to be afraid by your parents for your own safety. As a child the fear protected you from doing reckless and stupid behaviors. The problem is that you have carried that belief into adulthood. Fear is now making you weak because it is stopping you from taking radical bold action with women. Undo your childhood conditioning.

Four things that keep men in their cages: (1) fear of disapproval, (2) overthinking, (3) being stuck in endless research, and (4) caring what other people think. FUCK what anyone thinks. Be extremely aggressive in going after your goals in the sexual marketplace.

FEAR IS THE GREAT PARALYZER. IT IS HESITATION, FEAR OF REJECTION, FEAR OF DISAPPROVAL, FEAR OF BEING EMOTIONALLY HURT, AND BEING STUCK IN PERPETUAL THINKING THAT HAS KILLED MANY SEDUCERS - SOMETIMES BEFORE THEY HAVE EVEN STARTED SEDUCING. SOME MEN SPEND THEIR ENTIRE LIVES STUCK IN THIS PRISON OF FEAR - WITHOUT EVEN BEING AWARE OF IT. THEY'LL CLAIM THAT THAT THEY ARE BRAVE MEN, WHEN THE TRUTH IS THAT THEY HAVE PUSSIES THAT ARE DEEPER THAN A WOMAN'S PUSSY.

CONDITION YOURSELF TO BE FEARLESS IN THE SEXUAL MARKETPLACE, AND YOU WILL BE UNSTOPPABLE. WHEN YOU DON'T GIVE A FUCK ABOUT REJECTION THEN YOU WILL BE FREE TO MAKE MANY MOVES THAT YOU DIDN'T THINK WERE EVEN

POSSIBLE BEFORE._YOU WILL START TO SEE DOORS OF OPPORTUNITY THAT WERE ONLY DREAMS BEFORE. WHEN YOU DON'T CARE WHAT OTHER PEOPLE THINK OF YOU THEN YOU WILL BE EMPOWERED TO DO WHATEVER THE FUCK YOU WANT, WHENEVER YOU WANT TO. YOU WILL BE A SEXUALLY LETHAL FORCE TO BE RECKONED WITH.

DOING AT LEAST 1 THING THAT SCARES YOU EVERY DAY COULD MEAN DIFFERENT THINGS FOR DIFFERENT PEOPLE - DEPENDING ON YOUR SKILL LEVEL:

- THIS COULD MEAN HITTING UP THE GIRL THAT YOU HAVE A CRUSH ON AND MAKING A REAL-MAN MOVE ON HER - BY INVITING HER ON A DATE TO A LOCAL EVENT AND THEN AGGRESSIVELY PHYSICALLY ESCALATING DURING THE DATE - EVENTUALLY ENDING AT SEX IN YOUR CAR.
- THIS COULD MEAN CALLING UP A GIRL JUST TO PRACTICE YOUR FLIRTING SKILLS; THEN INVITING HER TO YOUR HOUSE TO DRINK WINE AND CATCH A MOVIE (IMPLEMENTING THE CLASSIC NETFLIX AND "CHILL" SEDUCTION MOVE).
- THIS COULD MEAN SPARKING A CONVERSATION WITH THE CUTE GIRL AT THE BUS BY ASKING FOR "DIRECTIONS" AND THEN MAKING AN OBSERVATIONAL COMMENT - LEAVING WITH A PHONE NUMBER AND A FUTURE DATE, OR TAKING HER ON A DATE RIGHT THERE AND THEN.
- THIS COULD MEAN JOINING A DANCING SOCIAL CLUB AT A COLLEGE CAMPUS, ATTENDING ALL OF THEIR EVENTS, HITTING UP ALL THE GIRLS IN THE SOCIAL CLUB, AND MAKING AN AGGRESSIVE DIRECT MOVE ON THE ONE THAT IS MOST RECEPTIVE TO YOUR ADVANCES, SO AS TO NOT WASTE YOUR FUCKING TIME WITH BULLSHIT.

You won't know how far you can go until you risk going too far. As a general rule: it is better to go too far and then recalibrate than it is to not risk at all and then never know what is possible. A woman will forgive a man who is too bold (emotionally stimulating) and then re-calibrates, but she will rarely forgive a man who isn't bold enough and is thus boring (emotionally un-stimulating).

I'm asking you to take a leap of faith and start making EXTREMELY BOLD MOVES in the sexual marketplace to start getting laid like a sexy seducer - instead of just waiting around for shit to happen by itself.

- **Create a lifestyle that involves meeting women on a daily basis.** On your way to work (or on your way back from work) stop by places that have a lot of beautiful women, and strike up conversations with them. When the conversation turns hot, invite them to a local Starbucks. End with a phone number and plans for a date at an exciting local event in your city. It's impossible to get good at something you don't do, so make sure meeting girls is something you do regularly; no excuses here.
- **Start hitting on girls - with the CLEAR INTENTION of fucking.** When you have the intention of "FUCK ME, or FUCK OFF" then you'll aggressively and proactively lead the interaction towards sex - automatically screening out time wasters. Women can sense sexual intent, and if they're still around then they've given passive permission for you to continue to escalate the interaction towards a BANG. No more wasting time on 30 minute interactions to nowhere. No more wasting time on endless conversations that

aren't leading to anything specific. Either make reasonable progress towards YOUR PENIS inside her VAGINA - or she fucks off of your life.

- **Every weekend invite your female orbiters on one-on-one dates** - with the intention of bringing them to an isolated area where you will escalate to the point of sex. Having a texting penpal is worth zero. If she won't show up on a date so you can stick your penis inside her hole, she is worthless. Don't accept friendship status because you have enough friends; nor should you accept penpal status, if she isn't willing to meetup then she is a waste of psychological space.
- Start touching women much more - constantly progressing up the physical intimacy level. If you can't even hold her hand, how do you expect sex to occur? **Get her used to the good feeling of being touched by you.**
- Escalate faster and harder. Life is too short to play the failing perpetual indirect game. Make tons of moves in the sexual marketplace and make them fast, because one day you'll be dead; before that day: you'll create sexual chaos - even if the world burns in the process. WIN AT ALL COSTS. This is the PSYCHOPATHIC EDGE. As long as you aren't breaking any laws, every dirty move in the book is fair game.
- Verbalize sexual frames. Simply stating a sexual compliment implies that you want to FUCK, and sets the stage for further escalation. By behaving like a lover, you won't be friend-zoned. **Dirty talk leads to sex occurring -** even if she doesn't respond to your dirty talk. Escalate on a physical level, emotional level, verbal level, and logistical level.

- Implement specific techniques mentioned in this book to spike the odds of sex occurring. Conscious implementation of seduction theory will lead to your skills becoming as sharp as a ninja blade. **Always sharpen the blade.**

The time to act was yesterday, but the second best time is: NOW.

By purchasing this book, you told me something about yourself. You are willing to invest in yourself to:

- learn **valuable practical knowledge** (highly specific behavioral things that you can do in the field to spike attraction),
- **internalize key mindsets** (ways of thinking that ,
- develop **seductive character traits**,
- create a **seductive lifestyle** that leads to banging pussy on auto-pilot,
- have **fundamental habits** that put you in the best position to BANG,
- be on your **path to greatness**, and
- sharpen your high-demand **value-generating skills** with women.

because you believe in a bright future.

Part I

1

👉LAW #101: LIVE OUTSIDE YOUR COMFORT ZONE.

MOTHERFUCKER!!!

STOP 🛑

EVERYTHING

THAT YOU ARE DOING RIGHT NOW AND LISTEN TO ME, MOTHERFUCKER.

HERE IS MAJOR RED FLAG that you aren't where you need to be in life right now: 🚩 **If you are deep inside your comfort zone then chances are that you aren't growing that much.**

Some men spend their entire lives in the comfort zone and then they wonder why their lives are so *average.*

Don't you fucking get it, son? Pain is your friend.

Growth happens in the uncomfortable zone. Get comfortable with to being uncomfortable. Get used to the pain of pushing yourself much harder than you ever thought you could push yourself. Embrace the pain of being miles away from the comfort zone. Get into the PAIN ZONE because NO PAIN MEANS NO GAIN.

The life of a beta male is pathetic and boring. Don't let that be your destiny.

If you keep doing what you're doing then you'll keep getting the results that you are getting. It's time to LEVEL UP.

I'm going to ask you to do something that is going to make you feel *uncomfortable.* [1]In fact, I'm going to tell you to do things in this book that will make you feel *VERY UNCOMFORTABLE* and I expect you to do them with 100% effort.

INPUT DETERMINES OUTPUT.

What you put into your development is what you will get out of it. You are worth investing in. **If you put in a mediocre effort to rise to the top of the sexual marketplace, then expect mediocre results.** If you go all in, then your results will reflect that level of effort. I WANT YOU GO ALL IN to improving your sex life.

This books is for people that are serious about fucking beautiful women in the vagina, so I expect you to do the exercises or turn the fuck back now.

If you do this single mental exercise properly, it will change your life right now. Turn the page and let's get started…

---

1. LEVELING UP happens outside your comfort zone. Get "comfortable" with being uncomfortable. Embrace the pain of pushing yourself further than you ever thought was possible for you.

2

PRECISE VISUALIZATION

MENTAL EXERCISE: PRECISE VISUALIZATION

TAKE a small step outside your comfort zone **at this exact moment** and ponder these potentially disturbing questions:

- **"What do you truly truly truly desire with women?"**
- **"If you could have anything in the world with women (with no chance of rejection) then what would you like?"**
- **"If you could live out your wildest fantasy with a woman - without any chance of failure than what would it be?"**
- **"What is a secret fetish that you want to experience?"**
- **"[In the case of a long-term relationship], what qualities would you want to see in the woman who you'd like to see as your life partner?"**

Be brutally honest with yourself. You don't have

to share the answers with anyone - except yourself. Visualize that reality coming true in your mind. Describe it in detail. Picture it CLEARLY. See it coming the image coming to life in your mind.

I'll give you a few minutes to visualize this image of success, and to manually write down what you want on a piece of paper. [1]Studies show that writing down your goals substantially increases the chances of achieving them, so write down the kind of woman that you want (even if you have to use code words to be discrete).

Take a few moments to write down the goal that you have for yourself for women.

Fill out this sentence: "I want to ____________."

❄

---

1. Figuring out what you want in a woman who you are going to be in a relationship with can take years, so your vision will become more sharpened as you accumulate more experience. The more women you enter in relationships with, the more you will understand which women are relationship quality versus which women are just worth nothing more than fucking. By experiencing a lot of women, you'll be able to narrow down qualities that you want in a sexual partner.

3

THE LAW OF THE UNIVERSE

LISTEN TO ME, my son…

If you can visualize it, you can achieve it.

In fact, YOU CAN ACHIEVE ALMOST ANYTHING WITH WOMEN THAT YOU SET YOUR MIND TO ACHIEVE.

If you can visualize it in your mind's eye then you can turn it into a reality - with consistent conscious action over a long period of time. No one becomes a Casanova overnight, but if you keep working on it - leveling and improving one key behavior at a time - then you will achieve the Apex of Apexes in the Sexual Marketplace.

See yourself achieving your vision. This exercise will fuel your self-belief. **In the sexual marketplace, you get what you believe you deserve.**

Reward her good behavior with greater amounts of your attention, calculated emotional expression, and increasing amounts of physical intimacy. In contrast, punish bad behavior by withdrawing attention. Attention is the currency in the Womaneverse. 🔑 The key is: frame your TOUCH as a REWARD GIVEN.

99.99% of the limitations that you perceive are merely illusions created by social conditioning. Society brainwashed you to be a conforming sheep because it is easier to profit from you in this way. You "can't" do certain things because you simply believe you "can't" do them; your limiting beliefs limit you because you believe in them.

- If you think you "can't" get a girl because she is "outside of your league" you won't get her.
- If you think you "can't" do something sexually with a woman then you won't be able to do so.
- If you think your situation is "hopeless", it will be.

The visualization exercise (nicknamed "PRECISE VISUALIZATION") will condition your mind to believe that it is possible for you to succeed in the sexual marketplace. **Once**

you believe that it is possible, then you will push yourself to make it happen; visualize your vision every morning as soon as you wake up. In stark contrast, if you think your odds of succeeding in the sexual marketplace are slim to null then you won't even try. It all starts with self-belief.

When you enter interactions with women with a CLEAR INTENTION of what you want then your words and behaviors will automatically be aligned to turning that into a reality. This is why it is so important to frequently visualize the vision that you want to bring to life. By picturing in your mind's eye what you desire, you're able to leverage the unconscious mind to work in the background - subtly influencing your actions - to create that reality.

Women will fall into the projected role, or filter themselves out and not waste your time. By having a dominant masculine sexual persona, you will find that many women will play the projected sexual and feminine role that you expect them to play. In other words, having a strong dominant masculine polarity leads to a woman exuding a submissive feminine polarity. **Put simply: being a sexual man inspires her to be a sexual woman.**

Beliefs are contagious.

- Believe that you are worthy of her, and she will believe that you are a good catch.
- Believe that your penis is a pleasure generating machine, and she will view sex as a reward.
- Believe that touching is the most normal thing to do in the world, and she will accept this as the reality.

ACHIEVING CLARITY AND WHY IT MATTERS.

I cannot overemphasize the importance about being ultra clear over what you want in the sexual marketplace, and visualizing your goals come to life in your mind - as soon as you wake up in the morning.

Go as far as making visual signs around your house that remind you of your goal to help you focus on making progress on that goal every single day. Create an environment and lifestyle where you're constantly reminded of the goals that you're focusing on. Have an accountability wingman who you meet with once a week to discuss the progress that you've made so far on your goals since the last seven days.

When you know what you want out of the sexual marketplace then your unconscious mind goes to work towards making that happen. **You'll surprise yourself when you suddenly catch yourself taking automatic action towards your goal - without even being aware of it; this is because you had a fierce desire that was cultivated my verbalizing your visions and goals at the exact moment that you wake up.** Condition your mind and it will work for you - not against you.

A lot of perpetual procrastination happens because the goals that you have in your life right now are too fuzzy and vague. You have to clarify them by getting more specific, verbalizing and writing them down.

What exactly do you motherfucking want? When you know the answer to that and review that goal every morning at the moment that you wake up, then you'll put yourself in the best position towards turning that goal into a reality.

The law of the universe states:

When there is clarity, there is motivation.

4

TAKE DAILY CONSISTENT MASSIVE ACTION TOWARDS YOUR GOAL.

Condition your mind.

SUCCESSFUL SERIES ENTREPRENEURS started out broke, but were able to go from zero to hero. They came from nothing, but were able to rise to the fucking top. Why? Because they knew that where they were now, was nothing compared to where they will be in the future - **with daily, consistent, conscious massive action.** *The goal is to get into the daily behavioral tendency of pushing yourself far outside your comfort zone.* Stories were told of how they would:

- Enter a bank and write themselves a fake check for a $100,000 in order to condition their mind to believe that this lifestyle was even possible. **This conditioned their mind that this reality was possible AND likely for them - enough for them to be unconsciously motivated to pursue it.**
- Enter a Ferrari dealership and drive around a Ferrari for a test drive (pretending to be interested

in buying it) in order to condition their mind that they have the potential to actually buy it for real.

- Donald Tump discussed how his friend needed to buy First Class airplane tickets because it put his mind into the right frame of mind that was conducive to success. His friended needed to cultivate the self-image of a WINNER, and that was exactly what led him to keep WINNING. **Having a WINNING MINDSET leads to having WINNING BEHAVIORS leads to WINNING.**

The same can be said about sexual entrepreneurs. You might not be where you want to be right now, but by putting in real work and effort then you will be. Regardless of how bad or seemingly hopeless your situation seems right now, never never never never give up hope. I forbid you from ever giving up hope on yourself. **Understand this: no matter how bleak your current situation is, the future can be incredibly bright.**

DO A DEEP DIVE INTO IMMERSIVE ACTION

Imagine yourself putting in a solid 4 hours of work every day of the year (and keeping track of those 4 hours with an accountability journal) - practicing the skills that you need to absolutely KILL IT in the sexual marketplace; in a year from now, would you not be absolutely savage?

YOU will be the one with tons of options, and have the capacity to reject lower quality woman - rather than the other way around. Don't underestimate yourself and where you can be in a year of intense, radical, consistent, conscious massive action. **Believe in the beauty of your potential and you will be able to change the world.**

- If you are happy with the results that you are getting right now in life then by all means keep doing what you are doing.
- If you want take your life to the next fucking level then you must change your perception and behaviors.
- You can't higher-level results with same level behaviors. You need to UP YOUR GAME to UP YOUR RESULTS. If you keep doing the same things you'll keep getting the same kind of consequences. You can't be a part of the 1% of men by doing what the 99% of men are doing.

Don't be so fucking easy on yourself. Push yourself harder. Life begins outside your comfort zone so GET UNCOMFORTABLE.

Key takeaway points:

- **Higher level behaviors = higher level results.**
- **More action = more results.**
- **Believe you can and you will. Believe you can't, and you won't.**
- **The unconscious mind can be a hidden helper, or a hidden sel-sabotager - depending on how you program it. Program it with visualization exercises and by creating an intense desire to win at all costs.**

❄

5

☛LAW #102: HAVE ESCALATION CONFIDENCE.

ACTIONS AND RESULTS FOLLOW SELF-BELIEF, **which is why making physical escalation with BULLET-PROOF CONFIDENCE IS PARAMOUNT.**

TOUCH A WOMAN'S BODY LIKE A YOU TOUCH A CUP OF COFFEE - WITH FULL BELIEF THAT IT WILL WORK AND ZERO HESITATION/ANXIETY. IF YOU TOUCH WITH CONFIDENCE, A WOMAN WILL FALL INTO THAT FRAME AND BELIEVE THAT IT'S ACCEPTABLE - JUST LIKE SHE KNOWS 1 + 1 = 2; SHE WON'T BE HELD BACK BY HER ANTI-SLUT DEFENSE.

As you'll see later in this book, I explain that when you touch a woman's body you should do it from a firm belief that it will work. Your expectation and intense self-beliefs:

- **"I am going to touch your body in the erogenous zones, and you're going to enjoy it."**
- **"Touching is no big deal, and a very normal aspect of interaction."**

- **"We both have beautiful bodies. And we want to enjoy each other with those bodies because it feels good, and deepens our connection."**
- **"My touch is a reward for good behavior."**

is conveyed to the woman through subtle nuances, and she falls into the frame. If your perceptions have high conviction, a woman will simply adopt them as their own because he mind is highly suggestible. A woman's mind is not as strong as a High Status Alpha Male's mind, and can be overtaken.

Contrary to the #MeToo movement's erroneous conclusions, don't ask a woman permission to touch her body (asking for permission is giving away social power, conveys self-doubt and puts her in the leaderhip role). Asking a woman what to do is handing away your balls on a silver platter. A woman is already giving you permission based on the way that she conducts herself around you; if you see multiple indicators that she is attracted to you then those are green lights for you to act upon the sexual opportunity that has presented itself to you. Saying something like: "Do you like me?" conveys self-doubt in your high worth.

Assume permission is already given:

- based on the situation,
- her prior actions,
- the frames that were set, and
- body-language

Then smoothly escalate incrementally.

Condition a woman to follow your lead through small hoops, submit to you mentally, and hold the frame that YOU ARE THE PRIZE; then you'll have the best conditions to train her to be metaphorical sexual slave - hooked on the value that you provide. Confidence is conveyed by simply acting - not by asking for permission to act. JUST TOUCH HER BODY - don't ask her if you can. ASSUME THE SALE - rather than asking for the sale.

Confidence isn't just the fucking key 🔑 to fucking pussy. It is the fucking key 🔑 to life.

IF YOU HAVE A STRONG FRAME AND SKILLS, YOU CAN GET AWAY WITH ANYTHING. As long as your frame is BULLETPROOF and with INTENSE CONFIDENCE then you'll have the ability to do almost anything with women and it will still work. A woman's mind is malleable; you can shape it according as you see fit. A woman can be conditioned - like a dog - to please you sexually.

The good news is that your limiting beliefs have power over you only because you believe in them. Unlearn that which you have learned. Replace old limiting beliefs with new empowering beliefs. Accumulate evidence that your old beliefs were wrong (also known as The Selective Confirmation Bias technique), and find pieces of information that reveal that you are The Fucking Boss.

Just like beliefs creates behaviors, behaviors create beliefs. No matter where you are, act like the FUCKING BOSS. This will accomplish a few things things:

- (1) You will feel like the boss,
- (2) you will have body-language that conveys power,
- (3) women will become attracted to you, and men will respect you, and
- (4) you'll eventually internalize the "I AM THE BOSS" MINDSET.

In conclusion:

1. Assume permission was already given, so don't ask for permission. If anything, she will say "no", but will still respect you for having the balls to go after what you want. If she's still around after that then she has given passive permission for you to keep escalating at a later time.

2. Touch a woman's body with full belief in yourself. You will either convey confidence or self-doubt based on the way that you touch her body. If you touch with ESCALATION CONFIDENCE then she will fall into your frame that touching s normal, and a healthy part of interacting with you.

3. Understand that it's imperative to lead a woman into the behavioral tendencies of submitting to your perspective of the world, following your leadership, complying with your requests, and accepting your sexual advances. Women will follow you if you know where you are going, you are competent at what you do, and you lead with fierce confidence. **When you dominate a woman's mind, you will likewise dominate her body. If she follows you in mundane matters, she will follow you in sexual matters.**

6

☛LAW #103: TAKE ACTION EVERY DAY. NO DAYS OFF.

Create positive actions on autopilot.

MANY OF THE **actions that you do on a daily basis are unconscious - as if you're driving on autopilot.** By changing your belief system, you'll change their accompanying behaviors. The aim is to reprogram your unconscious mind to one that is conducive to your success.

- For instance: by having the belief that you are of high worth, you'll naturally ooze sexy confidence.
- Another example: by simply knowing that you can achieve any sexual fantasy as long as you can see it in your mind, you'll push yourself to turn it into a reality.
- Final example: by knowing that women get intense pleasure from sex, and enjoy sex (more more than society allows them to share publicly), then you'll be able to own your sexual intent and be relaxed around women during sexual interactions.

The first limiting belief that I want you to let go of is that women don't want to fuck, and that women don't enjoy sex. **Women are highly sexual beings. They just hide it because society will judge them for it.**

You can have your wildest sexual desires come true just by having the MOTHER FUCKING FUCKING FUCKING BALLS TO GO AFTER IT!!!!

YES. **I AM TALKING TO YOU.**

I AM GOING **TO SAY IT AGAIN.**

YOU CAN HAVE **your wildest sexual desires come true just by having the MOTHER FUCKING FUCKING FUCKING BALLS TO GO AFTER IT!!!!**

THE PROBLEM IS that society has brainwashed you into being a sheep 🐑 because this way you'll be much easier to control. You were raised to be a nice gentleman, people pleasing, and to be extra friendly - which has made you weak. You've allowed care-takers to make you feel guilty for going after what you want, and thus, you've become a shadow of a real man. TAP INTO YOUR PRIMAL INSTINCT, and have the balls to TAKE WHAT YOU WANT IN THE SEXUAL REALM. We live in a world of incredible abundance. All you must do is to have the balls to fucking TAKE WHAT YOU WANT - without being paralyzed by the fears of disapproval and without being stuck in the trap of endless analysis.

You intuitively know what you need to do to get laid. You simply need to tap into that primal instinct and act upon it. **Use horniness as fuel and motivation to push your-**

self to take radical action in the field - despite any emotional resistance, fear, and anxiety that you might feel holding you back. **Doing the exercise of clearly visualizing what you want is crucial because when you have an exciting vision, you'll naturally want to ACT to turn that vision into a reality.**

The reality is that you have to be sexually aggressive with women in order to achieve your sexual goals. If you are not then don't expect things to magically fall into place by themselves. Women have been conditioned to wait to be acted upon - rather than to be the one who is doing the acting. This is why, as a man it is your responsibility to ACT in a manner that leads to SEX - even if it's being pushy - because if you don't make shit happen, it might not happen. You cannot rely on a woman to have sex on the agenda, or to behave in a manner that is conducive to sex occurring. **That is your role as a man to actively create the conditions for sex to occur and to push that agenda into the mind/body of a woman - or it simply won't happen.**

Kill the sheep mindset of being a prey and waiting for others to come and save you. Adopt the predator mindset of being the one who makes things happen. While being a leader means that you have greater amounts of responsibility than others, it also gives you more power.

❄

Create a hoop for her to jump through and prove herself to you: "Whats your favorite place - on your body - to be kissed - besides your lips?" When she answers the question, she's unconsciously agreed for it to happen because of the principle of commitment and consistency (the tendency to be consistent with prior behaviors/statements in order to avoid the uncomfortable feeling of cognitive dissonance). In other words, a woman is unconsciously motivated to stay consistent with her actions. This is why once you get into a routine of having sex with a woman, she will behave according to that routine - almost automatically - because the body is hardwired to to use "biological shortcuts" to offset cognitive loads.

WOMEN DESIRE the pleasure that you have to offer them (they even have an entire organ just to experience sensual pleasure). I hearby give you permission to be an ALPHA SEXUAL PREDATOR STARTING NOW.

To get sex, you have to aggressively go after it. **You have to be proactive towards leading interactions towards sex.**

- If you wait for a woman to make the move, you might just die waiting.
- If you wait for things to "magically" fall into place by themselves, you might spend your entire life in passive-mode.
- If you wait for opportunities to fall into your lap then even if they occur, you will still waste time

waiting and you won't have as many opportunities if you simply took action to create them.

Here is the truth: living a life in passive mode just sucks; you have no control. It is far better to be highly proactive in making shit happen. In the game of seduction it is usually the man with enough balls to TAKE WHAT HE WANTS SEXUALLY that gets what he wants.

This is a key rule for dealing with women: **ABC.**

ALWAYS BE CLOSING.

Have the killer instinct to go after what you want in life - whether its the pussy of beautiful women, or turning a passion project into a reality. KILLER INSTINCT isn't just about fucking pussy. It is about being a man who seals the deal and executes. 99.99% of guys talk a big talk, and then do nothing. You have to be a man who fucking executes, and gets shit done; this is true in regards to:

- getting sex DONE ✅,
- getting business deals DONE ✅,
- getting shit handled until that shit is DONE ✅.
- Whatever life throws at you, get it DONE ✅,

- starting this moment right now.

One day you will be dead; before that happens live life to the fullest. A life of playing it safe like a timid soy boy is not a life worth living. GROW BIG BALLS AND TAKE WHAT YOU WANT FULL FORCE - without feeling guilty or shameful. Let go of cultural conditioning that frames sex as "dirty". HAVE GOALS AND EXECUTE THEM LIKE THE TERMINATOR.

The Terminator doesn't allow emotions to get into the way. YOU ARE A MACHINE. YOU GET GOALS DONE -

whether it's a certain number of approaches that you have to do every single day, or its a certain number of hours you have to spend training your flirting skills with women (7 hours a week of practice), or it's a calling up at least one woman a day for conscious practice: YOU GET IT MOTHERFUCKING DONE.

YOU FUCK PUSSY THE WAY YOU FUCK YOUR GOALS. RELENTLESSLY GOING AFTER WHAT YOU WANT UNTIL YOU ACQUIRE IT. AND WHEN YOU HAVE IT, YOU FUCK IT FULLY - WITH EVERYTHING YOU'VE GOT. LEAVE NO UNFAIR ADVANTAGE UNDERUTILIZED.

❄

I AM GOING to teach you how to achieve lustful physical intimacy with women. HERE IS LESSON #1, SEXY PLAYER. **The secret to getting good with women is really the secret to getting good at anything: you have to do a lot of it.** Humans get good at what they do frequently, BITCH!!! FUCK YOU if you disagree with this advice.

I don't care how much pickup theories you know, how many books you've read, or how many hours you've spent on YouTube. If you don't actually go out, and practice the skills of meeting women EVERY DAY then your skills will remain stagnant and your results will be ZERO. Taking daily action is PARAMOUNT.

If the only thing you learn from this book is the EXTREME IMPORTANCE of practicing your skill with women EVERY SINGLE MOTHER FUCKING DAY OF YOUR LIFE then this book would have been worth it. TAKE NO TRAINING DAYS OFF. Make every day count by

being 365/365 consistent in taking raw action to bring you closer to your vision.

- Repeat after me: I will make it a top tier priority to take action with women everyday!!!!
- Verbalize this right now: I will make it a top tier priority to take action with women everyday!!!!
- SAY IT!! I will make it a priority to take action with women everyday!!!!

This means YOU. And this means TODAY. Let these self-suggestions and affirmations sink into your unconscious mind. **Verbalize these mantras on a daily basis over a long period of time to have them integrated into personality.**

Figure out the Ask yourself this question: at my current rate of progress, where will I be a year from now?

- Well, if you're putting in 5 approaches a day: then you will be an approaching master.
- Alternatively, if you're lacking in attraction-generating skills then putting in an hour of flirting practice a day would be the lifestyle habit to develop.
- Some men have the tendency to approach a lot of women (because they have an active social lifestyle that involves going to various events and spending time in high vagina-traffic areas), and collect a lot of phone numbers, but then they don't actually follow up. Their sticking point is: creating a Day Two. So for these type of men, it is advisable to spend at least 30-60 minutes a day practicing the art of following up on leads. Just start calling up phone numbers, engaging in brief conversations, flirting and being the one to end the convo first.

Find out what your sticking points are and then do clock in conscious practice to overcome them - on a daily basis. **You get good at what you practice doing.** Whatever your sticking point is: focus on spending a specific time each day on consciously doing the right behaviors to become good at that area of the seduction process. Turn weakness into strength, and liabilities into assets. The game is 100% learnable.

99% of your competition is too fucking lazy to put in the hustle to become highly competent in the areas of generating value that women care about, so if you actually put in conscious time and energy to develop the skills to generate the form of value that women care about then you will absolutely KILL IT in the sexual marketplace. Women are value-consumers and are highly attracted to value-givers. **Become highly competent in giving the form of value that women want to take.** This could mean:

- being good at approaching,
- being good at saying interesting things (such as cold reads, warm reads, astrology, palm reading, positive psychology, spirituality etc) that capture the mind of a woman,
- being good at flirting in a way that spikes her emotions,
- being good at humor in a manner that uplifts her spirits,
- being good at taking women on amazing experiences via dates,
- being good at touching a woman's body in a manner that gives her maximum pleasure, etc.

The problem is that a lot of guys have loser habits and loser hobbies that aren't conducive to developing these sets of skills. If a guy spends his evenings binge watching on TV shows then he is not spending his evenings developing competency in these valued skills. Simply becoming aware of where your time is going is absolutely essential in investing it in the right places.

❄

Decide that the pain of staying the same is greater than the pain of change. Contemplate your fate if you stay on your current path of progress and skill level.

- Do you want to settle with old, ugly, fat, broke girls who gives you attitude , drain your bank account, and then have the audacity to treat you like shit? FUCK NO!!! You don't have to settle for low quality garbage when you have the skills to meet new women!!!!!
- Do you ever want to be in a situation where you see cute girls, but are paralyzed from taking action because you're too much of an ignorant pussy? FUCK NO!!!!! Invest in the knowledge of practical pickup, and sharpen your skills on the daily.

Here's the truth: YOU can meet women ANYTIME and ANYWHERE.

If you don't truly believe this then it's because you have been brainwashed by angry, hypersensitive #MeToo feminists. FUCK what they think. It's WHAT YOU THINK THAT MATTERS. Having the skills to go out TODAY and meet cute girls - who desire you - is a fucking superpower power. Learn these skills and reap the sexually charged benefits to years to come.

Guys stay in shitty, toxic-as-fuck relationships because they're afraid of leaving the girl because they think: *"oh no!!!!!!*

If this relationship doesn't work out then it would take FOREVER for me to find another girl like her."

When you know you've got SOLID GAME SKILLS to approach, meet and attract new women into your life then you will be fearless in existing relationships because you retain that sexy "walkaway power", and you will have tons of options to choose a *crème de* la crème if you're single.

INVEST IN YOURSELF by training high ROI (return on investment) skills **every day.** You'll thank me later. "In a year, you would have wished that you had started today!" So start TODAY.

❄

IF YOU DON'T WANT to have a decade long learning curve before getting **REAL RESULTS** then listen the fuck up. I am going to be explaining the big secrets on how to accelerate the process of getting good with women, that I wish someone would have told me when I first started over a decade ago. I would have killed for someone to tell me this shit.

There are three ways to gain useful, practical knowledge about succeeding with women:

- (I) Reading stuff online - like this book - gain academic knowledge, and contemplate what you have read.
- (II) Take action in the real world, gaining experience and reflect on what you have went through.
- (III) Do nothing because "real men" already know what it takes to succeed with women and if it was "meant to be" then everything would happen on its own. Rot away playing video-games, watching movies and binge-sleep.

I. KNOWLEDGE THROUGH RESEARCH

In the first method, you are usually reading random pieces of information about succeeding with women and HOPING that it is relevant to your current situation.

- You are piecing these pieces of random information together with the intention of gaining a clearer picture of the whole map and integrating them into a holistic system.
- You verbalize out-loud the key concepts that you have learned to help internalize and reinforce them in your mind.
- You arm yourself with as much useful knowledge that you can, so that you will be ready to act decisively when opportunities arise.
- You hope that you'll remember your training through research when opportunities present themselves to implement what you've learned.

II. KNOWLEDGE THROUGH EXPERIENCE

In the second method, you are going out in the real world, approaching, striking up conversations, flirting, creating attraction, qualifying, vibing, closing and **DOING WHATEVER IS NECESSARY TO WIN** . After a "Daygame session", or a time of going out and approaching women, you spend time reflecting to maximize that which is gained.

During a reflection (also known as "writing a field report") contemplate these questions:

- "What did I do that WORKED and GENERATED REAL MOTHERFUCKING RESULTS? This way I can keep doing it!"

- "Why did it I do that DIDN'T WORK, so I can reassess the strategy and see if it can be improved upon?"
- "What did I do that GENERATED NEGATIVE RESULTS, so that I can cease doing that immediately."
- "What the fuck can I do to TAKE THINGS TO THE NEXT LEVEL?"
- "Based on my current level of progress where will I be six months from now?"

During the contemplation of the experience, it helps to be in an isolated, inspiring environment such as a nearby park, or taking a relaxing walk to help you think. Enter into a relaxed state of mind that is conducive to thinking. When you're thinking think about:

"What key behaviors implemented on a daily basis would absolutely change everything for me and lead to you 10Xing my results?"

Good questions lead to good answers, and that is a fucking killer question.

Make a list of the key-take aways in a journal (or laptop) and be willing to review them frequently. Review is essential for internalization. You will notice that a lot of seduction advice is common sense, yet it is still often ignored and not implemented, so review is an essential boost to one's game and to keep crucial principles of game in the forefront of your mind. Knowledge is not skill; skill comes from relentless conscious practice and implementation of abstract concepts in the field.

DAILY DOZEN

You are more likely to implement what you've learned if you take the time to review it on a daily basis over a long period of time. Make a list of the top dozen things that you need to remember and then review that list every day for 100 days. You will suddenly catch yourself becoming better at the key points mentioned in your daily dozen.

Set aside your ego and remember that the arrogant cannot learn; one must be willing to acknowledge that he does not know everything before he can learn something. Be humble enough to keep reviewing the key concepts that you have noted for yourself; **repetition is what leads to internalization**.

CONCLUSION

The second method of going out, taking action and then reflecting on what you have learned is a SUPERIOR METHOD to the first method which is reading, and thinking about what you have the read. The second method ensures that the information is highly relevant and highly personalized to YOU SPECIFICALLY. Seeing is believing, so the lessons that you gain from personal experience tend to stick HARD. Furthermore, it takes ACTION to develop skills and generate results (no amount of reading can substitute for this).

You want to be reading high quality content AND also taking real world action. The time that you spend reading should not exceed the time that you spend acting. If you spend almost all of your time reading and none of your time acting then you are a mental masturbator in great need of a punch to the face to WAKE YOU THE FUCK UP.

❄

THE THREE MAJOR STEPS TO UNFUCKING YOUR SEX LIFE:

- 1. **Set a time during the day where you will focus on generating new leads** by approaching women at your local college campus, social events, coffee shops, book stores, or even supplementary hitting cup women online through dating sites such as bumble and Tinder. Incorporate this activity into your daily life with a ZERO EXCUSES MENTALITY. [1]
- 2. **Set another time during the day where you will follow-up on new leads that have generated through texts and calls.** There is little point in approaching women if you collect numbers that you don't even call and don't bother to follow up. Set at least 30 minutes a day for this crucial daily training activity. NO MOTHER FUCKING EXCEPTIONS. NO DAYS OFF YOUR TRAINING.
- 3. And set a day during the week when you will invite these girls out on dates that lead to banging a woman in the pussy - **HARD**. TAKE ACTION TODAY. Yes, I am talking to YOU.

When thinking about the day's experience, reassess your mating strategy:

- - double-down on what is working with women,
- - let go of that which isn't working with women,
- - immediately cease that which is hurting your odds of success with women, and
- - consider alternative mating strategies.

Focus on doing more of the 20% that is bringing you 80% of your results.

The bomb of a question is "How does one know what is working with women and what isn't working with women? After all, women may be too polite to express immediate verbal repulsion for a tactic that doesn't work so it can be difficult to assess the efficiency of game tactics?"

Learning how to analyze women and reading body-language is how you can tell what is working with women, and what isn't working with women. Her words may lie but her body and actions will speak the truth. **THE BODY DOES NOT LIE. THE BODY IS CONSTANTLY INVOLUNTARY SIGNALING THE TRUTH ABOUT A WOMAN'S TRUE FEELINGS.** A woman betrays herself with actions - which reveal the truth of the situation. By speed-reading the non-verbals you can get an accurate picture of the situation and act accordingly. **She could be down to fuck right now but you missed out on the opportunity because you didn't know how to read the signals that she was sending it out.**

❄

THE GAME IS 100% LEARNABLE

Did you know that 10% of men get 90% of the women?

Some men mistakenly believe that "one is either born with the ability to seduce women, or is screwed to be lonely (or stuck with ugly, old and overweight women with bad attitudes)." They think "if you aren't born with the magical gift of being charismatic, sexy and charming then it's game over". NOTHING could be further than the truth.

GO FROM ZERO TO HERO

The beauty of the dating game is that it is 100% learnable. You can go from zero to hero! Regardless of your past mistakes you can start over, learn the sets of skills it takes to succeed with women (from approaching, flirting to texting and physical escalation), and have sex every weekend of your life with a new beautiful woman (or even every day if you are inclined). It is 100% possible. The only limits are the limiting beliefs you have been brainwashed to believe.

The question is not "can it be done?" But the question is "will you invest in yourself to succeed?"

Use these affirmations:

- **"The sexual game is learnable and I will learn it!"**
- **"I commit myself to learning how women operate!"**
- **"I will take action every day to practice my skill in the field!!"**

Here is a cold reality: regardless of how women pretend to be, they actually enjoy primal sex with powerful men. They need the touch of a high status man to make them feel good about themselves and be satisfied as a woman. By having intercourse with her, you are doing her a HUGE FAVOR of providing pleasure and filling her cravings - like an Alpha Male. If you don't bang her, another guy will.

You owe it to yourself to learn every single day the specialized knowledge and practice the specialized skills that it takes to succeed with women. **Train hard every day. In a year from now, you would have wished that you had started RIGHT NOW.**

❋

Real question: out of the year's 365 days, how many days do you make COUNT? [2]

TO HAVE A SUCCESSFUL YEAR, you have a series of success days. Think about how far you will be able to go if you practicing your chosen skill set (whether it's approaching, making moves, conversation, or flirting) for an hour a day every single day for a year. You would be miles ahead of the competition! You would be light-years ahead of where you are now! You would be so fucking good that you wouldn't even recognize yourself anymore.

365 days of consistent conscious practice of at least one hour a day on your chosen high return on investment skill will lead to absolutely remarkable transformation and results. Practice doesn't make perfect but it sure as hell makes you better than when you first started. In fact, practicing pushing towards sex - in real world situations - is the fastest way to learn the game - even faster than reading a book. You'll learn much faster from taking MASSIVE amounts of RAW ACTION in the field than you will from reading books.

Imagine how fucking amazing your game will be if you spent at least 1 hour a day hitting up women - either on Tinder, POF, Fetlife, OkCupid or in a relatively safer post-corona vaccine world: coffee-shops, libraries, college campuses etc.

Don't even be afraid of making mistakes or humiliating yourself in the process of learning the game. The faster you slip and the more times you slip, the faster you'll learn from the mistakes and improve. More failure means more lessons. Mistakes are successes when you learn from them. Each experience - regardless of whether the outcome was negative or positive - was a valuable learning experience.

The fear of rejection is what paralyzes guys from taking action. When you're afraid of disapproval then you remain in the mental prison of limiting yourself to only actions that will gain approval from women. For your own sake, give zero fucks what anyone thinks and then you will take true freedom. You will then be sexually fearless. Women desire to be used by you for their body - even if they are ashamed to admit this. BE SEXUALLY FEARLESS and almost ANYTHING IS POSSIBLE.

In the field of seduction, I strongly encourage you to take some time to really think about the one key behavior implemented daily that would make all the difference in your sex life, and then put in the effort to create that habit into your lifestyle. At the beginning that habit will take a lot of start-up energy, but if you continue to consciously implement that positive seductive habit into your lifestyle then it will eventually become an ingrained habit and then the maintenance cost of keeping it around will be relatively very minimal.

After that single high ROI habit is internalized, the next step in the process is to stack another high ROI habit. Keep stacking high ROI habits until from the dawn to midnight, you implement a series of high ROI habits. It all starts with choosing one positive habit that will make the biggest positive impact on your sex life, and then consciously implementing it on a daily basis. Hang a visual reminder on the door to your house so that every time you leave or enter your home, you're reminded of your task.

THE 5 KEY POINTS TO TAKING ACTION EVERY DAY

- **Massive action:** the action that you take should be high in quantity. Do a deep dive of an immersive action of several hours a day towards your goals.

- **Radical action:** the action that you take should be high in quality.
- **Consistent action:** don't take any fucking days offs. Every day is training day. Hang a calendar on your door, and put red check marks to show that you've taken action on that particular day. When you leave your home, you will be reminded of your goal through that visual reminder.
- **Conscious action:** keep your goals at the forefront of your mind. Verbalize your goals, and visualize your vision every morning as soon as you wake up.
- **Accountable action:** hold a weekly meeting with someone who is pursuing the game goals as you are, and discuss the prior week's successes. Having at least one wingman will create a sense of accountability (you can't fuck up because other people are depending on you).

---

1. It's incredibly important to have no training days off because once you start taking days off then having excuses becomes the new norm. When you unconsciously realize that you could take an excuse if you really wanted to, then somehow your brain will constantly find excuses to take a day off. **What the heart desires, the mind will rationalize.** The higher intelligence a guy is, the more likely it is that his brain will create highly convincing excuses to take the training day off. Dumb idiots fuck more women than high IQ guys because they are stupid to come up with reasons why they shouldn't take action with women today; they turn off their brain and just take HUGE AMOUNTS OF ACTION IN THE FIELD - eventually stumbling upon sex. The more action you take, the more you leverage the numbers to your favor, and the more "lucky" you get. Further, the more action you take, the better you become at taking action.
2. A lot of guys have super productive and killer weekdays but lose the progress that they've made by completely fucking up their weekends. The key is to be ULTRA PRODUCTIVE every day by entering a zen like hyper focus state, being acutely aware of your goals, verbalizing your vision every morning, and executing your daily goals like the fucking terminator at FULL FORCE. NO DAYS OFF. Be a weekend warrior, motherfuker.

7

👉LAW #104: HAVE CLEARLY DEFINED GOALS. REVIEW DAILY.

IT'S ABSOLUTELY **paramount to know what you want out of the sexual marketplace.** This is the single most important principle in the entire red pill philosophy. If you know what you want out of this entire game, you put yourself in the best position of getting there. Define your vision clearly in your mind. **Fuzzy goals lead to semi-results; clearly defined specific goals lead to SOLID RESULTS.**

TAKE A FEW HOURS TO ANSWER THESE CRUCIAL QUESTIONS

- Do you want to just have sex or do you want to have a long term relationship? Do you just want raw animal pleasure, or something more meaningful?
- What kind of qualities do you want to have in a sexual partner, or girlfriend? Do you want a party animal who frequents bars and clubs, or someone who is more ambitious and career oriented?

- What kind of man do you want to be, and what specifically are you doing to get there? Do you want to be a low key 9-to-5 corporate soldier who does everything by the book, or a ruthless business man who runs an empire?
- Which guys do you know specifically that are ultra successful with women, and what do you need to do to hang around them - so that you can study their behavioral patterns? Do you hang around places or attend networking events that would allow you to meet charismatic Alpha Males who you could learn from by the power of role-modeling?
- Is your vision based on something that you personally want, or something that society (consumerism) has brainwashed you to believe is valuable? Do you personally like the girl, or do you just like her because other guys would like her?
- How much time do you need to spend every single day meeting women, practicing attraction-generating techniques, and following up on leads to achieve competent seduction skills? Do you have an accountability partner, or some way of holding yourself accountable to do doing this?

If you don't know where you are going, you will get nowhere. Take a moment to visualize your ideal self with girls.

- What kind of man do you want to be?
- What kind of high-demand skills do you want to develop?
- What kind of lifestyle do you want to have?
- What kind of beautiful girls do you want to have in your life?

- What kind of responses do you want to elicit from women?
- KNOW WHAT YOU WANT. Are you interested in being a player who gets laid with a new girl every week every time his week, or do you want to have a relationship with a single beautiful women (but have the sharp skills to get new beautiful women if you want to)?
- If you could be anything with no chance of failure then what you would be?

Work towards your vision every day!

Create a vision of success with women, and make progress towards that vision every single day for a year (by taking action every day, and having a series of consciously implemented habits). Just make sure that it's a vision that you actually want and have chosen for yourself - rather than other people have chosen for you. It's your fucking life, so choose something that resonates the most with you - not what others have chosen for you. Ask yourself "Why am I in this game?"

- Don't game for validation. Let go of the need to learn pickup-skills to impress other guys. Don't learn game skills to impress random people on the internet. Don't get a specific girl that you're not attracted to, just because other guys are attracted to her. Don't game because you feel worthless about yourself, and when other beautiful women express interest in you then suddenly you start to feel important; that's an endless blackhole that never ends. Get ego validation from within. **You are highly valuable regardless of your**

specific results with women, and regardless of what women think about you.

- Don't learn the game just because you weren't popular in high-school and this is your way of turning a childhood fantasy into a reality. Many of the childhood dreams were formulated when your brain wasn't fully developed and you didn't yet have a mature view on the world. **Learn the fundamentals and highly competent game skills in order to be in the most conducive state to achieving specific goal(s) in the present**,[1] while letting go of the goals of the past and silly notions of what's what pursuing - when you had an inaccurate perception of reality.
- Don't game because you're using women for a sense of happiness. This is an ENDLESS THIRST TRAP. Draw state from within.

Some girls in particular are beautiful on the outside, but ugly on the inside. They might be pleasant to look at, but they are toxic when you're in a relationship with them then their real version comes out. The way that a woman behaves in a relationship is different than the way she behaves during the initial pickup phase.

Game to achieve a specific result that is personally valuable to you. Know what the END GAME is for you. One day you will cease to exist; everyone on this planet is a ticking time bomb - with his life force slowly dripping away with each passing moment. Before the life force fades into oblivion on this planet, know what you want to achieve as a final destination.

If you aren't clear about what you want to have then you really decrease your chances of getting it, so the first step to having a successful entrance in to the sexual marketplace is being clear about the destination. It goes without saying that regardless of your destination, it is still worth having high-tier highly competent GAME SKILLS (such as knowing how to meet new women, spark intrigue, ignite chemistry, form an emotional bond, physically escalate, follow up on more dates, keep up contact through texts/calls/video calls etc) and keeping those GAME SKILLS SHARP.

Do you want:

- Something casual which is just being friends with benefits[2].
- Something non-committal such as having a long term open sexual relationship.
- The full blown hardcore path, a woman to raise a family with.

The strategies used to lead you towards the END GAME will be based on what that END GAME is.

Again: if you don't know what you want, don't expect to suddenly get it. **You have to know what you want out of this game, create a game-plan to get it, and consciously work on a daily basis to reach this vision - consistently for years.** It is an active ongoing journey to achieve the END GAME - not something that should be left to chance.

Contrary to what Hollywood movies have implied, the nice anxious guy doesn't get the girl. In the real world, the girl just ignores the weak beta. No, she doesn't see his golden heart, past the weak external surface. The nice guy doesn't stand a chance. Your life would be so much more awesome if you were an Alpha Male. The defining trait of the Alpha Male is that he is extremely aggressive in going after what he wants in life, and he doesn't give a fuck if anyone disapproves.

It's not enough to know what you want. You need to a create a specific play-by-play plan of action on how you are going to get there, review your progress

on a daily basis, and refine the plan on a weekly basis. A third time: don't expect yourself to magically get to your destination without conscious effort. **You have to hustle to develop yourself to be a TOP TIER MAN because women fuck the #1 guy that they have access to - not second place.** BE THE BEST POSSIBLE OPTION in a woman's life.

TAKE POWER because it gives you the ultimate sex appeal. THIS IS THE GAME OF POWER IN SOCIETY AND WHY IT MATTERS:

Women want powerful men, which forces you into playing the game of power, and mind games designed to get power. Be on a path towards the top.

This comes from years of conscious personal development, taking action every single day, having a mentor who is highly successful[3], and being at the APEX of the social food chain. The path to power is open to anyone who has the fucking balls to climb it. Unfortunately most men would rather give into instant gratification and mindless distractions (Netflix, Oculus Quest 2, Cyberpunk video game, fruitless conversations with the boys that leads nowhere) than to climb the path to the top, but those that do climb to the top are able to achieve sexual results like no one else. The path to the top of the social totem pole can take years, but it is a prudent mating strategy for the long term. **Be on a consistent path towards apex power in society.**

While a broke loser (with no future) can still get you laid with girls as long as he has:

- BULLET-PROOF CONFIDENCE 🔥,
- GIGANTIC BALLS, 🏀🏀
- TENDENCY FOR RELENTLESS ACTION TAKING 🗡️ ,

- DOESN'T GIVE A FUCK IF YOU DISAPPROVE OR REJECT HIM BECAUSE HE LEVERAGES THE NUMBERS and knows his approach to sex funnel conversion rate, 👉👌 and has
- STRONG 💪 GAME SKILLS.

eventually the girl will realize that he has nothing else going for him. She will come to realize that it's all a facade, and he isn't a viable option for a long term relationship because of his loser status in society. Players like this can get girls, but they can't keep them because of how incompetent they are in the game that matters the most of all: the game of life.

BE THE COMPLETE PACKAGE, MOTHERFUCKER.

---

1. Having GAME SKILLS is like having a car. It is a tool to be used. You can use it to get laid with beautiful woman, or to find a relatively high quality woman to enter into a relationship with. Alternatively, you can use GAME SKILLS to land mutually lucrative business deals that bring in serious cash flow directly deposited into your bank account. You develop GAME SKILLS by being acutely aware of what specific goals you are trying to achieve with women, contemplating the best strategies/plan to achieve them, and practicing every single day - while taking the time to reflect and refine your strategies/plan based on results accumulated. Focus the most on what is giving you the most results. If during your experiences, you notice that something is taking away from your results then stop 🛑 doing that shit. Do more of what works, less of what doesn't, and keep experimenting on various new strategies. Another way to accelerate the learning curve is to find a role model who is already successful in doing what you want to do, and observing him - even if you have to pay him for the privilege.
2. When a woman is attracted to you then she'll say whatever is necessary for herself in order to justify her actions and avoid feeling guilty/seeing herself as a slut in her self-image.
3. Humans are hardwired to learn the fastest by observing others (Social Learning Theory). Simply watching an Alpha Male behave in a matter that is sexy to women is a shortcut to internalizing the behaviors yourself. Read that again: **observation is a shortcut to integration.**

The issue is that not everyone has a role model that they can emulate. Some guys were raised in a single mother household - with an absent father. In the ideal scenario, they would have learned how to interact with women by growing up in a household where the father interacts with the mother in a manner that is conducive to a healthy sexual relationship; they would have had gems of masculine wisdom dropped by their Alpha father during heart-to-heart talks.

8

👉LAW #105: REMIND YOURSELF OF YOUR VISION EVERY MORNING.

STOP what you are doing right now and ask yourself these questions:

- "WHERE DO I WANT TO BE SIX MONTHS FROM NOW?
- WHAT ABOUT FIVE YEARS FROM NOW?
- WHAT IS THE PURPOSE OF MY LIFE?"

Visualize your destination clearly in your mind. Develop a fiery vision that propels you forward. When you have an exciting meaningful mission in life, you'll be jumping to get out of bed in the morning instead of hitting the snooze button for the fifth time - moaning "uhhhhhhhhh not another boring day!!".

Friedrich Nietzsche said " ***He who has a why to live can bear almost any how.*** " Remind yourself of your vision and the reasons behind why you started your journey every day!! Remember: WHY YOU DECIDED TO START YOUR JOURNEY and WHY IT'S IMPORTANT FOR YOU TO REACH YOUR DESTINATION to accomplishing your goals. Then you will live a life of passion, purpose and fulfillment.

"To live is to suffer, to survive is to find some meaning in the suffering" says Friedrich Nietzsche. The philosopher explains the secret to being BULLETPROOF and ANTI-FRAGILE. When you have meaning in your life then you will be be able to ENDURE anything that life throws at you!! When you have a purpose to live for then you will find inner-strength that you did not know that you had, and will be able to HANDLE ANY CHALLENGE.

KNOW WHAT YOU ARE LIVING FOR. Set specific measurable goals that will get you closer to fulfilling that purposeful, meaningful vision. Then execute those goals with everything you've got!! MAKE EVERY DAY COUNT.

Friedrich Nietzsche teaches: ***"That which does not kill us makes us stronger."*** Do not be afraid of challenge. Every-time you survive a challenge, you grow wiser, smarter and tougher. Even if you did not achieve your specific goal, you still learned more about what it takes to succeed. When you take action, you'll experience one of two outcomes: you either win, or you learn more about winning.

Every time you approach a woman you win. You either girl the girl, or you learn more about getting the girl. THERE IS NO SUCH THING AS AN APPROACH THAT IS NOT A WIN.

Don't be afraid of trying your best in the field and making mistakes; be afraid of not even trying. Often one learns more from mistakes and losses than successes. Knowing what NOT to do is just as important as knowing what you should do.

Review your vision every single morning when you wake up. Be a man who lives passionately on his purpose. A woman does not want to be the purpose of your life but a helper to helping you succeed in your purpose in life.

9

☛LAW #106: LEARN USEFUL KNOWLEDGE FREQUENTLY.

TREAT A WOMAN AS SHE ACTUALLY IS - NOT AS YOU WISH SHE WAS

ADMITTING reality for what it truly is can be painful. It's easier to just put one's head into the sand, ignore the truth and pretend:

> *"EVERYTHING is just fine; my life is perfect! I don't need to improve because I am perfect! Anything bad that happens to me is not my fault. It's someone else's fault!!!"*

It's easier to imagine that reality is what we want it to be - instead of confronting it for what it actually is. In the novel "Don Quixote", Don Quixote behaves as if the world is an idealized fantasy (gaining a sort of self-sabotage bliss from ignorance) and as a result of living a life of delusions, he fails on an epic proportion.

Your perception of the world is your map of reality. To succeed in the game of life, one needs an accurate map of reality. As a man, you must confront hard truths - no matter how painful they are. **The raw truth can HURT LIKE A**

MOTHERFUCKER, but ultimately it will empower you.

The red pill is to embrace the dark side of female nature - no matter how painful it is - and act accordingly. Women are not just sunshine and rainbows. They have a dark side to them. **Red pill isn't about hating women. It is about accepting women for what they are and behaving accordingly - not for what they are not.**

The red pill isn't about hating society and hating people. It is about accepting the world for what it is. Then doing what is in your best-interest - just like women are doing what is in their best interest. **You have no one to truly rely on, but yourself. A woman's love is always conditional. Always take care of number one: you.**

CHOOSE THE RED PILL AND SEE HOW FAR THE RABBIT HOLE GOES...

There are many difficult to swallow red-pill truths about women and life, but once you embrace reality for what it is then you will be in the best position to succeed in the brutal game of seduction. After all, seduction is war.

- **The hard reality is that a woman will always prioritize her own agenda over yours.**
- **The hard reality is that women say they want nice guys, but chase bad boys.** Look to a woman's actions, micro expressions and body-language ascertain the truth of the situation.
- **The hard reality is being a people pleaser, being addicted to approval and praise, and putting everyone's goals ahead of your own: will get you nowhere in life.**

- **The hard reality is that women will play the role of an innocent prude to a nice guy, but be a dirty slut to a batboy who TURNS HER ON.**

Invest in yourself by learning red pill truths and other pieces of valuable useful knowledge on a daily basis. Don't waste time on junk activities like watching movies and TV Shows; invest that time into learning things that will prove useful to you!

10

☛LAW #107: CREATE WINNING HABITS.

A WOMAN WILL PRIORITIZE herself above all. Her own (unconscious or conscious) agenda will always be pushed forward. That's why one of the best pieces of conversation advice is to stack observations about her. **Cold reads are very effective when dealing with women because her favorite subject in the world is herself. When you share thoughts about things that you have noticed about her then she will be captivated.**

Just like a woman prioritizes herself, it's your job to prioritize yourself! Just like she is looking out for herself, you must look out for yourself! She's getting value out of you and that's why she is sticking around. **Women are attracted to value-givers.** As a man of high-status you are a value-giver because you have abundance in your life. It is important that you take value, as well. A mutually beneficial exchange of emotional value is what will keep the connection alive, and how society has functioned since the dawn of time.

You must take care of your mind, and body. These are machines and when you take care of them, they will take care of you. **Purge yourself of negative emotions, negative people, negative situations, and negative**

self-talk. Focus on positive emotions, people that inspire you, situations conducive to your growth and thoughts that motivate. Part of taking care of yourself is to realize the importance of mental health. Make research and daily learning a priority. For 2020, aim to be high energy, highly motivated and disciplined to accomplish a lot - every single day.

Now is the time to ponder 2020 resolutions. Ask yourself: "Which one positive behavior implemented daily would lead to a remarkably positive change in my life?"

- Quitting all TV shows, movies and video-games; then replacing those time sinks with reading and/or watching courses on areas that you want to improve in.
- Eliminating toxic people from your life who drag you down because they don't have much to offer. You may have found yourself prioritizing them, when they wouldn't prioritize you in return. Instead, reinvest the energy into higher-quality people who have much more to offer.
- Aiming for hotter, sexier and more beautiful girls. Don't feel guilty for cutting out ugly women from your life. You have spent years developing yourself as a man, and you deserve women of beauty in your life.

Focusing on developing a chain of positive daily behaviors such as working out, reflecting on ways to improve your life, and eating healthy. First you build your habits and then those habits build you. Successful seducers have a set of connected habits that lead them to automatic seduction; they almost can't stop meeting women and having sex because it's so naturally integrated into their lifestyle.

Be the person that you wish you were every single day for

the rest of 2020, and you'll thank yourself for this resolution in 2021.

Do not allow social anxiety, depression or panic attacks to stop you from living life to the fullest! Some men have been haunted by these weak emotions for years. In fact, they have been haunted for theses emotions for so long that they have considered them to be a normal way of being. **You have the kill the weaker version of yourself, so that the stronger version of you can take over!**

There is a constant battle between the weaker version of you and the stronger version of you. It is the version that you feed that becomes stronger!

It is time to undo that cycle of pain and self-sabotage! It doesn't matter who you were in the past, or how many mistakes you made. Let go of the past and start again this very moment!

Many men have an acute fear of beautiful women that paralyzes them from taking action. When they are in the presence of a beautiful woman they stumble over their words, and exude nervousness - instead of calm strength and certainty in their own high worth.

What kills fear and social anxiety?

The answer is simple but incredibly powerful. It is action! The more action you take towards achieving your goals, the less intensity of negative emotions you will feel.

Action is the cure against fear, social anxiety, and general nervousness around someone attractive who is the opposite sex.

When you do that which you are afraid to do, the fear vanishes. When you take action to have intercourse with beautiful women, you will continue to internalize the mindset that there is nothing to be afraid of but your own illusions that there is something to be afraid of.

You can learn more from simply confronting your fears and doing that which terrifies you than you will learn from hours of mental conditioning (with affirmations and self-suggestion). Never underestimate the sheer power of action.

You build your personality one step at a time with every action that you take.

It is of paramount importance to develop the action habit. The action habit is simply the positive lifestyle route of taking action every single day to make your vision a reality. If your vision is to be better with beautiful women, to have a beautiful girlfriend, or to have a rotation of women who you are having intercourse with it: it is imperative to set daily goals to achieve that.

You can learn all the theory in the world, but if you don't take action then you will get nowhere and even a guy with poor game will still outshine you. Develop the daily action habit!!!

11

👉LAW #108: CREATE A MOMENTUM OF NON-STOP WINNING.

THE UNCONSCIOUS MIND is always soaking in the actions that one takes. Self-sabotage actions create a turbulent mind. In contrast, one who takes MASSIVE ACTION - inspires himself and sends a message to the unconscious mind that if he applies himself then he will eventually emerge victorious. **By behaving like a warrior then one develops the mind of warrior because the external awakens the internal.**

12

☛LAW #109: DON'T BE A LITTLE BITCH.

INSTEAD OF OF COMPLAINING, **being bitter and focusing on the negative in life: take serious amounts of action to achieve what you want out of life.** The key is to take action consistently EVERY SINGLE DAY and start today.

- The life that you want to live isn't going to magically unfold unto itself.
- The beautiful women aren't going to suddenly fall out of the sky into your lap.
- Dreams don't come true simply by themselves.

<u>You have to know what you want, and actively take steps to turn that dream into a reality every day because it won't happen by itself.</u> You have to take a proactive approach - rather than a passive approach. Being bitter and complaining about how bad you have it isn't going to change anything. Playing the victim card and giving a laundry list of excuses isn't going to change anything either. Take responsibility for your life starting this moment!

TAKE YOUR HEAD OUT OF THE SAND AND

OPEN YOURS EYES. IF YOU ARE A LITTLE BITCH, YOU WILL GET NOWHERE IN LIFE.

The lesson is simple: don't be a little bitch.

The biggest danger for men is that they expect their problems with girls to magically be fixed by themselves. Things are not going to magically fix themselves. Things are not going to magically come together on their own. You need to develop a TAKE FUCKING CHARGE perspective on life.

You have to create a vision. Then set goals that are designed to get you closer to that dream you have in your mind's eye. **Once those daily goals are defined clearly, attack them with FULL FORCE. Attack! Attack! Attack!**

"Obey the Law of Reality. What is the Law of Reality? It is exactly what you think. Instead of REACTING to reality as burned Nice Guys do, you end up EMBRACING reality. When people follow the Law of Reality, the entire world seems filled with marvels." - Pook

13

☛LAW #110: DON'T BE A SHEEP.

"THE WAY IS the default life most men revolve around. The Way is routinely celebrated and held up as the only Way. The Way consists of the following:

- Go to school. Get good grades. Do the senior prom, go to school dances, give a girl your high school class ring, and other garbage like that.
- Go to college. Get even more good grades. Participate with the campus activities, especially the feminist ones. Celebrate the Vagina Monologues. Become a mangina and write against evil patriarchy and how women need more rights and security.
- Get a job, not in something you like, but in something that provides security. Make money by working harder.
- Meet a girl, fall in love, and marry her. Participate in the elaborate wedding and the honeymoon to a place you didn't choose.
- Buy a big house because of the expectation of kids.

- Once married, the other married guys show you how the system works by showing you the home improvement activities you now get to engage on. Yes, you get to go buy hammers and screws to continually improve the house. Lawn care, house care, car care, yes, your purpose is to maintain this physical shelter and make it look 'acceptable.'
- Have a kid or two. Wife gets fat and cuts her hair. You must accept this. You will now work 24 harder and be forced to get promoted due to the rising costs. You have become the wage slave.
- Keep doing this for decades until your soul evaporates. As your body breaks down (it will at this fast pace), let your wife play the role as the 'nurse' as you begin to make continual trips to the hospital.
- Die.

Sounds fun doesn't it? It certainly doesn't sound appealing to me. Keep in mind that I am not knocking college, good grades, children, home improvement, and all that. **What I am knocking is the pre-formulated life. This 'default' view is life in the Matriarchy**. And this is if you are lucky and were not divorced." Pook

Don't be a sheep. Think for yourself. Don't mindlessly do what the current culture of the times tells you to do. Don't be another sheep conforming to the masses.

The average person is a broke beta. Just doing what everyone else is doing will make you average. FUCK being like everyone else. Achieve greatness!

When it comes to seduction being a rebel and breaking conformity is one of the most exciting masculine character traits that TURN WOMEN ON.

14

☛LAW #111: DON'T BE BE HUNG UP ON A FORMER LOVER.

WHEN YOU CHASE an ex girlfriend then you may end up compromising your self-esteem and confidence levels. You're essentially communicating the message of:

"I am willing to give away all my power, and beg for you to come back. I will get on my knees and degrade myself, just to show you how much I want you! Tell me who I need to be and I will be that person for you! I will do anything and be anyone. Just take me back!"

While it may sound like this would work, it's actually really damaging to a person's self-esteem to communicate this message because it communicates to one's inner-game that he is not valuable as he is right now. **Even if he gets the girl back, this insidious low-value frame in the relationship is damaging and comprises his self-concept and place in the sexual marketplace. If you have to beg, apologize profusely, and degrade yourself to get a girl to be with you think about what that does to your self-image.**

Furthermore, women seek confident and powerful men. Breaking down with a frame like this, shows that he never really was confident to begin with. **A confident man doesn't break down immediately the moment some-**

thing goes wrong; he keeps assuming that he has value. Giving away one's power actually has the opposite of its intended effect because ultimately women desire powerful men and giving away one's power damages his perceived image.

Here's the truth: a person live in a hallway of infinite doors (opportunities). Each door has tremendous value inside, upon opening it. Sometimes one door was open but then suddenly shut. Instead of looking at the other doors, the man can't help but stare at the closed door and keep knocking it endlessly This causes a lot of needless suffering and sadness. It also causes one to miss out many, many, many present opportunities in his existence - just because he can't adopt to the current situation. **By focusing on what someone doesn't have instead of focusing on being grateful on what someone does have, and the present available opportunities: a lot of needless suffering is caused.**

Life is a series of creating and ending connections. It is normal for connections with women to be only temporarily. Think about your teachers in college; did you feel sad that the connection finished the moment the semester ended? No. Because you understood the nature of life: all things are temporarily. Understand this: everything in this world is temporary - even life itself. In this world, we are just passengers passing by a series of moments in this journey and in the end there is death. It is an illusion that you can have a beautiful woman forever. The secret to getting over an ex-girlfriend is to realize that you've never really had her on "lock" in the first place because of the temporary nature of existence, and to get a new, better girl. **No matter how "special" the first girl was, there's another girl out there that is younger, hotter, and you can have more chemistry with.**

A person's emotions tricks him into thinking that she is special, unique and one-of-a-kind. The truth is that she is like many, many other girls: just an ordinary girl who will one day grow old, disgusting and die. **The emotions you felt with her came from investing into her, and the same feel-good emotions can be created again with a woman of your choice.** Emotions are often not real but rather are based on illusions.

Just try to be prudent about which girl you allow yourself to develop feelings for before developing those feelings; falling in love with a gold-digger who doesn't actually like your personality but is in it for the money and pragmatic perks can almost destroy someone's life. **One has a certain level of control of himself before he becomes susceptible to losing control; the trick is to take charge during that temporary moment of clarity.**

It is a woman's nature to not have loyalty. She is only loyal to herself and the value that she gets from being with you (either present or potential). Her loyalty to you is actually just her loyalty to herself. A woman is loyal to the value that she receives from you. **When that value fades, she will be gone. And all of that which you have done for her in the past will be conveniently forgotten.**

Hence, forming a connection based on a woman liking your personality is more stable than forming a connection based on temporary/dynamic factors such as social status, and wealth. **While the latter can get you in the door, it's the former that keeps the interaction alive during the volatile nature (inevitable ups and downs) of socials status and wealth.** Put simply: giving emotional value based on purely having a charming, charismatic personality that she appreciates is more stable than giving emotional value based on social status, perceived wealth (fancy dates/expensive experiences) and provider based "game".

What is game? **It's developing one's sexy personality, exuding that sexy personality systematically, and having girls in your life like you for (relatively) you** -

without having to take out your wallet and compensate with alternative pragmatic perks. Playing provider "game" is not real game. Almost anyone can get a girl temporarily by dishing out cash left and right.

The irony is that women may ask you to change. If you comply, a part of her resents that she had this power over you and that she is dating a submissive boy. **Change enough times (turn "pussy whipped") and you've lost the exciting unpredictability, rebel, dominant, powerful "I don't give a fuck" persona that got her interested in the first place.** Keep things fresh and exciting - without being a boring conformist who always says "the politically correct nice thing". If you get your ex girlfriend back by doing everything that she wants and fulfilling her every whim, then the excitement that she had from you being an unpredictable uncontrollable rebel is gone. It's not even worth losing your frame and dominant nature to get her back because the sexual attraction will be more "obligatory" instead of "lustful". Keep assuming value and status - all the time.

A larger part of wanting to get your ex back comes from the human instinct to respond to things that are closed, by wanting them more. The oldest trick in the book is playing hard to get because it's human nature to want a dangling string that disappeared more than a string that's on your lap. **Put simply: you just want her because she said "no".**

Keep in mind that if you get her back - all the same problems will be present - except now she has even less respect/attraction for you because she knows you crawled on your knees to beg for her to return. It's more efficient to train one's mind to snap back into the present moment, be able to move on and get a new girl fast - rather than dwell on the past - replaying the same mistakes in his mind over and over falling deeper into self-pity/misery.

Let go of the past. **Spending too much time thinking**

about it means that you're missing out on the opportunities in the present. Bring yourself to the HERE and NOW. The things in store for you in the present and future will be better than that which has already transpired in the past. Train hard every day; take daily action; you will win and conquer the world.

15

☛LAW #112: DON'T DWELL ON THE PAST.

REPEAT THIS MANTRA OUTLOUD FOUR TIMES

- **THE PAST IS DEAD!!!!**
- **THE PAST IS DEAD!!!!**
- **THE PAST IS DEAD!!!!**
- **THE PAST IS DEAD!!!!**

Don't dwell on the past. It is over and done with. Those stuck on the past are missing out on something much more important: the present.

The easiest way to get over a former lover is to replace her with a better lover. Don't be afraid to put yourself out there and interact with many women. When one puts himself in the way of opportunity then many opportunities will come. Don't wait for the perfect girl to fall out of heaven. Be proactive in finding her. She is out there. Just like you are looking for her, she is looking for you.

Even when you are not doing pickup and meeting women, focus on developing yourself to maximize your SMV.

Some men have been stuck in toxic relationships in the

past. The women put them down, compromised their sexual market value, and confidence levels. These men have been around toxic women for so long that they have habituated being stressed and abused as the new "norm". Standing up for yourself is not being an asshole. You deserve better!!!! **Condition yourself to be extremely aggressive in going after what you want in life!!**

Some guys are so stuck obsessing over a former relationship that they had with a woman that they have little psychological energy left to meet new women. If you're focusing on the past, you might miss out on opportunities on the present. FUCK THE PAST! Bring yourself to the present.

You can't change what has already happened. Thinking about it is useless to you. Replaying prior mistakes in your mind only causes you greater suffering. You can be addicted to a certain kind of suffering; you can be addicted to mental anguish and hence, you keep thinking negative thoughts. PURGE YOURSELF OF NEGATIVE THOUGHTS AND EMOTIONS. Bring yourself to the present moment because life happens in the NOW!

16

☛LAW #113: DON'T HANG OUT WITH LOSERS.

IT IS healthy to be part of a supportive peer network. Having friendships with men that care about you (and you care about them) is incredibly beneficial for one's mental health. You have a lot to offer to the world, as does the world to you!

Do you know what is FOUR or FIVE TIMES more effective than a resume for getting a dream job? It is: getting a recommendation from someone within that organization. Social skills can be used to land you a working position of your dreams - among a multitude of other benefits. If you're an entrepreneur, then the same can be said for landing a mutually lucrative business partnership.

Be part of a mastermind group of people that share similar life goals as you do will advance your personal goals. Find ambitious, driven men that are highly motivated to succeed in the game of life. Befriend them. They will keep you inspired to keep taking action and reaching your full potential. Run with lions and you'll become a lion. Hang out with losers

DITCH THE LOSERS. CREATE A TRIBE OF WINNERS.

☛LAW #114: THINK POSITIVE.

YOU CAN BE happy no matter what!! Happiness is a state of mind. One should be happy and calm regardless of external circumstances. Positive Intelligence Quotient (PQ) measures to what extent your mind is serving you instead of sabotaging you. The great news is that PQ can be improved!

Once upon a time there was a wealthy man who enjoyed traveling to exotic places. He was always looking for the next big purchase and exciting experience that would bring him happiness. "If only I had a better car then I would be happy. If only I went on vacation to the Egyptian pyramids then I would be happy."

The wealthy man was drinking his cold beer on the beach when noticed an ordinary man with plain looking clothes laying on the beach. This laying man wore simple clothes but he was extraordinary happy. In fact, he was the happiest man that he has ever seen in life.

"Why are you laying on the beach when you could be making money?" asked the wealthy man. "Why do I need to make more money?" asked the plain man. "So you can buy more things and have more luxuries. Then you can be happy." The plain man replied "I am not wealthy like you, but I am happy with what I have now. I already am happy and I already have everything that I need."

The wealthy man then realized that happiness is not dependent on external stimuli such as having a beautiful woman, or having the latest iPhone. Happiness is a state of mind. A man can be happy regardless of outside conditions. Happiness comes from appreciating and having gratitude for the many gifts that you have now.

"When I will be successful then I will be happy" is a fallacy because there is always a higher level of success that one can achieve. **As soon as you get the latest XYZ then there is another thing that your heart will desire.** Science reveals that happiness is the first key to achieving success. **If you are happy then you will have a lot of physical and mental energy that will fuel the path to achieve your dreams.**

Being happy doesn't mean ceasing the pursuit of higher social status or wealth. **Even if one is striving to achieve these goals, he should do so from an emotional position of happiness and energy - rather one from a position of sadness and depression. When one is happy then he will have a lot more energy to conquer challenges and WIN AT ALL COSTS than if he is sad.**

One of the main secrets to being happy is developing positivity. By being positive one will increase his physical and mental energy to achieve much more in life. Positivity is the ability to stay focused on what is good in his life - instead of obsessing over what is wrong.

If one is dealing with a difficult situation then it is optimal to "change what he can" but "let go of what he can't". Instead of complaining bitterly, ask yourself "Is there something I can do about the situation? If there is then let me make a plan of action to do it!!!" Instead of complaining perceptually, figure out what your goal is and create a plan to achieve that goal.

Have you noticed that children are almost always happy? Dwelling on the negative in life is a habit that is developed in adulthood. **A big secret to happiness is to focus on what is good in your life and the good things that will come into the future - instead of spending a lot of**

time thinking about what you are missing and replaying miserable events (like prior breakups with ex girlfriends) in your mind. Don't torture yourself by thinking negative thoughts. Thinking negatively makes you feel like shit and can result in negative behaviors. Think positive to feel positive to take positive action.

Additional happiness comes from having a clear meaningful vision about something that you want and making progress towards it every day.

Thinking positive is highly relevant to the game of seduction for if a man thinks negatively and believes that he "can't" get a girl then this limiting belief fucks him up. In the game of seduction, you get what you believe you deserve. You have to sincerely believe that you are the prize and that the girl is incredibly fortunate to be with you; then she will be yours.

18

☛LAW #115: PUT YOURSELF FIRST.

THE PSYCHOPATH ISN'T OVERLY concerned with doing the "right, honorable" thing. Why? Because women aren't honorable. Why should you give women an advantage that they wouldn't give you? Instead of prioritizing her by being a selfless provider and protector of women (who don't appreciate this), focus on prioritizing yourself, pursuing your own goals and dedicating yourself to reaching the full potential. **PUT YOURSELF FIRST.**

There are many horror stories of men who have dedicated significant chunks of their life in service of a woman, only to be savagely rejected and left to the dust when the woman found a better man. Instead of focusing on being a selfless provider to women who don't follow the guidelines of honor, focus on your on self-development, career path/business ventures and reaching your full potential. **YOU OWE IT TO YOURSELF TO TAKE CARE OF NUMBER ONE: YOU.**

LOOK IN THE MIRROR.

Sometimes men would prefer to live in denial because it means less responsibility. "I don't have to learn anything because I'm already perfect just the way that I am!" the overweight pimple faced nerd says while playing video-games for hours, and gulping down his 2nd bottle of soda.

"Just be yourself" is not good advice for losers who are heading nowhere in life; it's an excuse to rationalize being lazy and avoid feeling guilty.

Sometimes the biggest red pill to swallow is the fact that one has a lot of room for improvement in his life. If "you suck" admit that "you suck" because that creates a vacuum for you to fill with self-development.

He who thinks he knows everything will learn nothing; he who thinks he is already perfect will fail to develop himself to higher levels. **He who thinks he is already doing everything he can, won't even try to push himself harder.** He who plays the victim card and blames everyone else for his lack of success, will fail to take responsibility and grow.

If you keep doing what you're doing, you'll keep getting the same kind of results with women that you've always been getting. Don't settle for your current level in life; he who settles, stops growing. There is always a higher level in the game of life. It's time to pivot. It's time to transform yourself!

If you're not developing and reaching higher and higher levels then you are descending into lower levels. **Fall in love with the process of becoming the best version of yourself!**

19

☛LAW #116: FUCK WHAT ANYONE THINKS.

ONE OF THE main fundamental problems that men have with women is the overall timidness and fear. Approach anxiety comes from giving too many fucks. Approach anxiety and approach fades away when you realize that the vast majority of interactions with women that you have won't even matter in a year.

For instant perspective ask yourself:

- **Will this matter a year from now?**
- **Will this matter five years from now?**

What matters most isn't the girl or the results that you get, but the person that you become in the process.

If you do at least 1 real man approach every single day for a year then you will emerge as a GOD AMONG MEN when it comes to approaching women. This is relevant to LAW #8: TAKE ACTION EVERY DAY. Some of the things that hold men back is:

- -> I don't want to bother her,

- -> I don't want to make her feel bad,
- -> I don't want other people to think negatively about me if the interaction turns sour, - I don't want to risk rejection or failure or feeling bad about myself,

But if you truly do not give a fuck from the bottom of your heart then you will take action. FUCK WHAT PEOPLE THINK. In a century, you and everyone will be dead. Their thoughts don't matter. The approach that you're about to make is a lot more meaningless and insignificant than you realize.

- **STOP giving a fuck about things that don't matter and aren't worth giving a fuck about.**
- **START being extremely aggressive in going after what you want in life.**

The psychopath's edge is that he doesn't give a fuck about what other people think, or the cultural rules. This allows him to push interactions further and take ultra bold actions that other men would not be able to do. The psychopath isn't held back by excessive worries about making women feel ultra comfortable; **he physically escalates because he is a man who makes moves in life to take what he wants.**

Most men are tied down by the cultural norms and unofficial rules of society on how they are SUPPOSED TO BEHAVE. These men consider to be themselves as "cultured" and "sophisticated" but really they are just brainwashed slaves to the social conditioning of the times. Instead of doing what you're SUPPOSED TO DO, think for yourself and carve your own path.

The very fact that you are approaching women during the daytime is a stamp of badassdom. It takes balls to walk up to female strangers and start interactions that lead towards sex. It takes balls to call up girls, flirt, invite out, physically escalate, tease, and bang hard. If this isn't you then GROW BIGGER BALLS NOW.

You don't have to take out your wallet and serve women to have sex with them. This comes from an inferiority complex, deep rooted insecurities and a culture that brainwashes young men into believing that pedestalizing women is the path to sex. In truth, women are disgusted by men that worship them.

- **FUCK what she thinks.**
- **What matters is what YOU THINK.**

Some men spend years of their life trapped in a prison within their mind. "What is this prison?" you wonder. It is a prison that stops you from doing what you truly want to do, and stops you from living life to the fullest. "Tell me what this prison is you!" you state.

It is a prison of worrying of what other people think.

You may have spent years being too afraid of pursuing your desires, and seizing that which you fancy because "PEOPLE WOULD JUDGE ME NEGATIVELY FOR IT."

- You wouldn't approach a cute girl because you were afraid that others would see and think negatively of you.
- You wouldn't escalate an interaction with a woman to a Rated R level because you were paralyzed by the possibility of a woman's disapproval and rejection.
- You wouldn't push the boundaries of what's possible because you were afraid that someone wouldn't like it. Perhaps someone would be pissed, and how could you run the risk of offending someone?

So you've been playing it extra safe for years of your life - or perhaps all of it. All of this was unconscious, or partially conscious. As a result, you have been living a fraction of the potential that you could be living in.

I'm going to tell you a secret that could change your life if you applied it. **What people think of you is not important.**

In fact, they rarely think of you at all because they're too busy obsessing over their own lives.

FUCK WHAT OTHER PEOPLE THINK.

Let them think what they want. Don't let it stop you from aggressively pursuing your goals in the game of life. The next time you see a beautiful woman and want to approach her, do it. Don't let the fear of "What would people say about me? What if she doesn't like it?" stop you.

FUCK what they say. FUCK her opinion. FUCK society's rules. Don't worry what she will think of you if you approach, say something, or make a move. It's not what she thinks that matters, but what you think that matters.

Alphas run the world because they take decisive action. They aren't frozen by social fears, or analysis paralysis. Instead of living your life to please the perspective of others, realize that their thoughts hold little weight. In a century, they will all be dead.

Live your life to pursue your own goals, vision and purpose - not for the sake of getting external approval from random strangers, or praise from people in your life. Don't be easily manipulated by dosages of approval or disapproval from women.

20

☛LAW #117: SEIZE POWER.

IN ANY RELATIONSHIP, **THE ONE WHO NEEDS THE OTHER LESS HAS MORE POWER!**

What this means for you is that you want to foster independence by having a certain level of psychologically aloofness.

YOU GAIN POWER BY REALIZING THAT YOU DON'T NEED HER BECAUSE YOU CAN EASILY GET OTHER GIRLS, AND YOU ACTUALLY DO HAVE MULTIPLE GIRLS IN YOUR ROTATION.

6 Key Mindsets to REGAIN THE POWER in a Relationship

- 1 -> You don't need her to be happy. You draw state from within.
- 2 -> You don't need her for intercourse. Intercourse is easily available for those that have at least intermediate game skills.
- 3 -> You don't need her for fun. You are self-amused.

- 4 -> You don't need her for female energy because you can easily meet and fuck tons of other girls.
- 5 -> You don't need her for self-esteem and confidence because you are internally validated.
- 6 -> You don't need her for direction because you have your own cool shit going on and life purpose to live for.

4 Red Flags that you're Living in Scarcity; You find yourself saying these things:

- "I can't leave her because then it will be impossible to find another girl."
- I can't leave her because she is the hottest girl that I can get."
- "There isn't enough pussy. The marketplace is too saturated and competitive."
- "I would do anything to her because I'm in love with her."

4 Green Flags that you're living in Abundance; You find yourself saying these things:

- -> "I'm not afraid to walk away when a girl crosses my personal boundaries - despite being clearly told what my personal limits are and having received a warning prior."
- -> "I'm not afraid to walk away because I know that I can easily get other girls."
- -> "Competition is a sign of healthy marketplace and a healthy level of demand. TThe world has abundant pussy. (If you don't believe this then move to a city and go to a nearby college campus social events during active semester hours where girls literally throw themselves at you as long you

aren't BRAIN-DEAD. Seeing is believing). And there is always room in the top for the APEX ALPHA GOD which is I."
- -> "I give value to women but I don't allow myself to be exploited. I don't identify with feelings or random thoughts of oneitis. I live my life according my decisions and use my willpower to act on these decisions - despite potentially opposing emotions."

From the moment you first see her and open you mouth, you should start the interaction on a dominant note. How the relationship starts sets the tone for the entire ensuing relationship. Start strong right off the bat.

Women may claim that they want power in a relationship, but the moment that they get it: they quickly lose respect and attraction for the man. Women desire powerful men. Hence, men play power-games and must seize social power in the situation. Play the dominant leadership role in your interactions with women and watch her attraction levels for you skyrocket.

21

☛LAW #118: ALWAYS RETAIN "WALK AWAY POWER".

DON'T ALWAYS TRUST YOUR FEELINGS.

MEN CLINGING on to woman that abuse and exploit them is a MENTAL SICKNESS. These men justify being taken advantage of by calling it "love" and have a perceived overinflated, idealized version of that woman. Contrary to how you feel, she isn't "special" or "magically unique".

- -> She isn't your fucking "SOUL MATE".
- -> She isn't the "ONE AND ONLY".
- -> She isn't "THE ONLY ONE WHO WAS MEANT FOR ME".

Society has brainwashed you into believing that if you develop feelings for a girl then that girl must be your "SOUL MATE" and now you have to be willing to go through any amount of verbal, emotional abuse to make things work. Even if she gets old, ugly, spoiled and has predatory gold-digging tendencies, you should still cling on to her because who are you to deny faith and destiny?

UNDERSTAND THIS MOTHERFUCKER:

The more time you spend going after a girl that doesn't give a fuck about you, or that has friendzoned you then the less time you have for beautiful girls that do give a fuck about who you are and are joyful over the idea of physical intimacy.

You can pour water into a rock or you can pour water into a seed that will grow into a beautiful flower. The choice is yours. **Spending time with a girl that is a dead-end is like pouring water over a rock that won't sprout into anything.** It's much better to spend that time with a girl that would actually lead to something. Make reasonable progress at a steady rate and if you hit a wall then smash that NEXT BUTTON!!!

If you have been friend zoned then escalate hard. There are two things that will happen:

- (1) You will get laid.
- (2) You will know exactly where you stand and will stop wasting away valuable time.

The last thing that you want to do is to keep staring at a door instead of knocking at it. If you knock at a door then it will either open (good) or it will remain shut (also good because you are no longer wasting time staring at the door and can move on to find other doors to knock on). Don't waste away valuable time playing super slow indirect friendzone game with girls. Life is too short for that. MAKE MOVES.

REMEMBER TO TAKE ACTION, TODAY!!!

The frame is: fuck or bounce. We either make reasonable progress towards sex, or you get the fuck out and stop wasting my time. The right women will stay in your sex funnel, and the wrong women will reject themselves out of the funnel (which is exactly what you want). Your aggressive progress towards sex serves as a filter for higher quality sexually receptive women and saves you from lower quality time-wasting attention-tiger women.

22

👉LAW #119: REJECT UNWORTHY WOMEN.

PROTECT YOURSELF AGAINST FEMALE EXPLOITATION.

- Don't waste valuable psychological resources on dead-ends. Make moves relatively quickly to test and assess her potential, so you don't invest time in something that isn't an optimal lead.

- Have clear boundaries and communicate them. If those are violated, walk away. Your energy is better spent on more promising leads, or generating new leads. ALWAYS ALWAYS ALWAYS retain "walk away" power. Ensure that you have leverage, and self-respect to keep your standards.

- Don't do the friendship first, fucking second route. Once a woman gets used to seeing you as friend, it can be hard for her to change those behavioral patterns. Create a dominant, Rated R, man-to-woman frame from the very start and sustain it throughout the interactions.

- It's imperative to know what you fucking want out of the field. Life rewards the "specific ask" and punishes the "vague wish"; in other words, the concrete goals should be clear in your mind. When entering pivotal situations, understand the agenda, and optimal outcome.

- **Respect yourself enough to walk away from one sided "friendships" with women who you want to fuck, or being in a sexual relationship with a woman of low quality (ugly, old, lots of attitude, gold-digging tendencies, needy, non-optimal logistics etc).** Your time is worth money. Have standards for those who you allow into your inner-circle. If a woman takes up your attention, psychological resources and time, but keeps you in firmly in the friend zone then it's time to cut your losses immediately. Don't waste another valuable unit of psychological energy on her. If you are digging yourself into a deeper hole then stop digging now!!! Immediately transition to generating more leads or following up on existing more promising leads.

Her past will let you know what kind of person she is, and what you can expect from her. Don't accept the BS of "Oh, I've changed." Who she was in the past will let you know what she will do in the future. If she has dates assholes then you know what kind of guy gets her gears turning. **At the core, all women are the same and have primitive drives that determine behaviors;** they still have quirks that can be utilized by a man with an insightful eye.

- **Have a purpose that is more important to you than pussy. If you stand for nothing, you fall for anything.** If you live for a meaningful vision then you'll naturally be immune to female manipulation, and be too busy to get sucked into female drama designed to boost her ego.

23

☛LAW #120: BE RADICALLY BOLD.

THERE WILL COME a time when you will die and everything that you have ever loved will be gone from you forever. Until that moment happens, it is upon you to live each day to the fullest and its maximum potential so when the day of death occurs you can honestly say "I have lived a good life and pushed things to the max."

UNDERSTAND THIS:

- **You are a biological ticking time bomb. Look back at your past years. Are they full of regrets of cowardice escape or are they full of pride for the bold, fearless massive action that you took?**
- **Who you are now is the result of past behavior and who you will be in the future will be the result of your present behavior.**
- You're reading this book because you want to get more results with women. You are sick and tired of stagnation. **Then heed my words now when I**

tell you this: STOP being held back by social inhibitions, social conditioning and thinking-paralysis. START pushing your interactions with women MUCH HARDER. You are capable of far more with women than you have ever imagined, but you don't even realize this because you've lacked the balls to act with extreme boldness.

If you follow the last bullet-point, then this alone will improve your game by 300%.

<u>The truth is that boldness turns women ON.</u>

The men that she has encountered in the past are conformists that remind her of the boring average guy. She is bored of seeing the same thing over and over again. "Yet another guy who says and does the same things that the last 1,000 guys did before him." Be different by being ultra bold and taking social/sexual risks.

Don't just be different for the sake of the women but be different because you inherently disagree with the philosophy of just doing what everyone else is doing. **LAW#5**: **THINK FOR YOURSELF. Remember: you can't be in the top 1% of men by doing what the 99% (masses) are doing.**

24

☛ LAW #121: BE BULLETPROOF IN YOUR FRAME.

EVEN UNDER THE face of an impeachment inquiry, Trump retains his confidence and calmness. Trump has an impressive ability to keep calm under high amounts of social pressure that would normally break the average man.

One of the key features of being attractive is to be emotionally centered, calm and non-emotionally reactive - even in the face of social chaos and explosive, world tearing shit-tests. **A shit test is a confidence test and you pass it by remaining calm even under the face of intense social pressure - NOT by losing your shit or by throwing a man-child tantrum.**

You have to be able to lead a woman physically, logistically, AND mentally. This means having a stronger frame. You should have more conviction in your perception of reality than the woman has in her perception of reality. Even if her frame is as strong iron, your frame should be even stronger. Even the starkest of feminists secretly desires to be dominated by a more powerful and competent man than herself - both physically and mentally.

Having a stronger frame than a woman boils down to being a man who leads others to victory. If your life is shit and everything you touch turns to shit then it will be challenging for women to trust your perception; **they'll think "this guy is a broke unpopular loser living with his mom; what the fuck does he know?".** In contrast, if you are a winner and you have the tendency to WIN IN EVERYTHING THAT YOU DO then women (and men) will be more prone to be influenced by your perspectives in life. Lead the men and the women will follow.

Even if you are not where you want to be in life, it is within your best interest to learn how to lead women. Leading a woman will turn her ON (because dominance is one of the main attraction switches). Part of leading a woman is having a stronger frame. It's not always easy to have a strong frame because often women can have strong frames themselves; the key is to have more confidence in your frame than she has in her frame.

25

☛ LAW #122: LET YOUR EGO WIN.

THE EGO CAN BE FRIEND, or it can be your enemy. It all depends on how you use it. **The ego is a force to be harnessed.**

I have frequently brought up the fact that a seducer should - quote - "Let his ego win." Firstly, this is contrary to the popular advice of "Your ego is not your amigo", and "Ego Destruction". So what does all of this mean? What is the difference between letting your ego win and when should would one embrace ego destruction?

PART I.

LET YOUR EGO WIN.

When you're approaching and interacting with women:

- Seize social power.
- Frame yourself as the prize and a highly valuable being.
- Be highly dominant and lead like a warrior.

- Exude extremely powerful body-language.
- Have standards and be willing to walk away if they aren't met.
- Be clear in what your goal is for your interactions.
- Be assertive.
- Be highly aggressive in going after what you want in life.
- Make bold moves to get what you want.
- Be socially fearless.
- Be comfortable with social tension.
- Give zero fucks what anyone thinks.
- Take control of the social situation. Disrupt her patterns.
- Don't play by her rules. YOU have the stronger frame.
- Be a rebel. FUCK the rules of society. Do what you want.

What do all of these traits have in common?

They all let your ego WIN. In other words, after doing them you DO FEEL LIKE A BOSS. You actually feel sexier when you behave in the more extreme end of the Alpha Spectrum. This is win/win. Your ego wins because it feels important and is motivated to stay in the game; the girl wins because she becomes more attracted.

Winners take all; losers take nothing. In the game of seduction, it's the men at the top that have the lion's share and the men at the bottom have nothing. There is an unequal distribution.

If someone has been a Beta all his life then it can be strange to suddenly start valuing himself above all else, and take a dominant role in interactions - instead of a submissive role. It can feel like he is being an asshole. It can feel "too much". **Of course, it will feel like this because he has been conditioned his entire life to put others before**

himself; then he wonders why he hasn't gotten ahead in the game of life?

A lifetime of servitude of others, ignoring one's own best-interests, letting one's ego leads to defeat. **This is why when you focus on LETTING YOUR EGO WIN then you will get further ahead in life and you will learn to enjoy the game of life much more.** By enjoying the game, you will be motivated to master the game, prevent burn out and sustain long-term motivation. THAT and APPROACH HOTTER GIRLS.

Being an asshole is more fun than being a nice guy.

- You don't have to be an asshole.
- You don't have lose your soul to the darkside.
- You don't have to hate women.
- You don't have to avoid doing kindness or acts of altruism.

But at the very least, get rid of self-sabotage behaviors such as:

- Submissive body-language (perma-smile, perma-eyebrows raised, excessive nodding)
- Under-valuing yourself,
- Putting up with BS from people that you don't want to put up with,
- Being stuck in abusive one-sided relationships, and
- Not being able to say "no" and doing favors you don't feel like doing.

26

☛ LAW #123: BE FEARLESS OF REJECTION.

PART II.

DESTROY YOUR EGO.

EVERY MASTER WAS ONCE A BEGINNER. You aren't born with excellent skills. You are born with shitty skills. That being said, by dozens of hours of relentless practice you will be able to eventually turn those shitty skills into excellent skills.

- Not every man is able to get passed the dozens of hours of looking stupid and foolish.
- Not every man can push the past the pain period, dry spells and have delayed gratification.
- Not every man is able to withstand the social pressure and humiliation of not looking like he knows what he is doing.

These men with fragile egos who can't handle a rejection would rather suck at doing something to avoid looking silly by others than to approach through the pain and eventually succeed. These men expect to get results without paying their dues in terms of practice, persistence and just putting in the time/effort/training.

You'll suck at the beginning. You will look like shit. It will hurt. People will judge you negatively and laugh at you. Then you'll keep at it, ignoring the hits your ego has taken and keep refining your method overtime. The more you practice, the better you will get it. Before you know it, you'll be at an intermediate level getting results. Then as the years will pass by, you will become pretty good at what you do. This is the nature of the game.

There is no way around paying your dues by putting in the action - just like you can't build muscles by reading about working-out, you actually have to work out. PUT IN YOUR DUES.

A BULLETPROOF man is able to kill his ego when necessary. When you're approaching you are making the ego vulnerable to rejection. You are making yourself vulnerable to pain. And that's what you have to do to get good. **When you are fearless of rejection and getting your ego burned then women lose their power over you.**

Understand that getting your ego burned when interacting with women is part of the territory. Unless you're playing super-safe (which is not recommended) you will be rejected and it will hurt. And that's okay. It is through the pain of being uncomfortable that one grows the most. **APPROACH THROUGH THE PAIN.**

27

☛LAW #124: BRING THE VALUE IMMEDIATELY.

THE TRUTH IS that women are lonely, insecure, sad and bored out of their fucking minds. They need a COOL MOTHERFUCKER to come into their life and save them from themselves. THAT COOL MOTHERFUCKER IS YOU.

If you believe that approaching is "bothering women" then you have a severe misunderstanding of how the game works. Would you feel guilty if you approached a woman to offer her a million dollars? No!!!! Fuuuuuuck no!!

You have to understand that when you approach a woman you have a tremendous amount of value to offer and that emotional value that you are going to be giving her is going to brighten up her day, put a smile on her face and make her feel good. Hence, there is no reason to be shy, reserved or timid about this.

Here are some ways that you can deliver value upon the approach:

- **1. Cold reads**
- **2. Having a great vibe**
- **3. Having great energy**

- **4. Being interesting and funny**
- **5. Being enthusiastic, happy and positive about life**
- **6. Sharing your purpose and exciting things that you're going through**
- **7. Delivering a compliment that will build up her ego, but following up with a tease so that your perceived high-status is maintained.**

1. Cold reads

Women love to know how they are perceived by other people. You will notice that sharing insights about who she is, will spike up her curiosity. If there is something interesting/unique that you noticed about her then share it!!! Don't be afraid to express the full force of your personality and share things about her that she may not have realized herself. You will be shocked by the alarmingly positive response that you will get by being brutally honest about your perception of her - even by commenting on her body-language.

There is much to say about this subject alone because this tactic has tons of nuance and application (from commenting to her energy levels, to her body-language), but this short paragraph will open the door on its own.

2. Having a great vibe!

She is sad and miserable. When you come in with happiness then you are lifting up her spirits and making her feel ALIVE again. When you feel really good, those good emotions will transfer on to her. Remember: women like to spend time around men who make them feel good and this is the best way to do that. The self always shines through.

3. Have great energy!

She might be tired and exhausted from a hard day of work. When you interact with her by having higher levels of energy than her then that is uplifting and energizes. Women feed off the energy of men like vampires.

Advanced note: don't be too high energy and too animated during the daytime because that's just weird. You want to meet her where she is at and be a bit higher energy than that - slowly bringing up her energy with time. But you don't want to be at 100 points of energy right off the bat, if she is at 20.

4. Be interesting and funny!

She is bored out of her fucking mind because her day is mundane and repetitive. A bold, socially confident and assertive man who comes up to her smoothly with something to interesting to say is a pleasant distraction from the harsh realities of life that she is trying to escape from.

5. Be enthusiastic, happy and positive about life!

She might be depressed and sad - especially if she is insecure and going through though shit. When you are happy and have lots of good emotions, then she feeds off that. The Law of State Transference states that women feel what you feel. If you feel happy, she will be uplifted from her state of depression and feel happy as well.

This is why passing shit-tests is so important. If a man suddenly loses his feel-good vibe when a woman says some stupid shit then the good emotions are compromised and she realizes that his vibe wasn't that strong to begin with. When you feel amazing, she will feel amazing.

6. Sharing your purpose and exciting things that you are going through

There is a reason why women spend so much time reading books and watching movies. They want a pleasant escape from the harsh realities of life. When you share the exciting new things that you are going through in life then she is able to magically escape her painful existence and world, to join your more exciting and fun world. This is what women mean when they say that they want prince charming to sweep them off their feet. "You won't believe what just happened to me today..."

7. Compliments followed by a tease

Compliments have a negative reputation in the seduction community because guys mistakenly believe that its supplication. While only complimenting without teasing is supplication, this isn't what we are doing here. You are complimenting her to show her that you have standards and she is meeting them. You don't just want to fuck any piece of meet with two legs and a hole in-between. You want to fuck special girls who meet your high standards of which she is one of them. **To avoid appearing like she is your superior and dismissing excess tension created by showing interest, you calibrate by poking fun at her, negs and teases.**

LAW #8: DAILY ACTION IS KING.

Don't just read this theory but also keep in mind to apply it in real life. After all, the goal of knowledge is application. **Without daily action, you have nothing, your skills will remain the same and the results will be null.**

28

👉LAW #125: EXUDE EXTREME CONFIDENCE IN YOURSELF.

ALWAYS. Always. Always. Exude extreme confidence. Confidence (or lack of) is written on your face. Here is a rule for dealing with people: displaying irrational confidence is better than exuding rational self-doubt.

Have confidence:

- in your self-worth,
- that women will be fortunate to be with you,
- that what you have to say is valuable,
- that being with you is an excellent move for her, &
- whatever life throws at you, you'll WIN.

CONFIDENCE COMES FROM GETTING YOUR LIFE TOGETHER:

- Have a meaningful vision.
- Set specific measurable goals.
- Make a concrete step by step plan to achieve those goals.

- Review your goals and plans frequently.
- EXECUTE daily.
- Have a mastermind group of men with similar goals as you - where valuable ideas are shared.

CONFIDENCE COMES FROM COMPETENCE. ONE GAINS CONFIDENCE BY BECOMING EXCEPTIONAL AT A FIELD THAT IS VALUED IN SOCIETY.

Be aware of factors that can undermine confidence:

- Being around people who put you down.
- Setting goals and then NOT executing them.
- Lacking competency in a valued field.
- Giving into social inhibitions.
- Having negative self-talk.
- Dwelling on mistakes - instead of focusing on strengths.
- Overthinking and doubting past actions,
- Caring too much about what other people think,

Figure out:

- - what is easy for you to do but comes hard to others?
- - what are you good at doing?
- - what are you passionate about?
- - what is there a market demand for?

When you find something that meets this criteria, figure out how to monetize it.

CREATE A MOMENTUM OF NON-STOP WINNING

The unconscious mind is always soaking in the actions that one takes. Self-sabotage actions create a turbulent mind. In contrast, one who takes MASSIVE ACTION - inspires himself and sends a message to the unconscious mind that if he applies himself then he will eventually emerge victorious. **By behaving like a warrior then one develops the mind of warrior because the external awakens the internal.**

BECOME VALUABLE.

1. Be exceptionally good at one high-demand set of skills. Then you can exchange your expertise for someone else's expertise. If you're really good at X then you can be a part of a team of other experts who are good at Y, Z, and A. Together as a team you can succeed. You always need to have something to bring to the table.

2. Be good at one set of skills that is not common place. This means that you are not easy to replace because this unique set of skills is hard to find. For instance: cross platform social media automation etc. The harder and more your unique your value proposition is, the more non-replaceable you are; you can sell water for $10,000 in a desert because there's nothing else like it in the area.

3. The Textbooks Basics are Always Relevant

- Keep your word.
- Have a proven track record of success.
- Have a good reputation with prior business contacts.
- Be professional because you take your job seriously.

- Look successful; perceived worth goes a long way.
- With the information revolution, there is no excuse for ignorance. Learn everyday.

29

☛LAW #126: ABC

ALWAYS BE CLOSING

IN THE SEDUCTION community there is an over inflation of the importance of approaching, and opening. You'll hear things like "Do 5 approaches a day for a year". While approaching is certainly of paramount importance, if you only focus on approaching then you will only be good at that phase in the Hello to Sex Funnel.

It's important to practice other aspects in pickup - besides approaching. You can be a master at approaching women, striking up conversations, flirting to spike attraction and so on, but if you fail to close then you will fail in general. Just like it's important to practice approaching skills, it's important to practice closing skills.

I want you to attempt to close - even if there is a possibility of rejection.

If you only attempt to close women who are you are 100% certain will be receptive to your advances then you will inevitably miss out on a lot of opportunities. I highly advise that you push yourself to attempt to close even if you are only 50/50% certain that she will go for it. By playing the numbers, you'll get rejected more, but you will also have more success. Ironically, the guys who get rejected a TON also get laid a TON because THEY PLAY THE NUMBERS in a matter that is statistically advantageous.

The more doors you knock on, the more doors will open, and the better you will be knocking on doors. **The more approaches you do, the more results you will get.** Further, the more doors you knock on, the more you will get a sense of which doors are worth knocking on in the first place; you'll develop a 6th sense of knowing ahead of time that a particular opportunity is worth your time versus a particular opportunity leads to a path that goes nowhere.

Another important point: the more doors you knock on, the greater your capacity to knock on more doors. For instance: if you do at least 1 approach a day for a year, then within a couple of months you'll naturally find yourself doing a few approaches a day. This phenomenon of natural progression in FUNDAMENTAL GAME SKILLS is true because once you're in THE ZONE, approaching becomes easy to you and you'll get a kick out of it. You might be having so much fun that you'll do a dozen approaches in a single day.

USE MOMENTUM AS A MOTIVATIONAL FORCE. The more action you take, the greater power you have to take even larger amounts of action. Just like success breeds success, action breeds more action. It's a positive cycle that reinforces itself with time.

One of the greater ironies of the game is that rejection can be incredibly motivating to improve your game skills. It's ironic because one might think that rejection is discouraging. Let me explain.

You can read this book in your pajamas, leaning back in your comfy chair, drinking your Starbucks Hazelnut Coffee, next to a blasting radiator, while listening to relaxing Spanish guitar music, and learn about 10 things to NOT do with women. When you're in the field, MAYBE you'll remember those 10 things and avoid them OR maybe you'll forget the theory that you learned and make the mistakes anyways. That's the inherent problem with learning self-help theory from reading books like this: you hope the lessons stick and become integrated into your behaviors, but they don't always do.

In stark contrast, when I was in Union Square I met this very young, gorgeous girl on the street. We started talking, and she seemed really interested in me. She even told her friends (with serious body-language) that she met this cool guy and she was going to hang out with him. She then followed by asking about my name. I was trying to be playful, so I made up some silly playful name - to tease her. I was following standard old school pickup theory, but misapplied in the context that I was in.

That instantly ended the interaction, and she immediately left. The pain that I felt from this short interaction was VERY REAL. It hurt like a motherfucker. It was the psychological equivalent of being punched in the face. And I learned from that moment that not telling your name to women sets of red flags 🚩 because it seems like I'm trying to hide something.

She's thinking *"He's not telling me his name because he wants to be anon. And he wants to be anon because he is going to do terrible shit to me and get away with it."*

From that moment I learned the importance of sharing personal information to win over a woman's trust, and make her feel comfortable - especially when approaching as a stranger from the street.

PAIN was a way for me to internalize the lesson much better than any book could ever teach me. When you have skin in the game, the lessons stick harder than when you're a 1,000 miles away from the field and learning about the game from the safety of your own room, under the protection of a computer screen. There are hundreds upon hundreds of short stories just like this one. Since I started in the Summer of 2012, I have done over three thousand approaches (and counting) as a pickup-artist. It was the PAIN of failure that showed me the light.

The pain that comes from rejection is a HUGE MOTIVATOR to improve yourself, if leveraged correctly with the right mindset. The mindset is: every mistake is a success if you learn from it. I want you to leverage the numbers by doing a TON OF APPROACHES. Have a minimum approach quota and meet it every single day. **Hang a calendar at the door of your house, so you can be reminded of the daily positive habit that you have to meet.**

- - Yes, your ego will sustain burns.
- - Yes, if she says "no": you will feel like shit.
- - Yes, if she does a hard NO, then you might find yourself questioning everything.

But it's still worth going for the close. Because statistically speaking, if you attempt to close women who even have a 1 out of 30 chance of having sex with you, you will get laid on every 30th try. Those odds are not bad.

Let me put it to you this way, and let's take an extreme example to help illustrate the point further. Suppose that only one out of 300 women who you hit on is interested in you on a physical level, and the 299 are absolutely disgusted by you - even going out of their way to make it clear about how much of a fucking loser you are, or pointing out how creepy your advances are.

But 1 out of 300 turns out to be a cute, young woman who you are friends with benefits with (over a short period of time), or 1 out of 300 turns out to be a long term sexual partner.

Wouldn't it have been worth it to endure 299 burns, to get that 1 success? FUCK YES.

I'm not saying you should SPAM APPROACH, which is putting in a very low effort on each woman you walk up to - just so you can meet your daily quota. On the contrary, you have to care about each approach enough to give it a valid try. However, I would also like you to not get hung up on having the perfect line because that sort of perfectionism will keep you stuck forever. The goal is for you to do a FUCK TON of approaches, and put in a reasonable amount of effort to make each approach count - even if it's just for the practice alone.

As a seducer, putting in effort every day through the medium of ACTION is the most important habit that you can develop. Some of that ACTION should be a way for you to be meet new women - either on a daily basis, or a weekly basis. Some of that ACTION should be you following up on leads, taking them on dates, calling them up, and of course fucking the shit out of them. You get better at what you do frequently - not so much what you read a lot about - so get the fuck out there in the cold fierce field and TAKE RAW ACTION WITH WOMEN. The more women you approach, the more you will get rejected, but also the more experience you will develop, the more your skills will be sharpened, and the more lays you will accumulate.

Don't say "I'll do it right after I finish X". FUCK THAT. That's a never ending cycle. There will always be some excuse to protect your ego from the pain of possible rejection. Take action today! This means YOU, and this means NOW.

30

☛LAW #127: EMBRACE THE SEXUAL TENSION.

EMBRACE THE SEXUAL TENSION. **Be 100% comfortable in the sexually charged situation.** Nice guys crumble under it, and start saying stupid shit to relieve the tension. Nice guys can't handle the tension and start saying all sorts of nice things that make women feel excessively comfortable - killing the excitement of the situation. Being excessively friendly kills the thrill of the chase for women. Frame yourself as the prize that she is fortunate to be with.

Embrace the tension of the situation - without even flinching. Remember: nothing a woman says or does, should faze you. You are a man who is experienced with beautiful women and has seen it all before; imply social proof with your composure. No matter what happens, you remain calm and on your purpose in life. Always assume that it's STILL ON. She is still into YOU. When you assume attraction then you'll come across as sexy and confident. Don't convey self-doubt or talk about your failures with women.

31

RECAP

CREATE THE CONDITIONS FOR YOUR SUCCESS

- **Knowing exactly what you want with women** (have a vision, long-term goals, and short term goals),
- **having an intense beliefs that it's possible** (have very strong self-belief in your potential; know that it's possible just like you know that a table is a table),
- **have a clear INTENTION when interacting with women** (when it is clear to you that you want to FUCK her, and are not willing to put up with friend zone bullshit then your actions will set this frame; know what you want when interacting with women),
- **having a concrete plan of action of what SPECIFICALLY you're going to do to make progress towards that vision** (highly and highly specific practical steps; break down that

vision into very realistic micro-goals - also known as "baby steps"),

- **take substantial radical action every single day consistently and consciously** (develop the character trait of strong sexual hustle; if you're not a very serious action taker then nothing else works),
- **transform TAKING ACTION into a habit** (e.g. meeting women every day as part of your lifestyle should be something that you do automatically as part of your daily routine - rather than a conscious battle that you have to win every time),
- **stay ultra focused** (review your goals in the sexual marketplace every morning as soon as you wake up)
- **refining your plan of action based on the sexual marketplace's feedback** (reflection and review),
- **take the time to sharpen valued skills** (be the best at what you fucking do; practice your skills with women every single day and TAKE NO DAYS OFF),
- **condition your mind through self-suggestions** (affirmations, mantras, and visualization)

puts you in the best position to succeed.

Life is too short to play perpetual indirect game over a span of weeks, or months (or in some cases: years). The key is to continuously make reasonable FAST PROGRESS towards sex with every woman in your rotation - until one of two things happen: (1) sex, or (2) there is a clear "no" to the point where it's a waste of time. Accept the ending of the friendship as a risk very well worth taking. Don't leave any woman in limbo. Polarize a response by making moves. Be willing to burn the entire venue - metaphorically speaking - by having a polarized response from every woman in that venue. **Ironically being fearless of rejection, gives you sexy fearlessness and actually makes it less likely that you will be rejected.**

Part II

Seduction is a lifestyle, and a way of being. While Part I, I discussed crucial, fundamental concepts that put you in the best position to succeed with women (including completely un-fucking your life), in Part II: I will teach you HIGHLY SPECIFIC BEHAVIORAL TECHNIQUES (HSBT) that you should use on women to get them physically receptive to sexual advances, and eventually horny. **Be willing to review key points in this chapter multiple times for the concepts to really sink in.** Remember: what you get out of this book depends on what you put into it. You have to actually apply the concepts in real-world situations with women for this shit to work, and pull results for you.

REVIEW AND REPETITION OF KEY CONCEPTS = INTERNALIZATION AND INTEGRATION INTO YOUR LIFESTYLE.

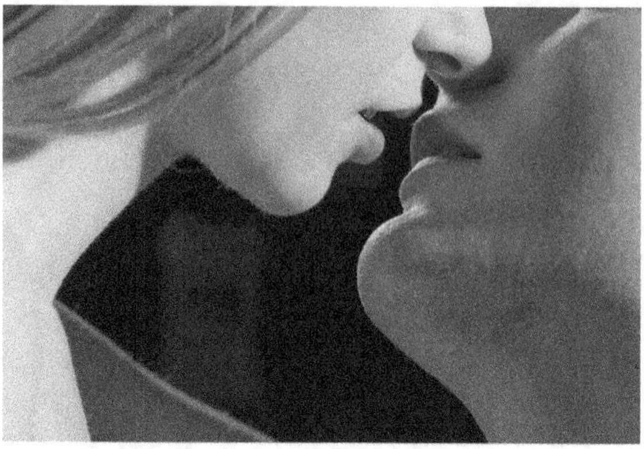

THE NUMBER ONE INDICATOR THAT A WOMAN IS SEXUALLY AVAILABLE IS THAT SHE IS RECEPTIVE TO PHYSICAL TOUCH.

32

CREATE PHYSICAL ADDICTION.

KEY I. 🔐

ASSUME "IT'S ALWAYS ON" 🔥.

WOMEN ARE like sharks that smell blood. Women can sense insecurity a mile away. Self-doubt is as disgusting to women as obesity is to men. Convey only strength, power, and confidence; never convey questions of your high worth.

This is especially true during the physical escalation process which is crucial for the relationship (and a lot of guys have anxiety when things sexual).

Every time you escalate you should do it form a position of 100% absolute certainty in yourself and what you are doing. This BULLETPROOF FRAME is essential because frame-breaks can kill the entire process. HOLD THE FRAME - especially during flinch points that would break lesser men.

THE MIND BODY CONNECTION

It's important to understand that women tend to develop feelings for men that they are physically intimate with. When a woman invests by having sex with you, she becomes more emotionally attached than before because **the mind follows the body. The mind will use rationalizations to justify what the body does;** in other words, once a woman has sex with then she will find 1,000 reasons why it was worth it, but before she has sex then she will find 1,000 reasons why it might be questionable.

MIND —-> BODY

KEY 1🔑 WHEN DEALING WITH WOMEN, WIN THROUGH ACTION - NOT SO MUCH LOGICAL ARGUMENTS. ASSUME PERMISSION WAS GIVEN AND JUST TOUCH HER BODY. ONCE TOUCHING HAS OCCURRED, A WOMAN WILL RATIONALIZE IT AWAY AS ACCEPTABLE. BUT IF YOU WOULD HAVE ASKED FOR PERMISSION THEN SHE WOULD HAVE SAID "NO" TO AVOID FEELING LIKE A SLUT.

ASSUME PERMISSION WAS ALREADY GRANTED,

so there is no need to ask for it. Women will fall into your frame.

Don't ask a woman permission to touch her body. Assume permission was already given and touch her body. Don't ask for the sale; assume it was already made.

By allowing touching to occur she will rationalize this to herself (in her mind) as acceptable behavior. If she's not okay with it then she will let you know. When it comes to dealing with women, it is better to be too bold and recover afterwards with a "mistakes were made" line, than it is to be too safe. Boldness makes women wet, but playing it safe bores them half to death.

Cognitive dissonance is a psychological phenomenon that occurs when women are not consistent with their prior actions. **A woman will align her set of beliefs with her behaviors**. Her belief system is shaped by the behaviors that she does, so if you create the behavior of her passively accepting your touches then you will also create the belief within her that touching is acceptable.

KEY II.

CREATE A PHYSICAL ADDICTION.

This is why the more a woman allows herself to be touched, the more she craves to continue to be touched and the more intimate you can push the touching to be; **oxytocin is highly addictive**.[1]

More importantly: her prior actions have been already rationalized with mentalities that are conducive to more physical interaction occurring. **Put simply: successfully executed touching leads to more touching, just like success breeds success.**

KEY 2A SMOOTHLY TOUCHING A WOMAN'S BODY LEADS TO MORE TOUCHING BECAUSE IT IS A SELF-REINFORCING POSITIVE FEEDBACK LOOP.

Now my dear son, you understand why you have to touch her body as frequently as possible. The more often you touch her body, the faster the self-reinforcing positive feedback works. Touching - even socially acceptable non-sexual touches - hooks her like glue.

KEY 2B TOUCH FREQUENTLY AND BE PATIENT. WITH TIME THE LINE OF ACCEPTABLE TOUCHING WILL INCREASE.

KEY III.

CLIMB THE COMPLIANCE LADDER.

Touching a woman even very low on the intimacy spectrum sets the stage for touching her in areas that are high on intimacy spectrum. **Physical intimacy on a lower level eventually leads to physical intimacy on a higher level.**

You see this concept of :

- "compliance leads to more compliance" ,
- "the compliance ladder"
- "yeses lead to more yeses", and
- "denial leads to more denial"

everywhere in game.

This is why you want to condition a woman to follow your lead with smaller compliance requests prior to bigger compliance requests. The more times a woman follows your lead, the more likely it is that she will continue to follow your lead. Once she gets used to light touches, light flirting, and light sexualization then she will be ready for higher intensity. Continue to push the line of acceptable behavior above and beyond the act of sex occurring.

KEY 3 **Condition a woman to follow your lead - even in mundane matters - and she will even follow your lead in sexual matters. In stark contrast, if a woman doesn't respect your authority in mundane issues then don't expect her to suddenly switch in the bedroom.**

KEY IV.

AFTER SHE IS HOOKED, TAKE IT AWAY.

THE CORE OF WHAT MAKES THE SEXCALATION METHOD WORK IS PULLING BACK IN THE RIGHT WAY. SMOOTHLY REJECTING A WOMAN ON A PHYSICAL LEVEL CAN MAKE HER CHASE - TWICE AS HARD.

- Start with light physical escalation known as Social Touch (using combination of techniques such as micro-escalation, bullshit baffles brains, leveraging social convention, and plausible deniability).
- **Touch early** - even within the first 3 seconds of meeting her - to establish the frame that you're a touchy guy.
- **Start subtle.** The very first touch can be quite subtle and/or "accidental", but you build from there based on her reactions (e.g. green, yellow, or red).
- **Touch frequently.** Have her become hooked to that level of touching (simply by touching often and letting oxytocin do the work for you).
- **Give tons of value.** Be fun to be with by giving emotional value, intrigue and having strong conversation skills. I recommend reading my other books "Conversation Casanova Mastery" and "Womenese 101".
- Then proceed with **heavy escalation**.

If she rejects the heavy escalation then you remove even the light escalation (taking 2 steps back - instead of just 1 step back) to create the conditions of where **compliance is more rewarding than denial.** Following your lead should be more emotionally enticing than being bored half to death by not following your lead. Let me break it down to you, my dear son; **create the conditions where doing what you want is more enjoyable than NOT doing what you want.**

So if a woman is doing what you want and allowing physical escalation to occur at a reasonable pace then she gets to experience:

- fun times,
- enjoyable conversation,
- validation from your attention,
- oxytocin-releasing social touch, and
- tons of value in general,

Get her into loving the value that you provide by giving a lot of it at first. However, if she's behaving like a bitch then you withdraw your valuable attention, and she LOSES EVERYTHING. She doesn't even get social touch. You even remove your proximity from her - creating geographical distance between you and her. **Make her metaphorically bleed from her loss.**

When this happens and you break rapport on an emotional/physical level then she will miss what she used to have with you. In fact, she will miss it so much that **she would rather embrace some level of discomfort and increase physical intimacy with you than continue to miss out on what she used to have with you.** The power of "The Sexcalation Method" is in taking away what you have given - just when she wants it most.

You have power over the woman once she becomes hooked to the value that you have provided. That power comes from being able to remove the value that she is hooked on. Remember: **you can't play hard to get if you're hard to want,** so first create WANT and then you can play HARD TO GET.

KEY 4 PULLING AWAY AND REJECTING A WOMAN ON A PHYSICAL LEVEL WILL MAKE HER WILD OVER YOU. ATTRACTION IS GENERATED WHEN YOU TAKE AWAY A FORM OF VALUE THAT SHE BECOME USED TO. VERBALIZING "THAT'S ALL YOU GET" CAN SOLIDIFY THE FRAME THAT SHE IS LOSING SOMETHING THAT SHE HAD.

❄

THE ART OF THE TAKE-AWAY

- 1. Give value.
- 2. Get her addicted to the value that you provide by being consistent in giving that value.
- 3. Continue to physically escalate. If she gives you any rejection on a physical level then withdraw the value that you've given her - removing ALL forms of touch and attention. Give her the gift of missing you. Then try again later.
- 4. When a woman is in a state of missing you, she will be susceptible to a more intense form of physical escalation than before.
- 5. Repeat steps 1-3 continuously pushing the boundaries of how far you can go with touching her body.

HOW TO GIVE PHYSICAL VALUE AND CREATE A PHYSICAL ADDITION.

The more you touch a woman's body (in the right way), the more oxytocin is released, and the faster she will become physically addicted to your touch. It's important that you touch her body in the right way for this to occur.

- Don't touch her body in a way that breaks her comfort threshold. **Calibrate.**
- Don't touch her body in an insecure manner that conveys doubt in what you're doing. **Have courage.**
- Don't bring attention to your touches during the social touches. **Distract her.**
- Don't go for too much, too soon. Pace yourself.
- Don't play the game blindly and ignore her body-language during the physical escalation process. **Read her reactions.**
- Don't go for heavy escalation in a public place because that signals to women you're a guy who just doesn't "get it". **Aim for isolation**.
- Don't fail to continuously escalate the level of physical touching. Always move forward.
- Don't expect a woman to initiate the touching and lead the interaction towards sex. **Own your masculinity.**
- Don't touch a woman's body during moments when she is upset, or angry. The aim is to associate your touch with positive emotions. **Anchor yourself.**

---

1. The more you time you spend with a woman, the more she comfortable she feels when spending time with you. The same concept applies to physicality: the more you touch, the more she feels comfortable with your touch. There is a process of desensitization that occurs from mere exposure.

33

SUMMARY OF KEYS #1-4

- 🔑 KEY #1: Win through action - not arguments. Don't ask for permission to touch. Assume permission was given. If anything, she'll say "no". **Touch early** on in the interaction to establish that you're a touchy guy from the start - immediately filtering out time wasters.
- 🔑 KEY #2: Touch **often** to maximize the power of oxytocin to create a physical addiction and get her hooked on the value that you provide.
- 🔑 KEY #3: Condition a woman to follow your lead - even in mundane matters. Start small to establish your foot in the door, but then increase the level of physical (and non-physical) compliance with time. Climb the compliance ladder. **Start subtle and increase the level of intimacy incrementally with time.**
- 🔑 KEY #4: When a woman gives compliance denial, remove all the fun, distance and touching entirely. Watch her metaphorically bleed for her loss, and miss what she had. **Then when**

initiating again increase the level of intimacy.

TOUCH EARLY, *and start subtle. Touch often. Get her hooked. Escalate by closing in the distance, increasing frequency, intensity of escalation and area of intimacy. If you notice resistance, go two steps back.*

34

OWN YOUR SEXUAL INTENT

FOR EVERYTHING you say and do, YOU HAVE TO OWN IT!!! YOU NEED TO HAVE 100% PURE DECISIVE BELIEF. If you physically escalate with this kind of extreme confidence, you will be successful.

A WOMAN CAN SENSE HOW MUCH YOU BELIEVE IN THE VALUE THAT YOUR TOUCH GIVES WHEN YOU TOUCH HER. IF YOU WANTED TO GIVE A STRANGER $1,000 THEN WOULD YOU BE HESITANT AND INSECURE ABOUT APPROACHING THEM? OF COURSE NOT. ONE KEY POINT TO REALIZE IS THAT YOU TOUCHING HER IS AS IF YOU'RE GIVING HER A $1,000.

No one is 100% sure of anything. For all we know Iran terrorists could launch a nuke, and many will die within a span of 12 minutes. But in the game, you have to at least pretend that you are 100% sure of what you are doing. **Lead with confidence and women will follow.**

Continue to physically escalate with hyper confidence - in a smooth progression - all the way to sex. At each step of the way, you need to have 100% BULLETPROOF HYPER CONFIDENCE in yourself, what you are saying to her, what you are doing to her, and what you stand for.

Women value men that value themselves. Further, women take cues based on your own level sense of self-belief and how you react to yourself, in order to unconsciously gauge how much they believe in you and how they should react to you. **When you believe in yourself, women believe in you.**

Get into the habit of using Tinder on a daily basis. Consciously endeavor to communicate with extreme confidence and intense conviction.

AVOID FLINCH MOMENTS

At no point in the smooth escalation should you have a moment where you flinch. Women can sense brief moments when you lose confidence, and that can be enough to lose the set. Seriously: it just takes one single moment - where doubt is written on your face - for the girl to be lost. When dealing with women, you need to exude a larger than life extreme level of confidence, and not convey self-doubt in yourself even when it seems "reasonable" to do so. When dealing with women, irrational extreme confidence is superior to rational humility. **No matter what a woman says, or does: retain emotional composure, bullet-proof confidence, and a positive vibe; this is true for each step in the physical intimacy ladder that you climb. NO FLINCHING IS ALLOWED.** Fuck that "look vulnerable" bullshit designed to keep you weak.

From "hello" to "sex" there should be no flinch moments. Just keep in mind that flinch moments are most likely occur during moments in physical escalation, so during that time: it is especially important to NOT flinch. Even if on the inside you feel like hell, on the outside: be a radiating sun. Happiness is sexy.

Utilize emotional regulation techniques such as:

- singing a song,
- self-amusement humor,
- affirmations,
- self-suggestions,
- dancing, and/or
- talking about subjects that you enjoy

to pump your own emotional state. Never show weakness. A woman is BIOLOGICALLY HARDWIRED to sexually reject men that are psychological weak. Keep emotional composure at all times, and utilizing emotional regulation techniques is an effective way of doing this.

❄

KEY #5 🔐

A WOMAN CAN FEEL YOUR CONFIDENCE WHEN YOU TOUCH HER BODY.

When you touch a woman's body, always touch her with absolute 100% certainty that what you are doing is giving her value, normal, and it is 100% expected for her to comply. Never flinch.

Stop feeling guilty for being sexual with women. If you feel nervous and anxious around sex, then just imagine how she will feel about it (women are mirrors to your emotional state). Let me break it down for you in the simplest way, so that you will have no excuses for fucking this up: if you feel anxious around physical escalation and sex, then she will too.

Women are a mirror.

- **Your vibe becomes her vibe.**
- **Your frames (perception of reality) become her frames.**
- **Your belief of your worth becomes her belief.**
- **Your behavioral patterns are then eventually mimicked by her.**

OWN YOUR SEXUAL INTENT

Own your dick. Cultural brainwashing has made you feel bad for enjoying life and having pleasure. Some men are addicted to feeling sad and miserable. There is a sick pleasure that comes from being a failure with women, and that sick pleasure might be a source of unconscious motivation to self-sabotage. Ask yourself if you're afraid of success.

Let go of prior conditioning that "sex is dirty" and rewire your brain into believing that "sex is a mutually enjoyable activity between two consenting mature adults". This is the frame that you should project when interacting with women.

Highly Specific Behavioral Technique #14 (HSBT): VERBAL ESCALATION: Verbalize sexual enjoyment, and what you are going to do to her sexually.

Verbalize your enjoyment of the physical process to encourage a woman to be more into it. Simply stating "this feels good" superimposes the frame that bodies are to be mutually enjoyed.

Have an unshakeable frame. Don't view sexuality as "creepy" or express any sort of shame over it. This is true even if she projects negative views on sexuality herself. When a woman says something that is judgmental then positively but firmly reframe it by behaving as if what she said was very weird. Reframe a woman's self-sabotage verbalized beliefs into positive ones that are conducive to sex occurring.

Highly Specific Behavioral Technique #19: REFRAME and REFOCUS

- Sex isn't "dirty". It is normal.
- Sex isn't "disgusting". It is enjoyable and fun.
- She isn't a "slut". She is adventurous.
- She isn't "drunk".[1] She is "partying".

REFRAME and REFOCUS are techniques that you can use to manage yourself, just like they are techniques that can be used to manage women. When a woman starts saying all sorts of negative things that can self-sabotage the interaction, reframe by deflecting with humor and then refocus by changing the subject into something that is more conducive to sex occurring.

While it is true that changing a woman's mood leads to changing her mind and it's an effective strategy, smoothly changing a woman's mind also changes her mood. **Changing her mind changes her mood, just like changing her mood changes her mind.**

Reframing is the art of using linguistics to paint a pretty picture that is easier to swallow for a woman who is looking for an excuse to be fucked and not feel guilty about it. She's already looking for a rationalization that she can tell her conscious, so give it to her.

KEY #6

ALWAYS BE ADVANCING FORWARD.

THE KEY **THAT UNLOCKS ALL THE DOORS 🔑 IS TO ALWAYS BE LEADING THE INTERACTION CLOSER TO SEX. ESCALATE. ESCALATE. ESCALATE.** If you don't do it then sex might never occur. Don't leave you sex life to chance; be proactive in making shit happen. If you can't escalate then take off your pants and see if you still have balls - or perhaps instead of balls there is a pussy inside there.

Escalate mentally, physically and logistically.

Escalate mentally by simply talking about sex, making sexual jokes, or sexual innuendos, or mentioning it casually.

🔥 Escalate physically by touching her body:

- in increasingly intimate areas,
- more frequently,
- greater intensity,
- longer durations,
- more obvious, and by
- closing in the geopolitical distance between the both of you.

🔥 Escalate mentally by:

- talking about sex *casually* as if it's the most normal thing to do in the world,
- always framing yourself as THE PRIZE,
- framing your touch as THE REWARD,

🔥 Escalate logistically by:

- getting her used to following you around the city,
- knowing where she lives,
- knowing where she works, and
- becoming a part of her lifestyle (either daily, or at a weekly basis).

SEE HER FOR THE SEXUAL CREATURE THAT SHE IS - NOT THE PRUDISH INNOCENT CHURCH GIRL SHE PRETENDS TO BE IN ORDER TO LURE A ROTATION OF WHITE KNIGHTS TO FINANCIALLY SUPPORTING HER

A woman is a sexual creature; she just shows her prudish nature to beta males with weak frames, losers, and guys that treat her platonically. Women WANT TO FUCK - just not with losers that worship the ground they walk on. Women WANT TO FUCK with guys that FUCK - not with sexually inept who don't understand a woman's sexual nature. If you think women are asexual then you are a fucking idiot who has fallen for cultural brainwashing; it's time to open your eyes, son.

Be one of the guys who "just gets it". You get "it" by engaging in a silent form of communication of both of your bodies touching each other at various points in the interaction - something that is happening, but does not have to be verbalized. **A woman sends SILENT SIGNALS that she wants to be fucked because society will judge her harsh (as a "slut!) if she says "I want to be fucked" explicitly.**

If a woman puts herself in a position to be touched:

- by accepting a date,
- going inside your home,
- initiating interactions,

- even though she knows that you are going to try to fuck her, then that is passive acceptance of the frame. It is clear that she wants to be fucked by you by the very fact that she showed up in the first place. **If she didn't want to be fucked she wouldn't put herself in a position to be fucked.**

At some point, when crossing from social touching to sexual touching: you will make your intent more blatant with a sexual compliment or a sexual statement of intention. When doing this, (again) convey 100% confidence and 100% full belief in yourself. When you OWN YOUR SEXUAL INTENT WITH BULLETPROOF CONFIDENCE; then women will start buying-into your frame. **HAVE NO SHAME IN YOUR GAME.**

When you have a strong sexual intent and OWN IT, you'll find that you will unconsciously start behaving in a manner that leads to sex occurring. When you feel like sex is "dirty" and "disgusting" then your unconscious mind will operate in the background to sabotage you. Believe it or not, some men are afraid of success, so they'll continue to sabotage themselves. Ask yourself as a serious question (that might sound a little too silly, but trust me on this one): **"Am I afraid of the repercussions of success to the point that I am intentionally sabotaging themselves?"**

CONDITION YOUR MIND TO WANT SUCCESS by verbalizing your goals out-loud, writing your goal on a piece of paper (then hanging that piece of paper on a place where you see it frequently) and visualizing your vision every morning when you wake up. Program your mind for success.

❄

KEY #7 🔓

YOU ARE THE FIRE AND THE GHOST.

DURING THE PROCESS OF CONTINUING THE PHYSICAL ESCALATION TOWARDS SEX, YOU WANT TO BE COMPLETELY RELAXED AND IN A GOOD MOOD.

EVEN IF SHE PUTS THE BREAKS ON, REMAIN EMOTIONALLY UNFAZED AND STILL IN A GOOD MOOD. DON'T GET "BITTER". JUST WITHDRAW ATTENTION AND TRY AGAIN LATER. "NO" MEANS "NOT RIGHT NOW, BUT MAYBE LATER." SHE CAN REJECT YOU KISSING HER 4 TIMES, AND STILL FUCK YOU IN THE END. AS LONG AS YOU PLAYFULLY DEFLECT HER REJECTION, IT HAS NO MEANING TO YOU AND THEREBY, HER.

A WOMAN DOES NOT EVEN HAVE TO LIKE YOU FOR SEX TO OCCUR. NOR IS SEX THE ULTIMATE COMPLIANCE GAUGE. IT'S SIMPLY AN ACT THAT YOU LEAD A WOMAN TO DO BECAUSE SHE IS GETTING POSITIVE ENERGY, EMOTIONAL VALUE, AND PHYSICAL FROM BEING PHYSICALLY CLOSER WITH YOU THAN BY BEING PHYSICALLY FURTHER AWAY FROM YOU. SEX IS JUST ONE FORM OF COMPLIANCE - ALONG A STRING OF COMPLIANCE BEHAVIORS THAT YOU HAVE ALREADY TRAINED HER TO DO FOR YOU.

HOW TO DEAL WITH PHYSICAL "REJECTION"

"No" means "not yet". Don't get emotionally bitter because then you will have shown that she has affected you in a negative way. Allowing a woman to affect you - on an emotional level - makes you look weak and it (ironically) rewards the very negative behavior that you're trying to stop. Hence, one of the IRON CLAD RULES OF DEALING WITH WOMEN is DON'T BE EMOTIONALLY REACTIVE.

Some men spend their entire lives in constant reaction-mode. They're always reacting to other people around them, being at the effect (not at the cause). They're letting their environment dictate their destiny. FUCK THAT! The correct path is to be proactive.

- YOU deal the cards.
- YOU be at the cause.
- YOU lead.
- YOU be the one who makes the decisions.
- She should be the one who is reacting to you, and playing by cards that you've dealt - rather than vice versa.

Be the one who is being reacted to - not the one who is doing the reacting.

It is preferable to just reframe her rejection of physical escalation as "she's not in the mood at this exact moment because her breakfast wasn't that good" instead of saying "I am ugly and unworthy of sex". Redirect blame to some arbitrary excuse to convey extreme confidence in the field, and verbalize it (for your sake and her sake). When you believe that you are sexy and blatantly disregard evidence to the contrary, women fall into that frame. **In general, it's not you PER SE that she is rejecting, but your approach and merely your presentation of yourself.**

If a woman rejects you on a physical level, you can still bounce back and fuck her later - as long as you don't take it personally, don't let it emotionally affect you, and don't show her that you've taken it as a legitimate rejection. **If you don't view her actions as a final rejection then she won't either.**

Laugh it off. Disregard it. Don't attach importance to her actions of rejecting your physical advances, and she won't attach importance to them either. If you take her actions as a rejection then they will become a rejection. Your perception will become her perception - which is why it's important that you view the situation in a positive light. **Remember: ideas are contagious.**

A confident man doesn't suddenly fall apart and crumble the moment a woman shows disinterest in him. He continues to retain his emotional composure and confidence levels. **Making a physical move on a woman is an incredible show of confidence.**

Be the fire.

- As the fire 🔥 , you are the one who is pumping good emotions unto others. You are the life of the party.
- As the fire 🔥 , you are self-amused and having a good time - NO MATTER WHAT.
- As the fire 🔥 , your life is awesome with her, or without her. You're always on the metaphorical fun bus - having a blast and ENJOYING YOUR EXCITING LIFE. Regardless of whether or not she hops on the fun bus, you will still be having fun.

Be the ghost.

- As the ghost 👻 , you are immune to the negative emotions of others. You deflect a woman's shit-tests with humor. You aren't emotionally affected by her bullshit, because you're too busy being on your purpose.
- As the ghost 👻, you aren't emotionally fazed if a woman is physically unreceptive at the current moment in time because you know you've got the game skills to get another a woman if you wanted to, and you can try again on that specific woman at a later time. **No matter what she does or**

says, you remain unflinching, unfazed and ON YOUR LIFE PURPOSE.

---

1. Stay legal. Don't have intercourse with women who are too intoxicated to understand what is going on. I had to put this in for legal reasons.

35

SUMMARY OF KEYS #5-7

- KEY #5: She can sense your level of confidence just by the way that you touch her. **Touch firmly with a sense of certainty.**
- KEY #6: Always continue to move the interaction towards sex for life is too short to waste away playing perpetual indirectly waiting games. The right kind of women will stick and the wrong kind of women will filter themselves out and stop wasting their time. **Be proactively in increasing the level of physical intimacy. Escalate on all three levels: physical, logistical and emotional.**
- KEY #7: **Don't get bitter or butt-hurt, if you've been rejected on a physical level.** Remain emotionally unfazed, still having a good time and on your life mission. Try again later.

36

UTILIZE LOVER EXCLUSIVE BEHAVIORS.

ESCALATE MOTHERFUCKER! ESCALATE!!

ONCE SHE GETS USED to light touching, light flirting, and light sexualization then she will start to get a bit bored with that (although hooked), and she will be ready for a greater level of physical intimacy. Now that she been (for lack of a better word) "groomed"/"prepped", you can pick the fruits of the tree and GO HARDER. Prior escalations have set the stage for future escalations; it is a process that takes time to unfold and requires patience.

KEY #8 🔐

BE AGGRESSIVE BUT PACE YOURSELF

Rushing for too much, too fast can lead to compliance denial. But consistently going for a little at a time, and building with time will eventually lead to full compliance.

That being said, take this advice with a grain of salt and be cognizant of the particular woman you are dealing with (as well, as the unique situation that you find yourself in). **For instance: a more promiscuous woman can be fucked on the same day** that you meet her (even within a couple of hours), as long as you have strong confidence in yourself and what you're doing; so, you can progress physically at a faster pace. There is no reason to escalate slowly if she is down to fuck right now, and you can escalate crazy fast. If I see a guy running nice guy conversations with a woman who is DOWN TO FUCK NOW then I'm going to punch him in the face.

Signs she is down to fuck tonight:

- #1) She brings up the subject of sex first.
- #2) She give you bedroom eyes.
- #3) She initiates touch.
- #4) She is VERY emotional and submissive - instantly complying to moving within the venue.
- #5) She leaves her friends to be with you in isolation.
- #6) There is no hesitation or resistance when you touch intimate areas of her body. She doesn't move back, flinch, get tense, or ask "What are you doing?"
- #7) She's going out of her way to gulp down more alcohol.
- #8) She compliments your body, or smell.
- #9) She emphasizes parts of her own body by "accidentally" lifting her skirt/shirt, and seeing if you noticed it.
- #10) She is really dependent on you for some particular form of value, and will do anything for it - including not object when you physically escalate to the hilt during the date. Keep in mind that you should NOT explicitly state quid pro quo for

multiple reasons (besides the reason that it is very illegal, it also conveys that you're extremely insecure and this alone can end potential relationships). Don't go overboard with Tip #10. Keep in mind that when you have game, sex is free.

There are a lot of subtle indicators that a woman is a slut, but that's beyond the scope of this book. However, I'll casually drop this gold nugget here: **a promiscuous woman will engage in instant gratifications that compromise her long-term future such as drug abuse (alcohol, weed, pills), and will mention a large number of prior relationships.** If all of her friends are guys then chances are that she is a slut because the only form of value that she has to offer is her body.

CLIMB THE STEPS OF THE COMPLIANCE LADDER.

YOU WANT TO START SUBTLY WITH LIGHT FLIRTING, LIGHT VERBALIZATION OF SEXUAL FRAMES, AND LIGHT TOUCHING. ONCE YOU SEE THAT SHE IS RECEPTIVE TO THESE THEN CONTINUE TO ESCALATE TO HEAVIER FLIRTING AND HEAVIER TOUCHING. LOWER LEVELS OF PHYSICAL INTIMACY, PRECEDE HIGH LEVER LEVELS OF PHYSICAL INTIMACY IN THE METAPHORICAL COMPLIANCE LADDER.

Women are like frogs. If you put a frog into a pot of boiling water then it will immediately jump out. But if you put a frog into a pot of warm water (very subtle) and then slowly increase the temperature - while keeping the frog distracted and giving it food then the frog will stay there until the water's boiling part.

Likewise, don't scare off a woman by being deeply sexual

right off the bat.[1] At the beginning, you're a fucking stranger. It's not normal for strangers to express high levels of interest from the very start. It's creepy if someone you never met before is suddenly incredibly unexplainably highly interested in being with you.

Start off with light flirting, and lightly showing intentions. You think she's cute, and attractive, but you aren't sold yet. You are skeptical of her worth. You begin with subtle light touching that you don't draw attention to. **As time goes on, and you see that she is receptive to lower levels of escalation then increase the intensity of the escalation.** Read her body-language to read her level of receptiveness and comfort threshold. The key is to always keep advancing towards sex and escalating on different levels - without giant gestures, without giving a massive speech confessing your deep feelings for her, and without going too fast to the point where the woman feels uncomfortable.

Constantly lead the interaction towards sex at a reasonable pace of progress. Not so fast that she freaks out and gets uncomfortable (breaking her comfort threshold), but not so slow that the interaction is boring, you're unmotivated to continue to pursue, and you're wasting everyone's time. Remember: a woman is designed to wait on the man to act on her, and to be acted upon by a man. **Hence, physical escalation is your responsibility**, so don't wait for a woman to make shit happen on a sexual level; be proactive in making sexual shit happen on your own. Highlight that last passage. Understand this right now at this moment and you'll save yourself a lot of headache.

That being said once sex is occurring create the frame that you want to **"make love with her"** - not just "to her". Create physical hoops for her to jump through. Initially, guide her physically to touching your body - by literally taking her hand and putting it in right spots; assuming attraction has been created, she'll catch on and play along. Create the frame that she is investing and chasing you - rather than the other way around.

THE DISNEY MYTH

There is no such thing as being super nice to women and then they suddenly fuck you "out of the blue" to "pay you back" for your niceness. Let go of the reciprocity-tripping fallacy and the Disney myth. Women don't owe you sex just because you were nice to them. Sex doesn't just magically happen by itself because you were nice to her and you were such an amazing friend.

You have to create a romantic/sexual frame and lead things towards sex from the start. You have to constantly be leading the interaction towards sex by escalating on an incremental basis. You have to lead. Women find a man who is a dominant decisive leader incredibly attractive, so take that role in the dynamic between you and her.

If you let a woman lead then you might end up with just being with your hand. **A woman often doesn't have sex on the agenda; it's not prudent to let her lead the interaction because her end-game may not end with sex.** Don't leave your sex life to chance, or hope. Leave your sex life to skill. Further, a woman may do all sorts of things that self-sabotage the interaction, so it's smart for you to take charge and lead from the start. Take control of the situation.

BEHAVE LIKE THE FRIEND, AND YOU'LL BE FRIENDZONED.

If you behave only like a friend, she'll treat you into like a friend and eventually you fall into the friend-zone. You put yourself into the friendzone by being "too friendly" and ONLY doing the things that friends normally do to each other. If you always behaved like a friend towards her then why are you surprised that you are in the friendzone?

You should have behaved, like a man who is interested in a woman would behave, to establish a sexual frame and sexualize the interaction. This can be done directly or indirectly. **Utilize sexually-charged behaviors and not just friendly behaviors to create the right frame.**

The Main Keys:

- Do NOT hide your dick.
- Do NOT behave towards a woman like you are only her friend.
- Do NOT allow a mutually-reciprocated pattern of friend-only behaviors to occur.

THE DIRECT PATH

Behave in a manner that makes it very clear that you are not just a friend. Do things that one who is just a friend would not do. These are known as lover-exclusive behaviors. By behaving like one who is sexual being and sexually interested in her you'll create a lover frame. By treating her as a sexual being, she'll fall right into that frame of being a sexual being who enjoys pleasure.

- Explicitly state your sexual intent
- Describe in detail (with humor at first) what you are going to do to her body
- Pay her a sexual compliment
- Touch her body in intimate areas

THE INDIRECT PATH

The best way to avoid the friendzone is not get

there in the first place. Start interactions with the right man-to-woman frame. After all, how you start an interaction sets the tone for the entire interaction. This can be done with flirting, making moves, touching her body frequently, and sexualized comments. **Often a man finds himself in the friendzone due to a lack of action. He didn't do things that lovers do, so he wasn't categorized in her mind as a lover.**

Remember: it is your actions (or lack of actions) that will create the frame the interaction. If your actions are 100% friendly and 0% sexual then you'll find yourself in the friend category. If your actions contain an element of sexuality then you'll find yourself in the lover category.

Flirting, touching her body frequently, making moves, hitting on her, and stating sexualized comments are specific behaviors that lovers tend to do; hence, if you do them then you will be categorized as a lover. **Create seductive perceptions, behave like a lover and treat her like a lover to enter the loverzone**.

BALANCE

Sometimes an indirect path is used prior to using a direct path because it warms up a woman to the situation and prevents her from being scared off by a man who is too aggressive, and too pushy. **As in all things in life, balance is key. Just like when cooking a meal, the right amount of salt makes a meal delicious, but too much salt makes the meal unbearable.** Likewise, you don't want to be constantly hammering sex all the time. Nor do you want to come on too strong too fast. Read the room. Read her body-language. Find the right balance.

1. A good pickup process doesn't look that glorious, stylish and flashy. In fact, it can look pretty boring because it doesn't even look like a pickup (to the untrained eye). It looks like a normal fun interaction between two people. If your pickups look like pickups (instead of spontaneous "accidental" interactions that lead to sex) then chances are that you're coming across as too try hard.

37

SUMMARY OF KEY #8

- 🔑 KEY #8: Pace yourself. Pushing for too much too fast can lead to negative compliance momentum - where "no" leads to more "no"s down the line. **It's better to go for less initially. Gauge her body-language response. Then escalate at a pace (increasing the intimacy level of your touches at an incremental level) that is according to where she is at.** Highly interested body-language (green light) means that you can escalate crazy fast. Neutral body-language (yellow light) means that you should escalate at a reasonable pace. Negative body-language (red light) mean that you should escalate with micro-escalations with releases/indicators of disinterest (to release tension).

38

THE "FUCK OR BOUNCE" MENTALITY, NEVER BE FRIENDZONED EVER AGAIN

ACT like a friend and you'll be friend-zoned. Behave like a lover, and you'll see her sexual side. **It's your behaviors (what you think, say, and do) that create the mutually acknowledged reality (aka frame).**

Hence, key #1 (mentioned prior): win through action - not through logical debate. If you ask for permission prior to physical escalation then you might find that the answer is "no" because she doesn't want to feel slutty. If you just ACT ON HER BODY then you'll spike her excitement (and endorphins) and she'll backwards rationalize her passive permission as a "yes".

You might be thinking "But that's irrational behavior?" The answer to that is that "Yes, women are creatures of emotion and emotion is not rational." The way of emotions is the way of women - both of which do not operate according to the laws of logic. Women do what feels good - even if it's not exactly rational.

KEY #9 🔐

GAUGE HER BODY-LANGUAGE RESPONSE AND CALIBRATE ACCORDINGLY.

While it is true that the one who is emotionally reacting more than the other has less social status, it is also true that you should **meet women where they're at**. Not being emotionally reactive does NOT mean:

- not being emotionally expressive, and
- not calibrating your strategy based on a woman's responses to your move.

On the contrary, **it is prudent to read a woman's responses to your physical escalation moves and calibrate accordingly.**

Every ping has a pong.

Women take cues on how to behave based on your behaviors. It's a Ping/Pong Effect. You do something (ping) that creates a psychological, emotional, and behavioral response (pong) from her.

- If your ping contains the frame "I am platonic" then her pong will likewise mirror that.
- f your ping contains the frame "I am interested in you like the way that a man is interested in a woman; I'll treat you like the sexual being that I know you are" then her pong will mirror that as well.

You do something, and she does something in response to what you did. Then you respond to her response. She responds to your response of her response. **The cycle of responding to each other (in that particular way)**

continues and the patterns of behaviors become reinforced with time. As a lot of time passes, you start to develop specific micro-habits of dealing with her, and she develops micro-habits of dealing with you. As mentioned earlier, **a woman is a mirror** to your mentalities, vibe, behaviors, and lifestyle.

The problem is that when a woman is used to treating you as a friend then it became difficult to alter those behaviors (because at this point they have become ingrained habits). Everything that you did with her was from a position of "I am your friend" instead of a position of "I am your lover"; **and every time she behaved according to that perception, the perception became reinforced.** It reaches a point where that perception is fully internalized and you've landed hardcore deep into the friend-guy territory - instead of being in sexual-territory.

This is why the friend-first-fuck-second method of seducing women doesn't work efficiently. Habits can be hard to break, and first impressions tend to be lasting. A woman tends to be consistent with her previous set of behaviors and prior ways of viewing the world - especially that they have been reinforced with many repetitions. Put simply: if she is used to treating you as a friend, then she has already developed those behavioral habits/internalized mentalities, and that shit can be hard to break.

SEVEN RULES OF THUMB:

- #1) **Behave like a friend, and a friend you shall become.**
- #2) **Behave like a lover, and a sexual partner you shall be.**
- #3) **Take forever to invite her out, and forget about you she will.**
- #4) Don't do anything at all, and the answer will always be "no". At the end your life, you'll regret

the things you didn't more than the things you did. When in doubt err on the side of boldness. **Doing ANYTHING in the sexual marketplace is better than doing nothing at all.**

- #5) Women value men that value themselves. **Behave like a king, and king she will see.** Pedestalize her and she won't be able to help, but look down on you.
- **#6) See her as a sexual woman, and behave like this portrayed self-image she will.**
- **#7) When physically escalating you have to accept the reality that you might lose the current state of friendship and be 100% okay with that.** If you're afraid to lose a woman you have already lost her because that neediness will leak out.

The best way to not be in the friendzone is to avoid getting there in the first place. You want to establish a man-to-woman frame from the very beginning. When starting interactions with women, you want to "hit the ground running" by setting the right lover frame from the very first seconds of encountering her. By doing this, you leverage human psychology (and the tendencies for behaviors to turn into habits) to your seductive advantage - instead of it working against you.

- This doesn't mean you should start interactions on a deeply sexual level right off the bat.
- This doesn't mean you immediately say things like "Wanna fuck?"
- This doesn't mean you should approach women with a hug that leads to finger-banging within 30 seconds.

Things like this will land you a verbal harassment lawsuit, or jail time. Coming on too strong and too fast can scare a cat off. **Pace yourself.**

FUCK OR BOUNCE

Always be making reasonable progress towards sex; and if you hit a blockade then she has to fuck off. It's FUCK OR BOUNCE. Always be advancing but be patient. Start subtle, and build on that incrementally. Start interactions with light touching, light flirting and light sexualization.

Women are better at reading body-language then men because they've been approached more, so they'll notice subtle indicators that you're sexually interested - even if you don't outright say it. Your body-language is always communicating the truth even if your mouth says nothing. Often you are communicating signals to women about your status within society - without even realizing it. [1] Start becoming conscious of the facial expressions (and other messages) that you are sending out.

Womenese is not just about being good at deciphering the signals that women send out that reveal the truth about the situation, but it is also about being able to send out signals that women will understand.

The "Fuck of Bounce" mindset is about respecting your own time. If you don't respect your own time then expect others to respect it.

---

1. For instance when a guy has a high-end suit, expensive car, and luxury watch, but cheap shoes

39

SUMMARY OF KEY #9

- 🔑 KEY #9: Don't game blindly. Make physical moves. Gauge a woman's body-language response and calibrate your strategy accordingly.
- Yes, you should NOT be emotionally reacting to her and you should NOT fall into her frame (both of these are low social status behaviors). However, it's still immensely helpful to be emotionally expressive and to strategize based on the current situation that you find yourself by meeting the woman where she is at.
- If you completely ignore where she is at and just fuck her, you'll find yourself with a sexual harassment and sexual assault charge; you have to read the situation.

40

VIEW HER AS A SEXUAL BEING.

View a woman as the person that you want her to be.

ONE OF THE **fundamental concepts of psychology is: who a person thinks he is, is how he will behave.** Self-image is the perception that you have of yourself. Self-image is incredibly important because how you view yourself is how you will behave and will determine what you are capable of achieving.

- If you view yourself as a courageous Alpha Male then you will do things that are aligned with that belief; you will be more prone to behave like an Alpha Male.
- If you view yourself as always tired and weak, then you will physiologically feel tired and weak. If you view yourself as a highly-motivated action-taker then you will find yourself always having energy to achieve your goals.
- If you view yourself as simp, then you will frequently find yourself taking out your wallet as a means to attract a woman into your life (because

you falsely believe that money is all that you have to offer).

The body is highly influenced by the mind, just like the mind is influenced by the body. The quality of one's behaviors are consistent with the quality of one's thoughts. Hence, it's important to view yourself in a positive light. This will give you greater levels of confidence, self-esteem and potential. **View yourself and the woman as sexual beings who enjoy living life to the fullest - including partaking of sensual pleasures from enjoying each other's bodies.**

When you have already conditioned a woman to follow your lead - mentally, logistically and physically - then she will naturally follow your lead once things turn sexual. Establish your dominance and lead from the very start. Get her into the behavioral pattern of being submissive and compliant. **It is easy to change a woman's perspective on sex when she is already used to (from prior interactions) accepting your frame as the dominant one and accepting your role as the leader.**

CREATE SEDUCTIVE FRAMES

There has been a famous study done about two different groups of students that were submitted into a school setting. For one group of students, the teacher was told that they were exceptionally gifted and highly intelligent. For the other group of students, the teacher was told that they were average. Over the course of the year, the teacher found himself treating the first group - as if they were very smart. The result was that treating the students as if they were high IQ radically boosted their test scores - even more than if they were treated as average. The point is: how you treat someone influences their self-image which influences their behaviors.

Treat a woman as a sexual being and you'll see her sexual

side. Treat a woman like she is a prude, and (you guessed it): that is the only side of her that you will see. Tell a woman she is "XYZ" and she'll behave to match that compliment. Create perceptions that give you a seductive advantage.

NORMALITY

A good frame to have is that being sexual is very normal, and the expected course of action between two adults who both like each other. If she mentions shame over being sexual then behave shocked. **You want to treat sex as if it is the most normal thing to do in the world.** Treat sex - like "of course (!) that is what two adults do together!" Have the frame that it would be WEIRD to NOT have sex. When you assume the sale has already been done and just TAKE WHAT YOU WANT, you'll find that women will often act in accordance with your expectations. Assume that she will agree to sex rather than asking permission explicitly.

- Don't view sex as a big deal and a "favor" that she does for you. On the contrary, view sex as the most normal action in the world between two consenting adults who like each other and favor that you do for her - because your dick generates pleasure in her body. Talking about sex casually, or embedded in stories is one way technique to normalize it, as I mention in other parts of this book.
- Don't make women feel guilty or shameful for being sexual with you. Have a non-judgmental perspective and make it clear that you don't kiss&tell. Discretion is a virtue.

View sex as a natural course of action that two adults frequently do. This means owning your sexuality and letting go of the conditioning that you had as child. You may have been brainwashed by your parents that your private parts are "dirty" and enjoying yourself is "disgusting". If you believe sex is "morally wrong" then you'll consciously or unconsciously transmit this viewpoint to her.

A SEXUAL STATE WILL AROUSE HER.

Sometimes a woman will pretend to be a prude and "innocent". She might say something like "I'm not that type of girl" or "You are the first guy that I have ever been with". Just smirk and know that she is lying to your face. Women are incentivized by society to not appear to be "easy" especially when they are seeking a long-term partner.

The key is to have a stronger frame than her. Even if she behaves like she "doesn't even know what sex is", have the stronger frame that she is a sexual-being and she enjoys sex. Keep sustaining this frame throughout the interaction and eventually she'll fall into it.

Continue to have sexual humor and dirty comments - to create a sexual frame - even if she doesn't play along the Rated R frame immediately. It can take a while for a woman to fall into the Rated R frame, but she will fall into to it eventually. The spoken word has real power.

A woman may not admit this because of her ego, but it turns her ON to be sexually desired by you. This lustful state transfers over to her, and activates her own primal desires. A woman is a mirror to your intentions, emotional state and arousal. This is because of mirror neurons within a woman's brain; **she can't help but be influenced by your sexuality, and respond with her own sexuality.**

KEY #10 🔐

VIEW HER AS A SEXUAL BEING

One of the primary keys to having sex is to view the woman as a sexual being. Women have twice as many nerve endings in their clit as you do as you in the head of your penis (8,000 versus 4,000), so it's essential to realize that women enjoy the pleasure of being fucked hard. They have been forced since their childhood to hide their sexual desire, but it still very real. When a woman plays along your seductive advances, she is unconsciously sending the message that she wants you to fuck her; otherwise, she would have walked off a long time ago. When you view a woman as a sexual being then a few things happen:

- You portray this self-image onto her. **When you view her as a sexual being then will start to view herself as a sexual being and then act accordingly.** One's self-image influences behaviors.
- You start behaving towards a sexual manner to her because you know that she actually enjoys sex - despite her prudish facade.

❄

SEXCALATION TECHNIQUE #10: CONVERSATION NORMALIZATION

Talking about sex leads women to wanting to having sex with you. The goal is to normalize sex by just having a conversation about it. Ask simple questions like "Where was the most exotic place that you've ever had sex in?"

SEXCALATION TECHNIQUE #20: THE PIERCING MOVE, MASSAGE HER THROUGH HER PANTS

Foreplay leads to sex. Massage her back and then stimulate her clit - even if she has her pants on.

- Stimulate her clit through her pants.
- Stimulate her clit by sliding your hand inside her pants and on top of her panties.
- Stimulate her clit by sliding your hand inside her panties.

When she is aroused then she won't be able to stop herself from fucking you. Suggest going to somewhere private and she'll quickly comply because she is horny. Already have a nearby fuck location in mind.

41

SUMMARY OF KEY #10

- 🔑 KEY #10: Self-image impacts behaviors. In other words, it's human nature to act in ways that are in accordance to one's identity. By changing how she views herself, you'll change what she does. Hence, see her as the sexual being that she is, so she'll behave like a sexual creature.

42

TEST HER.

CUT OUT THE NOISE. READ THE SIGNALS.

A WOMAN WANTS to be swept away into your sexual adventure - even if her ego prevents her from admitting this. A woman desires you to seduce her successfully and create an experience that leads to sex but she can't outright verbalize this because of the stigma associated with those words. **This is why often a woman knows that you desire her sexually and will play along your seductive advances** - while feigning ignorance and not outright saying "I know you want to fuck with me, so let's get to it." **She wants you to lead her through a mutually enjoyable experience that ends with sex and she'll play along to make that happen - without actually saying this directly**.

A woman doesn't want to stuff like "Do XYZ. The take me to GHG. Afterwards, say ABC. Then I'll spread my legs for mutual ecstasy." A woman desires a man that just-gets-it; if she has to explain what you have to do to fuck-her then it takes away from the experience.

Learn to read a woman's body-language signals to determine how sexually receptive to you she is, so you don't have to have to ask the insecure question of "Are you physically attracted to me?" Her body-language, micro-expressions and actions will reveal the truth of the situation. This way you can follow up on leads that have sexual potential and quickly reject leads that are time-wasting sexual dead-ends.

KEY #11

TRUST THE TOUCHING.

A woman can be verbally dismissive, but if she is physically receptive then this is the number one indicator that she is sexually available. **I repeat: touching is the number one indicator that she is sexually available**. Successful sexual touching leads to her becoming horny and having an uncontrollable desire to be fucked, which leads to her sex.

Learn to TRUST THE TOUCHING for the body does not lie. If she is allowing physical escalation to occur and she is into-it, then she is sexual available. Keep physically escalating all the way to sex. **Gain ground** by increasing the frequency, and intimacy level of your touches. When she's in the bed moaning from pleasure, she'll be thankful that you didn't pussy out. Persistence reveals confidence.

Touching a woman's body forces her to reveal the cards that she is holding. To put it bluntly in layman's terms: you know that she likes you when your dick is deep inside her mouth. You can be an amazing conversationalist and have a fun time on dates, but in the end what actually matters is touching her body and fucking the shit out of her. **Touch is the real barometer for where you are with a woman.**

YOUR TIME IS WORTH MORE THAN MONEY. Why? Because your time is worth more than life itself. The purpose of money is to help you live life.[1] Life is made of a series of moments that are measured in units of time.

I bet you wouldn't sell a year of life for $35,000 in cold hard cash because life (chunks of time in a sequential series) is priceless. Time is the most valuable resource that you own, so if a woman is taking up that time then she better be damn fucking worth it.

Testing a woman allows you to not waste time on sexual dead-ends, where you invest a lot of time and get almost nothing sexual in return. The more time that is wasted on sexual dead ends, the less time there is leftover for stuff that actually matters:

- investing in leads that are sexually fruitful.
- spending time generating new leads.
- focusing on improving high return on investment skills.
- increasing your sexual market value by improving yourself and refining skills of generating value deemed valuable to women (such as emotional and psychological value).
- focusing on your life mission.

It's worth noting that even if a woman is sexually available, it's important for her to invest into the relationship in order for her to value the relationship. It's human nature to disregard that which is free, while appreciating that which one works for. Create hoops for her to jump through; when she sweats on your behalf, reward her with touch and by giving her physical sensual pleasure.

TOUCHING TESTS (Also known as "Physical Pinging")

- Move in very close to her, and see if she stays put, or moves back.
- Squeeze her hand, and see if she squeezes back.

- Wrap your hand around her shoulder and see if she replicates this behavior for you.
- Take her hand and put it on your thigh. Hold it there with your own hand. Then remove your hand and see how long her hand stays on your thigh.

You want to consistently be touching a woman's body because it will give you a lot of information to work with. You'll always know where you stand. Make a move, gauge her response, recalibrate your strategy and then make another move.

Testing is what allows you to quickly read a woman's feelings towards you ("Is she a green, yellow, or red light?") and keeps you informed as to how fast you can escalate. The more information you have about where you stand, the better you will be able to progress forward towards a mutually enjoyable/beneficial long term sexual relationship with a holder of vagina.

---

1. The purpose of money is to help you live your life to the fullest. In contrast, it is absurd to believe that the purpose of life is to make money. Life is just units of time. If you believe money is important than time than you likewise believe that money is more important than life itself.

43

SUMMARY OF KEY #11

- 🔑 KEY #11: Time is your most valuable resource. It is prudent to know what you want out of the sexual marketplace, and thus be able to see if the woman you are dealing with possess what you want - by testing her. Tests allow you to ascertain the truth. I'm going to make the assumption that you are interested in sex, in which case, physical escalation will reveal if the woman is sexually available. **Touch is the number one indicator of sexual availability.**
- **Testing women is what lets you quickly see if a woman is worth your time, or not.** This alone will save you a lot of time. Women test men all the time and then accept/reject according to the results. It's time that you level the playing field and utilize the same tactics women use on men for your own benefit.

44

ALWAYS BE TOUCHING.

GET her body used to the enjoyable oxytocin that is released when you touch her frequently and she will come to crave that hormone. Her body is designed to pair bond. All you have to do is to touch her body and those natural feel-good hormones will be released. You are a man, and she is a woman; **nature has a way of naturally bringing things to sex - as long as you keep on touching her body all the time.**

KEY #12 🔐

NORMALIZE.

As long as you frame initial touching as casual, "not a big deal", have some "accidental touching", and don't draw attention to the touching then she will allow this to occur - without even realizing that her biological nature is designed to become addicted to touches.

Drawing attention to the touching by looking at your hand ✋ while you're touching her is insecure behavior. It shows self-doubt and places too much intenseness on the interaction. Physical escalation should appear to be spontaneous, in the moment and is part of the fun of the interaction. Focus on the conversation and look at her face while you're physically escalating. If you notice facial flinches or muscular tension then these are signs that you're about to breach her comfort threshold (or already have breached it), and it's time to withdraw touch. It is important that you withdraw the touch first before she does to create the perception that you are physically rejecting her - rather than the other way around.

Women CRAVE to be touched and sexually desired by a high-status man, but they just can't verbalize this because society will judge them as a stigmatized slut for doing so. Be part of the secret society that "just gets it". Touch her body often and consistently to have her hooked on that hormone. **Women desire to be desired and women crave physical intimacy - even if this is unconscious and even if her ego is too fragile to admit this.**

This principle that women are biologically designed to become addicted to sensual touching is also true in the later stages of seduction. Get her addicted to your body by giving her intense pleasure through triggering her G-spot consistently. Become the source of intense pleasure; a woman will become hooked on a man that satisfies her sexually. This is a little known secret that isn't spoken about: **being good at giving women sexual pleasure gets them hooked into having sex with you.**

Women don't respect a man that doesn't go after what he wants. When she is in bed before you, ravage her completely. Fuck her as hard as you can. Hold nothing back. Dominate her physically in bed. Pull her by the legs. Carry her. Put her in the positions hat you want. **Just like you want to dominate her body completely, you want to dominate her mind entirely; fuck her mind, just like you will fuck her body.** Women crave to be completely dominated in bed -

they just can't say this outright because they're afraid of being judged.

When a man is sexually uninhibited and completely free in his sexual expression then the woman falls into this frame and plays along. When you behave completely sexually unrestricted, you gives her permission to do so the same. It is absolutely crucial that you never judge a woman negatively for expressing her sexuality as this can cause her to shut down. Even if she expresses guilt or shame for being sexual, you should be quick to reframe it as "Sex being normal and natural" and that it's WEIRD to "not have sex."

As a man, it is your responsibility to lead sexually by example. This means having the stronger frame, and getting into a behavioral pattern of leading her (while she follows you).

IRON CLAD RULE OF TOUCHING WOMEN #4

You want to start this by taking charge from the very start of the interaction by touching early. This creates the frame that you're a touchy guy - the kind of frame that you want to have. Do this almost immediately - even touching on the opener itself (when possible). The touching starts "innocent" and very subtle (almost un-noticable). You start with "innocent" things (included in this category are "accidental" touches).

- High-five (the high five is also a good transition into a handhold)
- Handshake
- Tap her on the shoulder when you have an important point to make.

- Say something sweet and then hug her from the side. However, as time moves on this will progress to a frontal hug.
- When you sit down, you "accidentally" have your legs touching hers.
- When she starts laughing, touch her briefly on the thigh to associate good emotions with your touch.
- "Lets go here!" And take her hand to lead the way.
- When crossing the street or taking her through a crowded area, simply take her hand to guide her path. When you take her hand, maintain eye-contact - to show her that you are OWNING your actions.

YOUR TOUCHING IS OXYGEN.

Touch early and touch often.

A woman who has already been trained to be submissive and comply with your demands - will likewise follow your lead into the sexual realm. If you've conditioned her to do what you want with dozens of mundane tasks, and follow your directions in various simple things then when things suddenly get sexual then she will still continue to be in compliance mode. Every yes, leads to more yeses.

Use dosages of approval to reward good behavior, while withdrawing attention to punish bad behavior. Attention from high status men is the currency that women value. Now it's time to cross the bridge between social to sexual. A woman's body does a lot of the work for you; all you have to do is touch it in the right areas, at the right times, and in the right sequence.

IRON CLAD RULE OF TOUCHING WOMEN #6

ONCE YOU HAVE ESTABLISHED TOUCHING ON NORMAL SOCIAL AREAS, IT IS TIME TO VERBALIZE STATEMENTS THAT ARE MORE SEXUALIZED AND TO INCREASE THE INTIMACY LEVEL OF THE TOUCHING TO BE MORE SEXUAL.

As time moves on and her body-language is receptive then escalate the intimacy of the touching:

- Tell her that she has sexy legs and squeeze her leg with your hand.
- Tell her that she has a cute butt, and squeeze her but.
- Take her hand and put it on your lap.
- When her nipples are exposed, suck on them.
- When you're in a fuck location, just whip out your dick.
- When she's on your bed physically lift her up and position her in a way that is the most optimal way for mutual pleasure. Be very dominant.
- Some women enjoy having their hair pulled; this reinforces a dominant frame as touching a woman's face is a dominant gesture.
- Light choking can make her wet.
- Fuck her very hard. Hold nothing back.

IRON CLAD RULE OF TOUCHING WOMEN #7

BE THE ONE TO RELEASE FIRST.

This creates the frame that she is the one who is chasing you - rather than the other way around. With experience you can sense a woman's muscular tension and release the touching before she releases it - preemptively.

TRAIN HER.

If a woman resists, punish her by taking two steps back, moving physically away from her, and withdrawing attention. This technique is known by a few names including: negative punishment, freeze-out, physical blackmail, and soft nexting.

45

THE 1-2-3 COMBINATION PUNCH TECHNIQUE FOR ESCALATION

IRON CLAD RULE OF TOUCHING WOMEN #5

THERE IS A PHYSICAL ESCALATION WINDOW WHEN A WOMAN IS A HEIGHTENED EMOTIONAL STATE. ONE EFFECTIVE STRATEGY IS TO MAKE A WOMAN LAUGH OR SHRIEK FROM JOY, AND TOUCH HER BODY - IN AN INTIMATE MATTER - AT THE EXACT MOMENT WHEN THAT HAPPENS. HER LAUGHTER IS AN OPEN INVITATION TO TOUCH HER BODY IN INTIMATE AREAS.

Push/pull is an extremely effective tactic for heightening a woman's emotional state, and making her crazy about you.

- - Qualify/disqualify
- - Compliment/tease
- - Build rapport/break rapport
- - Statement of interest/statement of disinterest
- - Sending mixed signals

The more intense the emotional state a woman is in, the more susceptible she is to being manipulated

into sex. Game is manipulation, and manipulation is game; if that bothers you then put this book down because you aren't ready for the truth. A successful seducer is one who

- The goal is to spike her emotional levels to an apex state, so she is easier to manipulate and lead towards sex.
- Likewise, the goal is to condition a woman to do what you want (and following your leadership) through increasing levels of compliance, so that eventually you will lead her to sex.

IMPLANT THE IDEA OF SEX OCCURRING BETWEEN THE TWO OF YOU - INITIALLY WITH PLAYFULNESS AND HUMOR, BUT THEN WITH FULL-BLOWN SERIOUSNESS.

- "If no one was here right now, I would fuck you right here."
- "Its too bad that I'm a gentlemen or I would do dirty things. We can wait."
- "I can already tell that you last boyfriend didn't spank you enough."
- "Try not to throw your panties on me. I have to effect on women."
- "You just want to use me for sex. I Just want you to know that we're not having sex tonight."

Spike her emotions, watch her have an emotional high, and then escalate at that exact moment.

46

JUMP INTO THE DEEP END AND IMMERSE YOURSELF

- Go to Google Maps to search up local colleges. Then go to these college websites to see events that are listed. Go to one of these events to socialize. Alternatively, apply to be a college tutor.
- Hit up MeetUp and search for Yoga and Salsa Dancing events. Check on Google Maps for various dance clubs.
- If you live in a rural area where there are few beautiful women, then move to a highly populated city where the options are abundant. This will allow you to go to high vagina traffic areas where you can get a lot of practice done in short amounts of time.

WHEN YOU DIVE knee deep into situations where you are forced to interact with women and you're surrounded by many beautiful women, then you won't be able to help yourself but improve.

Picking up chicks in college is like taking candy from a baby. It is extremely easy. It's like throwing yourself in a ocean of VERY ATTRACTIVE fish (where you're forced to interact with this fish because it's everywhere); you're almost guaranteed to get laid by taking a college class - as long as you're not a pussy, take massive action and hit on every girl.

When you jump into a pool of sharks, you'll force yourself to swim or sink. You'll find strength and insights that you didn't know you had.

47

CREATE AROUSAL.

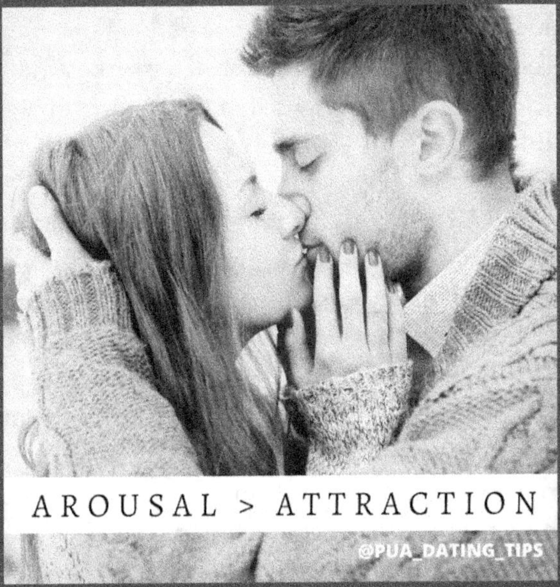

FEMALE AROUSAL IS a physiological response of a woman getting horny and wet. Arousal is physical process created by touching **highly specific areas on her body** that:

- have a lot of nerve endings,

- are highly sensitive, and
- are inherently sexual.

Arousal can be created at any time by metaphorically "punching in a specific code". If you touch specific parts of a woman's body and she becomes aroused, then she won't be able to stop herself from getting an uncontrollable intense desire for sex and fulfilling that desire with your penis. **Just like attraction is not a choice, arousal is not a choice;** both are hardwired biological responses to specific external stimulus.

- Lightly pulling her hair while kissing her
- Massaging her inner-wrist (a surprising area of the body that has nerve endings leading to the vagina)
- Touching/kissing her neck which is a sensitive area
- Caressing the area right about her butt and her inner-thigh.

Brute force is not always the key. Sometimes touching a woman lightly and slowly has a greater impact than touching a woman with intensity. One incredibly powerful technique is to touch a woman's neck with the extreme ends of your finger-tips - barely grazing her neck; there are special nerve endings that sense very light touch that aren't activated during heavy touch.

Keep in mind that a woman may be too humiliated to tell you upfront that your sexual touch is turning her ON. You'll be able to tell through her body-language. Is she moving closer? Are her eyes lighting up? Is she positioning your hand into certain places specifically and if so, which places? Further, you can directly tell her "Tell me what feels really good for you" to learn a woman's specific pleasure spots.

An overall theme of dealing with women in sexual situations is to be very dominant in the bedroom. Be willing to physically lift her up and position her in the places that are the most optimal for mutual pleasure to occur. Tell her to say specific things that make things hotter.

One extremely powerful and absurdly effective technique is to play the daddy and his little girl role-play. I cannot over-empahize how powerful this single technique is. In fact, this one technique is worth the price of this entire book. Create the imaginary role-play that you are her dominant daddy, and she is your submissive little-girl. Refer to yourself in third person with statements such as "Daddy is going to [xyz]" and use the nickname "little girl" when referring to her. For whatever reason, this turns women ON 🔥 like nothing else.

Part III

48

THE SEXCALATION SYSTEM, THE ESCALATION MODEL

PHASE #1: BREAKING THE TOUCH BARRIER

- Touch very early.
- Start very subtle.
- Start with micro-escalation.
- Touch everyone.

The overall philosophy to Phase #1, is that it's harder to get your foot in the door than it is to enter into the house. Being small, subtle, and brief makes it much easier to start. *But once your foot is in the door, you've opened multiple pathways of escalation from there. This is similar to the business realm: getting a consumer to spend his first $1 is harder than getting a consumer to go from $1 to $50.*

Once a woman is okay with even the smallest tiniest level of physical escalation, she will eventually be okay with something 10X more intense and eventually sex itself because with game skills you can build on the opening that is given to you. It is human nature to get used to something fast; with enough times of repetition, even the "forbidden" becomes permissible. ***The point is that even the micro of micros escalation eventually leads to macro escalation.***

❄

PHASE #2: CONDITIONING HER.

- **Touch often to get her hooked.**
- Keep her mood high during the touching process. **Associate positive emotions with you touch.**
- **Use touching as a reward.** Don't frame it as a reward that she gives you. Remember: when done right, touching for women is enjoyable and intensity pleasurable, so it is a gift that you give.

The overall strategy to Phase #2 is that you want to get a woman to be physically addicted to your touch. *Oxytocin is addictive and is released during touching. This is done by touching her frequently. To amplify this even further, go for long durations (such as sitting close together or cuddling - when you're watching a 3D movie, reading a book, or falling asleep). Touch when the vibe is positive to anchor your touch with good emotions.*

The philosophy behind this is that you can't play hard to get if you're hard to want. By giving physical value, you're creating DESIRE in her body, and a WANTING in her mind - even if she is too humiliated to admit this to herself at the current stage. Then this form of value can be used as leverage later - by withdrawing it if she refuses to comply with more intimate touching (a sort of physical blackmail).

❄

PHASE #3A: BYPASSING DEFENSES FOR SOCIAL TOUCHING, SPECIFIC TECHNIQUES:

- **Touch during points, peaks, and questions.** Touch her body on the shoulder when verbalizing an important point in the conversation, or asking a question. Touch her arm to emphasize an important thing that you have to stay in the conversation. When she experiences an emotional peak, there is brief window of escalation when you can touch her a more intimate part of her body.
- **Any excuse is a good excuse for social touching** until the plausible deniability barrier is crossed into sexual touching. Utilize every excuse for social touching. **During sexual touching, you don't need excuses anymore** and you kiss her/finger her whenever you want - as long as your frame is strong and it's done with an ultra high level of confidence.
- SOCIAL TOUCHING EXCUSE **#1: Leverage social conventions.** Huge during greetings and goodbyes - as is standard social convention. Hugs are preferable to handshakes, but if you do end up using a handshake then have it last a few seconds longer than normal.
- SOCIAL TOUCHING EXCUSE #2: **Utilize accidents.**
- SOCIAL TOUCHING EXCUSE #3: **Create advantageous situations.**
- SOCIAL TOUCHING EXCUSE #4: **Tap into her need to feel safe. Don't ask. Assume. Take her hand and lead.**
- SOCIAL TOUCHING EXCUSE #5: **Tap into her need to look good. Fix her up - her**

clothing, her posture, or taking the hair out of her face.

❄

PHASE #3B: BYPASSING DEFENSES FOR SOCIAL TOUCHING, GUIDELINES

- Don't draw attention to social touching by looking at it.
- Distract her during the social touching. Utilize "Bullshit Baffles Brains" technique.
- Be the life of the party. Be fun to keep her hooked into the interaction, and having her listen to you - instead of having her focused on the touching that is happening in the background.

❄

PHASE #4: BYPASSING DEFENSES FOR SEXUAL TOUCHING, GUIDELINES

- Know where her comfort threshold is (by sensing muscle tension, hesitation, micro-expressions, withdrawal), and preemptively release first. **Physically reject her to make her chase.**
- **Release and increase.** Always move forward. Be the one to release before she does - preemptively. If you sense she is getting uncomfortable then take a few steps back (removing even social touch), and she'll miss the prior the level that she got hooked to.
- **Punish bad behavior with negative punishment.** Freeze-out when getting

compliance denial. Withdraw attention, fun, distance, and all forms of touching (including social touching which she has already been conditioned to enjoy).

❄

PHASE #4B: BYPASSING DEFENSES FOR SEXUAL TOUCHING, HIGHLY SPECIFIC BEHAVIORAL TECHNIQUES (HSBT)

- **Take her on an exciting date to prevent triggering anti-slut defense,** but have her meet you at your house (keep door wide open). Men want to skip to the end results versus women want to experience the process.
- **Make the meetup easy for her by ordering an Uber to her location, and have the Uber go straight to your house.**
- **When leading her, put your hand on her lower back.**
- **Sit next to her - not across from her.**
- Netflix and chill works. The silly meme is true.
- Escalate with a specific compliment.
- Introduce sexuality with humor.
- Normalize sex by talking about it.
- Create an emotional high with shock humor. Then escalate like crazy during a high.
- Isolate.
- Signal discretion.
- Do a simple back massage. Massaging her in the areas of the body that has more nerve endings has a greater impact.
- Physically pick her up and position her.

- Make her horny by massaging her sensitive, pleasure zones such as the clit - even if it's done through her jeans (eventually proceeding to slipping your hand inside her jeans and rubbing her clit through the panties).

Physical aesthetics:

- Trim pubic hair.
- Get rid of acne.
- Work out daily.
- Dress wealthy.

Have a lifestyle that includes meeting women on a daily basis. Practice high demand skills every day - no excuses. Practice every part of the roadmap that leads to sex.

49

ILLUSTRATIONS

During the pickup phase, hug from the side; then transition to frontal hugs. Does she lean in (and press her body against yours) when you hug her? Do her hands curl when you do a high five? Does she linger in the hug, or does she release quickly? Gauging physical indicators of interest lets you know where you stand, and how fast you can escalate. Life is too short to play waiting games; **escalate as fast as possible without breaking her comfort threshold, but not faster.**

During the date, site next to her - not across from her. Sit so close that your legs are touching. Logistics is important to find the venue that will allow this to occur (times, locations, and menu) prior to even taking her there. You should have an arsenal of places that you are used to taking women to, so that when you arrive you already know the venue and have situational confidence. You'll be able tell how much she is enjoying the moment by sensing genuine smiles, sensitivity to laughing, which direction her feet at pointing towards, whether or not she initiates subjects of conversation at her own initiative etc. Even if you can tell that she is enjoying the venue, don't stay for too long because it can stale. It is preferable to take a woman to multiple venues to create a time distortion effect where she feels like she has known you for longer than she actually has.

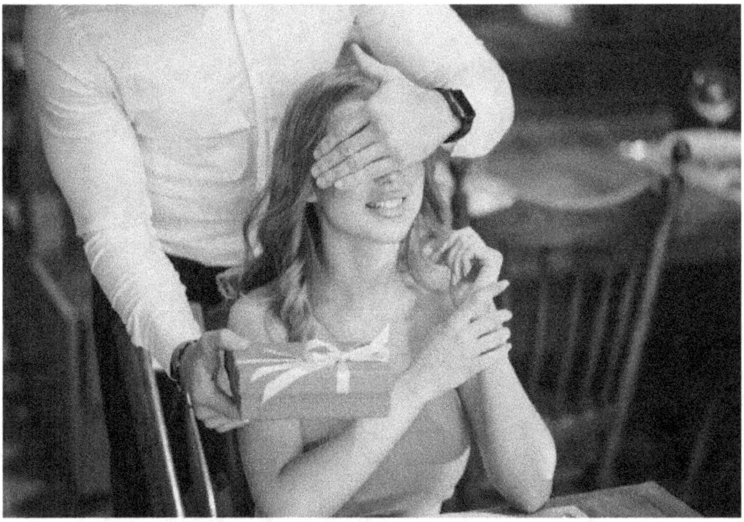

Playfully touch her. Humor lets you "get away" with things you otherwise could not.

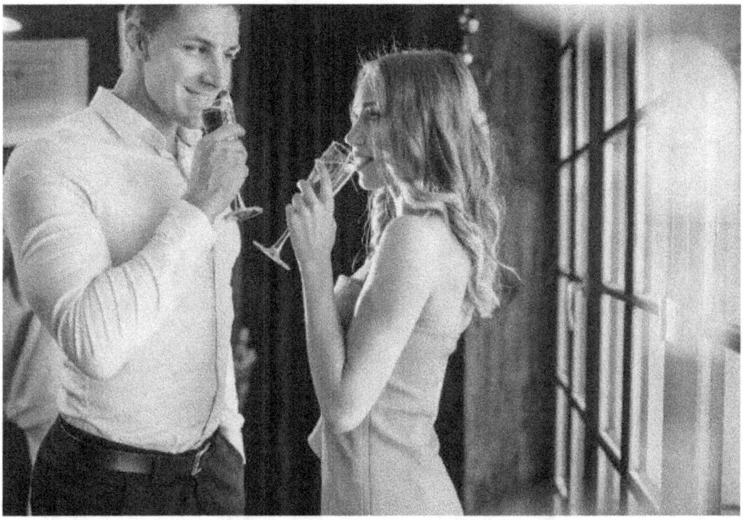

A bit of wine lowers a woman's inhibitions.

Take a fork of food, and flirtatiously feed her - while calling her cute to reward compliance.

Sexual arousal is contagious. You can transfer your lust unto her. Whisper in her ear, and then kiss her neck.

Travel excites women like nothing else. It's like a glitch in the matrix that is absurdly effective on women. Even mentioning the fact that you've been to multiple countries - embedded in stories through good story-telling delivery - works like magic. On your IG bio, put different flags to show that you're a well traveled man. Take her to an exotic location and make her horny by rubbing her clit through her pants. Once she is horny, take her to a super-close-by fuck location (while keeping her distracted with conversation/music videos the entire way), and fuck her brains out in a discrete isolated location - such as a nearby bathroom , hotel room, her place, or your place. It helps a lot to rent an apartment that is very close to the place where you will be meeting a lot of very young 18-20 year old women (such as a college campus).

50

SPECIFIC LINES TO USE

Negging

- "I don't think you and I are going to get along."
- "I'm not sure about you yet."

Screening Questions

- "Is there more to you than meets the eye?"
- "If you had no chance of failure and you could be anything you want to be in the world, who would you want to be?"

Escalation Lines

- "Gosh. You smell good. I'm trying so hard to NOT make out with your right now."

For Dates

- Don't do coffee dates. Every person is doing that, so it's very boring for women. Be more creative. Use this line: "We're having a dinner party. I'm having some collected friends. We're all gathering tomorrow at 8:00pm; I'd love for you to join us."

For Releasing

- "Slow it down speed-racer."

Part IV

51

Plausible Deniability

What is anti-slut defense?

WOMEN DON'T WANT to feel slutty because they have been conditioned by society that being too promiscuous is evil. She was just brought up to feel this way. She doesn't want to see herself as a slut - even in her own eyes - and certainly in the eyes of other people (who will judge her negatively for it).

Don't take it personally.

Don't take anything a woman says or does personally. Focus on your improving your game skills overall rather than obsessing over getting a specific girl. Accept women for what they are and playing the game accordingly, rather than getting bitter over what women could be (but aren't). Life is harsh and then we die; fucking deal with it. Complaining about things won't change them, so instead use that same energy to focus on that which is within your realm of control.

Do you only want a 1 night stand and not see her again next morning, or do you want endless nights of sex?

You can still get 5 minute lays (and not see her again afterwards when she has Buyers Remorse the next morning), but if you want to have a LONG TERM SEXUAL RELATIONSHIP then it is recommended to spend 7 hours getting to know the girl and taking her on various dates before fucking her. By taking things a bit slower and getting to know the girl before fucking her then she will feel like the sex is in the context of a potential relationship - rather than a promiscuous one night stand.

<u>CREATING PLAUSIBLE DENIABILITY FOR THE WOMAN IS A GOOD STRATEGY TO BYPASS HER ANTI-SLUT DEFENSE.</u>

What is plausible deniability?

Take the responsibility for physical escalation off her so that she doesn't feel slutty, and put it on yourself. It is your responsibility as a man to lead the interaction towards sex because a woman may feel too slutty to be sexually aggressive - even if she wants to have sex with you. **I repeat: if a woman really likes you, her ego may get into the way of making moves towards you.**

Make the girl feel less slutty by being the sexual aggressor - instead of putting the responsibility on her. When taking a woman to your apartment, she knows that you are going to try to fuck her, but it's still better for you to create a context that is a more romantic, **<u>so sex can seem like it just happened as a byproduct - rather than her direct intention for it to happen.</u>**

<u>Create an excuse and she'll happily play along.</u> Remember WANT to be seduced. And they WANT to be seduced by guys who just GET IT. Women know what the fuck is going on, but they'll feign ignorance because they would rather enjoy the process and play along (allowing themselves to be swept by the magic of your game) than by focusing on the result and verbalizing what is happening.

Tell her that you're inviting her to your apartment to see the AMAZING VIEW from the roof etc. Create an excuse for her, so she doesn't feel morally guilty later and when she tells her friends about what happened: she will have a legitimate story about that ends in "then things just naturally progressed and we had sex."

Keep in mind that not every girl feels anti-slut defense. Some women are more open minded. However, there are enough women who do experience anti-slut defense mechanisms for me to dedicate a chapter to countering it. Plausible deniability in a nutshell is feeding a woman an excuse that she can tell herself to avoid feeling guilty about having sex outside of wedlock, and doing something that in many cultures is frowned upon.

52

Micro Escalation

THIS IS escalation that happens so quickly and so brief that it doesn't even feel like actual escalation. This is ideal for when you are breaking the touch barrier by introducing the behavioral habit of touching her body. Starting very subtle gets your foot in the door. From there, increase the level of touch incrementally at a reasonable pace all the way to sex.

The reason why micro-escalation is effective is because it's so subtle and brief that a woman won't even object to it. Then before she knows it, she has been conditioned to accept your touch as the new norm.

One can go from 1mph to 100mph if there's gasoline, but one can't go from 0mph to even 1mph without gasoline. Her accepting your touch - even on the tiniest level - is the gasoline in this metaphor. Once you get in the foot in the door then you can eventually escalate radically, but if your foot isn't even in the door, then further escalation is impossible. That's why a woman accepting even the smallest of touches opens the floodgates for the future.

53

Crazy Fast Escalation

WHEN A WOMAN IS EXPERIENCING an emotional high then that is a point in time when you can escalate very fast. The reason for this is because intense emotions shut off the logical, conscious part of a woman's brain that would normally say "hey, you shouldn't do that because of XYZ."

This is why loud parties in college often lead to sex occurring; women are in an intense emotional state and aren't thinking about their actions - including giving into physical instant gratification. If she's highly emotional then she is more susceptible to manipulation.

Good game is about pumping up a woman's emotional state and then escalating during her emotional highs.

54

Bullshit Baffles Brains

THE CONSCIOUS MIND contains the super-ego which is the critical part of the brain. It is the logical part of the brain that can find objections about why she shouldn't be having sex with you, and why shouldn't be increasing the physicality because of stupid reason X, or Z.

In contrast, the primal and emotional sides of the brain are the parts of her that loves instant gratification - including physical pleasure and riskier behaviors. **Activating a woman's primal and emotional sides will unleash her wild sexual side.**

As I mentioned earlier, one effective strategy for keeping the conscious mind away from blocking out sex from occurring (by coming up with bullshit logical reasons) is to get a woman into a highly emotional state. When a woman is in a highly emotional state, her logical part of the bra**in is turned off. She is too busy being wild to think critically. During these moments of susceptibility, there is a brief window when you can escalate crazy fast (gain a lot of ground in a matter of just a moment).** She is too busy having fun to be conscious (and to care) about what is happening.

Taking a woman to an exotic location through the use of traveling can put her into a highly emotional state and make her incredibly sexually submissive - as long as you capitalize on this scenario fast before she settles in. It's a cheesy tactic (just like Netflix and Chill), but it works.

Traveling with her to an exotic location for a date looks like a sleazy gimmick, but it's actually a highly effective strategy towards making a woman incredibly receptive to intimate physical escalation. Don't do boring coffee dates like the average guy because she's seen that a million times before; be more creative.

Once you've established the habit of erotic touch or having sex then it will be easy for you to continue to do so. The key is to break that ground in the first place. This means that you don't need to travel every time you want to have sex with her (because that's absurd and not even remotely sustainable in the long term). However, it is a highly effective strategy for getting laid the first time with her. Once you've had sex with a particular girl once then the future times are as easy as a walk in the park **- as long as you keep doing the things that made you attractive to her in the first place.**

Another effective strategy for getting a woman to accept physical escalation is to keep her conscious mind distracted with random shit, so she isn't overly self-conscious about the aggressive escalation that is happening at the moment.

It doesn't matter that much what that shit is as long as it's captivating enough to have her distracted enough to not pay attention to the fact that you're physically escalating. In fact, even if it's complete bullshit - as long as it's intriguing bullshit - then it will keep her mind NOT paying attention to the fact that you are physically escalating. When her mind is distracted then you can physically escalate a lot faster. Hence, watching a movie is a good starting point for physical escalation - especially if it's a scary movie and the lights are off. The stupid memes about “Netflix and Chill”are true.

55

Releasing

- Being the first one to release the touch is important because it gives you social power, and creates the frame that you are THE SELECTOR. **Creating physical rejection is a powerful tool because it makes a woman DESIRE YOU.**
- **Sense when she is about to release the touching, and be the one to do it first - preemptively.** The oldest trick in the book is that women want what they can't have; don't you know that? 😏

KEEP in mind that this particular piece of advice is very counter-intuitive. Most guys will take as much touching as they can get for as long as they can. I am telling you to push her off - literally. While you might get a bit less touching by being the first one to remove the touching, you've still won because you've created a greater level of desire within her and that desire will lead to more touching down the line. 👉👌

www.ingramcontent.com/pod-product-compliance
Lightning Source LLC
Chambersburg PA
CBHW061128120626
46546CB00005B/1704
9781960655004